The Economics of Immigra

The Economics of Immigration provides students with the tools needed to examine the economic impact of immigration and immigration policies over the past century. Students will develop an understanding of why and how people migrate across borders and will learn how to analyze the economic causes and effects of immigration. The main objectives of the book are for students to understand the decision to migrate; to understand the impact of immigration on markets and government budgets; and to understand the consequences of immigration policies in a global context.

From the first chapter, students will develop an appreciation of the importance of immigration as a separate academic field within labor economics and international economics. Topics covered include the effect of immigration on labor markets, housing markets, international trade, tax revenues, human capital accumulation and government fiscal balances. The book also considers the impact of immigration on what firms choose to produce, on the ethnic diversity of restaurants and on financial markets, as well as the theory and evidence on immigrants' economic assimilation. The textbook includes a comparative study of immigration policies in a number of immigrant-receiving and sending countries, beginning with the history of immigration policy in the United States. Finally, the book explores immigration topics that directly affect developing countries, such as remittances, brain drain, human trafficking and rural–urban internal migration. Readers will also be fully equipped with the tools needed to understand and contribute to policy debates on this controversial topic.

This is the first textbook to comprehensively cover the economics of immigration, and it is suitable both for economics students and for students studying migration in other disciplines, such as sociology and politics.

Cynthia Bansak is Associate Professor of Economics at St. Lawrence University, USA.
Nicole B. Simpson is Associate Professor of Economics at Colgate University, USA.
Madeline Zavodny is Professor of Economics at Agnes Scott College, USA.

 A range of further resources for this book are available on the Companion Website:
www.routledge.com/cw/Bansak

The Economics of Immigration

Cynthia Bansak, Nicole B. Simpson and
Madeline Zavodny

Routledge
Taylor & Francis Group

LONDON AND NEW YORK

First published 2015
by Routledge
2 Park Square, Milton Park, Abingdon, Oxon OX14 4RN

by Routledge
711 Third Avenue, New York, NY 10017

Routledge is an imprint of the Taylor & Francis Group, an informa business

British Library Cataloguing in Publication Data
A catalogue record for this book is available from the British Library

Library of Congress Cataloging in Publication Data
Bansak, Cynthia.
The economics of immigration / Cynthia Bansak, Nicole Simpson and Madeline Zavodny.
  1. Emigration and immigration–Economic aspects. 2. Emigration and immigration–Government policy. 3. United States–Emigration and immigration–Government policy. 4. Immigrants–Employment. 5. Emigration and immigration–Social aspects. 6. Manpower policy. 7. Government spending policy. I. Simpson, Nicole (Economist) II. Zavodny, Madeline. III. Title.
JV6217.B36 2015
304.8–dc23   2014039396

ISBN: 978-0-415-74705-9 (hbk)
ISBN: 978-0-415-74706-6 (pbk)
ISBN: 978-1-315-79725-0 (ebk)

Typeset in Perpetua
by Sunrise Setting Ltd, Paignton, UK

Contents

Figures

Tables

Boxes

Preface

This book is aimed at students taking an undergraduate or introductory course on the economics of immigration. The book is also appropriate for undergraduate or graduate interdisciplinary courses on immigration. There are several excellent books that explore the economics of immigration at a more mathematical level and a number of books aimed at academics doing research on immigration. But we found while teaching undergraduates at our respective liberal arts colleges that there isn't a book that provides a thorough introduction to the subject area from an economic perspective. This book fills that gap.

The economics of immigration illustrates a number of more general economic concepts. Immigration affects the labor market in the country where immigrants go. It affects a number of other markets in both receiving and sending countries. It has implications for governments and taxpayers and for employers and native-born workers. It raises interesting issues regarding selection, human capital accumulation and future generations. Students of the economics of immigration will learn how to apply basic economic principles to a variety of concepts in this book.

The economics of immigration also has important policy implications. Immigration policy is controversial in many countries. This book discusses why this is so. The book also provides an overview of immigration policy around the world, including in the United States. The book includes facts and theories regarding legal and unauthorized immigration there and elsewhere.

This book assumes that students have had at least an introductory course in microeconomics and are familiar with basic macroeconomics. The book keeps mathematical details to a minimum. The appendix to Chapter 1 provides a review of basic tools necessary to understand the models presented in the book.

We made an effort to make this book contemporary. When appropriate, the book includes brief overviews of historical trends and issues, but our focus is the most up-to-date migration data, theories and findings.

The book is written for a semester-long course. We expect that courses would spend about a week on each chapter. Each chapter provides suggestions for further reading on particular topics. Most of these suggestions are chosen because they are accessible to undergraduate students, particularly those published in the *Journal of Economic Perspectives*. The suggested readings also include "must-read" classics in the field. Some of these are quite mathematical, but most include economic intuition that is more accessible. For a shorter course, instructors may wish to skip the policy section of the book (Chapters 13 and 14). Chapter 4 on selection also could be skipped or covered in considerably less detail. Many of the other chapters cover selection since that is one of the most central topics in the economics of immigration.

The companion website to this book, http://www.routledge.com/books/details/9780415747066/, provides a number of suggestions for class activities related to the book. We have found that the subject lends itself well to classroom debates. The website has suggested debate topics. The website also has PowerPoint slides of the tables and figures from the book as well as the links to Internet resources given in the book.

We would like to thank many people who helped with the writing of this book. Our research assistants, Xiomalys Crespo, Annie Hines, Jordan Kuchan, Chris Junqing Ma and Sifael Ndandala, provided excellent help. Our editor, Emily Kindleysides, and editorial assistant, Laura Johnson, were instrumental in keeping us on track. We are grateful to the anonymous external reviewers for their invaluable feedback. We also thank our colleagues and collaborators for many helpful conversations on this topic over the years, including Catalina Amuedo-Dorantes, Michael Clemens, Pia Orrenius, Giovanni Peri and Chad Sparber. We particularly thank Animesh Giri, Ethan Lewis, Pia Orrenius, Chad Sparber and Allan Zebedee for proving feedback on parts of this book. Finally, we thank our families for their support while we wrote this book: Allan, Tyler, Zoey and Jackson; Brendt, Thomas and Katelyn; and George, Corbin and Joseph.

Part 1

Trends in Immigration

1   Why Study the Economics of Immigration?

Economics is the study of how societies allocate scarce resources. Immigration is the movement of people across national borders. It may not be obvious what these two topics have in common. But they actually have quite a bit in common. More people moving to a country can mean more workers producing more things, which reduces the level of scarcity and raises the standard of living. Or, more people moving to a country can mean more people competing for scarce resources, which reduces the standard of living.

Which of these two opposing views is correct? The economics of immigration applies economic tools to the topic of immigration to answer questions like whether immigration affects wages, poverty and income inequality in a country. The economics of immigration examines many other consequences of immigration as well, such as the effects on tax revenues and government expenditures, the effects on how and what firms decide to produce and the effects on innovation and technology, to name just a few. The economics of immigration also examines questions like what determines whether people choose to move and where they decide to go. It even examines how immigration affects the ethnic diversity of restaurants and financial markets! The economics of immigration is a booming field within economics.

More than 230 million people, or 3 percent of the world's population, are immigrants (United Nations, 2013). Immigration is a truly global concept—virtually every country in the world continually experiences both inflows and outflows of people. Some countries, like Australia, Canada and the United States, have long histories of receiving large numbers of immigrants. Other countries, like Ireland, Italy and the United Kingdom, sometimes have had more people leaving than entering, or a net outflow of people, but at other times have had more people entering than leaving, or a net inflow of people. Developed and developing countries alike experience out-migration by people looking for better opportunities elsewhere while also experiencing in-migration by people from other countries looking for better opportunities there.

Although 230 million immigrants globally seems like a lot of people, it pales in comparison to the number of people who would like to move to another country. Gallup polls indicate that more than 640 million people—13 percent of the world's adult population—would like to move permanently to another country (Gallup, 2012a). Among people who would like to move, the United States is the most preferred destination (23 percent), followed by the United Kingdom (7 percent) and Canada (6 percent). About 1.1 billion people—26 percent of the world's adult population—would like to go to another country temporarily in order to work (Gallup, 2012b). Almost one-half of adults living in sub-Saharan Africa would like to move to another country temporarily in order to work, and one-third of them would like to move abroad permanently.

One reason why so many people would like to work or live in another country is that they may earn much more if they move. Michael Clemens, Claudio Montenegro and Lant Pritchett (2009) have calculated what they call "the place premium," or the wage gains to immigrants who move to the United States. The average worker who migrates from Yemen, a country in the Middle East, to the United States earns 15 times more in the United States than in Yemen—$1,940 a month in the United States versus $126 a month in Yemen, adjusting for the exchange rate and differences in prices (purchasing power parity) across the two countries. The average worker who moves from Mexico to the United States earns 2.5 times more, and the average worker from Haiti earns 10 times more.

The possibility of large income gains is not limited to immigrants who move to the United States, or even to industrialized countries in general. Developing countries attract immigrants from even poorer countries. For example, Thailand has some 2.5 to 3 million migrant workers, most of them from neighboring Myanmar (World Bank, 2013). Gross domestic product (GDP) per capita is almost five times higher in Thailand than in Myanmar. But as Myanmar's economy has begun improving in recent years, fewer people are migrating to Thailand and some migrants are returning home, creating concerns that Thailand may experience a labor shortage in the coming years.

There are other reasons for moving to another country besides to work, of course. People may want to move to another country in order to study or to join family members. More than four million students were enrolled at a university outside their country of citizenship in 2010 (OECD, 2012). The United States is the top destination for foreign students (19 percent), closely followed by the United Kingdom (18 percent). Many foreign students view studying abroad as a temporary move, but some do so hoping that it will enable them to live permanently in that country. Likewise, some people who move to join family members who live or work abroad may view it as a temporary move, while others view it as a permanent move.

From an economic perspective, the key question in immigration is not why so many people become immigrants, but why so few. If more than one-quarter of the world's population would like to move to another country at least temporarily, why has only 3 percent of the world's population actually done so? Policies that limit immigration are one reason. Countries impose many restrictions on immigration. These restrictions discourage some potential migrants from moving at all, and they cause others to migrate illegally instead of legally.

Being unable to afford to immigrate, either legally or illegally, is another reason why some people who would like to move to another country do not do so. Moving is costly. Legal migrants may need to pay for a passport and a visa and hire a lawyer or an agent to help them migrate. They also have to pay for transportation. Workers from Bangladesh spend between $1,935 and $3,870 to obtain low-skilled jobs in the Middle East, for example (World Bank, 2013). This is 2.5 to 5 times the average annual income in Bangladesh. Only people who can save or borrow that much can access jobs in the Middle East, which pay far more than jobs in Bangladesh. The people who may gain the most from migrating may be the least able to afford to do so. Likewise, illegal migrants may need to pay a smuggler to help them enter a country illicitly. This can cost hundreds, thousands, or even tens of thousands of dollars, depending on the distance, difficulty and discomfort involved.

There are non-monetary costs to moving as well. Migrants may miss their families, their friends and their culture. If their family stays behind, migrants may not be there as their children grow up or when their parents die. Immigrants who are unable to return home regularly may not be able to attend family weddings, birthdays, graduations, funerals and other important events. They may struggle to learn another language and to adapt to another culture. Such non-monetary costs, often called "psychic costs," may be even higher than the monetary costs.

Immigration has been rising globally during the past few decades and is likely to continue to become more common. Although immigrating is expensive, its cost has fallen over time. In addition, incomes have risen in much of the developing world. As average incomes rise, more people can afford to migrate. Immigration is also rising because people are more aware of better opportunities elsewhere. Cell phones and email have made it easier for immigrants to let friends and family members back home know when jobs are available abroad. Television, movies and the Internet have made people more aware of global differences in living standards. A "youth bulge" in many developing countries has increased the population of young adults, the group most likely to migrate in search of better opportunities. Repressive political regimes in some countries have motivated people to leave voluntarily in some cases and led to refugee crises in other cases.

Types of immigrants

Immigrants can be classified into different, sometimes overlapping groups. This book uses the term immigrants to mean people who are not citizens at birth of the country in which they currently live. (A section called "Economics of immigration terminology" later in this chapter discusses this definition further.) One way to classify immigrants is based on whether they choose to move or are forced to do so. Other ways include their duration of migration, whether they migrate legally and how skilled they are.

Most of the world's immigrants are voluntary immigrants—they choose to move. People choose to move for a variety of reasons, including to work, to study and to join family members. But there are two important exceptions: refugees and asylum seekers (sometimes jointly called humanitarian immigrants), and victims of human trafficking.

Refugees are people who leave their home country because of persecution, war or violence. At the end of 2013, there were 16.7 million refugees worldwide (UNHCR, 2014).[1] The number and location of refugees can change quickly if a war or violence erupts. For example, more than two million people fled Syria during the first two years of the civil war that began there in 2011 (UNHCR, 2013).

Some refugees return home when conditions improve, while others are never able to return. Many live for years in desperate conditions in neighboring countries that do not welcome them. Some are ultimately resettled by the United Nations High Commissioner for Refugees (UNHCR) in countries that agree to accept them. In many industrialized countries, refugees are eligible for public assistance programs.

Refugees are often confused with asylum seekers. Asylum seekers are international migrants who apply for asylum, or protection as a refugee, after entering a foreign country. In essence, asylum seekers are people who have left their home country and whose claims for refugee status have not yet been evaluated. The country they are in must determine whether they meet the grounds for being considered a refugee. The UNHCR specifies those grounds as a well-founded fear of persecution in the home country for reasons of race, religion, nationality, political opinion or membership in a particular social group. Asylum seekers who are denied refugee status usually must leave the destination country and are deported back to their origin country, although they sometimes stay and become illegal immigrants. Distinguishing legitimate asylum seekers from economic migrants—people who move for a better life but do not meet the criteria to be considered a refugee—can be difficult.

Victims of human trafficking are migrants who are deceived or coerced and then exploited. They are typically forced to work against their will for little or no pay and are not free to leave. The U.S. State Department (2013) reports that as many as 27 million people are victims of human trafficking today, although not all of them have moved across an international border. Some victims of human trafficking start out as voluntary migrants but are instead enslaved or exploited. For example, women might believe they are going abroad to work as housekeepers but are forced into prostitution after they have left home.

A second way to classify immigrants is based on whether they are permanent or temporary. Migrants may be "birds of passage," migrants who plan to work abroad for a while in order to earn enough money to return home and buy land, start a business or retire (Piore, 1979). Workers also might move temporarily in order to send money home to support their relatives. Other motives for temporary migration include studying and visiting family members. Temporary migrants are sometimes called "sojourners." Permanent migrants are immigrants who do not return to their origin country to live. Some of them choose to become citizens of their new country while others do not. People who intend to be temporary migrants may end up becoming permanent migrants, and vice versa. Immigration policy can affect this choice. For example, policies that make it difficult for migrants to move back and forth may prompt them to settle permanently in the destination and bring their families there.

People who are very short-term migrants—people who travel to another country to visit but not to live, such as people taking a foreign vacation or taking a business trip to another country—are not considered immigrants, even temporary ones. They are visitors. It is not clear exactly how long a stay needs to be to distinguish a visitor from a temporary immigrant. Is someone who stays for six months every year with her children who live in another country a visitor, a temporary immigrant or a permanent immigrant? When someone has moved to a new country and no longer has a residence in another country, he is clearly an immigrant. But is someone who has homes in two countries then an immigrant in neither country? There is no clear answer to these questions from an economic standpoint.

Another way to classify immigrants is based on whether they are legal or not. Legal immigrants have permission to enter and live, at least temporarily, in a country. Illegal immigrants do not. There are two main ways that people can become illegal immigrants. They can enter a country illicitly, such as by crossing a border without permission. (The U.S. government refers to this as "entry without inspection.") Or, people can violate the terms of a visa, such as by overstaying a temporary visa and not leaving when they are supposed to. Another way that people can violate the terms of a visa is by working while on a visa that does not allow them to work. As of 2009, the United Nations Development Programme estimated the number of illegal immigrants worldwide at 50 million.

Classifying immigrants based on their skill level is particularly common in economics. Skill is a multifaceted concept and hard to observe, so economists often use education as a proxy for skill. What is considered a high skill level in one country may be different from what is considered a high skill level in another country. In most industrialized countries, adults who have not completed high school (secondary school) are considered low skilled while those who have completed college (tertiary education) are considered high skilled. In a developing country where most of the population has little formal education, people who have completed primary school might be considered skilled. The skill level of immigrants relative to the skill level of natives in the destination and relative to the skill level of non-migrants in the origin plays an important role in determining the economic impact of immigration.

Immigration is controversial

In most countries, immigration is a controversial topic. Immigration has distributional consequences—some groups benefit from immigration while other groups are harmed. Some of the benefits of immigration are broadly diffused, making them hard for people to observe, while some of the harms are concentrated within regions, industries and skill levels and therefore result in strong opposition to immigration. The biggest beneficiaries of immigration are usually the immigrants themselves, who typically earn more or have a better life after moving to a different country. (This is not true for all immigrants, of course.) The businesses that hire immigrants clearly benefit as well.

People may oppose immigration because they believe they will compete with immigrants for jobs or will pay more in taxes as a result of immigration. They may view immigrants as taking their jobs, receiving more in public assistance than they pay in taxes, taking spots in universities that would otherwise go to native-born students and so on. Such beliefs are not always true, as this book explains, but many people hold such views nonetheless. In addition, people may be concerned that immigration will lead to changes in their country's culture, such as whether people speak the same language and share similar values. Whether people know any immigrants, and what those immigrants are like, is likely to affect how people feel about immigration.

Studies show that people tend to be most opposed to immigration by workers with similar or lower education or skill levels and if they live in areas with large numbers of immigrants (e.g., Scheve and Slaughter, 2001; Mayda, 2006). This suggests that people are concerned about labor market competition from immigrants. Such concerns are among the major reasons why countries impose restrictions on immigration and why immigration policy generates considerable debate.

Immigration versus international trade

Immigration may be a substitute for international trade. Instead of goods being shipped across borders, workers may move across borders and produce goods that otherwise would be imported. Alternatively, immigration may be a complement to international trade. Multinational corporations may transfer workers across offices in different countries, for example.

In addition, immigrants may create trade relationships with partners back in their home country, resulting in more international trade.

The economic impact of immigration is similar to the economic impact of international trade in some ways, according to economic theory. Both immigration and international trade are the result of cross-country differences in prices—the price of labor in the case of immigration, and the price of goods in the case of international trade. Workers move from countries where their earnings are relatively low to countries where their earnings are relatively high. Much like the movement of goods across borders causes prices to move closer together across countries, immigration causes wages to move closer together across countries. These wage changes benefit some workers while hurting others. For example, a large influx of less-educated immigrants may reduce wages among competing less-educated native-born workers who are substitutes for those immigrants, and it may boost wages among more-educated native-born workers who are complements for those workers. It may also raise wages among workers in the origin country, who now face less competition in the labor market there.

The effects of immigration are unlike those of international trade in some ways, however. The movement of people can affect a society in more dimensions than the movement of goods. Immigrants may bring new ideas, and they may start new companies. Almost 20 percent of Fortune 500 companies—the largest companies headquartered in the United States—were founded by immigrants, and another 20 percent by the children of immigrants (Partnership for a New American Economy, 2011). One of the two founders of Google, Sergey Brin, emigrated from Russia to the United States with his parents as a child. Jerry Yang, the founder of Yahoo!, is from Taiwan. Pierre Omidyar, an immigrant from France, created the auction website eBay.

Another way in which immigration is different from international trade is that immigrants are consumers. Immigrants buy goods and services in addition to producing them—they increase demand for goods and services in a country. Having more consumers in an economy may at least partially offset any negative effects of more competition in the labor market.

Immigration tends to be more controversial than international trade. Part of the opposition to immigration is rooted in cultural issues, not economic ones. Immigrants may look different from the people already living in a country. They may speak a different language. They may eat different foods that smell odd. They may celebrate different holidays and raise their children differently. These are not directly economic issues, but they may have economic implications. For example, immigrants who learn the language spoken in the destination country are likely to be more successful in the labor market than immigrants who do not. But if the number of immigrants who all speak the same language is large enough, it may not be necessary for them to learn the destination's language in order to be successful. In such cases, natives who speak only their country's language may be at a disadvantage in the labor market. Such changes may spur considerable tension.

Immigration policy

The fact that every country imposes barriers to immigration, and a few to emigration—people leaving a country, as opposed to people entering a country—as well, suggests that countries are concerned about the consequences of immigration. Many countries try not only to limit the number of immigrants entering their country but also to shape the characteristics of the inflow. Countries typically want to attract immigrants whose skills are in relatively short supply there and immigrants who are relatively wealthy. They may want to discourage entry by immigrants whose skills are relatively abundant among current residents or who are likely to impose a fiscal burden by receiving more in government services than they pay in taxes.

Countries use a variety of admissions policies to try to affect the size and characteristics of their immigrant inflows. Australia and Canada, for example, have point systems that award points to potential permanent immigrants based on various characteristics, such as age, education and occupation. Potential migrants who exceed a points threshold can gain admission. Countries in the European Union (EU) currently allow citizens of other EU countries to enter freely to work but have relatively strict policies for immigration by non-EU citizens. The United States admits permanent immigrants primarily on the basis of family ties to U.S. citizens or permanent residents. It also admits some immigrants, particularly relatively skilled immigrants, temporarily and permanently based on employment.

Immigration may affect not just the receiving country but also the sending, or origin, country. Concern that these effects are negative is the main reason that some countries impose restrictions on emigration. Emigration reduces the size of the population of the sending country. If the people who leave are not representative of the country as a whole but are instead concentrated among certain skill, education or occupation groups, the distribution of wages may change. For example, if most emigrants are unskilled workers, wages among unskilled workers are likely to rise relative to wages among skilled workers. Emigrants may send money back to family who remain in the origin country, further changing the distribution of income. If most emigrants are skilled—the so-called brain drain—economic growth may slow in the sending country as skilled workers leave. However, it is possible that the sending country benefits via "brain gain" if emigrants return after acquiring skills abroad or if the possibility of emigrating causes residents to acquire more skills.

Immigration and immigration policy affect the distribution of income globally as well as within countries. Gordon Hanson (2010) and Michael Clemens (2011) have both forcefully argued that an easing of restrictions on immigration by developed countries would be one of the most effective ways to reduce global income disparities. Clemens reports that the potential gains from reducing restrictions on immigration are 50 to 100 times the potential gains from reducing restrictions on trade in goods and services or on capital flows.

Economics of immigration terminology

Economists sometimes use terms differently than other people do. For example, "rent" in economics means not just how much it costs to lease an apartment or other space but also economic profit. This different usage of terms applies to the economics of immigration. To make matters more complicated, different immigration-related terms can have different meanings in different countries. For example, in the United States, immigration law uses the word "immigrant" to describe only legal permanent residents, people who have legal permission to live permanently in the United States but who have not yet become naturalized U.S. citizens. The Department of Homeland Security, the main government agency in charge of enforcing immigration laws in the United States, considers everyone in the United States who is not a U.S. citizen to be an "alien," a quite different use of the term than most movies!

Whether and how someone can become a citizen of a country varies considerably across countries. In the United States, some people born abroad can become naturalized U.S. citizens. This typically requires living in the United States legally as a permanent resident for at least five years and then passing a test about the U.S. government, a background check and an interview. Everyone born in the United States is a U.S. citizen, regardless of whether her parents are U.S. citizens or even legally present in the country. This policy is called *jus soli* (Latin for "right of the soil") or "birthright citizenship." Most countries in the Western Hemisphere have a *jus soli* citizenship policy.

Many countries have *jus sanguinis* (Latin for "right of blood") citizenship policies. Citizenship is granted based on parents'—or sometime even grandparents'—citizenship. As a result, even some people born in a *jus sanguinis* country to people born in that country are not citizens of that country. These policies are common in Europe, Asia and Africa. Countries with a *jus sanguinis* policy often distinguish between "foreigners" and "citizens" instead of between "immigrants" and "natives." Some countries with a *jus sanguinis* policy allow residents who were born elsewhere, or were born in that country to non-citizen parents, and meet certain conditions to gain citizenship. In addition to its *jus soli* policy, the United States has a *jus sanguinis* policy that confers U.S. citizenship at birth on children born abroad to most U.S. citizens.

How to refer to immigrants who are not legally present in a country is controversial. Opponents of this group usually use the terms "illegal immigration" and "illegal immigrants" to stress its unlawful nature. Groups that are more sympathetic often use the terms "undocumented immigration" and "undocumented immigrants." Both sets of terms have become value laden. The U.S. government usually uses the terms "unauthorized immigration" and "unauthorized immigrant," which are more neutral. In Europe, the terms "irregular immigration" and "irregular immigrants" are usually used. This book uses all of these terms interchangeably and without any value-laden intent.

People may have permission to live in a country legally but only on a temporary basis. International students who study abroad are an example of legal temporary migrants. Other groups include diplomats and workers who have a visa that allows them to work for a specified period under certain conditions. The United States officially refers to such migrants as "nonimmigrants." To the U.S. government, nonimmigrants include visitors for business and for pleasure. The economics of immigration devotes little attention to visitors and, as noted earlier, does not consider them to be immigrants because they do not live in the new country.

Economists who study immigration usually use "immigrants" to mean people who live in a country they are not a citizen of by birth, regardless of whether they are living in that country legally or illegally, permanently or temporarily, and regardless of why they entered. This book follows that convention. Unless specified otherwise, immigrants means people who are not born a citizen of the country they live in. "Natives" means people who are born a citizen of the country they live in. Comparisons between immigrants and natives are common in the economics of immigration.

The country immigrants are from is called the origin country, the home country, the source country or the sending country. The country immigrants move to is called the destination country, the host country or the receiving country. This book uses these terms interchangeably.

Finally, understanding the difference between stocks and flows is important in immigration. A stock is a measure at a point in time. A flow is a measure over an interval of time. For example, the stock of immigrants in the United Kingdom was about 7.8 million people in 2013. The net flow of immigrants into the United Kingdom during 2000–2013 was about 3.1 million people.[2]

A basic model of immigration

One of the main models used to examine the economic effect of immigration focuses on immigrants as workers. In this model, wage differences across countries motivate people to move. Immigrants move from countries with lower wages to countries with higher wages. As immigrants move, wage differences shrink and perhaps ultimately disappear.[3]

Figure 1.1 shows the labor markets for two countries. The country with higher wages before immigration is the destination country, and the country with lower wages is the origin country. In each country, there is a demand for labor that is based on the value of workers' output, as reflected by the downward-sloping labor demand curves. Each country also has a supply of labor. The supply of labor is assumed to not depend on the wage, or to be perfectly inelastic (a vertical line). This assumption is made for simplicity, but the general results of the model carry through if the labor supply curves are upward sloping. Before immigration occurs, natives of each country supply all of the labor in that country. The pre-immigration labor market equilibrium in the destination is L_D workers and wage W_D in Figure 1.1(a), and L_O workers and wage W_O in the origin in Figure 1.1(b).

Suppose that some workers migrate from the origin to the destination, and workers are perfect substitutes across the two countries. Perfect substitutability means that a native-born worker in the destination is interchangeable with an immigrant worker from the origin. As this migration occurs, the labor market equilibrium in each country changes. The new equilibrium in the destination is L_{D+M} workers at wage W_{D+M}, and L_{O-M} workers at wage W_{O-M} in the origin. Immigration thus results in the number of workers in the destination increasing

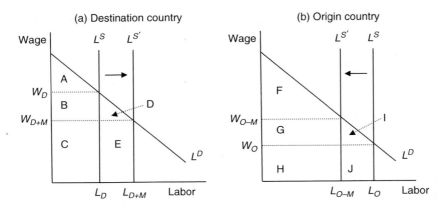

Figure 1.1 The labor market in the destination and origin countries before and after immigration.

Before immigration, L_D workers are employed at wage W_D in the destination. In the origin, L_O workers are employed at wage W_O. After immigration, L_{D+M} workers are employed at wage W_{D+M} in the destination, and L_{O-M} workers are employed at wage W_{O-M} in the origin.

and the number of workers in the origin decreasing. The wage in the destination falls, and the wage in the origin rises.

Immigration creates winners and losers in this model, as listed in Table 1.1. Immigrants earn higher wages and are clearly better off. In the destination, they earn an amount given by area E in Figure 1.1(a). In the origin, they earned only area J in Figure 1.1(b). Immigrants gain since they are moving from a lower-wage country to a higher-wage country. Competing native-born workers in the destination are worse off because their wage falls. Before immigration, they earned the sum of areas B and C. After immigration, they earn only area C. Area B in Figure 1.1(a) thus represents the losses to competing native-born workers in the destination country.

Meanwhile, competing native-born workers in the origin who do not migrate are better off because they earn more. Before immigration, they earned area H in Figure 1.1(b). After some workers leave, they earn the sum of areas G and H. They thus gain area G.

The destination country as a whole is better off because of immigration, and the origin country as a whole is worse off, ignoring the gains to the immigrants. Area D in Figure 1.1(a) represents the social welfare gains in the destination, while area I in Figure 1.1(b) represents the social welfare losses in the origin. For the destination, this gain in social welfare occurs because factors of production other than competing native-born workers—employers, for example—gain from the lower wage and increased production that result from immigration. For the origin, the loss in social welfare accrues to factors of production other than native-born workers as the wage rises and production decreases as a result of emigration.

Immigration is what economists call potential Pareto superior. Within the destination country, the gains to employers and society as a whole would be big enough to compensate the native-born workers if there were a costless way to redistribute some of those gains from the winners to the losers. Similarly, the gains to immigrants would be big enough to compensate the origin country for its loss in social welfare.[4] In reality, however, redistribution is not costless and rarely occurs enough to fully compensate losers. This is one reason why countries impose barriers to immigration (and sometimes to emigration).

The social welfare gain in the destination country is called the "immigration surplus." This immigration surplus is bigger the larger the number of immigrants. It is also bigger the more

Table 1.1 Winners and losers from immigration

Group	Gain (or Loss)
Immigrants	$E - J$
Destination country:	
Competing workers	$-B$
Other factors of production	$B + D$
Social welfare	D
Origin country:	
Competing workers	G
Other factors of production	$-(G + I)$
Social welfare	$-I$

Welfare gains and losses accruing to different groups in Figure 1.1.

the wage falls as the number of workers increases. Estimates suggest that this immigration surplus is quite small for the United States. For example, the U.S. Council of Economic Advisors estimated in 2007 that the immigration surplus is about $37 billion a year, or 0.28 percent of GDP.

Globally, the potential gains to more immigration are far bigger. Clemens (2011) estimates that if one-half of the population in poor regions of the world were to migrate to rich regions, global GDP would increase by 20 to 60 percent. Most of these gains would accrue to the immigrants themselves, and there could be sizable changes in average wages in poor and rich regions alike, but the world as a whole would clearly be better off if more people migrated. Again, the question is not why so many people become immigrants but rather why so few.

The simple model presented here makes a number of assumptions. As already noted, it assumes that labor supply is perfectly inelastic. This means that wages change as a result of immigration but employment of natives does not. It also assumes that immigrants are perfect substitutes for natives—the labor supply curve in the receiving country shifts to the right by an amount equal to the number of immigrant workers. But immigrants may instead be imperfect substitutes or complements for natives. It assumes that workers are homogeneous, or that there is only one type of worker. But there may be multiple types of workers who have different skill levels. It assumes that the amount of capital in each country is fixed. Immigrants may bring or attract capital, increasing the marginal productivity of labor in the receiving country and perhaps decreasing it in the sending country. This would change the demand for labor. It assumes that markets are perfectly competitive. Workers are paid the value of their marginal product. Chapter 7 presents models that relax some of these assumptions.

A global overview of immigration

Figure 1.2 shows immigrant shares—the percentage of the population that is foreign born—by country in 2010. The darker a country, the higher the share of its population comprised of immigrants. Some of the most immigrant-intensive countries are well-known immigrant destinations, such as Australia, Canada and New Zealand. Others may be a surprise, however, such as Saudi Arabia. Three of the countries with the highest immigrant shares in the world—Qatar (87 percent), United Arab Emirates (70 percent) and Kuwait (69 percent)—are in the Middle East, and a number of other Middle Eastern countries also have high immigrant shares. These countries have large numbers of foreign workers there on a temporary basis working in construction, private household services and the like. Qatar's immigrant share is expected to rise even further as the country builds stadiums and hotels and adds more infrastructure as it prepares to host the soccer World Cup in 2022.

Some of the countries with high immigrant shares are so small they don't show up on the map. These include small island nations that are territories of Britain or the United States, such as the Cayman Islands (63 percent) and the U.S. Virgin Islands (57 percent). In Asia, they include Hong Kong and Macao, which are special administrative regions of China, and Singapore.

Poor countries tend to have low immigrant shares. Most countries in Africa, Asia and Latin America had immigrant shares below 5 percent of their population in 2010. There are

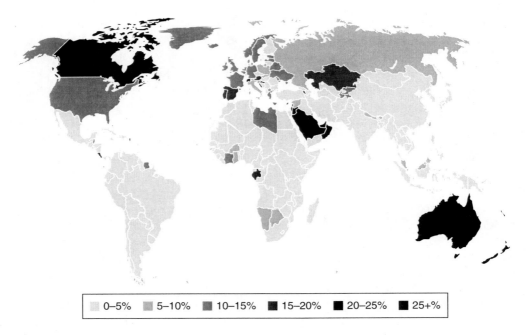

Figure 1.2 Immigrant shares around the world, 2010.

Source: World Bank (http://econ.worldbank.org/WBSITE/EXTERNAL/EXTDEC/EXTDECPROSPECTS/0,, contentMDK:21352016~pagePK:64165401~piPK:64165026~theSitePK:476883,00.html [5 November 2013]).

exceptions, however. These tend to be countries with even poorer neighbors, such as Gabon in Africa and Costa Rica in Latin America.

Many European countries have moderately high immigrant shares. The highest immigrant shares in Europe include Switzerland (23 percent in 2010), Ireland (20 percent) and Austria (16 percent). Within Europe, immigrant shares are lowest in eastern and southeastern Europe, where countries tend to be poorer.

Figure 1.3 shows emigrant shares, the percentage of a country's population that has left that country. These shares are shown relative to the population living in a country (including immigrants), not relative to the number of people born in that country. It is therefore possible for the emigrant share to exceed 100 percent. This is the case for Dominica, a small island in the Caribbean that has more emigrants than it has residents. Many other small countries have high emigrant shares as well, perhaps because there are fewer opportunities in small countries. Many small countries with high emigrant shares were (or still are) territories of a larger country that allows territorial citizens to immigrate without any restrictions. For example, Puerto Rico's emigrant share was 43 percent in 2010, almost all to the United States, and Suriname's emigrant share was 39 percent, almost all to the Netherlands.

Emigrant shares tend to be low for many of the same countries that have low immigrant shares. This may be because many people in those countries are too poor to leave, and those countries are so poor that few people want to go there. There are some interesting exceptions, however. For example, Lesotho has an emigrant share of 21 percent, almost all to

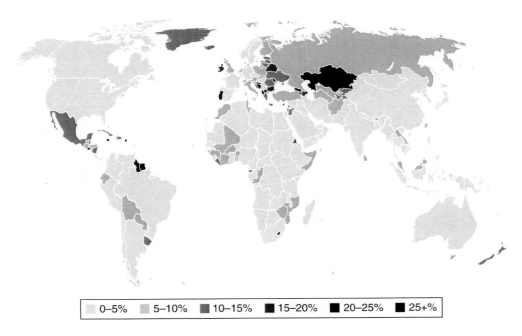

Figure 1.3 Emigrant shares around the world, 2010.

Source: World Bank (http://econ.worldbank.org/WBSITE/EXTERNAL/EXTDEC/EXTDECPROSPECTS/0,,
contentMDK:21352016~pagePK:64165401~piPK:64165026~theSitePK:476883,00.html [5 November 2013]).

South Africa, which surrounds it; Lesotho's immigrant share is only 0.3 percent. Australia represents the other extreme—it has an immigrant share of 26 percent and an emigrant share of 2 percent.

A few countries have relatively high shares of both emigrants and immigrants. Kazakhstan, for example, has an emigrant share of 24 percent and an immigrant share of 20 percent. This is partly due to the country's central location, which makes it a destination country for migrants from other Central Asian countries and a sending country to Russia and Europe. Portugal is another country with relatively high emigrant (21 percent) and immigrant (9 percent) shares.

An overview of U.S. immigration

The United States is the world's top immigration destination, with more than 42 million foreign-born residents in 2010 (U.S. Bureau of the Census, 2012). About 13 percent of the U.S. population is foreign born. Estimates suggest that about one-quarter of immigrants living in the United States are unauthorized (Hoefer, Rytina and Baker, 2012; Passel, Cohn and Gonzalez-Barrera, 2013). Mexico is the top source country of U.S. immigrants overall and of unauthorized immigrants. The number of immigrants from Mexico is so large that the World Bank considers Mexico–United States to be the largest migration corridor in the world. However, other origin countries account for a growing share of unauthorized immigrants.

Much of the discussion in this book focuses on the United States. Because the United States is such a major immigrant-receiving country, the literature on the economics of immigration to date has largely been about the United States. There are many interesting studies of other countries, some of which are discussed in this book, and researchers are increasingly turning their attention elsewhere. In addition, migration data are getting better around the world, giving researchers the chance to carefully analyze other migrant flows.

The rest of this book

This book begins its exploration of the economics of immigration by looking at immigrants and the immigrant experience. Chapter 2 examines who becomes an immigrant and why. Chapter 3 examines where immigrants go and how long they stay there. It also discusses what determines where immigrants choose to live within the receiving country. Chapters 2 and 3 expand on the patterns suggested in the discussion of Figures 1.2 and 1.3.

One important question in the economics of immigration is whether immigrants are positively or negatively selected relative to the sending or receiving country populations. Chapter 4 presents the canonical model of selection and empirical evidence on selection. Patterns of selection affect how well immigrants do in the destination country, the topic examined in Chapter 5. Chapter 5 also looks at whether immigrants assimilate, or become similar to natives of the destination country, and patterns of naturalization—becoming a citizen of the destination country—and of intermarriage between immigrants and natives. Chapter 6 discusses the children and other future generations of immigrants and their experiences from an economic standpoint.

The book then focuses on economic theory and empirical evidence about the effects of immigration. Chapter 7 presents theoretical models of how immigration affects the labor market in a receiving country. Chapter 8 presents the empirical evidence on immigration's labor market effects in the United States and elsewhere. Chapter 9 discusses theory and evidence on the effects of immigration in other markets in receiving countries. The chapter discusses how immigration affects housing markets, technology and prices, to name a few topics. Chapter 10 looks at immigration's fiscal impact, or how it affects government revenues and costs in receiving countries.

Chapter 11 looks at how migration affects source countries. Emigration may have an adverse effect, particularly if it results in brain drain. Alternatively, emigration may have a positive effect. Emigration may relieve economic pressures created by a fast-growing population, and emigrants may send back remittances that help their families and communities. Chapter 12 discusses theory and evidence in several interesting new areas of research on the economics of immigration. These include how immigration affects happiness, crime and education.

Understanding the economics of immigration requires understanding immigration policy. Policy affects the number and characteristics of immigrants. Policy plays a key role in determining whether people migrate legally or illegally, and policy affects where migrants go and how they do when they get there. Many topics in this book therefore integrate discussions of immigration policy in the United States and other countries. In addition, Chapters 13 and 14 are devoted to immigration policy. Chapter 13 discusses U.S. immigration policy in depth, and Chapter 14 discusses immigration policy in other countries.

What this book does not cover

How many immigrants should a country admit? Which immigrants should a country admit? This book does not answer questions like these. These are normative questions—answering them requires making value judgments. But your—and policymakers'—answers to them probably depend on the economic effects of immigration. This book presents the main economic theories and empirical evidence related to immigration. These theories and evidence are positive, or factual predictions and descriptions. Normative analysis addresses what "should be," while positive analysis addresses what "is."

One of the main goals of this book is for you to understand the positive economics of immigration—the theories and empirical evidence. Another goal is for you to be able to make informed economic arguments about normative issues related to immigration. Making informed normative arguments—and designing informed immigration policies—requires understanding the economic theories and empirical evidence. For example, the model of the immigration surplus predicts that, as a whole, the receiving country gains from immigration. However, immigration is redistributive. Native-born workers lose while employers gain. Immigration policy therefore involves deciding whether to favor the interests of workers or the interests of employers. This is a normative decision, but policymakers would benefit from knowing the evidence on how big the tradeoff is before deciding on a policy.

Like much of economics, this book focuses on averages. It discusses the average immigrant, the average native and so on. Of course, there really is no average person. Instead, there are distributions of characteristics, like education, and distributions of outcomes, like earnings. Not all immigrants are the same, and neither are all natives. As you read this book, remember that, just as all people are not the same, all people will not be affected in the same way by immigration.

Because this book examines immigration through the lens of economics, it does not examine many topics related to immigration that are worth considerable attention and discussion. For example, this book devotes little attention to humanitarian issues related to immigration, such as how many refugees a country should admit and what should be the grounds for granting asylum. This book also devotes little attention to geopolitical issues related to immigration, such as treaties that allow workers to move freely across international borders in some parts of the world. It does not examine the philosophical issues related to whether a country should restrict immigration.

The economics of immigration takes national borders for granted. It typically analyzes issues from the perspective of a single country, not from a multinational or global perspective. It typically assumes that the welfare gains to immigrants themselves should not be counted as part of the welfare gains (or losses) from immigration. The immigrantion surplus in the receiving country (and loss in the sending country) in Figure 1.1 does not include the wage gains that accrue to immigrants. Although the discussion indicates the global gains to migration, economics typically does not examine this—instead, it looks at welfare gains or losses for the receiving and sending countries separately. Policymakers likewise typically focus on effects on their own country, not global effects. The policies that destination countries adopt play a central role in determining how many people migrate and where they go, but those policies may not take into account effects on immigrants or on sending countries.

Analyzing issues from a multinational or global perspective might change some of the conclusions that economics reaches and the policies that countries adopt. As you read this book, think about what other assumptions economics makes and how changing those assumptions might change the conclusions that economics reaches. Also think about what immigration policies you think countries should adopt, and why.

Problems and discussion questions

1   What are the main reasons people migrate? What factors are likely to influence how many people migrate and their reasons for migrating?
2   What factors are likely to influence immigrants' choice of destinations?
3   What types of immigrants are likely to go to poor, developing countries, and what types of immigrants are likely to go to rich, industrialized countries?
4   How would the effects of migration on employment and wages in the sending and the receiving countries be different from Figure 1.1 if labor supply is responsive to wages? What if labor demand is not responsive to wages?
5   What types of barriers to immigration or emigration might a country impose, and why? What are the likely economic effects of such barriers?
6   Describe an interesting migration flow. Do some research on that migration flow. Why did these people leave their home country, and where did they go? How many migrated? Was the migration temporary or permanent?
7   Using the Internet, create a list of countries with *jus soli* and *jus sanguinis* citizenship policies. Do you see any patterns?

Notes

1   There are another five million registered refugees who are displaced Palestinians.
2   Based on United Nations data available at http://esa.un.org/unmigration/TIMSA2013/migrant stocks2013.htm?mtotals [9 June 2014].
3   Because migration is costly, not enough migration is likely to occur for wage differences to disappear entirely. However, Figure 1.1 shows the case where wage differences disappear entirely since that is the simplest case to illustrate.
4   The economist Jagdish Bhagwati proposed in the 1970s that low-income countries impose a tax on their citizens abroad in order to offset this loss. His proposal has come to be known as the "Bhagwati tax."

Internet resources

The International Organization for Migration has an interactive map of where immigrants go and where they are from by country, available at http://www.iom.int/cms/en/sites/iom/home/about-migration/world-migration.html.

The U.S. Department of Homeland Security's glossary of immigration-related terms is available at https://www.dhs.gov/definition-terms. Its annual Yearbook of Immigration Statistics is available at http://www.dhs.gov/yearbook-immigration-statistics.

The World Bank's resources on migration and remittances are available at www.worldbank.org/prospects/migrationandremittances.

Suggestions for further reading

Clemens, M.A. (2011) "Economics and emigration: Trillion-dollar bills on the sidewalk?" *Journal of Economic Perspectives* 22(3), pp. 83–106.

Clemens, M., Montenegro, C. and Pritchett, L. (2009) "The place premium: Wage differences for identical workers across the US border." Harvard Kennedy School Faculty Research Working Paper Series RWP09-004. John F. Kennedy School of Government, Harvard University.

References

Clemens, M.A. (2011) "Economics and emigration: Trillion-dollar bills on the sidewalk?" *Journal of Economic Perspectives* 22(3), pp. 83–106.

Clemens, M., Montenegro, C. and Pritchett, L. (2009) "The place premium: Wage differences for identical workers across the US border." Harvard Kennedy School Faculty Research Working Paper Series RWP09-004. John F. Kennedy School of Government, Harvard University.

Gallup (2012a) "150 million adults worldwide would migrate to the U.S." Available at: http://www.gallup.com/poll/153992/150-Million-Adults-Worldwide-Migrate.aspx. [9 January 2014].

Gallup (2012b) "More adults would move for temporary work than permanently." Available at: http://www.gallup.com/poll/153182/Adults-Move-Temporary-Work-Permanently.aspx. [9 January 2014].

Hanson, G.H. (2010) "Why isn't Mexico rich?" *Journal of Economic Literature* 48(4), pp. 987–1004.

Hoefer, M., Rytina, N. and Baker, B. (2012) "Estimates of the unauthorized immigration population residing in the United States: January 2011." Available at: https://www.dhs.gov/publication/estimates-unauthorized-immigrant-population-residing-united-states-january-2011. [10 January 2014].

Mayda, A.M. (2006) "Who is against immigration? A cross-country investigation of individual attitudes toward immigrants." *Review of Economics and Statistics* 88(3), pp. 510–530.

Organization for Economic Cooperation and Development (OECD) (2012) "Education at a glance 2012: OECD indicators." Paris: Organization for Economic Cooperation and Development.

Partnership for a New American Economy (2011) "New American Fortune 500." Available at: http://www.renewoureconomy.org/research/new-american-fortune-500/. [5 November 2013].

Passel, J.S., Cohn, D. and Gonzalez-Barrera, A. (2013) "Population decline of unauthorized immigrants stalls, may have reversed." Available at: www.pewhispanic.org/files/2013/09/Unauthorized-Sept-2013-FINAL.pdf. [10 January 2014].

Piore, M.J. (1979). *Birds of Passage: Migrant Labor and Industrial Societies.* Cambridge: Cambridge University Press.

Scheve, K.F. and Slaughter, M.J. (2001) "Labor market competition and individual preferences over immigration policy." *Review of Economics and Statistics* 83(1), pp. 133–145.

United Nations (2013) "Total international migrant stock." Available at: http://esa.un.org/unmigration/TIMSA2013/migrantstocks2013.htm?mtotals. [9 January 2014].

United Nations Development Programme (2009) "Human development report 2009." Available at: http://hdr.undp.org/en/content/human-development-report-2009. [9 January 2014].

United Nations High Commissioner for Refugees (UNHCR) (2013) "Syria regional refugee response." Available at: http://data.unhcr.org/syrianrefugees/regional.php. [1 November 2013].

United Nations High Commissioner for Refugees (UNHCR) (2014) "UNHCR global trends 2013." Switzerland: United Nations High Commissioner for Refugees.

U.S. Bureau of the Census (2012) "The foreign-born population in the United States: 2010." Available at: http://www.census.gov/prod/2012pubs/acs-19.pdf. [9 January 2014].

U.S. Council of Economic Advisors (2007) "Immigration's economic impact." Available at: http://
georgewbush-whitehouse.archives.gov/cea/cea_immigration_062007.html. [8 January 2014].

U.S. State Department (2013) "Trafficking in persons report 2013." Available at: http://www.state.
gov/j/tip/rls/tiprpt/2013/index.htm. [5 November 2014].

World Bank (2013) "Migration and remittance flows: Recent trends and outlook, 2013–2016."
Available at: http://siteresources.worldbank.org/INTPROSPECTS/Resources/334934-1288990
760745/MigrationandDevelopmentBrief21.pdf. [1 November 2013].

Appendix

This appendix provides a quick refresher on basic microeconomic tools that this book uses. These tools include supply and demand analysis, elasticity, consumer and producer surplus and present discounted value.

Supply and demand

Neoclassical economic analysis is rooted in supply and demand. In a supply and demand diagram for a product market, quantity is on the horizontal axis and price is on the vertical axis. The supply curve usually slopes up, and the demand curve usually slopes down. Producers' desire to maximize profits underlies the supply curve. If producers can make more profit at any given output price, they will produce more. Changes in factors that determine profitability, other than output price, shift the supply curve. These factors include input costs, such as wages and the prices of raw materials, and technology. If profit increases per unit produced, holding output price constant, producers increase supply and the supply curve shifts to the right. This would occur if input costs fall or production technology improves. If profit decreases per unit produced, holding output price constant, producers decrease supply and the supply curve shifts to the left. This would occur if input costs rise or production technology worsens.

Consumers' willingness to pay underlies the demand curve. Changes in preferences, income and the prices of related goods shift the demand curve. If more consumers want to buy a product, holding its price constant, demand increases and the demand curve shifts to the right. If fewer consumers want to buy a product, holding its price constant, demand decreases and the demand curve shifts to the left. In a market-clearing equilibrium, the intersection of the demand and supply curves determines the equilibrium price and quantity.

This book applies supply and demand analysis to the labor market as well as to the product market. In a supply and demand diagram for a labor market, the number of workers (or the number of hours worked) is on the horizontal axis and the wage is on the vertical axis. People's willingness to work underlies the labor supply curve. (Note that in the labor market, workers are the supply side, not firms.) If more people are willing to work at a given wage, the labor supply curve shifts to the right. Since immigration usually means more workers, immigration shifts the labor supply curve to the right in the destination. (In the origin, labor supply shifts to the left as workers leave the country.) Firms' willingness to hire workers underlies the labor demand curve. Labor demand is called a "derived demand"—firms' willingness to hire workers depends on, or is derived from, demand for the product. If firms can profitably sell more output because demand for their product rises, then they are willing to hire more workers at a given wage and the labor demand curve shifts to the right. For example, if the output price increases, firms will hire more workers in order to increase production. If workers become more productive at a given wage, firms also will hire more workers.

Elasticity

Elasticity of supply or demand is the responsiveness of the quantity supplied or demanded to changes in price (wages, in the case of labor supply and labor demand). The more the quantity supplied or demanded changes when price changes, the more elastic supply or demand is said to be. Supply or demand is perfectly inelastic if it does not respond at all to changes in price. A perfectly inelastic curve is a vertical line. Supply or demand is perfectly elastic if it is infinitely responsive to changes in price. A perfectly elastic curve is a horizontal line. Most of the time, supply and demand are not perfectly elastic or perfectly inelastic but instead somewhere in between. Economists often focus on the perfectly elastic or inelastic cases, however, because they are interesting to think about and are the basis of some models (like perfect competition).

Elasticity is measured as the percentage change in quantity for a percentage change in price, or

$$\frac{\%\Delta Quantity}{\%\Delta Price} = \varepsilon. \tag{A1.1}$$

Elasticity equals zero for a perfectly inelastic curve, and it equals infinity for a perfectly elastic curve. Supply or demand curves are considered inelastic if the absolute value of ε is between zero and one, and elastic if the value of ε is greater than one but less than infinity.

Figure 1.1 in the main text of Chapter 1 shows a perfectly inelastic labor supply curve. The labor supply curve is perfectly inelastic if workers' willingness to work does not change as the wage changes. Since most people need to work in order to pay their bills, most people probably have very inelastic labor supply curves. Although in reality labor supply curves probably have some elasticity to them, they are very inelastic for most groups of workers in developed countries. The labor supply curve also is vertical if the income and substitution effects cancel out. The income effect for labor supply is that most people are less willing to work as their income goes up as a result of higher wages. They work fewer hours in order to have more leisure. The substitution effect is that the opportunity cost of not working increases as the wage goes up—leisure becomes more expensive as the wage increases, and people substitute away from leisure and towards working more hours. The income effect implies a negatively sloped labor supply curve, while the substitution effect implies a positively sloped labor supply curve. If the two exactly cancel out, the labor supply curve would be vertical and perfectly inelastic. These opposing effects mean that the labor supply curve could be positively sloped at low wages but negatively sloped at high wages, or "backwards bending."

Consumer and producer surplus

Consumer surplus measures the difference between willingness to pay and price actually paid for all units purchased. Graphically, it represents the area below the demand curve and above the price line for the quantity purchased. (See Figure A1.1.) Producer surplus measures the

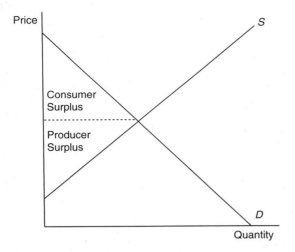

Figure A1.1   Consumer and producer surplus.

Consumer surplus is the area between the demand curve and the price line for the quantity purchased. Producer surplus is the area between the price line and the supply curve for the quantity sold.

difference between the price received by firms and the price at which firms are willing to sell for all units actually sold. Graphically, it represents the area below the price line and above the supply curve for the quantity sold.

If the demand and supply curves are straight lines, then consumer and producer surplus are triangles. Their values are then easily calculated using the formula for the area of a triangle (½ base × height). The sum of consumer and producer surplus is called "social welfare" or "economic surplus" and represents how well off producers and consumers are together. Note that social welfare says nothing about the distribution of welfare, and the consumer and producer surplus triangles do not have to be the same size. If social welfare increases, it does not necessarily mean that both producers and consumers are better off or that all consumers are better off, just society as a whole as measured by social welfare.

Present discounted value

The twin concepts of present discounted value (also called present value) and future value are used to show the time value of money. They also allow economists to compare future and current values. A given amount of money usually does not have the same value at different points in time. Inflation is one reason that a dollar today is not worth the same amount as a dollar in the future. When inflation occurs, the purchasing power of a given amount of money decreases. For example, suppose you have $100 hidden in your mattress at the beginning of the year. Over the year, the price level—the average price of goods and services—rises by 5 percent. Your $100 now can buy 5 percent less than it could before. Inflation has eroded the value of your money. In order for you to have the same purchasing power at the end of the year as you had the start of it, you'd need to have $105.

Most people don't hide money in their mattress, especially when the inflation rate is hig Instead, they put it in the bank so that they can earn interest. Suppose that you put $100 in the bank at the start of the year, and the bank pays you an annual interest rate of 3 percent. At the end of the year, you have $103. Suppose you then leave your $103 in the bank for another year at 3 percent annual interest. At the end of the next year, you have $106.09 (the 9 cents comes from the interest on the interest, or the compound interest).

The present discounted value formula expresses the relationship between present and future values. This formula is

$$Present\ value = \frac{Future\ value}{(1+r)^t} \, ,$$
(A1.2)

where r is the interest rate and t is the number of time periods (usually years). As the interest rate or the number of time periods increases, the present value decreases, all else equal. This book uses present value to compare the present value of income if someone migrates to the destination with the present value of income if that person remains in the origin. As discussed in this chapter and again later in the book, the income gains to migration are substantial for most immigrants.

People Become Immigrants

People have always migrated. The movement of early humans out of Africa across Eurasia set the stage for later migrations across the globe. Early humans migrated primarily in search of food and safety. Although the details have changed, people migrate today largely for the same reason: to have a better life. They move to another country because of better opportunities to work or to study, or to join family members. Others become immigrants not because they are pulled by better opportunities or family but rather because they are pushed out and need to move in order to escape violence or oppression.

Immigrants are from virtually everywhere. However, more people leave some countries than others. This chapter examines the push and pull factors that underlie the decision to become an immigrant. Immigration policies and migration costs also play important roles in the decision to migrate. The chapter develops an economic model of individuals' decision to migrate and an aggregate model of migration flows between pairs of countries that incorporate such factors. It then examines the empirical evidence on these models with regard to sending countries.

Where are immigrants from?

Table 2.1 lists the top 15 source countries of immigrants worldwide. Many of the world's most populous countries are on the list: China, India, Pakistan, Bangladesh, Russia and Mexico. But some other big countries are not on the list, such as the United States, Indonesia and Brazil. Few people are likely to leave the United States since it is among the world's wealthiest countries, but it is surprising that Indonesia and Brazil are not on list. Proximity to a rich country seems unlikely to fully explain the list. Some of the countries on the list are not near a rich country, while some countries that are not on the list are near a rich country.

Another surprise is that not all of the major immigrant-sending countries are poor. Some of the countries on the list are indeed quite poor, but the United Kingdom and Germany are most definitely not. Just because a country has a relatively high average income does not mean that no one in that country is better off if she migrates.

The emigration rates shown in Table 2.1 provide another way of looking at whether a country is a major immigrant-sending country. The emigration rate—the number of immigrants from that country relative to its current population—for the top 15 immigrant-sending countries by absolute number of migrants ranges from 68 percent in the West Bank and Gaza to just 0.9 percent in India and 0.6 percent in China. Part of this variation is due to the size of

Table 2.1 Top 15 immigrant-sending countries and their emigration rates

	Number of migrants (millions)	*Emigration rate (%)*
India	14.2	0.9
Mexico	13.2	10.7
Russia	10.8	7.9
China	9.3	0.6
Bangladesh	7.8	3.3
Pakistan	5.7	2.5
Ukraine	5.6	14.4
Philippines	5.5	4.6
Afghanistan	5.1	8.1
United Kingdom	5.0	7.5
Germany	4.0	4.3
Kazakhstan	3.8	23.6
Poland	3.7	8.2
West Bank and Gaza	3.6	68.3
Egypt	3.5	4.4

Source: Number of migrants from United Nations, Department of Economic and Social Affairs (2013). "Trends in international migrant stock: Migrants by destination and origin." Available at: http://esa.un.org/unmigration/TIMSO2013/migrantstocks2013.htm?msdo [12 December 2013]. Emigration rates from World Bank (2010). *Migration and Remittances Factbook 2011*. Available at: http://econ.worldbank.org/WBSITE/EXTERNAL/EXTDEC/EXTDECPROSPECTS/0,,contentMDK:21352016~pagePK:64165401~piPK:64165026~theSitePK:476883,00.html [17 December 2013].

the sending countries. If China's emigration rate was the same as the West Bank and Gaza's, it would have more than 900 million emigrants, or almost three times the current total number of migrants worldwide! The bigger the country, the lower its emigration rate tends to be, all else equal. As discussed in Chapter 1, small countries tend to have higher emigration rates, perhaps because economic opportunities are more limited there.

Most of the world's poorest countries would not be on a list of top immigrant-sending countries either by absolute number of migrants or by emigration rate. Most of the poorest countries in the world are in sub-Saharan Africa, where emigration levels and rates tend to be relatively low. Afghanistan is the poorest of the countries listed in Table 2.1, with a GDP per capita of only $687 in 2012 (World Bank, 2014). But that's 2.5 times bigger than GDP per capita in the Democratic Republic of the Congo or Burundi—countries that are not on the list. Yet Afghanistan's emigration rate was more than six times the Democratic Republic of the Congo's rate, and twice Burundi's rate. The poorest of the poor may not be able to afford to migrate even though they have the most to gain by doing so.

Push and pull factors

Push factors are conditions that propel people to leave the origin country, while pull factors are conditions that entice people to enter a destination country. Push factors matter more for some groups of immigrants, while pull factors matter more for other groups. For most immigrants, however, both push and pull factors are at play in the decision to become an immigrant.

Virtually every push factor has a corresponding pull factor, and vice versa. For example, a high cost of living in the origin country is a push factor while a low cost of living in the destination country is a pull factor. For many factors, what matters to potential immigrants is relative values, or the difference between countries—is the cost of living lower in the destination country than in the origin country?

The economics of immigration focuses on the role of economic push and pull factors in determining whether people become immigrants. Labor market conditions and economic growth in both sending and receiving countries are key economic factors, particularly for work-based immigrants. As John Hicks, a Nobel Prize winner in economics, wrote in 1932, "Differences in net economic advantages, chiefly differences in wages, are the main causes of migration" (Hicks, 1932: 76). High wages and strong economic growth in a receiving country act as a pull factor, while high unemployment in a sending country acts as a push factor. Other economic factors that motivate some people to become immigrants include the opportunity to get a better education and the availability of more generous welfare benefits in another country. Better access to advanced technologies may be a pull factor for some scientists and medical professionals, while poor health care may be a push factor for people who are ill.

Political and social factors also affect the decision to become an immigrant. Some of these factors are intertwined with economic factors. For example, corruption may push some people who want to run a business but are unable or unwilling to pay the bribes necessary to do so into becoming immigrants. Meanwhile, enforcement of private property rights may act as a pull factor for people who want to run a business without having to worry that the government will confiscate their assets. For many immigrants, having family or friends who live abroad—what economists and sociologists call "networks"—is a pull factor. As discussed later, having a network can also enable migrants to bear migration costs and can even lower migration costs. Other political and social push factors that influence the decision to become an immigrant include discrimination, violence, political oppression and having to serve in the military in the home country.

Wars and changes in national borders have caused some of the largest immigration episodes in history. The end of World War II resulted in more than nine million people migrating across Japan, Korea and the former Manchuria as the Japanese army demobilized, ethnic Japanese moved back to Japan from other parts of Asia that the country had occupied, and foreigners were deported from Japan (Araragi, 2013). At the same time, millions of ethnic Germans moved from Soviet bloc countries to Germany and Austria (Gibney and Hansen, 2005). When India was partitioned upon becoming independent from Britain in 1947, more than seven million Muslims moved to Pakistan from India, and a similar number of Hindus and Sikhs moved to India from Pakistan (Zamindar, 2013).

Natural disasters and famines have also caused several major migration episodes. For example, one to two million Irish emigrated during the 1845–1852 famine, and at least another one million died (Ó Gráda and O'Rourke, 1997). More recently, emigration from Honduras tripled after Hurricane Mitch devastated that country in 1998 (Kugler and Yuksel, 2008). As sea levels rise in the coming decades because of global warming, millions of people are likely to leave low-lying countries around the globe. Other climate changes due to global warming, such as desertification and food shortages, are also likely to lead to substantial migration.

Attractive amenities may lure some immigrants to particular destinations. Amenities are location-specific, immobile factors, such as beautiful scenery, a pleasant climate and a good quality of living. The desire to be near mountains, the beach or good museums may attract some immigrants, particularly wealthy people or retirees who have more leisure time to enjoy such amenities.

Figure 2.1 summarizes the push and pull factors that influence immigration flows. These push and pull factors suggest different reasons for immigration for different groups of immigrants. Work-based immigrants and foreign students move primarily because of the push and pull of relative economic conditions in the origin and destination countries. Family-based immigrants are pulled to join relatives living abroad. Refugees are pushed by political and social conditions, typically war or conflict; other conditions, such as famine, may be a factor as well. Asylum seekers are pushed by political and social conditions as well, but economic factors may also play a role in their decision to migrate. The fraction of asylum seekers officially recognized as refugees and awarded asylum is low—typically less than 40 percent globally (UNHCR, 2013). The fraction of asylum seekers actually awarded asylum is so low because receiving countries often decide that asylum seekers are economic migrants, not people fleeing persecution.

The relative importance of push and pull factors in a given migration stream can change over time. For example, political upheaval or economic distress may prompt emigration from

Push factors	Pull factors
Economic	Economic
High unemployment	Demand for labor
Poverty	High wages
High taxes	Strong economic growth
Poor health care	Opportunity for advancement
Overpopulation	Schooling
	Technology
Political and social	Generous welfare benefits
Discrimination	Low cost of living
War or oppression	
Corruption	Political and social
Crime	Family and friends
Compulsory military service	Rights and freedoms
	Law and order
Other	Safety
Natural disaster	
Famine	Other
Climate change	Amenities

Figure 2.1 Immigration push and pull factors.

a country to a particular destination. Once there, migrants may recruit their friends and families to join them. Employers may become accustomed to hiring a steady stream of readily available migrant workers. What started as push-driven migration thus transforms into pull-driven migration.

Whether a country is an origin or a destination country can change over time as well. Some countries undergo the "migration transition" of moving from experiencing sizable net outflows to simultaneously experiencing both inflows and outflows that roughly balance out to experiencing sizable net inflows. And some of those countries eventually experience net outflows once again. South Korea and Ireland are examples of countries that underwent the migration transition but then experienced net outflows during the late 1990s and late 2000s Asian and global financial crises, respectively.

Push and pull factors may affect whether immigration is permanent or temporary. Moves that were planned to be temporary may become permanent if push conditions in the origin country worsen or pull conditions in the destination country improve. Conversely, moves that were planned to be permanent may become temporary if push conditions in the origin country improve or pull conditions in the destination country worsen. Changes in immigration policy may also cause temporary stays to become permanent, or vice versa.

Push and pull factors affect legal and illegal, skilled and unskilled immigrants alike. Some factors may play bigger roles for one group than the other as a result of immigration policy. For example, if a country admits immigrants based primarily on family ties, the pull factor of family may matter a lot for legal immigrants. Meanwhile, the push and pull of relative economic conditions may matter more for illegal immigrants than for legal immigrants. In many countries, illegal immigrants enter mainly to work, while legal immigrants enter for a wider variety of reasons, including family ties. As a result, relative economic conditions may matter more for illegal immigrants than for legal immigrants. Regardless of their legal status, skilled and unskilled workers alike are affected by the push and pull of relative economic conditions.

The opposite of the push and pull factors listed in Figure 2.1 will cause some potential migrants to remain in their home country. Better economic, political, social and other conditions at home—or worse conditions elsewhere—will reduce migration. The opposite of the pull factors may also divert some migrants from a particular receiving country to a different country. For example, worse economic conditions in the United States may cause some people to migrate to, say, Canada instead. This may be preferable to remaining home and not migrating at all. Of course, countries do not deliberately seek undesirable conditions in order to discourage potential immigrants from coming there. Instead, they are likely to adopt restrictive immigration policies.

The role of immigration policy

Public policies play an important role in determining whether people become immigrants. Sending country governments may make it difficult for people to leave, such as by requiring an exit visa or charging a fee. Such policies allow sending countries to influence the number and characteristics of emigrants. For example, countries may refuse to issue exit visas to highly skilled workers or to political dissidents. Restrictions on emigration beyond requiring a passport are uncommon today, although a few countries still have them, most notably North Korea.

Restrictions on immigration—who can enter a country—are far more common. Virtually every country in the world imposes some limit on the number of immigrants and tries to influence the characteristics of immigrants. This is usually done by determining who can qualify for a visa that allows them to work or live, either temporarily or permanently, in a country. Some countries do not require that foreigners have a visa, particularly if they are only in the country on a temporary basis and are not working there. Such policies, called visa waiver programs, are usually limited to countries that have reciprocal arrangements and are not major sources of unauthorized immigrants. Visa waiver programs are usually aimed at tourist and business travelers and involve a time limit—often three or six months—and do not allow visitors to work in the country they are visiting.

Most of continental Europe has gone even farther and joined the so-called Schengen area. People who travel from one of the 26 member countries to another are not asked to present their passport or a visa when entering or exiting. The Schengen Borders Agreement even extends to people who are not citizens of the member countries. The agreement only allows people freedom of movement, not necessarily the right to live or work in any of the member countries.

In addition, some groups or pairs of countries have agreed to allow each others' citizens unrestricted access to their labor markets. Examples include the European Economic Area (the European Union plus Iceland, Norway and Liechtenstein); the Mercosur bloc in South America (Argentina, Brazil, Paraguay and Uruguay plus Bolivia and Chile); and Australia and New Zealand. Under the 1992 North American Free Trade Agreement (NAFTA), skilled professionals have relatively free movement across the Canadian, Mexican and U.S. labor markets.

The United States has a complex system of immigration quotas and admissions requirements that heavily favors potential immigrants who are closely related to a U.S. citizen or a permanent resident or who are highly skilled and have a U.S. job offer. Immigrants who do not fit into one of those categories typically find it very difficult to migrate legally to the United States. Some immigrants enter as refugees or asylum seekers, of course. A few enter under the unique diversity lottery program, which allocates up to 55,000 permanent resident visas per year to people from countries with historically low rates of immigration to the United States. For fiscal year 2014, more than 9.3 million people entered the diversity lottery, meaning that less than 1 percent ultimately won a visa (U.S. State Department, 2013).

The low success rate among diversity lottery entrants points to the excess demand among potential immigrants to the United States (and other developed countries). Far more people want to enter developed countries than those countries are willing to admit. In the United States, there are lengthy backlogs for some categories of numerically limited permanent resident visas. More people have been approved to receive those visas than are admitted under the annual quotas, so many people must wait years or even decades before they can receive a legal permanent resident visa. Some of those people live in the United States on a temporary visa while waiting for a permanent resident visa; others wait in their home country or another country. Most years, employers submit far more applications for numerically restricted categories of temporary foreign workers than the numbers of visas available. One consequence of this excess demand for visas is that some people enter illegally, while others enter legally on a temporary visa but then illegally overstay their visa. The large number of asylum seekers in developed countries is another consequence of excess demand for visas.

Migration costs

Costs also play a role in determining the size and composition of immigrant flows. Migration costs usually include a passport fee charged by the origin country and a visa fee charged by the destination country. These costs are nontrivial. Table 2.2 lists passport fees in various countries and some common visa fees in the United States. Migrants also bear transportation costs, which may be substantial if traveling a long distance. Decreases in transportation costs are a major reason why immigration has become more common over time.

Undocumented migrants who enter a country illicitly avoid passport and visa fees. However, they often must pay a smuggler to help them enter a country. The United Nations Office on Drugs and Crime (2014) estimates that human smugglers operating between East, North, and West Africa and Europe and between South and North America earn more than $6.75 billion annually. The costs of using a smuggler typically far exceed passport and visa fees. Undocumented immigrants who enter a country illicitly are not trying to avoid paying passport and visa fees but rather cannot get a visa.

Table 2.2 Passport and visa fees

Passport fees around the world in local currencies

Australia	A$208	Mexico	1795 pesos
Canada	C$87	New Zealand	NZ$150
China	200 yuan	Russia	2500 rubles
France	89 €	Singapore	S$80
Germany	59 €	South Africa	R190
India	1000Rs	South Korea	55,000 won
Indonesia	250,000 rupiah	Thailand	1000 baht
Ireland	80 €	Trinidad & Tobago	TT$250
Israel	NIS 220	United Kingdom	£77.50
Japan	16,000¥	United States	US$135

U.S. visa fees

Nonimmigrant (temporary) visas:		*Immigrant (permanent) visas:*	
Visitor or student	$160	Diversity lottery	$330
Temporary worker	$190	Family-based	$650
Fiancé(e) or spouse of U.S. citizen	$240	Intercountry adoption	$720
Treaty trader/investor	$270	Employment-based	$985

Passport fees are for adult applicants as of 2011. U.S. visa fees include petition fees charged by the U.S. Department of Homeland Security for family- and employment-based immigrants and are as of November 2013.

Source: HM Passport Office (2011) "International passport comparisons." Available at: https://www.gov.uk/government/publications/international-passport-comparisons [15 November 2013]; U.S. Department of State (2013) "Fees for visa services." Available at: http://travel.state.gov/visa/temp/types/types_1263.html [17 November 2013]; and U.S. Department of Homeland Security (2013) "Forms." Available at: http://www.uscis.gov/forms [17 November 2013].

The costs of entering a country illicitly usually rise as that country increases border enforcement. As border enforcement increases, entering a country becomes more difficult, and immigrants entering illicitly are therefore more likely to need to hire a smuggler. This increase in demand for smugglers increases the price of hiring them. At the same time, increased border enforcement makes it more difficult for smugglers to enter the country. This increases smugglers' costs and therefore further increases their price.

Figure 2.2 shows a supply and demand framework for smuggling services. The quantity of smuggling services demanded falls as the price increases, creating a negatively sloped demand curve. Meanwhile, more people are willing to act as a smuggler as the price increases, creating a positively sloped supply curve. Increased border enforcement causes demand to increase and supply to decrease. The decrease in supply is due to higher costs. For example, smugglers are more likely to be apprehended and find it more difficult to smuggle people into a country as border enforcement increases. As the figure shows, increased border enforcement results in an unambiguous increase in the price of smuggling services. However, the net effect on quantity—the number of people who hire a smuggler—is ambiguous. The increase in demand causes quantity to increase, while the decrease in supply causes quantity to decrease. The net effect is uncertain. Other factors that might shift the supply or demand for smuggling services include changes in smugglers' other labor market opportunities and changes in visa availability.

Research indicates that smuggling prices along the U.S.–Mexico border increase by 3 to 6 percent when U.S. border enforcement, as measured by hours worked by the U.S. Border Patrol, increases by 10 percent (Roberts et al., 2010). Hiring such a smuggler—called a *coyote*—to help cross the Mexico–U.S. border cost about $2,500 in 2013.

High direct costs of migrating may lead to trafficking. Immigrants who are not able to bear the costs of migrating, either legally or illegally, may make a deal with an employer or a smuggler who promises to help them migrate in exchange for the immigrant working to pay off the debt. These arrangements, called "debt bondage," are akin to the indentured servitude agreements that enabled poor Europeans to immigrate to the United States in previous centuries. Just as some indentured servants were exploited and mistreated back then, so are some

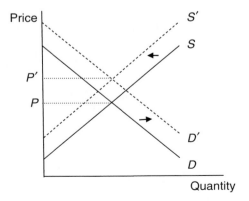

Figure 2.2 The market for smuggling services.

An increase in border enforcement increases the demand for smuggling services and decreases supply. This results in a higher price.

immigrants who enter into debt bondage contracts today. Away from home, unable to speak the local language and with few resources, immigrants who enter into debt bondage contracts are vulnerable to further abuse. They may be forced to work indefinitely as prostitutes, in factories and restaurants, or as household slaves. The higher the costs of migrating, the less likely it is that an immigrant can afford to pay those costs in advance, and therefore the more likely it is that an immigrant enters into a debt bondage contract.

There are other, indirect costs of migrating that many immigrants incur, not just those who are unauthorized or victims of human trafficking. Immigrants may experience psychic, or non-monetary, costs of missing family and friends and having to adjust to a new culture and a new language. They may have difficulty finding work, particularly initially. They may need to go back to school to acquire occupational certifications that are valid in the new country, such as the licenses required in the United States to sell real estate, to cut hair and to practice medicine or law. They may lose their eligibility for a pension program or their right to vote in their home country, and they may need to pay taxes in both the origin and the destination countries.

Some immigrants pay an extraordinarily high price for attempting to migrate: they die. Some unauthorized migrants, refugees and asylum seekers undertake perilous journeys that put them at risk of dying. Between 1990 and 2012, more than 2,200 migrants died in Arizona while trying to enter the United States from Mexico (Binational Migration Institute, 2013). Crossing the border on foot through Arizona involves a two- or three-day trek through a remote, mountainous desert where temperatures often reach 115° F (46° C) degrees or higher during the summer and drop below freezing during the winter.

As high as the death toll of attempting to enter the United States is, it appears to be even higher elsewhere. Since 2000, more than 1,400 migrants have died at sea while trying to reach Australia (Australian Border Deaths Database, 2014). The United Nations High Commissioner for Refugees (2012) declared the Mediterranean Sea the deadliest stretch of water in the world for migrants, with more than 1,500 people drowned or missing in 2011 alone while trying to cross from Africa to Europe.

Immigration paradigms

This book focuses on the neoclassical model of immigration. This model is rooted in individual utility maximization, although it can easily be extended to include the family, the household and the community. There are at least three other paradigms that people who study the economics of immigration should be familiar with: the new economics of migration, dual labor market theory and world-systems theory (Massey et al., 1993). Other disciplines, particularly sociology, often focus more on these paradigms than on the neoclassical model.

The new economics of migration paradigm focuses on immigration as a collective decision made not only to maximize income but also to minimize risks and loosen constraints that result from incomplete markets. Markets are incomplete when supply is not sufficient to meet demand in an economy (or vice versa). For example, families in agricultural areas may not be able to insure against crop losses. There is no market for crop insurance in some countries. They may therefore send a family member to work in an urban area or abroad in order to diversify their income and reduce risk. Financial markets are limited in many developing countries, making it difficult for people to borrow enough money to buy land or start a business. Moving abroad to earn funds may be the best solution to incomplete financial markets.

Dual labor market theory posits that immigration is the result of industrial countries' need for a continual stream of low-skilled, low-wage labor (Piore, 1979). Labor markets in industrialized countries are divided, or segmented, into a primary sector of high-skilled, high-wage jobs and a secondary sector of low-skilled, low-wage jobs. Natives are reluctant to take low-skilled, low-wage jobs, but immigrants will, at least initially, because they have a different frame of reference than natives. Immigrants from poorer countries tend to perceive such jobs more positively than natives of rich countries do. In this theory, immigration is largely a response to firms' demand for workers, and firms may actively recruit workers abroad.

World-systems theory argues that, as capitalism spreads globally, it creates dislocations that lead to migration. For example, international trade may lead to lower prices for goods that are not a country's comparative advantage. Comparative advantage is when a country can produce a good at a lower opportunity cost than other countries. That is, a country with a comparative advantage in a good gives up the fewest resources to produce that good. If a country that opens up to international trade no longer produces a good because another country has a lower cost of producing that good, people who used to produce that good lose their jobs and may become immigrants.

The push and pull factors discussed above include facets of all of these paradigms, particularly the new economics of migration. The neoclassical model developed below can also be modified to include some facets of these paradigms. This book focuses on the neoclassical model because it is the main paradigm in economics.

The migration decision

One of the canonical assumptions of neoclassical economics is that people are utility maximizers. People act on the information they have to make decisions that make them as well off as possible—to maximize their utility—given the constraints they face. In most economic models of the decision to migrate, people's utility depends only on their income, net of migration costs, and income varies across locations. In more complex models, utility depends on multiple factors, such as family members' preferences, and can be uncertain. Formal models of migration were first created by Larry Sjaastad (1962) and others to understand internal migration and then later applied to international migration.

Individuals have a utility function represented by U. For simplicity, the model only compares utility across two locations, the origin and the destination. The destination can be thought of as the best of all possible destinations for a potential immigrant. Individuals thus compare their utility based on their income in the origin and in the destination, net of migration costs, and decide whether to remain in the origin or move to the destination. People move if

$$U(\text{Income in Destination} - \text{Migration Costs}) > U(\text{Income in Origin}) \tag{2.1}$$

and stay in the origin country if the inequality is reversed. People are indifferent about moving if the two sides of the equation are equal.

Box 2.1 Internal migration

Internal migration—the movement of people within national borders—far dwarfs international migration. Economics defines internal migration as moves that result in a change in a person's economic environment. Moving within the same city or region is not internal migration, while moving across a country usually is.

Globally, at least one in eight people are internal migrants, or people who live in their birth country but not in their birth region. Perhaps the largest migration episode in human history is the rural to urban migration movement that has been underway in China since 1978. About 250 million people have moved from rural areas with few economic opportunities to cities with plentiful factory jobs. However, the *hukuo* system acts as a barrier to internal migration in China. Under the *hukuo* system, households are registered to live in a certain region. People have less access to social services, including health care and education, if they live outside that region. Many migrants therefore have left their children behind in rural areas to be raised by grandparents or other relatives.

The United States has had two major long-term migration episodes. The first is the westward movement of the population as the United States acquired new territories in the late 1700s and 1800s. Transportation improvements, most notably the transcontinental railroad, facilitated this movement. The second is the movement of blacks from the South to the North during the 1900s in pursuit of better employment and educational opportunities. Smaller but notable internal migration episodes include movement to California, first by poor farmers during the 1930s Dust Bowl and then by skilled workers joining the state's burgeoning aerospace industry in the 1950s and 1960s, and then an exodus from California in the late 1990s and 2000s as the state's economy slowed relative to the rest of the United States.

Another major example of internal migration is from eastern to western Germany. From 1949 to 1990, East and West Germany were separate countries. East Germany was a socialist state that tried to limit out-migration to the more prosperous West Germany. In the first two years after the fall of the Berlin Wall and collapse of communism, more than 7 percent of the former East Germany's population moved to western Germany. The young and the high skilled were particularly likely to move (Hunt, 2006).

Economics views internal migration, like international migration, as motivated by differences in incomes and living standards. Migration costs are typically much lower for internal migration than for international migration, and there are usually fewer policy barriers to internal migration. Internal migration also often does not require learning a new language. It is therefore no surprise that internal migration is much more common than international migration.

Internal migration is quite common in the United States. About 1.5 to 3 percent of the U.S. population migrates internally each year, and slightly less than one-third of the U.S.-born population lives outside their state of birth. Internal migration in the United States declined by about one-half over the 1990s and 2000s. Greg Kaplan and Sam Schulhofer-Wohl (2012) conjecture that this decline is due in large part to two factors. The first is shrinking geographic differences in the returns to skills as occupations have become more evenly spread across the country. Cross-state differences in earnings within occupations have fallen over time. This reduces workers' potential gains to moving if they plan to stay in the same occupation. The second factor is better information about job opportunities in other parts of the country as a result of the Internet and declining travel costs.

European countries tend to have lower mobility rates than the United States. Raven Molloy, Christopher Smith and Abigail Wozniak (2011) show that only Denmark and Hungary have higher within-country mobility rates than the United States, and only Demark and Finland have higher overall mobility rates (any move at all). Mobility between European countries appears to have been flat or increasing during the early 2000s, perhaps because of rising economic integration there.

Internal migration can be a stepping stone toward international migration or a substitute for it. When people migrate internally, they may develop networks that facilitate international migration. Alternatively, people who can improve their educational and employment opportunities by moving internally may not need to leave the origin country.

If utility increases linearly with income, the model can be simplified by just comparing income in the origin and in the destination, net of migration costs. In this case, if utility depends only on income in the origin and in the destination, people decide to move if

$$Income\ in\ Destination - Migration\ Costs > Income\ in\ Origin \tag{2.2}$$

This simple income-maximization model predicts that increases in a person's income in the destination country will make migration more likely, holding constant income in the origin country and migration costs. Increases in migration costs will make it less likely a person migrates, holding constant income in both countries. Increases in a person's income in the origin country will make it less likely that person migrates, holding constant income in the destination country and migration costs.

The utility- or income-maximization model can be made more realistic in several ways. It can incorporate the fact that income depends on wages and probabilities of being employed. It also can incorporate differences in the costs of living in the origin and destination countries. The model can incorporate a time horizon to indicate that migration may occur only for a certain period, such as while someone is of working age. When a time horizon is added, future income is discounted to its present value. (The appendix to Chapter 1 explains present discounted value.)

In a more realistic model that includes these factors, people migrate if

$$\sum_{t=1}^{T} \frac{\widetilde{Wage_t} \times \widetilde{Prob\ Emp_t} - \widetilde{Cost\ Living_t}}{(1+\delta)^t} - Migration\ Costs >$$

$$\sum_{t=1}^{T} \frac{Wage_t \times Prob\ Emp_t - Cost\ Living_t}{(1+\delta)^t} \tag{2.3}$$

where the terms on the left-hand side (those with a ~ over them) indicate the destination country, the terms on the right-hand side indicate the origin country, and t represents time (usually measured in years). *Wage* is earnings among people who are employed, *Prob Emp* is the probability of being employed and *Cost Living* is the cost of living. The term δ is the discount rate, or the time value of money. The model assumes that migration costs are a one-time cost paid up front when a person migrates. Migration costs therefore are not discounted.

The time horizon of the model, T in equation 2.3, may vary across people. People may decide whether to migrate based on income and cost of living differences for the rest of their lives, their working lives or a shorter time horizon. People with shorter time horizons are less likely to migrate since there is less time to "earn back" the cost of migrating. This may be one reason why young people are more likely than older people to move. (Differences in risk preferences by age are another reason, as discussed later.)

Looking at the present discounted value of income in the origin and in the destination, net of migration costs, makes it clearer that immigration can be viewed as a form of investment. Much like students boost their future earnings by bearing the costs of attending college, immigrants boost their future income by bearing the costs of migrating. Immigrants may even earn less initially after they move than if they had stayed home, but their lifetime income is higher. The model predicts that they won't move otherwise.

Like the simple model, this more complex model predicts that people will be more likely to migrate as the wage in the destination country increases and less likely to migrate as the wage in the origin country increases. People are also more likely to migrate as the probability of finding a job in the destination country increases and less likely to migrate as the probability of finding a job in the origin country increases. An increase in the discount rate reduces the time value of money and makes future income less important in the migration decision. If income increases over time at a different rate in the destination country than in the origin country, for example, this will have a bigger effect on the migration decision for a person with a low discount rate than for a person with a high discount rate.

In the model, an increase in migration costs makes it less likely a person migrates. Migration costs include direct costs, like transportation, as well as indirect costs, like missing family and friends. Migration costs tend to increase with the distance between the origin and the destination. Economists often use distance as a proxy for migration costs since it is fairly easy to measure. In addition, the cultural and linguistic differences between countries may increase as distance increases, causing the psychic costs to be higher. More restrictive immigration policy increases migration costs but can be harder to quantify. Having a larger network of family and friends in the destination is likely to reduce migration costs. Networks pass along information about how to migrate and about opportunities abroad. Speaking the destination country language may also lower migration costs by making it easier to enter a country.

Some of the factors that affect migration costs also affect income in the destination. Having a larger network makes it easier to find a job and housing in the destination. Larger networks also may lead to a better-paying job in the destination. Immigrants who speak the destination country language have more and better opportunities there. More restrictive immigration policy may boost immigrants' incomes by keeping the supply of immigrant workers in the destination country labor market low. This creates a paradox—restrictive immigration policies that raise incomes in the destination country make immigration more attractive while they simultaneously make it more difficult to migrate legally. Illegal immigration is often the result. However, unauthorized immigrants tend to earn less than legal immigrants, making it less desirable to migrate illegally than legally.

This model can explain not only why people move but also why some people move again. Some people become return migrants by moving back to their home country. Changes in conditions in the origin country relative to the destination country, such as a relative increase in wages or the probability of employment in the home country, may cause a person to return migrate, for example. Some other people become repeat migrants by moving on to yet another destination country. Conditions in that new destination may have improved relative to the place where the migrant currently is, making it more desirable to be in the new destination than in the current destination.

This model of the migration decision can be adapted to include some of the other push and pull factors discussed earlier, but not all of them. The model in equation 2.3 focuses on labor market outcomes and the cost of living. The model can easily be modified to incorporate taxes and government transfers, like social insurance and public assistance programs, that affect incomes. It implicitly includes economic growth, which affects future wages and employment probabilities. If economic growth is stronger in the destination country than in the origin country, future income is likely to increase faster in the former than in the latter. Schooling and health care also may affect future wages and employment probabilities. For example, migrating may enable someone to obtain more education, which boosts earnings in the destination country. (Obtaining education abroad may also boost earnings in the origin country, but education usually is the most valuable in the country in which is it obtained.)

The model can also incorporate political and social factors that affect earnings, such as discrimination, insofar as such factors affect earnings or the cost of living. Crime and corruption, for example, might raise the cost of living in a country. The model does not easily include factors that do not affect earnings or the cost of living, such as religious freedom.

This model applies well to economic migrants, people who migrate to work or study. It can be stretched to apply to migrants who move to join family or friends. Such migrants may have lower migration costs because family or friends who have already migrated may be able to pay those costs. Having family or friends in the destination country may also boost the probability of finding a job or reduce the cost of living there. The model does not apply well to refugees, asylum seekers and other involuntary migrants, nor to migrants moving because of a natural disaster or famine. Such migrants move in part for economic reasons, such as the inability to earn a living, but primarily because of other factors not captured by the model.

The model does a particularly poor job of explaining migration because of better amenities in the destination country than in the origin country. Areas with more amenities are likely to have a higher cost of living since more people want to live there. A model like equation 2.3 therefore predicts that people are less likely to migrate to areas with amenities that are reflected in a higher cost of living. However, access to amenities increases people's utility, so a more general model of utility that is not exclusively focused on income may explain why people move to areas with better amenities.

Family decision-making

The migration decision may be made by an individual or by a family. A family may want to remain together—everyone moves or everyone stays. Alternatively, a family may decide that one member will migrate in order to boost total family income. If a family decides to remain together, it chooses whether to migrate based on what makes the family as a whole best off. But that decision may not make each individual within the family better off. For example, a wife may earn more if a family moves, but her husband may earn less. The family moves if the wife's gains are greater than the husband's losses, net of migration costs. In this case, the husband is a "tied mover," or someone who moves because of his ties to another migrant. If the family stays because the wife's gains are smaller than the husband's losses, the wife would be a "tied stayer."

Figure 2.3 illustrates the joint decision. The horizontal axis shows the wife's private gains from migration, which is the present value of the change in her income less her migration costs (ΔPV_W). If she were single, she would move if those gains were positive. This occurs in region C, D or E in the figure. The vertical axis shows the husband's private gains from migration (ΔPV_H). If he were single, he would move if his gain were positive, which occurs in region A, B or C in the figure. The couple benefits from moving if the sum of their net gains is positive.[1] The 45° line in the figure shows the sum of their net gains. To the right of this line, the sum is positive; to the left of this line, the sum is negative. The couple therefore jointly benefits from moving if they are in region B, C or D.

Another possibility is that one or more members of a family migrate while others stay behind. Those with the biggest gains from migration are the most likely to migrate, of course. For families, having some but not all members migrate may be a way to reduce risk. Immigration or internal migration is a way for a family to diversify its sources of income. Rural families can reduce the likelihood that a bad harvest will devastate the family if a family member works in a factory in a city, for example.

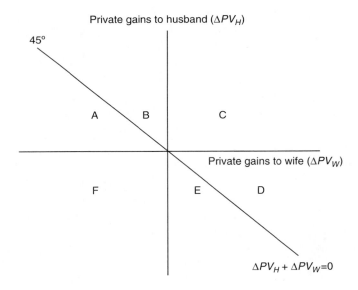

Figure 2.3 Immigration under joint decision-making.

The husband gains from moving in regions A, B and C. The wife gains from moving in regions C, D and E. The couple jointly gains from moving in regions B, C and D.

Family members who migrate can send back remittances to those who stay behind. Remittances are money sent by immigrants to people back in the origin country. Those who migrate first also may pave the way for the rest of the family to migrate later. Remittances sent back by immigrants may fund migration by other family members, and immigrants may be able to sponsor their relatives for visas. In many cases, there is an expectation that an immigrant will send remittances home to replace the income that person contributed to the family when he was working in the origin country.

Uncertainty

Although migration can be a way for families to reduce risk, moving is often a risky activity. The model in equation 2.3 already includes the risk of not finding a job. It can be adapted further to include uncertainty by using the expected values of income and migration costs. Equation 2.3 can also incorporate a measure of the variation in those values to account for the disutility of uncertainty—most people dislike not knowing what their income will be, and they dislike fluctuations in their income.

Income may be more uncertain in the destination country than in the origin country since immigrants are likely to have less knowledge about their prospects abroad than at home. Income also may be more variable abroad than at home since immigrants may have fewer family and friends to rely on for help in bad times. On the other hand, the destination country may have a more generous social insurance and public assistance system, reducing uncertainty and fluctuations in income.

The model can also include a measure of potential immigrants' tolerance for risk or their risk aversion. Some potential immigrants may be quite willing to bear risk, while others may not. The model can incorporate utility functions that allow for varying degrees of risk aversion. If income is more uncertain in the destination country than in the origin country, people with less tolerance for risk will be less likely to migrate for a given difference in expected income. Risk aversion may depend on factors such as age, with older people more risk averse; on sex, with women more risk averse; and on the number of family and friends in the destination country, with people with smaller networks more risk averse.

Do potential immigrants have accurate expectations about their incomes if they move? Previous immigrants are one of the main sources of information about incomes abroad.[2] Previous immigrants may exaggerate their success, creating over-optimistic expectations about incomes abroad. Alternatively, previous immigrants may downplay their incomes abroad in order to reduce expectations about how much money they can send to family and friends. Relatives who live abroad are likely to be a source of information about income, but do potential migrants with relatives abroad have better estimates of their incomes if they move than potential migrants without relatives abroad?

To examine these questions, David McKenzie, John Gibson and Steven Stillman (2013) surveyed Tongans who applied for visas to move to New Zealand about what they expected to earn if they moved. The economists compared potential migrants' expectations to their actual earnings if they moved. They find that men underestimated their likely earnings in New Zealand by almost two-thirds prior to moving; women estimated their likely earnings quite accurately. In recent years, Tongan men experienced much larger earnings gains than women when they moved to New Zealand, a fact that potential migrants did not seem to know. In addition, men who had non-immediate relatives living in New Zealand tended to underestimate their earnings more than men with no relatives living in New Zealand or with close relatives living there. This suggests that immigrants understate or do not report their earnings to their extended family back in Tonga.

The role of immigration policy

The model does not directly incorporate immigration policy in either the destination country or the origin country. It assumes that people can move if they want to, and it says nothing about whether migration is legal or illegal. It can apply to legal and illegal, skilled and unskilled immigrants alike. The model can easily incorporate immigration policies that are based on quantifiable factors, such as policies in destination countries that allow only people with incomes or education above a certain level to move there. This can be done by making the ability to migrate subject to meeting such conditions.

However, the model cannot easily incorporate immigration quotas, which limit the number of immigrants allowed to legally enter a country. This is because the model is at the individual level, not at the aggregate level—it says nothing about the number or share of people who want to move, only whether an individual wants to move. One way to incorporate restrictive policies like quotas is via migration costs, which can be modeled to increase as immigration policies become more restrictive. The gravity model, explained next, can better incorporate immigration quotas.

The gravity model of migration

The utility- or income-maximization model discussed above is a microeconomic model. It models whether a person benefits from migrating. Economists are interested not only in whether a certain person becomes an immigrant but also in how many people in total or what proportion of a country's population become immigrants. The gravity model is frequently used to model migration at the macroeconomic level. The model is implicitly rooted in utility or income maximization—it assumes that people base their decision to migrate on whether migration makes them better off.

The gravity model is based on Isaac Newton's law of gravity, which states that the attraction between two bodies is directly proportional to the product of their masses and inversely proportional to the distance between them. George Zipf applied this idea to migration in 1946.[3] In the gravity model, the volume of migration between two countries is equal to a constant times the product of those countries' population, and inversely proportional to the distance between them, or

$$Migration\ from\ Origin\ to\ Destination = c \times \frac{Population\ of\ Origin \times Population\ of\ Destination}{Distance\ between\ Origin\ and\ Destination} \quad (2.4)$$

where c is a constant for a given origin and destination pair. Intuitively, the bigger the population in each of the countries, the bigger the number of people who benefit from migrating.

Further, the effect is multiplicative, not additive. The bigger the population of the other country, the more opportunities there are there, which increases the number of people who benefit from moving. In addition, the bigger the distance between two countries, the higher migration costs are. Fewer people will therefore benefit from migrating.

Migration between two countries is also likely to depend on relative income in those countries. Migrants are expected to flow from countries with relatively low incomes to countries with relatively high incomes. The gravity model of migration flows from the origin to the destination is better written as

$$Migration = c \times \frac{Population\ of\ Origin \times Population\ of\ Destination}{Distance\ between\ Origin\ and\ Destination} \times \frac{Income\ in\ Destination}{Income\ in\ Origin} \quad (2.5)$$

When the model is applied to data, GDP per capita is often used as a proxy for income.

Applications of the gravity model also often include other variables that proxy for migration costs or the benefits of migrating. For example, the benefits might be higher (and the costs lower) if more people have already migrated from the origin to the destination. The benefits are likely to be smaller the higher the cost of living in the destination relative to the origin. The benefits are likely to be bigger if people in the two countries speak the same language. Migration costs are likely to be lower if two countries have historical ties, such as one being a colony of the other, and if two countries are contiguous.

Applications of the gravity model may also include variables that measure the restrictiveness of immigration policy. For example, immigration quotas are expected to reduce immigration flows, while liberal immigration policies, like belonging to the Schengen Borders Agreement or the European Economic Area, are expected to increase immigration flows.

Like the utility- or income-maximization model, the gravity model applies best to economic migrants. It has limited applicability to family-based migrants, although a bigger population in either the origin or the destination may increase the number of family members who have already migrated. It also has limited applicability to refugees and asylum seekers.

The gravity model applies to both temporary and permanent migration. Most data on migration flows or immigrant stocks do not distinguish between temporary and permanent migrants, making a model that applies to both useful. It also applies to both legal and illegal immigration and to skilled and unskilled immigrants. Data on flows and stocks often do not distinguish between legal and illegal immigrants, while data on stocks and flows by education level are increasingly available.

Empirical evidence

Economists use the utility- or income-maximization model to estimate the determinants of migration when using individual-level data and the gravity model when using aggregate data. More data on migration are available at the macro level than at the micro level, so the gravity model is more commonly applied to data than the utility- or income-maximization model. Traditionally, most studies used data on immigration only to one country, but large datasets on bilateral migration flows—flows between pairs of countries—have been created in recent years. Some of the results of studies using those data are consistent with theoretical predictions while others are not.

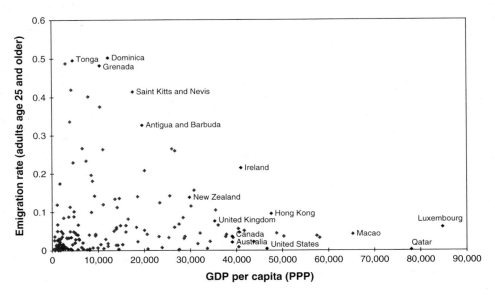

Figure 2.4 Emigration rate and source country GDP, 2010.

Source: Emigration rate from Brücker, H., Capuano, S. and Marfoulk, A. (2013) "Education, gender and international migration: Insights from a panel-dataset 1980–2010." Available at: http://www.iab.de/en/daten/ iab-brain-drain-data.aspx [12 December 2013]; GDP per capita (PPP) data from World Bank (2013) "GDP per capita, PPP." Available at: http://data.worldbank.org/indicator/NY.GDP.PCAP.PP.CD [17 December 2013].

The role of economic conditions

The utility- or income-maximization and gravity models predict that as income in a country increases, emigration from that country should decrease and immigration to that country should increase, all else equal. Figure 2.4 gives an initial look at the relationship between emigration and income in the origin country, a push factor. (Chapter 3 looks at the role of income and other pull factors in where immigrants go.) The emigration rate is based on the number of adult immigrants aged 25 and older in 20 Organization for Economic Cooperation and Development (OECD) countries in 2010. GDP per capita, converted into U.S. dollars using purchasing power parity (PPP) rates, in 2010 serves as a measure of income. The figure shows a sizable cluster of countries with low incomes and low emigration rates. Several notable countries are indicated by name, but each diamond in the figure indicates a country.

Unlike the negative prediction of the model, there is no clear pattern in the figure— higher incomes in the origin country neither discourage nor encourage emigration. Other studies likewise fail to find a significant relationship between emigration and origin country GDP per capita (e.g., Mayda, 2010).[4] Some studies even find a positive relationship, perhaps because higher incomes or stronger economic growth in the origin enable people to cover the costs of migrating (e.g., Greenwood et al., 1999). (As discussed in Chapter 3, research does typically find a positive relationship between immigration and destination country GDP per capita.)

The lack of a negative relationship in the figure does not necessarily mean that income in the origin country does not affect whether people move. The data only include immigrants to

20 countries, almost all of them high income. Data that include all destinations might show a different pattern. In addition, the figure compares the stock, or the accumulated number, of emigrants as a fraction of the origin country population with GDP in the origin country at a point in time. The gravity model is about flows of migrants, not stocks. Current income in the origin may not be closely related to what income was in the origin when emigrants left, and emigration may have affected average incomes in the origin. However, research by Anna Maria Mayda (2010) finds a similar null result using annual data on flows (although still using only a sample of OECD destination countries).

Mayda (2010) finds that the relationship between origin country income and emigration becomes negative—as predicted by theory—when destination country immigration policies become less restrictive. Restrictive immigration policies may dampen the effect of push (and pull) factors by preventing some people from migrating. People who would like to move from low-income to high-income countries may not be able to do so (at least legally) because of restrictive immigration policies.

Some indirect evidence suggests that income in the origin country does affect whether people migrate. Research shows that birth rates and rainfall—variables that are related to income—in Mexico affect whether people migrate from there to the United States. The size of birth cohorts in Mexico is positively related to the Mexico–U.S. emigration rate (Hanson and McIntosh, 2010). A bigger birth cohort means a bigger increase in labor supply when a cohort reaches working age. The increase in labor supply reduces wages, all else equal. Population growth in Mexico can account for two-fifths of emigration from there to the United States between 1977 and 1997. Population growth has slowed dramatically in Mexico over the last few decades. If this theory is correct (and if nothing else changes), that portends a drop in Mexico–U.S. migration in the future. The level of rainfall is important to agricultural communities in Mexico—too little rainfall can mean crop failures and lower incomes in rural areas. Low rainfall is associated with more emigration from rural areas (Munshi, 2003).

Research suggests that emigration flows respond more to long-run trends in income than to short-run fluctuations in income (Simpson and Sparber, 2013). For most people, whether to migrate is a major decision made in response to long-standing circumstances, not a response to temporary shocks. Migration tends to respond slowly over time to changes in economic, political and social factors, not quickly. Refugee movements can be an exception, however. They often occur quickly in response to abrupt, major changes in political and social conditions.

The availability of social insurance programs appears to affect whether people migrate. Research finds that immigration to the United States is lower from countries that have public health insurance and unemployment insurance programs (Greenwood et al., 1999). Immigration to the United States is higher from countries that require employers to make severance payments when they dismiss workers, perhaps because such funds enable people to move. Employment-related funding of old-age and sickness programs in the origin increases immigration to the United States, presumably because such funding raises the tax burden on workers. Taxes also matter, at least for football stars (see Box 2.2, "Football players and tax rates").

The role of migration costs

The models also predict that as migration costs increase, emigration should decrease. Researchers typically use the distance between countries, whether countries share a common language

Box 2.2 Football players and tax rates

The utility- or income-maximization model and the gravity model predict that high tax rates in a country should encourage emigration and discourage immigration, all else equal. Research shows that this is the case for a group of highly compensated workers: European football players. Top football (soccer in the United States) players earn millions of dollars a year, giving them a potential reason to move in response to tax rates. Their mobility was limited until 1995, however, because the European Football Association required that teams could not field more than three foreign players in any club competition. Most national competitions had a similar rule. As a result, clubs had few foreign players. The European Court of Justice ruled against the three-player rule in late 1995, paving the way for football players to move across countries.

Henrik Kleven, Camille Landais and Emmanuel Saez (2013) use data on the rosters of football clubs in 14 European countries from 1985 to 2008 to examine how top marginal tax rates on labor income are related to the immigrant shares of clubs before and after 1995. Before 1995, immigrant shares were unrelated to tax rates. After 1995, however, clubs in countries with higher tax rates had lower immigrant shares. Moreover, native-born players were more likely to be playing in another country the higher the tax rate in their origin country. Higher tax rates thus encouraged emigration and discouraged immigration by football players. Interestingly, clubs in countries with higher tax rates earned fewer points in European Football Association competitions after 1995. Countries with higher tax rates were less able to attract or retain good players, and so they lost more matches.

and whether countries have a colonial history as proxies for migration costs. Studies typically find the distance between two countries is negatively related to the scale of migration between them, while having a common language is positively related to the scale of migration between two countries. Studies typically find that having a colonial relationship is positively related to the scale of migration between two countries.

Although the models treat migration costs and income in the origin as separate variables, they may jointly affect whether people emigrate. Timothy Hatton and Jeffrey Williamson (2005) observe that there is an inverse U-shaped relationship between economic development in a country and emigration. They show that increases in income in middle- or high-income countries, like those in much of East Asia, South America and Western Europe, appear to reduce emigration rates to the United States. Increases in income in low-income countries, like those in much of Africa, appear to boost emigration rates to the United States, in contrast.

Hatton and Williamson offer two potential, non-mutually-exclusive explanations for this pattern. First, at low levels of average income in the origin, few people may be able to finance an international move. As average income rises, more people can afford to move. But when average income becomes high, the gains from moving are smaller. Second, the structural and demographic changes that often cause or accompany rising incomes—such as moving from an agricultural to an industrial economy, opening up to more international trade and declining childhood mortality—may generate more migration in early stages than later on.

Another example of the joint effects of migration costs and income is the effect of women's rights in the origin country on emigration. At low levels of women's rights, women may face prohibitively high costs of migration. For example, they may be required to have their husband's or, if single, a male relative's permission to leave the country. Women also have limited earnings opportunities in countries with low levels of women's rights. As women's rights increase, women may be more able to leave. But their labor market opportunities likely improve as well, which reduces their incentive to emigrate. Research shows an inverse U-shaped pattern between women's rights and the emigration rate of highly-educated women relative to highly-educated men (Nejad, 2013). Saudi Arabia is on the left-hand side of the inverse U, with increases in women's rights predicted to increase emigration by women relative to men there, while Costa Rica, Greece, Malaysia and Turkey are all on the right-hand side of the U, with increases in women's rights predicted to decrease emigration by women relative to men.

The role of migrant networks

The existence and size of migrant networks also influence whether people become immigrants. Networks typically lower the costs of migrating while raising the benefits. Based on surveys conducted in rural Mexican communities between 1987 and 1992, Douglas Massey and Kristin Espinosa (1997) show that the odds of the average young adult male becoming an undocumented U.S. immigrant were about 4 percent each year. If a man's parent has migrated, the odds that he himself will migrate increase by more than one-half; if he has two siblings who have migrated, the odds more than double. The higher the fraction of people in his hometown who have migrated to the United States, the more likely he is to migrate. More generally, the higher the share of a country's population already living in the United States, the higher that country's emigration rate to the United States. Research shows that the annual flow of immigrants increases by 4.7 people if the stock of immigrants from that country increases by one thousand people, although the effect dies out as the migrant stock gets bigger (Clark, Hatton and Williamson, 2007).

Empirical evidence on refugees

A study by Susanne Schmeidl (1997) of refugees between 1971 and 1990 shows that the number of refugees depends primarily on political, not economic, conditions. Specifically, the number of refugees fleeing a country is bigger when a country is experiencing genocide or a civil war, especially a civil war that involves foreign intervention. The number of refugees is not directly related to economic conditions, as proxied by energy consumption per capita and population density. However, the effect of genocide or a civil war on the number of refugees appears to be larger in poorer countries than in richer countries. People in more developed or more population-dense countries appear to be more likely to remain in their country during genocide or a civil war. Conventional economic models like those presented here thus have limited applicability to refugees.

Research indicates that the number of asylum seekers likewise depends on political conditions. The number of asylum applicants from a source country is higher when a country is experiencing conflict, political oppression or human rights abuses (Neumayer, 2005; Hatton, 2009). However, economic conditions in the origin country appear to matter as well. This suggests that at least some asylum seekers are economic, not humanitarian, migrants.

The role of immigration policy

Immigration policy in receiving countries plays an important role in determining the number of people who become immigrants. For example, the 1986 Immigration Reform and Control Act, which gave legal status to 2.7 million unauthorized U.S. immigrants, led to substantial increases in the number of legal and illegal immigrants from Mexico entering the United States to reunite with family members who had acquired legal status (Orrenius and Zavodny, 2003, 2012). The yearly probability of undocumented migration to the United States rose from 4 percent to 35 percent for young Mexican men who lived in a household where someone received amnesty under a 1986 U.S. legalization program (Massey and Espinosa, 1997).

Immigration policy also determines where people go. The next chapter turns from looking at why people become immigrants and where they are from to where they go when they become immigrants.

Problems and discussion questions

1   Explain which push and pull factors apply to the following groups of immigrants: economic migrants; foreign students; family members; refugees and asylum seekers; and victims of human trafficking.

2   Using exchange rates, such as those available from the World Bank, convert the passport visas for various countries in Table 2.2 into a common currency. Which country has the highest fee, and which has the lowest? What factors do you think determine how much a country charges for a passport?

3   Why would a country waive visa requirements for immigrants from some countries but not from others?

4   Explain in what region(s) in Figure 2.3 the husband or wife is a tied stayer or a tied mover.

5   Suppose a person has a utility function that increases linearly with net income. Suppose the person can earn the equivalent of $8,000 if employed in the origin country and $12,000 if employed in the destination country. At what level of migration costs is this person indifferent to moving if the probability of employment is 100 percent in both countries? If migration costs $1,000, and the person has a 90 percent chance of being employed in the origin, how high does the probability of employment in the destination need to be for this person to be willing to move?

6   Describe the differences between a person with a low discount rate and a person with a high discount rate. How does the discount rate affect the decision to migrate? Do you think you have a high or low discount rate, and why? Similarly, how does risk aversion affect the decision to migrate?

7   Describe the determinants of an interesting migrant flow. Which push and pull factors influenced that flow?

8   A couple is considering moving to Tokyo from New York. Ashley's cost of moving is $300, and Casey's cost of moving is $600. Ashley earns $500 in New York and $550 in Tokyo (after converting earnings from yen into dollars). Casey earns $200 in New York and $1000 in Tokyo. Will they move as a couple? Is one of them a tied mover or a tied stayer?

9   Using the supply and demand model of smuggling services, explain how an increase in the number of visas affects the quantity and price of smuggling services.

10   Think about a friend's or relative's migration experience. Describe where that person came from, and when, how and why that person migrated. Consider the following questions: Was that person a voluntary or involuntary migrant? Did networks help that person migrate, and how? What push factors may have contributed to her decision to migrate?

Notes

1   The model assumes that the net gains can simply be added, or there are no spillovers from one spouse to the other as a result of where they live and there are no savings in migration costs when both spouses move.

2   The mass media can be another source of information. Research shows that, in Indonesia, access to cable television reduces internal migration by giving people more information about labor markets in potential destinations. See Farré and Fasani (2013).

3   Zipf analyzed internal migration, but the model applies to international migration as well. The gravity model has also been used to model bilateral trade patterns, or imports and exports between pairs of countries.

4   A notable exception that does find a negative relationship between outflows and origin country GDP per capita is Pedersen, Pylikova and Smith (2008). Results in studies that use the ratio of origin to destination GDP per capita, adjusted for PPP, are mixed. One study that finds no significant effect is Grogger and Hanson (2011). Studies that find significant negative effects include Hatton and Williamson (2005) and Clark, Hatton and Williamson (2007).

Internet resources

Herbert Brücker, Stella Capuano and Abdeslam Marfouk have made data on immigrants in 20 OECD destination countries by year, gender, country of origin and education level available at the Institute for Employment Research's website (IAB): http://www.iab.de/en/daten/iab-brain-drain-data.aspx.

The OECD's International Migration Database has data on stocks and flows of immigrants for OECD countries by nationality and country of birth: http://stats.oecd.org/Index.aspx?DataSetCode=MIG.

Suggestions for further reading

Hatton, T.J. and Williamson, J.G. (2005) "What fundamentals drive world migration?" In: Borjas, G.J. and Crisp, J. (eds.) *Poverty, International Migration and Asylum*. Hampshire, UK: Palgrave-Macmillan for WIDER, pp. 15–38.

Massey, D.S. and Espinosa, K.E. (1997) "What's driving Mexico-U.S. migration? A theoretical, empirical, and policy analysis." *American Journal of Sociology* 102(4), pp. 939–999.

Sjaastad, L. (1962) "The costs and returns of human migration." *Journal of Political Economy* 70(5), pp. 80–93.

References

Araragi, S. (2013) "Japan: Collapse of empire and repatriation." In: Ness, I. (ed.) *The Encyclopedia of Global Human Migration.* Wiley. Available at: http://onlinelibrary.wiley.com/book/10.1002/9781444351071 [8 May 2014].

Australian Border Deaths Database (2014) "Australian border deaths database." Available at: http://artsonline.monash.edu.au/thebordercrossingobservatory/publications/australian-border-deaths-database/ [10 February 2014].

Binational Migration Institute (2013) *A Continued Humanitarian Crisis at the Border: Undocumented Border Crosser Deaths Recorded by the Pima County Office of the Medical Examiner, 1990–2012.* Arizona: University of Arizona.

Clark, X., Hatton, T.J. and Williamson, J.G. (2007) "Explaining U.S. immigration, 1971-1998." *Review of Economics and Statistics* 89(2), pp. 359–373.

Farré, L. and Fasani, F. (2013) "Media exposure and internal migration: Evidence from Indonesia." *Journal of Development Economics* 102, pp. 48–61.

Gibney, M.J. and Hansen, R. (eds.) (2005) *Immigration and Asylum: From 1900 to the Present.* Santa Barbara, CA: ABC-CLIO.

Greenwood, M.J., McDowell, J.M., Waldman, D.M. and Zahniser, S.S. (1999) "The influence of social programs in source countries on various classes of U.S. immigration." *Journal of the American Statistical Association* 94(445), pp. 64–74.

Grogger, J. and Hanson, G.H. (2011) "Income maximization and the selection and sorting of international migrants." *Journal of Development Economics* 95(1), pp. 42–57.

Hanson, G.H. and McIntosh, C. (2010) "The Great Mexican emigration." *Review of Economics and Statistics* 92(4), pp. 798–810.

Hatton, T.J. (2009) "The rise and fall of asylum: what happened and why?" *Economic Journal* 119(535), F183–F213.

Hatton, T.J. and Williamson, J.G. (2005) "What fundamentals drive world migration?" In: Borjas, G.J. and Crisp, J. (eds.) *Poverty, International Migration and Asylum.* Hampshire, UK: Palgrave-Macmillan for WIDER, pp. 15–38.

Hicks, J. (1932) *The Theory of Wages.* London: Macmillan.

Hunt, J. (2006) "Staunching emigration from East Germany: Age and the determinants of migration." *Journal of the European Economic Association* 4(5), pp. 1014–1037.

Kaplan, G. and Schulhofer-Wohl, S. (2012) "Understanding the long-run decline in interstate migration." *National Bureau of Economic Research Working Paper* No. 18507. Cambridge, MA: National Bureau of Economic Research.

Kleven, H.J., Landais, C. and Saez, E. (2013) "Taxation and international migration of superstars: Evidence from the European football market." *American Economic Review* 103(5): 1892–1924.

Kugler, A. and Yuksel, M. (2008) "Effects of low-skilled immigration on U.S. natives: Evidence from Hurricane Mitch." *IZA Discussion Paper* No. 3670, Bonn, Germany: Institute for the Study of Labor.

Massey, D.S., Arango, J., Hugo, G., Kouaouci, A., Pellegrino, A. and Taylor, J.E. (1993) "Theories of international migration: A review and appraisal." *Population and Development Review* 19(3), pp. 431–466.

Massey, D.S. and Espinosa, K.E. (1997) "What's driving Mexico-U.S. migration? A theoretical, empirical, and policy analysis." *American Journal of Sociology* 102(4), pp. 939–999.

Mayda, A.M. (2010) "International migration: A panel analysis of the determinants of bilateral flows." *Journal of Population Economics* 23(4), pp. 1249–1274.

McKenzie, D., Gibson, J. and Stillman, S. (2013) "A land of milk and honey with streets paved with gold: Do emigrants have over-optimistic expectations about incomes abroad?" *Journal of Development Economics* 102, pp. 116–127.

Molloy, R., Smith, C.L. and Wozniak, A. (2011) "Internal migration in the United States." *Journal of Economic Perspectives* 25(3), pp. 173–196.

Munshi, K. (2003) "Networks in the modern economy: Mexican migrants in the U.S. labor market." *Quarterly Journal of Economics* 118(2), pp. 549–599.

Nejad, M.N. (2013) "Institutionalized inequality and brain drain: An empirical study of the effects of women's rights on the gender gap in high-skilled migration." *IZA Discussion Paper* No. 7864, Bonn, Germany: Institute for the Study of Labor.

Neumayer, E. (2005) "Bogus refugees? The determinants of asylum migration to Western Europe." *International Studies Quarterly* 49(3), pp. 389–409.

Ó Gráda, C. and O'Rourke, K.H. (1997) "Migration as disaster relief: Lessons from the great Irish famine." *European Review of Economic History* 1(1), pp. 3–25.

Orrenius, P.M. and Zavodny, M. (2003) "Do amnesty programs reduce undocumented immigration? Evidence from IRCA." *Demography* 40(3), pp. 437–450.

Orrenius, P.M. and Zavodny, M. (2012) "The economic consequences of amnesty for unauthorized immigrants." *Cato Journal* 32(1), pp. 85–106.

Pedersen, P.J., Pylikova, M. and Smith, N. (2008) "Selection and network effects: Migration flows into OECD countries 1990–2000." *European Economic Review* 52(7), pp. 1160–1186.

Piore, M.J. (1979) *Birds of Passage: Migrant Labor and Industrial Societies.* Cambridge: Cambridge University Press.

Roberts, B., Hanson, G., Cornwell, D. and Borger, S. (2010) "An analysis of migrant smuggler costs along the Southwest border." *Office of Immigration Statistics Working Paper.* Washington, DC: U.S. Department of Homeland Security.

Schmeidl, S. (1997) "Exploring the causes of forced migration: A pooled time-series analysis, 1971-1990." *Social Science Quarterly* 78(2), pp. 284–308.

Simpson, N.B. and Sparber, C. (2013) "The short- and long-run determinants of less-educated immigrant flows into U.S. states." *Southern Economic Journal* 80(2), pp. 414–438.

Sjaastad, L. (1962) "The costs and returns of human migration." *Journal of Political Economy* 70(5), pp. 80–93.

United Nations High Commissioner for Refugees (2012) "Mediterranean takes record as most deadly stretch of water for refugees and migrants in 2011." New York, NY: United Nations. Available at: http://www.unhcr.org/4f27e01f9.html [17 November 2013].

United Nations High Commissioner for Refugees (UNHCR) (2013) *UNHCR Statistical Yearbook 2011*, 11th edition. New York, NY: United Nations.

United Nations Office on Drugs and Crime (2014) "Smuggling of migrants: the harsh search for a better life." Available at: http://www.unodc.org/toc/en/crimes/migrant-smuggling.html [15 May 2014].

U.S. State Department (2013) "DV 2014: Selected entrants." Available at: http://travel.state.gov/content/visas/english/immigrate/diversity-visa/dv2014-selected-entrants.html. [15 May 2014].

World Bank (2014) "GDP per capita." Available at: http://data.worldbank.org/indicator/NY.GDP.PCAP.CD [20 February 2014].

Zamindar, V. (2013) "India–Pakistan partition 1947 and forced migration." In: Ness, I. (ed.), *The Encyclopedia of Global Human Migration.* Wiley. Available at: http://onlinelibrary.wiley.com/book/10.1002/9781444351071 [accessed 8 May 2014].

Zipf, G.K. (1946) "The P_1P_2/D hypothesis: On the intercity movement of persons." *American Sociological Review* 11(6), pp. 677–686.

3   Where Immigrants Go and For How Long

Why does the United States have almost 46 million immigrants while Fiji has only 23,000? After all, Fiji sounds like a very nice place to live. But Fiji is much poorer than the United States (and perhaps white sand beaches aren't everyone's idea of paradise). So then why does Norway—one of the richest countries in the world, with a higher GDP per capita than the United States—have only 700,000 immigrants?[1]

The theoretical models of migration presented in Chapter 2 predict that immigrant inflows increase as a receiving country's income increases and as its population rises. The models also predict that immigrant inflows increase if migration costs fall, migrant networks grow or immigration policy becomes less restrictive. As discussed in this chapter, empirical evidence indicates that economic conditions in potential destinations play an important role in whether people decide to migrate and where they go. Other characteristics of receiving countries, such as proximity to the sending country, appear to matter as well.

After examining where immigrants tend to go across potential destinations and why, this chapter examines where immigrants tend to go within destination countries. Whether immigrants are attracted to countries or areas within countries with relatively generous public assistance—the "welfare magnet" hypothesis—is of particular interest to many economists, policymakers and taxpayers. The chapter also discusses the determinants of whether immigrants remain in the destination country and for how long.

Immigrant destinations

A large share of immigrants go to just a handful of countries. Table 3.1 lists the countries with the largest number of immigrants. The United States tops the list. The United States accounts for less than 5 percent of the world's population but has almost 20 percent of the world's immigrants. Russia, which is second, receives large numbers of migrants from other former-Soviet Union countries. Germany is third, in large part because in the 1960s and early 1970s it recruited workers from Turkey who stayed and were joined by their families. Saudi Arabia and the United Arab Emirates, which have large numbers of temporary foreign workers who are not allowed to bring their families or stay permanently, round out the top five. The top ten destination countries account for more than one-half of all immigrants worldwide.

Immigrants go primarily to the countries listed in Table 3.1 for four main reasons. First, economic opportunities are better there than in immigrants' origin country and other

Table 3.1 Top 15 immigrant-receiving countries, 2013

	Share of global migrants (%)	*Number of migrants (millions)*
United States	19.8	45.8
Russia	4.8	11.0
Germany	4.3	9.8
Saudi Arabia	3.9	9.1
United Arab Emirates	3.4	7.8
United Kingdom	3.4	7.8
France	3.2	7.4
Canada	3.2	7.3
Australia	2.8	6.5
Spain	2.8	6.5
Italy	2.5	5.7
India	2.3	5.3
Ukraine	2.2	5.2
Pakistan	1.8	4.1
Thailand	1.6	3.7

Source: United Nations, Department of Economic and Social Affairs (2013) "Trends in International Migrant Stock: The 2013 revision." Available at: http://esa.un.org/unmigration/TIMSA2013/migrantstocks2013.htm?mtotals [3 February 2014].

potential destinations. These destination countries have relatively high incomes, either globally or relative to nearby countries. Second, having large numbers of immigrants means a country has networks of family and friends that lead to yet more immigration. Third, some high-immigration countries are geographically located near other populous, poorer countries. The cost of migrating to them is therefore relatively low for large numbers of potential migrants. Lastly, most of the countries listed in Table 3.1 have fairly generous immigration policies that allow large numbers of immigrants to enter legally, although there are certainly exceptions. These four reasons are discussed in turn below.

The role of economic conditions

Economic opportunities are a powerful force behind immigration. A country's immigrant share—the fraction of its population comprised of immigrants—is strongly positively related to its GDP per capita. Figure 3.1 shows the relationship between GDP per capita, adjusted for purchasing power parity, and the immigrant share across 172 countries. Outliers and some important destination countries are individually labeled in the figure. There is a large cluster of countries with both low GDP and a low immigrant share—poor countries do not attract many immigrants. Meanwhile, the richest countries in the world have immigrant shares well above the global average. Across these 172 countries, as GDP per capita increases by $1,000, the immigrant share rises by 0.5 percentage points.[2]

Economic conditions are a bigger pull factor than a push factor. Research usually finds that economic conditions in receiving countries matter more than economic conditions in sending countries (e.g., Mayda, 2010; Grogger and Hanson, 2011; Ortega and Peri, 2013). After all, billions of people live in relatively poor countries and never migrate—conditions there are

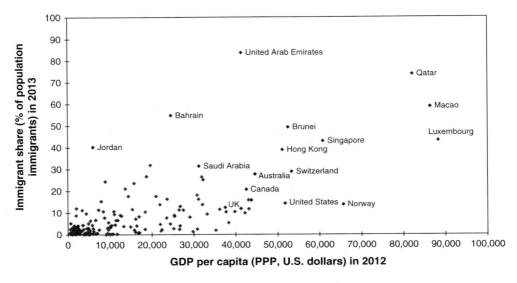

Figure 3.1 Immigrant share in 2013 and source country GDP in 2012.

Source: Immigrant share data from United Nations (2013) "Trends in international migrant stock: The 2013 revision." Available at: http://esa.un.org/unmigration/TIMSA2013/migrantstocks2013.htm?mtotals. [3 February 2014]. GDP per capita (PPP) data from World Bank (2013) "GDP per capita, PPP." Available at: http://data. worldbank.org/indicator/NY.GDP.PCAP.PP.CD [17 December 2013].

not bad enough for them to leave, or something else is holding them back. But once people decide to move, they are considerably more likely to move to a country with a higher average income than their origin than to a country with a lower average income.

Perhaps the most interesting countries in Figure 3.1 are those with relatively low GDP per capita but a high immigrant share. Jordan and Bahrain are notable outliers, for example. Jordan's central location in the Middle East makes it both a transit country and a destination. A transit country is one that migrants pass through on their way to their final destination. (See Figure 3.2 for a map of the Middle East.) Jordan has large numbers of migrants from other Middle Eastern countries, most notably Egypt, Syria and the West Bank and Gaza. Unrest in the region has caused its immigrant population to swell by 40 percent between 2010 and 2013 (United Nations, 2013). Like many other countries in the Persian Gulf region, Bahrain relies heavily on temporary foreign workers from Asia. Its immigrant share is lower than in its wealthier neighbors, such as the United Arab Emirates and Qatar, but higher than in its neighbors with lower GDP per capita, such as Saudi Arabia.

Research shows that economic factors other than average income matter as well. Immigration tends to be negatively related to a destination country's unemployment rate and its tax burden (e.g., Geis, Uebelmesser and Werding, 2013). Migrants are more likely to move to a country with a low unemployment rate than to a country with a high unemployment rate, and more likely to move to a country with low taxes than a country with high taxes. Migration flows slowed around much of the world during the 2007–2009 global financial crisis. Reduced demand for labor and higher unemployment rates in destinations reduced the incentive to

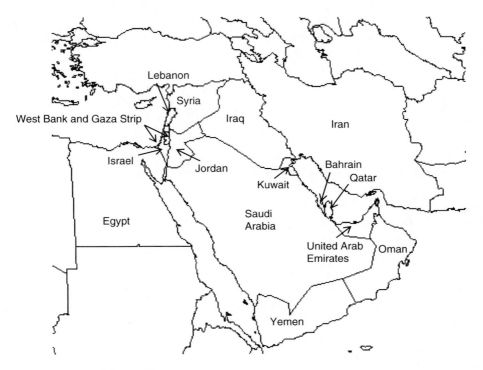

Figure 3.2 Map of the Middle East.

migrate, and many would-be migrants were less able to bear migration costs during the crisis. In addition, some countries tightened immigration policy during the crisis.

Countries can switch from being destination countries to being sending countries, on net, if their relative economic conditions worsen. Much of Latin America is an example. Argentina, Brazil, Chile, Cuba, Panama, Peru and Uruguay, among others, attracted European or Asian immigrants until about 1950. After that, relatively slow economic growth and political upheavals reduced the region's attractiveness. Emigration from much of the region began accelerating in the 1960s while immigration slowed. Spain and Ireland are examples of countries that switched from destination to sending countries in the 2000s as a result of the global financial crisis.

The role of migrant networks and migration costs

Networks play an important role in determining where migrants go. Networks provide information about potential destinations, funds that cover migration costs, and jobs and housing in the destination. Empirical studies tend to find that the number of people moving from an origin to a destination is strongly related to the number of previous immigrants from that origin living in that destination. In other words, immigrant stocks are a major predictor of immigrant flows. Research on immigration from 195 countries to 30 OECD countries finds that diasporas—people living outside their homeland—can explain more than 70 percent of the observed variation in migration flows (Beine, Docquier and Özden, 2011). Immigrant networks tend to matter the most for immigrants coming from poor source countries (Pedersen, Pytlikova and Smith, 2008).

The number of immigrants in a destination may also provide a signal to potential immigrants about relative economic conditions. Potential immigrants who are uncertain about where to go may opt to go where recent immigrants went because they believe those immigrants had good information—their presence in a destination signals that it is a desirable destination. Economists refer to this as "herd behavior" (Bauer, Epstein and Gang, 2007).

The importance of networks can make immigration a self-perpetuating process once the number of immigrants reaches a critical threshold. Bad economic, political or social conditions in an origin country—or good conditions in a destination country—may cause some people to move. Once those migrants are settled, their friends and families may join them even if the relative conditions that stimulated the initial migration have dissipated. The Nobel prize-winning economist Gunnar Myrdal (1957) referred to this as the "cumulative causation of migration."

One reason why networks matter so much is that family members often can sponsor their relatives for permanent residence. This can lead to substantial migration flows. Suppose a worker receives permanent resident status and brings her spouse. They both sponsor their parents and siblings. Those siblings bring their spouses, who in turn sponsor their parents and siblings, and so on. Economists and sociologists refer to this as "chain migration."

Chain migration is a major source of migration for countries that grant permanent resident status based partly on family ties to citizens or permanent residents. The United States grants more than 60 percent of its permanent resident visas based on family ties, or more than 600,000 immigrants a year in recent years. During 1996 to 2000, the average Asian immigrant who was the first in his family to move to the United States sponsored another four relatives; the average South American immigrant, more than five; the average European immigrant, one and two-thirds (Tienda, 2013). These differences by region are likely a result of differences in family size as well as relative economic opportunities and migration costs—families in Europe tend to be smaller and economic opportunities are better there than in South America and Asia, although migration costs are likely to be lower from Europe than from South America and Asia.

Migrant networks lower the cost of migrating, as do shorter distances. A study of immigration from 102 countries to 15 high-income OECD countries finds that increasing the great-circle distance—the distance "as a crow flies"—between an origin and a destination by 10 percent reduces migration flows by almost 12 percent (Grogger and Hanson, 2011).

Distance can be not only geographic but also cultural and linguistic. Immigration flows are bigger between countries that share a language or speak similar languages. Smaller cultural and linguistic distances reduce the psychic costs of migration. Immigrants who already speak the language or can easily learn it also have a significant advantage in the labor market. Having a colonial relationship leads to bigger flows between countries as well. This may reflect immigrants' preference to move to a country with a shared history and cultural ties. In some cases, it also reflects immigration policies that give admissions preference to residents of former colonies or even allow them to enter without restriction. For example, the 1962 accord that made Algeria independent from France gave Algerians relative freedom of movement to France.

The role of immigration policy

Immigration policy plays an important role in determining the number of immigrants, largely through its impact on migration costs. One study finds that when industrialized non-European countries, such as Australia, Canada and the United States, tighten immigration policy, immigration inflows fall within the same year (Ortega and Peri, 2013). Not surprisingly, research shows that the number of people who receive U.S. permanent resident visas is positively related to U.S. quotas on those visas (Clark, Hatton and Williamson, 2007). Immigration to Canada fell when the country introduced its point system in 1967, and then fell further when the country began requiring in 1982 that economic immigrants had a prearranged job offer that was approved by a Canadian employment center (Greenwood and McDowell, 1991).

Some evidence suggests that multinational agreements regarding immigration policy affect immigrant inflows. When countries joined the Schengen area, total immigration inflows into those countries dropped relative to other countries (Ortega and Peri, 2013). This may seem surprising since the Schengen agreement allows for free movement among members, which should increase inflows. However, members agreed to relatively strict border enforcement. This increased enforcement appears to have deterred immigration, on net—although inflows of citizens of other Schengen area countries increased, inflows of citizens of non-member countries decreased more. Research shows that more generally, migration flows from an origin are larger when a destination does not require that visitors from that origin have a visa (Grogger and Hanson, 2011).

Other countries' immigration policies may affect the number of immigrants to a particular destination. For example, Australia receives fewer visa applications from skilled migrants when the United States and Canada admit more skilled migrants (Cobb-Clark and Connolly, 1997). The converse was true historically: During the late nineteenth and early twentieth centuries, Australia's openness reduced flows to Canada (Timmer and Williamson, 1998). In addition, Brazil's subsidies to immigrants during that period reduced flows to Australia, and Argentina received more immigrants when the United States closed its borders in the 1920s. More recently, some EU member countries opted to allow more worker mobility than others when eight Central and Eastern European countries joined the EU in 2004. Some immigration from the new member states was diverted from EU members that restricted immigration, like Germany, to those that had relatively open borders, like the United Kingdom (Boeri and Brücker, 2005).

Immigration policy also influences how other factors affect immigration flows. Policies that regulate the number and characteristics of immigrants who can be admitted make immigration flows less responsive to changes in economic conditions. For example, a study of migration flows from 120 countries to 15 high-income destination countries shows that flows within the EU are much more responsive to destination country GDP per capita than are immigration flows overall (Ortega and Peri, 2013). EU citizens have considerable labor mobility across EU countries, allowing them to move easily in response to economic opportunities, while immigrants from non-EU countries face fairly tight restrictions that limit their responsiveness to economic opportunities.

Economic conditions, networks, immigration policy and migration costs may reinforce or offset each other when affecting where immigrants go. A major emigration episode from

Ecuador offers an example. Almost 5 percent of the country's population left after an economic crisis in the late 1990s. Most of the emigrants went to Spain or the United States. Although the United States is closer, had better economic conditions and had more Ecuadorians already living there, the number of Ecuadorians who migrated to Spain was about three times bigger than the number who migrated to the United States. Several factors can explain why Ecuadorians were more likely to go to Spain: Spain is more culturally and linguistically similar to Ecuador; Spain has a more generous welfare system than the United States; and Spain initially did not require that visitors from Ecuador have a visa, a policy that changed a few years into the crisis (Bertoli, Fernández-Huertas Moraga and Ortega, 2013).

Immigration to poor countries

Developing, or low-income, countries are the destination as well as the origin of many immigrants. In economics and political science, developing countries are sometimes called the "South," and industrialized countries the "North." The largest number of migrants—82 million people as of 2013, or 36 percent of all migrants—are South–South migrants (Martin, 2013). Important South–South migration corridors include Ukraine to Russia (which is considered a South country by the World Bank's Migration and Remittances unit) and vice versa; Kazakhstan to Bhutan and Russia; and Afghanistan to Pakistan (International Organization for Migration, 2013).

Migration costs are typically lower for South–South migrants than for South–North migrants. (South–North migrants are about 35 percent of all migrants, just slightly less than the share of migrants who are South–South.) The income gains are probably smaller as well for South–South migrants than for South–North migrants. Immigrants from developing countries may find that their skills are more transferable to other developing countries than to industrialized countries, but they may also face more competition for jobs and lower average wages. In addition, public assistance is typically much more limited in developing countries than in developed countries.

Interestingly, about 14 million people, or 6 percent of all migrants, are North–South migrants. Important North–South migration corridors include the United States to Mexico and South Africa; Germany to Turkey; and Portugal to Brazil. Some of these migrants are retirees drawn by the lower cost of living in developing countries, while others are workers seeking better opportunities. Many North–South migrants are the descendants of migrants from the country they move to.

Differences across types of immigrants

Economic migrants who move to work or study should be more affected than family-based migrants by economic factors in the origin and destination. Both groups are affected by immigration policy, albeit by different aspects. Whether an immigrant is even considered an economic migrant or a family-based migrant can depend on immigration policy. If immigration policy is more favorable toward family-based migrants than economic migrants, potential migrants may find a relative or spouse to sponsor them for admission. Marrying in order to move or remain in a destination is the plot of romantic comedy movies, but it also happens in real life.

Industrialized countries therefore may screen immigration applicants sponsored by a spouse to make sure that the marriage is legitimate, and immigrants suspected of fraudulent marriages can face deportation or criminal charges. (See Box 3.1, "Immigration and fraudulent marriages in the United States.")

The destinations of two groups of immigrants merit special attention: unauthorized immigrants, and refugees and asylum seekers.

Unauthorized immigrants

Accurate data on the number of undocumented immigrants entering or living in a country are difficult to obtain. Few large-scale government surveys ask immigrants about their legal status, and those that do may not receive truthful answers since unauthorized immigrants usually try not to make their presence known. Estimates of the number of unauthorized immigrants are often calculated using the residual method: the estimated number of legal immigrants is subtracted from the total foreign-born population. The difference, or residual, is the estimated number of unauthorized immigrants:

$$\text{unauthorized immigrants} = \text{all immigrants} - \text{legal immigrants} \tag{3.1}$$

The estimated number of legal immigrants, in turn, is based on government records of the number of people who have entered legally over time or adjusted from illegal to legal status,

---

Box 3.1 Immigration and fraudulent marriages in the United States

Foreigners who marry a U.S. citizen are usually eligible to receive a "green card," or legal permanent resident visa, in the United States. There is no numerical limit on the number of spouses of U.S. citizens who can receive a green card. More than 2.7 million green cards were issued to the spouses of U.S. citizens during fiscal years 2004 to 2013. This was by far the most common admissions category during that period, accounting for one-quarter of all green cards.

Although most of these marriages are legitimate, some are not. Fraudulent marriages may involve an exchange of money, or one spouse may be deceiving the other about his intentions. The foreign-born spouse must undergo an interview with a U.S. Citizenship and Immigration Services (USCIS) official. The interview is one way that USCIS tries to determine whether a marriage is valid or fraudulent. Couples suspected of fraud must meet separately with USCIS officials, who ask them an identical set of questions under oath. Spouses' answers are then compared to see if they gave the same answers. Officials ask to see photos and other evidence that the marriage is valid.

Green cards issued to spouses of U.S. citizens are provisional for the first two years. If the marriage ends within that period, the spouse's green card is usually revoked and he must leave the United States.

minus estimates of the number who have died, the number who have left the country and the number who have moved from legal to illegal status because they overstayed their visa:

$$\begin{aligned} \text{legal immigrants} = \text{ } &\text{legal entrants over time} + \text{adjusted to legal status over time} \\ &- \text{legal immigrant deaths} - \text{legal immigrant exits} \\ &- \text{visa overstayers} \end{aligned} \tag{3.2}$$

Since few reliable statistics on the number of unauthorized immigrants are available, the distribution of unauthorized immigrants across destination countries is uncertain. Globally, about 10 to 15 percent of immigrants are unauthorized (Castles et al., 2012). Virtually every country has some unauthorized immigrants. The United States probably has the greatest number of unauthorized immigrants globally given that it has the most immigrants overall and is a high-income country with many lower-income neighbors to its south. The United States has 11 to 12 million unauthorized immigrants, who comprise about one-quarter of its immigrant population (Passel, Cohn and Gonzalez-Barrera, 2013).

Unauthorized immigration is estimated to be about one-third of all migration to developing countries, on average (UNDP, 2009). This suggests that undocumented immigration is more prevalent in developing countries than in developed countries, although there are certainly exceptions. Unauthorized immigrants accounted for almost two-thirds of immigrants in southern and eastern Mediterranean countries (Algeria, Egypt, Israel, Jordan, Lebanon, Libya, Morocco, Turkey and Tunisia) in the mid-2000s (Fargues, 2009). The proximity of those countries to much poorer countries to the south plays a role in the large share of immigrants who are unauthorized there. Strong economic growth in those destinations during the late 1990s and early 2000s attracted migrants, legal and illegal alike. Legalization programs in some of those countries during the 1980s to 2000s may have encouraged further illegal migration.

The prevalence of unauthorized immigrants in developing countries may be surprising since those countries have lower incomes and are therefore less likely than industrialized countries to be attractive to immigrants. However, developing countries also tend to be near other developing countries, which are the source of most unauthorized immigrants. Immigrants who cannot afford to migrate to a far-away industrialized country may instead migrate to a closer developing country. In addition, developing countries may have more porous borders than industrialized countries that can afford more border enforcement. Migrating to another developing country may be the first step toward migrating to a developed country. Migration from Guatemala and Honduras to Mexico and then eventually to the United States is an example.

Industrialized countries may have enacted legalization programs that allow unauthorized immigrants to adjust to legal status, reducing their stock of unauthorized immigrants. On the other hand, legalization programs may attract more unauthorized immigrants. (Chapters 13 and 14 discuss legalization programs in the United States and Europe and evidence on whether legalization programs lead to bigger unauthorized inflows.)

Most unauthorized migrants move for economic reasons. Figure 3.3 shows the estimated number of unauthorized immigrants living in the United States and real GDP in the United States during 1990 to 2010. The two series follow a similar trend over time. In fact, inflows of

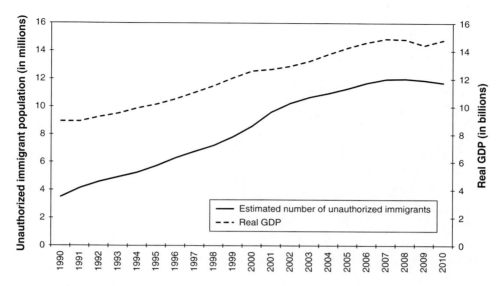

Figure 3.3 Unauthorized immigrants and real GDP in the United States.

Source: Warren, R. and Warren, J.R. (2013) "Unauthorized immigration to the United States: Annual estimates and components of change, by state, 1990 to 2010." *International Migration Review* 47(2), pp. 296–329; and Bureau of Economic Analysis (2014) "Gross domestic product." Available at: http://bea.gov/national/index.htm#gdp [1 July 2014].

unauthorized immigrants into the United States are more closely related to the U.S. business cycle than inflows of other groups of immigrants are (Hanson, 2006). The estimated number of unauthorized immigrants in the United States fell by almost one million during the Great Recession (Passel, Cohn and Gonzalez-Barrera, 2013). The decrease was primarily due to fewer unauthorized immigrants entering the United States, not to unauthorized immigrants leaving in large numbers.

Increased enforcement activity by a destination country is likely to reduce the number of unauthorized immigrants in that country. Enforcement can take many forms. Examples include patrolling land and sea borders; building fences; using unmanned drones; requiring people to show their legal right to be in the country in order to work, go to school or receive social services; and deporting unauthorized immigrants. (Figure 3.4 shows two men scaling the fence along the U.S.–Mexico border near Douglas, Arizona.) Increased enforcement may reduce inflows of unauthorized immigrants by making a country harder to enter (increasing migration costs) or by making it a less desirable place to live (reducing pull factors). Increased enforcement also may reduce the stock of unauthorized immigrants already in a country, either by deporting people or by making conditions worse so that people leave voluntarily.

Paradoxically, enforcement that succeeds in reducing the number of unauthorized immigrants in a destination also increases the attractiveness of that destination. An enforcement-induced decrease in labor supply raises wages, which are a pull factor for many unauthorized migrants. Figure 3.5 illustrates this in a supply and demand framework.

Figure 3.4 Border fence near Douglas, Arizona.

Source: U.S. Navy photo by Steelworker 1st Class Matthew Tyson/Released. http://en.wikipedia.org/wiki/Mexico%E2%80%93United_States_barrier#mediaviewer/File:US_Navy_090317-N-5253T-016_Two_men_scale_the_border_fence_into_Mexico_a_few_hundred_yards_away_from_where_Seabees_from_Naval_Mobile_Construction_Battalions_%28NMCB%29_133_and_NMCB-14_are_building_a_1,500_foot-long_concrete-lined_dr.jpg [3 September 2014].

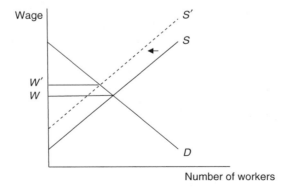

Figure 3.5 The effect of increased enforcement on wages.

An increase in border enforcement decreases the supply of unauthorized workers. This results in a higher wage.

Refugees and asylum seekers

Most refugees and asylum seekers initially flee to nearby countries. There are then three possible outcomes: they return to their origin, they remain in the host country permanently or they move to a third country. Refugees may move to a third country on their own, or they may be resettled in a third country by the United Nations High Commissioner for Refugees or as a result of an agreement between countries.[3]

Table 3.2 reports the distribution of refugees and asylum seekers across regions in 2013. (The table reports stocks by current residence, not origin.) Most refugees are in Africa and Asia because those regions are also the main origin of refugees in recent years. However, the number of refugees and asylum seekers and their distribution across areas can change quickly in response to events. For example, the number of refugees in Jordan and Lebanon more than doubled from 2012 to 2013 as a result of events in Syria. Meanwhile, most asylum seekers— people who say they are refugees but whose claims have not yet been evaluated—are in Africa and Europe. Germany, South Africa and the United States have been the top recipients of new asylum seekers in recent years.

The United Nations High Commissioner for Refugees (UNHCR) works to resettle refugees in third countries when it appears that they will never be able to return to their origin and integrating them into the current host country seems infeasible. For example, in 2013 the UNHCR helped more than 23,000 refugees from Myanmar, most of them living in Thailand, resettle in other countries. Most industrialized countries voluntarily accept a certain number of refugees each year. In the United States, this number is determined by the President in consultation with Congress. The United States agreed to accept up to 70,000 refugees in fiscal year 2014, for example. Australia, Canada and the United States together accepted 90 percent of resettled refugees in 2013.

During the late 1980s and early 1990s, Western European countries received an unprecedented number of asylum seekers, many of them from the former Yugoslavia. Germany received more than 1,000 asylum applications a day in 1992 (Martin, 2013). More than 90 percent of applicants were ultimately found to not qualify for refugee status. In the wake of the flood of asylum seekers, most European countries made it more difficult for migrants to apply for asylum. They began requiring visas for migrants from countries that were major sources of unfounded asylum seekers; imposed sanctions on airlines and ships that transported

Table 3.2 Populations of refugees and asylum seekers, 2013

Region	Refugees	Asylum seekers
Africa	3,308,674	449,345
Asia	5,983,280	168,510
Europe	1,156,398	408,790
Latin America and the Caribbean	90,785	23,808
North America	424,011	106,491
Oceania	40,714	14,818
Total	11,003,862	1,171,762

Source: United Nations High Commissioner for Refugees (2014) *UNHCR Global Trends 2013*. Geneva, Switzerland: United Nations High Commissioner for Refugees.

migrants without visas; narrowed the grounds for awarding refugee status; and sped up the application process, among other changes. They also began requiring migrants to seek asylum in the first safe country they reach. This means that most asylum seekers now must apply—and are supposed to remain—in Greece, Italy or Spain instead of wealthier Northern European countries with more generous public assistance programs.

Immigrant destinations within countries

The same factors that determine what countries immigrants go to also determine where they go within those countries. Economic conditions, the presence of other immigrants and geography play key roles in immigrants' location choices within countries.

Immigrants are typically highly geographically concentrated within destination countries. Within the United States, for example, one in four immigrants lives in California, one in ten in New York and one in ten in Texas. In 2010–2012, the top six states (California, New York, Texas, Florida, New Jersey and Illinois) together accounted for 65 percent of all immigrants living in the United States. The bottom six states (North Dakota, Wyoming, Montana, South Dakota, Vermont and West Virginia), in contrast, together accounted for only 0.3 percent.

Figure 3.6 gives another way of looking at the concentration of immigrants within the United States by showing the fraction of the state population comprised of immigrants. The darker

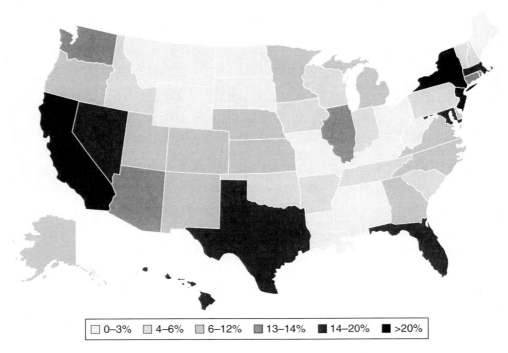

| □ 0–3% | □ 4–6% | ▨ 6–12% | ▨ 13–14% | ■ 14–20% | ■ >20% |

Figure 3.6 Percent of population comprised of immigrants in United States, 2010–2012.

Source: Authors' calculations using 2010–2012 American Community Survey data from the U.S. Bureau of the Census.

shaded states have a higher fraction of foreign born. The three darkest shades are above the national average of 13 percent, while the three lightest shades are below the national average.

The concentration of immigrants in certain states is the result of several factors. Most high-immigration states have traditionally been gateways into the United States. Because of geographic proximity and the locations of large ports, immigrants coming from Europe historically arrived primarily in New York; from Asia, California; from Latin America, Texas; and from the Caribbean, Florida. Although some moved on to other parts of the country, many remained in these gateways.

Historically and currently, immigrants tend to go to urban areas where there are already large numbers of immigrants and where jobs are available. This explains the large immigrant share in Illinois, the outlier as the only land-locked state on the list. Illinois was the center of the Midwest economy during the "age of mass migration" at the turn of the twentieth century, and the ready availability of jobs in meatpacking and other industries there attracted immigrants. Once diasporas were established there, the state continued to attract large numbers of immigrants.

During the 1990s and 2000s, however, immigrants became more dispersed throughout the United States. Immigrants moved to new destinations, primarily in the South and West. During the 1990s and 2000s, immigrant populations grew fastest in Arkansas, Georgia, Nevada, North Carolina and Tennessee. Much of this dispersion was the result of faster economic growth in the "Sunbelt" states than in other parts of the country. California saw its share of all U.S. immigrants slide from 33 percent in 1990 to 25 percent in 2010 as the result of a prolonged economic downturn combined with a state law adopted in 1994 that aimed to prohibit unauthorized immigrants from receiving publicly funded services.[4] Immigrants thus remain geographically concentrated in the United States, but less so than two decades ago.

The geographic concentration of immigrants is not unique to the United States. In Canada, almost 63 percent of recent immigrants live in Toronto, Montréal and Vancouver (Statistics Canada, 2013). About 35 percent of Canada's total population lives in those three metropolitan areas, in contrast. In Britain, two-fifths of immigrants live in London (The Economist, 2012). One-third of London residents are foreign born, versus 8 percent in the rest of Britain.

Within states or cities, immigrants tend to cluster in particular neighborhoods with other people from the same origin country. Such areas, termed "ethnic enclaves," often take on nicknames that reflect their demographics. New York City, for example, has neighborhoods nicknamed Chinatown, Little Italy and Spanish Harlem (comprised mainly of Puerto Ricans). Immigrants who live and work in enclaves may earn higher returns to their human capital and feel more comfortable since they live and work with other people who share their language and cultural background (Portes and Bach, 1985). Enclaves may provide immigrants with employment opportunities and protect them from discrimination. However, enclaves may offer primarily low-wage jobs and more competition for jobs from other immigrants. Living in an enclave may delay learning the language of the destination country and generally slow immigrants' assimilation. (Chapter 5 discusses this in more detail.)

The tendency of U.S. immigrants to live in enclaves has risen over the last 50 or so years. Research shows that segregation of U.S. immigrants declined from the turn of the twentieth century until the middle of the century and has been increasing since then (Cutler, Glaeser and Vigdor, 2008). Part of the reason why segregation has increased is that immigration to the

United States has increased—having more immigrants makes it easier for immigrants to live near their compatriots. In addition, immigrants whose languages are less similar to English and who are racial minorities are more segregated than other immigrants. The increasing share of immigrants from Latin America, Asia and Africa has therefore led to increased immigrant segregation.

Location choice and economic opportunities

Research shows that immigrants are attracted to areas with better economic opportunities within destination countries. For example, less-educated recent immigrants to the United States during 2000 to 2009 were more likely to go to states experiencing faster GDP growth (Simpson and Sparber, 2013). In addition, less-educated immigrants who arrived in the United States in the 1990s were less likely to settle in areas experiencing larger increases in labor force participation by less-educated U.S.-born women (Cadena, 2013). In other words, if competition for jobs was becoming tougher in an area, immigrants were less likely to go there. Less-educated immigrants also are less likely to live in states with relatively high minimum wages. A 10 percent increase in a state's minimum wage reduces the number of less-educated recent immigrants in that state by 8 percent (Cadena, 2014). All of these findings are consistent with the utility- or income-maximization models discussed in Chapter 2.

Economic migrants' location choices within a country are likely to be more responsive to local economic conditions than other migrants' choices since the former migrate primarily to work. David Jaeger (2008) shows this is indeed the case for U.S. immigrants who receive a green card on the basis of employment compared with immigrants who receive a green card based on family ties. However, Jaeger also shows that refugees' location choices within the United States are as responsive to economic conditions as employment-based immigrants' choices. This is somewhat surprising since refugees are assumed to be motivated more by push factors than pull factors. But once they are within the United States, wages and unemployment rates appear to affect their location choices. Many refugees are initially sent to a specific location in the United States, but they tend to quickly move to areas with better economic opportunities and where their compatriots have already settled.

Immigrants' location choices within a country tend to be more responsive than natives' choices to local labor market conditions. Newly arriving immigrants are essentially starting from scratch within the destination country—once immigrants have decided to move to a particular destination country, they have to decide where in that country to go. For most newly arriving immigrants, the marginal cost of choosing to go to one region of the country instead of another is small relative to the total cost of migrating. Natives, in contrast, already live in the destination country. Their marginal cost of moving to another region is also their total cost of migrating. Natives therefore may be less likely than newly arriving immigrants to respond to differences in economic opportunities across regions within a country.

Immigrants' responsiveness to local labor market conditions helps equilibrate differences in labor markets across the United States. Greater mobility speeds up economic convergence across regions of the country. George Borjas (2001) refers to immigration as "grease in the wheels of the labor market." He shows that the tendency of new immigrants to cluster in areas with better economic opportunities speeds up wage convergence and improves economic efficiency. For example, the distribution of less-educated Mexican immigrants across U.S. states changed quickly during the 2007–2009 Great Recession. This reallocation, in turn, substantially reduced the impact of the downturn on less-educated U.S. natives (Cadena and Kovak, 2013).

If immigrants tend to settle in areas where earnings and employment opportunities are relatively strong or rising, estimates of immigration's impact on labor market outcomes that do not account for this are biased. Naïve estimates will underestimate any negative impacts of immigration on labor market outcomes if they do not properly control for a positive relationship between immigrant inflows and economic conditions. Economists try to control for this bias by looking for factors that determine where immigrants settle that are unrelated to economic opportunities. (Economists call these "exogenous" sources of variation in where immigrants settle.) This is harder than it may sound. Economists typically use the distribution of earlier immigrants across areas to explain the distribution of recent immigrants across areas. But the economic conditions that attracted previous immigrants may have persisted over time and continued to attract recent immigrants.

One of the most promising exogenous sources of variation in where immigrants settle within countries is government policies that direct immigrants to settle in certain areas. Denmark, Israel and Sweden, for example, try to disperse refugees across their countries. Such settlement policies aim to accelerate immigrants' incorporation into the destination by directing them away from immigrant enclaves and to distribute the perceived burden of immigrants across the country. Germany offers an interesting example. When it began receiving large inflows of ethnic Germans from Central and Eastern Europe and the former Soviet Union in the late 1980s, Germany adopted a law that tried to disperse immigrants across counties based on their relative population sizes. However, there was no enforcement mechanism, and immigrants concentrated in certain areas. In 1996, most German states made immigrants ineligible for public assistance benefits if they did not live in their designated county. Compliance increased dramatically, and immigrants became more dispersed throughout the country (Glitz, 2012).

Effects on natives' locations

Where immigrants choose to live within destination countries may affect where natives choose to live. Natives may move out of—or not move to—areas where immigrants settle because housing costs increase, school quality worsens, their labor market outcomes worsen or they simply dislike living near immigrants, among other potential reasons. Alternatively, natives may be attracted to the same factors that attract immigrants to an area, such as good labor market opportunities or a low cost of living.

Whether immigrant inflows into an area result in native inflows or outflows is thus an empirical question. Knowing the answer to this question is important. Assessing immigration's impact on labor markets, housing costs and other economic outcomes requires understanding whether natives enter or leave areas that attract immigrants. Native outflows would reduce the strains potentially created by immigrant inflows on labor markets, housing costs, educational systems and the like. Not accounting for natives' offsetting migration would lead to an underestimate of any adverse effects of immigration. Native inflows would add to those strains, but their effects should be attributed to natives, not to immigrants.

Research findings on the question of whether immigrant inflows lead to native outflows or inflows are mixed. For the United States, some studies find that U.S. natives leave areas experiencing immigrant inflows, while other studies find that immigrant inflows do not lead to native outflows (e.g., Card and DiNardo, 2000; Borjas, 2006). One major reason why studies reach conflicting results even when they examine the same country is that they use different methodologies. This makes it difficult to know which set of results is correct. But even if research does reach a consensus on the effect of immigrant inflows on native outflows in the past in a country, the same effect may not occur in the future for that same country. Natives' response to immigration may depend on context. Under a different set of economic, political and social conditions or a different group of immigrants, natives might make different choices.

Enforcement and unauthorized immigrants' location choices

Increased enforcement is likely to discourage unauthorized immigration. It may also change where unauthorized immigrants go within a country. If enforcement is not uniform within a country, unauthorized immigrants are likely to settle in areas where enforcement is relatively lax. In the 1990s, the United States increased enforcement along the U.S.–Mexico border in California through Operation Gatekeeper and in Texas through Operation Hold the Line. Unauthorized immigrant crossings quickly shifted to Arizona. As a result, the unauthorized immigrant population grew more slowly in California and Texas and faster in Arizona and other states during the late 1990s and early 2000s (Bohn and Pugatch, 2013).

That population shift, in turn, may have spurred a number of states to adopt laws aimed at discouraging unauthorized immigrants from settling in their states. Such laws often require that employers verify workers' eligibility to work or face fines; reduce immigrants' eligibility for public assistance programs; and require that police officers verify people's legal status when arresting them or giving them a ticket. Studies indicate that such laws are effective at reducing the number of immigrants in a state. For example, a 2007 law in Arizona led to a 17 percent drop in the state's population of likely unauthorized working-age immigrants (Bohn, Lofstrom and Raphael, 2014). The laws appear to cause unauthorized immigrants to primarily move to states without such laws instead of leaving the United States (Amuedo-Dorantes and Lozano, 2014).

Welfare magnets?

One of the reasons immigration is controversial is concerns that immigrants are a fiscal drain, or that they receive more in government services than they pay in taxes. A related issue is whether countries with more generous public assistance programs attract more immigrants. This is often called the "welfare magnet" hypothesis or "benefit tourism." The welfare magnet hypothesis usually involves two related questions: are immigrants more likely than natives to receive public assistance, and do immigrants choose their destination based on the generosity of public assistance programs?

Evidence indicates that, in most industrialized countries, immigrants are more likely than natives to receive public assistance (Giulietti and Wahba, 2013). In the United States, about one-third of households headed by an immigrant participate in a major public assistance program, compared with about one-fifth of households headed by a U.S. native.[5] This pattern does not hold in all industrialized countries, however; immigrants are not more likely to participate in public assistance programs than natives in Ireland, for example (Barrett and McCarthy, 2008).

One important reason why immigrants are more likely than natives to receive public assistance is that they are more likely to qualify for it. Immigrants tend to be poorer than natives, making them more likely to be eligible for means-tested programs, or programs with eligibility based in part on having a low income. Immigration policies that affect the distribution of skills or other characteristics among immigrants therefore may affect immigrant–native differences in eligibility for public assistance programs.

If immigrants are attracted to destinations with relatively generous public assistance programs, countries that spend a greater share of GDP on public assistance programs should have higher shares of less-educated immigrants. Less-educated immigrants are more likely than better-educated immigrants to be eligible for means-tested programs. Figure 3.7 shows expenditures on social programs as a percent of GDP—a measure of the generosity of public assistance—and the share of immigrants who have at most completed primary school for 24 OECD countries. If the welfare magnet hypothesis is true, the relationship should be positive across countries. However, the data points in Figure 3.7 actually indicate a negative relationship, if any.

Other cross-country comparisons also do not indicate that countries with more generous public assistance benefits attract more immigrants. A study of 26 OECD countries finds that the generosity of public assistance programs, as measured by social expenditures as a percentage of GDP, is generally not related to the magnitude of migration flows into those countries (Pedersen, Pytlikova and Smith, 2008). However, immigrants from the poorest destination countries do appear to be more likely to migrate to countries with relatively generous programs within that group of 26 countries.

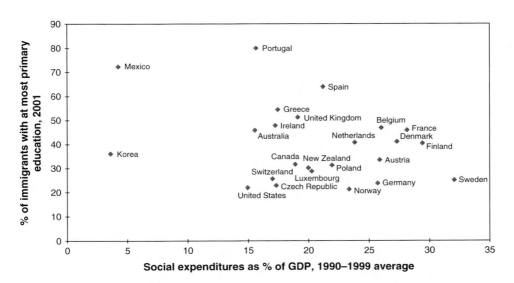

Figure 3.7 Percent of immigrants with only primary education in 2001 and social expenditures as percent of GDP in 1990–1999.

Source: Social expenditures data from OECD (2014) "Stats extracts." Available at: stats.oecd.org [11 March 2014]; immigration data from OECD (2006) "Counting immigrants and expatriates in OECD countries: A new perspective." *Trends in International Migration 2004*. Paris: OECD.

Immigration policy restrictions may limit immigrants' ability to move to countries in order to participate in public assistance programs. Employment-, education- or other skill-based restrictions on immigration implicitly limit the number of immigrants who are likely to qualify for public assistance programs. EU countries with more generous public assistance programs have higher shares of less-educated immigrants from other EU countries (from which people can migrate freely) than from non-EU countries (which face immigration restrictions) (Razin and Wahba, 2011). This suggests that admission restrictions may limit the welfare magnet effect.

Most evidence suggests that the generosity of public assistance programs plays relatively little role in immigrants' location choices within destination countries. For example, research finds that the generosity of means-tested program benefits does not affect the distribution of newly arrived immigrants across U.S. states (Zavodny, 1999; Kaushal, 2005). However, immigrants who receive welfare are more clustered in California, a state with relatively generous welfare benefits, than either immigrants who do not receive welfare or natives (Borjas, 1999).

Research may have difficulty finding evidence of a welfare magnet effect within or across countries if welfare magnet concerns lead to policy changes. In addition to restricting admissions of immigrants who are more likely to be eligible for public assistance, policymakers may change public assistance eligibility rules or benefits in response to concerns that immigrants disproportionately receive public assistance or migrate in order to receive public assistance. The 1996 U.S. welfare reform is a case in point.

In 1996, the United States enacted welfare reform. Changes were made to public assistance programs that affected all residents, but immigrants were specially targeted, as discussed in more detail in Chapter 10. About 45 percent of the projected savings from welfare reform were from denying benefits to immigrants (Martin, 2013). Some of the cuts were later reversed, but newly arrived immigrants continue to face more limited access to public assistance than U.S. natives or earlier immigrants.

Return and repeat migration

Not all people who migrate remain abroad. Some return migration is involuntary, such as when an unauthorized immigrant is deported or when a temporary foreign worker would like to remain in the destination but the worker's visa has expired. Some return migration is voluntary, perhaps because conditions in the origin or the destination have changed or because the immigrant had always intended to return home. Some return migration is due to migrants being overly optimistic about their prospects in the destination. Meanwhile, some immigrants who leave a destination are repeat migrants—also called secondary migrants and onward migrants—who move on to another country instead of returning to their country of origin.

This chapter uses the term "out-migrants" to refer to all immigrants who leave the destination country, or repeat migrants and return migrants together. Destination countries probably do not care whether out-migrants are return migrants or repeat migrants unless they want those immigrants to stay, in which case knowing where they are going is important to understanding why they are leaving. From the perspective of origin countries, return migration versus repeat migration is important since return migrants can have significant effects on their origin countries, as discussed in Chapter 11. Natives who leave—emigrants—are not included in this discussion.

Understanding the extent of out-migration and the characteristics of immigrants who leave compared with those who stay is important for several reasons. Immigrants who anticipate they might leave have less incentive to acquire skills that are valuable in the destination but not valuable in other places, such as learning a language spoken only in the destination. Such decisions, in turn, are likely to affect how immigrants do in the labor market and the extent to which they compete with natives or other immigrants for jobs. The impact of immigration on labor markets, tax revenues and public expenditures will differ depending on how many immigrants leave and on whether immigrants who do poorly in the destination leave while those who succeed stay, or the reverse.

Few countries collect comprehensive data on out-migration. The United States stopped counting out-migrants in 1957. In general, countries are less concerned about who exits than who enters. Since collecting data is expensive, it makes sense to prioritize data collection efforts. However, this limits researchers' ability to study out-migration.

Researchers estimate the number of out-migrants by comparing the number of immigrants at a point in time with a later count of the number of immigrants, adjusted for the number of immigrants who entered and the number who died. The number of out-migrants between time t and time $t+1$—between 2000 and 2010, for example—is then

$$\text{out-migrants}_{t,\,t+1} = \text{immigrants}_t - \text{immigrants}_{t+1} + \text{arrivals}_{t,\,t+1} - \text{deaths}_{t,\,t+1} \qquad (3.3)$$

Such estimates can be calculated for specific origin countries or other demographic characteristics, such as sex, age and education. Longitudinal surveys that follow people over time

---

Box 3.2 Evidence on U.S. out-migration

Using methods like equation 3.3, Robert Warren and Jennifer Peck (1980) conclude that the ratio of migration from the United States to migration into the United States was about 18 percent during 1960 to 1970. George Borjas and Bernt Bratsberg (1996) report that about 22 percent of people who received permanent resident status during 1970 to 1974 had left by 1980, and about 18 percent of people who had received permanent resident status during 1975 to 1980. Guillermina Jasso and Mark Rosenzweig (1982) find that as many as one-half of people who received permanent resident status in the United States in 1971 had left by 1979. The evidence thus suggests that out-migration from the United States is substantial.

The U.S. out-migration rate may have been even higher historically. A study by Oriana Bandiera, Imran Rasul and Martina Viarengo (2013) using administrative records on immigrant arrivals and the 1900, 1910 and 1920 Censuses concludes that for every 100 immigrants who arrived in the United States during 1900 to 1910, 58 to 63 immigrants left. During 1910 to 1920, the number rises to 75 to 81. This was the period when the immigrant share—immigrants as a fraction of all U.S. residents—was at a historic high. Given such high rates of out-migration, the implied numbers of immigrants who arrived in the United States relative to the size of the U.S.-born population at the time are simply astounding.

in the destination offer another way to estimate out-migration: people who no longer answer the survey may have left the country. Surveys in origin countries that include questions about whether people lived abroad are another window into return migration.

Table 3.3 reports estimated out-migration rates after five years—the fraction of immigrants who have left within five years of arrival—for several industrialized countries. All of the out-migration rates are substantial, ranging from about 19 percent to over 60 percent. Within most industrialized countries, immigrants from other industrialized countries are more likely to leave than immigrants from developing countries. For example, research finds that as income per capita doubles across origins, the out-migration rate from the United States increases by 4.9 percentage points (Borjas and Bratsberg, 1996). The earnings gains from migration are typically bigger for immigrants from developing countries than for immigrants from industrialized countries, giving the former more incentive to stay. Immigrants from closer countries are more likely than immigrants from further away to leave, all else equal.

Out-migration tends to be more common among economic migrants than among family-based migrants (Dustmann and Görlach, 2014). Refugees who have been resettled in an industrialized country are particularly unlikely to leave. This is in part because conditions in their origin country may never improve sufficiently for them to return. In addition, the standard of living in industrialized countries tends to be much higher, reducing refugees' incentive to leave. Undocumented immigrants tend to be more likely than legal immigrants to out-migrate.

The likelihood of out-migration tends to fall as immigrants' duration of residence in the destination increases. There are several possible reasons for this pattern. One is that immigrants who mistakenly believed that they would be better off in the destination quickly learn that they prefer being elsewhere, and they soon leave. Another possibility is that there are essentially two types of immigrants: those who intend to migrate only for a short period of time, perhaps to earn a certain amount of money in order to buy land or open a business in the origin, and those who plan to stay forever. As the first type leaves, the remaining immigrants will be increasingly composed of those who plan to stay forever. In addition, as immigrants stay longer in the destination, they may acquire more skills that are valued in the destination, while their skills that are valued in the origin may atrophy. In addition, immigrants tend to create networks in the destination and are joined there by friends and family, making it less likely over time that they leave.

Table 3.3 Estimated out-migration rates after five years

Country	Entry period	Out-migration rate (%)
Belgium	1993–1998	50.4
Canada	1996	23.7
Ireland	1993–1998	60.4
Netherlands	1994–1998	28.2
New Zealand	1998	23.0
Norway	1996–1999	39.6
United Kingdom	1992–1998	39.9
United States	1999	19.1

Source: OECD (2008) *International Migration Outlook 2008*. Paris: OECD.

Motivations for return migration

There are several reasons an immigrant may leave the destination. Economic models focus on voluntary reasons for leaving, which include a desire to live elsewhere; changes in exchange rates; having earned a targeted amount; having acquired skills that are valuable in the origin; and having failed in the destination.

Living in the origin may be cheaper and more preferable to immigrants than remaining in the destination. Lower prices and a desire to live in the origin provide a powerful reason for many immigrants to return migrate (Dustmann and Weiss, 2007). Immigrants may be particularly likely to retire to the origin country since the higher earnings in the destination that motivated them to move there are no longer relevant once they retire.

Changes in exchange rates may prompt return migration. If the value of the origin's currency increases relative to the destination's, a given amount of money earned in the destination buys less in the origin. Immigrants who migrated in order to send remittances back to the origin or to save to pay for future consumption in the origin may return migrate as the origin's currency appreciates and their earnings become less valuable. On the other hand, immigrants may remain longer in the destination as the origin's currency appreciates since they need to earn more in order to achieve the same level of purchasing power in the origin. In other words, a change in the exchange rate creates countervailing income and substitution effects. In the case of immigrants from the Philippines, the substitution effect outweighs the income effect for most migrants (Yang, 2006). For immigrants from Mexico, however, the opposite appears to be the case (Reyes, 2004).

Achieving a target level of savings is another reason immigrants may return to their origin country. As economic conditions in the destination improve, immigrants can achieve their target level of savings sooner. However, like exchange rates, changes in economic conditions in the destination have countervailing income and substitution effects. Although better economic

---

Box 3.3 Money isn't everything

Many factors, not just economics, determine whether people choose to migrate. Research suggests that lifestyle preferences may ultimately play a more important role than relative earnings in determining both emigration and return migration. John Gibson and David McKenzie (2011) surveyed former top students from three nations in the South Pacific about their earnings and migration histories. They find high rates of migration. They also find high rates of return migration. Among top students from New Zealand, two-thirds had ever migrated; Tonga, 83 percent; Papua New Guinea, 37 percent. Between one-fourth and one-third were return migrants. Although most of them said they can earn more abroad—they earn $1,000 more a week, on average, if they migrate—their location decisions were based more on lifestyle and family preferences than on income, macro-economic factors or credit constraints. For many people, desire to live near family and in a familiar culture overrides purely economic motives when it comes to the migration decision.

conditions mean that target savers can leave sooner because they were able to achieve their savings goal more quickly, some immigrants may stay longer in order to save even more. Research findings are mixed, suggesting that the relationship between return migration and economic conditions may depend on the context.[6]

The possibility of earning more in the origin as a result of migrating may motivate people to migrate and then return. Immigrants may learn a new language, create new networks, get more or better education and acquire skills that are valuable in their origin country. Living abroad even appears to boost creativity (Maddux and Galinsky, 2009). Irish workers who have emigrated and returned earn 7 percent more than comparable workers who have never migrated (Barrett and Goggin, 2010). Among Mexicans who return after migrating to the United States, the labor market experience they acquired in the United States is worth twice as much as the experience they would have acquired in Mexico had they not migrated (Reinhold and Thom, 2013). However, some studies do not find that return migrants earn more than people who never left. For example, Chinese venture capitalists who have migrated and returned—termed "sea turtles"—appear to be less productive than those who never migrated (Sun, 2013).

Immigrants may leave because they have not succeeded in the destination. However, earning less than expected in the destination may paradoxically prevent some immigrants from leaving. Much like potential immigrants may be too poor to migrate in the first place, immigrants who have not done well in the destination may not have the funds to finance their out-migration.

Circular migration

Some migrants engage in circular migration, or repeated moves between an origin and a destination. Immigrants who work in seasonal jobs, such as agriculture or construction, are particularly likely to engage in circular migration. Many programs that allow firms to hire low-skilled temporary foreign workers are designed to encourage circular migration. For example, Canada's program for seasonal agricultural workers allows workers from Mexico and the Caribbean to remain in Canada for up to eight months of a calendar year. Workers must return to their home country in order to be eligible to return to Canada, and workers from the Caribbean receive part of their pay only after returning to their home country. The *bracero* program that allowed Mexicans to do temporary agricultural work in the United States during 1942 to 1964 similarly withheld part of workers' pay until they returned to Mexico. Because of a combination of corruption and poor record keeping, Mexicans never received much of the funds that were withheld.

Research shows that stricter border enforcement reduces circular migration and increases duration of stay among unauthorized immigrants in the United States. Stricter border enforcement increases the cost of crossing the border illicitly. Some unauthorized immigrants who would otherwise return home to visit instead stay in the United States longer or even permanently as reentry becomes more difficult (Angelucci, 2012).

Chapters 2 and 3 focused on why people become immigrants, where they are from, where they go and for how long. The next chapter switches the focus to the characteristics of immigrants and out-migrants by looking at selection.

Problems and discussion questions

1   Explain how immigration policy can affect the number and type (economic, family-based, refugees, legal, illegal, etc.) of immigrants. Why might destination countries want to use immigration policy to affect the number and type of immigrants?
2   Why do immigrants go to poor countries?
3   Why do immigrants tend to be geographically concentrated within destination countries?
4   What factors led to the dispersion of immigrants across the United States during the 1990s and 2000s? What do you think happened to this dispersion after the 2007–2009 housing and financial crisis?
5   Why do some immigrants leave the destination country? Use the utility- or income-maximization model and the gravity model from Chapter 2 to explain out-migration.
6   How can countries reduce the likelihood of being a welfare magnet?

Notes

1   Based on United Nations (2013) and World Bank (2014).
2   This estimate is not controlling for other origin or destination country factors. Controlling for other observable factors, Mayda (2010) finds that a 10 percent increase in destination country GDP per capita increases an origin country's emigration rate by 20 percent.
3   For example, asylum seekers who arrive in Australia by boat are sent to a refugee-processing center in Papua New Guinea. If they are found to be refugees, they are resettled in Papua New Guinea, not in Australia. This so-called Pacific Solution is aimed at discouraging asylum seekers who undertake a risky sea journey to Australia from Indonesia.
4   Proposition 187 was a ballot initiative passed in California in 1994 that aimed to prohibit unauthorized immigrants from receiving publicly funded education, health care or other social services. The law was ultimately found to be unconstitutional but was an indicator of anti-immigrant sentiment in the state.
5   Major public assistance programs include public health insurance (primarily Medicaid and SCHIP; Medicare is not included), food stamps (SNAP), cash welfare (TANF or SSI) and subsidized housing. Calculations are based on 2011–2013 March Current Population Survey data for benefits received during the previous calendar year using data from IPUMS (King et al., 2010).
6   Some research finds that duration of stay is shorter when economic conditions in the destination country are better (e.g., Lindstrom, 1996). However, some studies find that the probability of leaving is lower when economic conditions are better (e.g., Aydemir and Robinson, 2008).

Internet resources

The Database on Immigrants in OECD Countries has data on a broad range of demographic and labor market characteristics of immigrants living in OECD countries and is available at http://www.oecd.org/els/mig/databaseonimmigrantsinoecdcountriesdioc.htm. Data that include non-OECD countries are available at http://www.oecd.org/migration/databaseonimmigrantsinoecdandnon-oecdcountriesdioc-e.htm.

Suggestions for further reading

Dustmann, C. and Görlach, J.S. (2014) "Selective outmigration and the estimation of immigrants' earnings profiles." In: Chiswick, B. and Miller, P.W. (eds.) *Handbook of the Economics of International Migration*, vol. 1A. Amsterdam: Elsevier.

Giulietti, C. and Wahba, J. (2013) "Welfare migration," in Constant, A.F. and Zimmermann, K.F. (eds.) *International Handbook on the Economics of Migration*. Cheltenham, UK: Edward Elgar, pp. 489–504.

Hatton, T. (2013) "Refugee and asylum migration," in Constant, A.F. and Zimmermann, K.F. (eds.) *International Handbook on the Economics of Migration*. Cheltenham, UK: Edward Elgar, pp. 453–469.

References

Amuedo-Dorantes, C. and Lozano, F. (2014) "On the effectiveness of SB1070 in Arizona." *CreAM Discussion Paper* No. 1423. London: University College London.

Angelucci, M. (2012) "US border enforcement and the new flow of Mexican illegal migration." *Economic Development and Cultural Change* 60(2), pp. 311–357.

Aydemir, A. and Robinson, C. (2008) "Global labour markets, return, and onward migration." *Canadian Journal of Economics* 41(4), pp. 1285–1311.

Bandiera, O., Rasul, I. and Viarengo, M. (2013) "The making of modern America: Migratory flows in the age of mass migration." *Journal of Development Economics* 102, pp. 23–47.

Barrett, A. and Goggin, J. (2010) "Returning to the question of a wage premium for returning migrants." *National Institute Economic Review* 213, pp. R43–R51.

Barrett, A. and McCarthy, Y. (2008) "Immigrants and welfare programmes: Exploring the interactions between immigrant characteristics, immigrant welfare dependence, and welfare policy." *Oxford Review of Economic Policy* 24(3), pp. 543–560.

Bauer, T, Epstein, G.S. and Gang, I.N. (2007) "The influence of stocks and flows on migrants' location choices." *Research in Labor Economics* 26, pp. 199–229.

Beine, M., Docquier, F. and Özden, Ç. (2011) "Diasporas." *Journal of Development Economics* 95(1), pp. 30–41.

Bertoli, S., Fernández-Huertas Moraga, J. and Ortega, F. (2013) "Crossing the border: Self-selection, earnings and individual migration decisions." *Journal of Development Economics* 101, pp. 75–91.

Boeri, T. and Brücker, H. (2005) "Why are Europeans so tough on migrants?" *Economic Policy* 44, pp. 629–703.

Bohn, S. and Pugatch, T. (2013) "U.S. border enforcement and Mexican immigration location choice," *IZA Discussion Paper* No. 7842. Bonn, Germany: Institute for the Study of Labor.

Bohn, S., Lofstrom, M. and Raphael, S. (2014) "Did the 2007 Legal Arizona Workers Act reduce the state's unauthorized immigrant population?" *Review of Economics and Statistics* 96(2), pp. 258–269.

Borjas, G.J. (1999) "Immigration and welfare magnets." *Journal of Labor Economics* 17(4), pp. 607–637.

Borjas, G.J. (2001) "Does immigration grease the wheels of the labor market?" *Brookings Papers on Economic Activity*, pp. 69–119.

Borjas, G.J. (2006) "Native internal migration and the labor market impact of immigration." *Journal of Human Resources* 41(2), pp. 221–258.

Borjas, G.J. and Bratsberg, B. (1996) "Who leaves? The outmigration of the foreign-born." *Review of Economics and Statistics* 78(1), pp. 165–176.

Cadena, B.C. (2013) "Native competition and low-skilled immigrant inflows." *Journal of Human Resources* 48(4), pp. 910–944.

Cadena, B.C. (2014) "Recent immigrants as labor market arbitrageurs: Evidence from the minimum wage." *Journal of Urban Economics* 80, pp. 1–12.

Cadena, B.C. and Kovak, B.K. (2013) "Immigrants equilibrate local labor markets: Evidence from the Great Recession." *National Bureau of Economic Research Working Paper* No. 19272. Cambridge, MA: National Bureau of Economic Research.

Card, D. and DiNardo, J. (2000) "Do immigrant inflows lead to native outflows?" *American Economic Review Papers & Proceedings* 90(2), pp. 360–367.

Castles, S., Cubas, M.A., Kim, C. and Ozkul, D. (2012) "Irregular migration: causes, patterns, and strategies." In: Omelaniuk, I. (ed.) *Global Perspectives on Migration and Development: GFMD Puerto Vallarta and Beyond.* New York: Springer, pp. 117–151.

Clark, X., Hatton, T.J. and Williamson, J.G. (2007) "Explaining U.S. immigration, 1971–1998." *Review of Economics and Statistics* 89(2), pp. 359–373.

Cobb-Clark, D.A. and Connolly, M.D. (1997) "The worldwide market for skilled migrants: Can Australia compete?" *International Migration Review* 31(3), pp. 670–693.

Cutler, D.M., Glaeser, E.J. and Vigdor, J.L. (2008) "Is the melting pot still hot? Explaining the resurgence of immigration segregation." *Review of Economics and Statistics* 30(3), pp. 478–497.

Dustmann, C. and Görlach, J.S. (2014) "Selective outmigration and the estimation of immigrants' earnings profiles." In: Chiswick, B. and Miller, P.W. (eds.) *Handbook of the Economics of International Migration,* vol. 1A. Amsterdam: Elsevier.

Dustmann, C. and Weiss, Y. (2007) "Return migration: Theory and empirical evidence from the UK." *British Journal of Industrial Relations* 45(2), pp. 236–256.

The Economist (2012) "Hello, world: Growth has brought foreigners, and foreigners have brought growth." June 30.

Fargues, P. (2009) "Work, refuge, transit: An emerging pattern of irregular immigration south and east of the Mediterranean." *International Migration Review* 43(3), pp. 544–577.

Geis, W., Uebelmesser, S. and Werding, M. (2013) "How do migrants choose their destination country? An analysis of institutional determinants." *Review of International Economics* 21(5), pp. 825–840.

Gibson, J. and McKenzie, D. (2011) "The microeconomic determinants of emigration and return migration of the best and brightest: Evidence from the Pacific." *Journal of Development Economics* 95(1), pp. 18–29.

Giulietti, C. and Wahba, J. (2013) "Welfare migration." In: Constant, A.F. and Zimmermann, K.F. (eds.) *International Handbook on the Economics of Migration.* Cheltenham, UK: Edward Elgar, pp. 489–504.

Glitz, A. (2012) "The labor market impact of immigration: A quasi-experiment exploiting immigrant location rules in Germany." *Journal of Labor Economics* 30(1), pp. 175–213.

Greenwood, M.J. and McDowell, J.M. (1991) "Differential economic opportunity, transferability of skills, and immigration to the United States and Canada." *Review of Economics and Statistics* 73(4), pp. 612–623.

Grogger, J. and Hanson, G.H. (2011) "Income maximization and the selection and sorting of international migrants." *Journal of Development Economics* 95(1), pp. 42–57.

Hanson, G.H. (2006) "Illegal migration from Mexico to the United States." *Journal of Economic Literature* 44(4), pp. 869–924.

International Organization for Migration (2013) *World Migration Report 2013: Migrant Well-being and Development.* Geneva: International Organization for Migration.

Jaeger, D.A. (2008) "Green cards and the location choices of immigrants in the United States, 1971–2000." *Research in Labor Economics* 27, pp. 131–183.

Jasso, G. and Rosenzweig, M.R. (1982) "Estimating the emigration rates of legal immigrants using administrative and survey data: The 1971 cohort of immigrants to the United States." *Demography* 19(3), pp. 279–290.

Kaushal, N. (2005) "New immigrants' location choices: Magnets without welfare." *Journal of Labor Economics* 23(1), pp. 59–80.

King, M., Ruggles, S., Alexander, J.T., Flood, S., Genadek, K., Schroeder, M., Trampe, B. and Vick, R. (2010) Integrated Public Use Microdata Series, Current Population Survey: Version 3.0. [Machine-readable database]. Minneapolis: University of Minnesota.

Lindstrom, D.P. (1996) "Economic opportunity in Mexico and return migration from the United States." *Demography* 33(3), pp. 357–374.

Maddux, W.M. and Galinsky, A.D. (2009) "Cultural borders and mental barriers: The relationship between living abroad and creativity." *Journal of Personality and Social Psychology* 96, pp. 1047–1061.

Martin, P. (2013) "The global challenge of managing migration." *Population Bulletin* 68, pp. 1–16.

Mayda, A.M. (2010) "International migration: A panel analysis of the determinants of bilateral flows." *Journal of Population Economics* 23(4), pp. 1249–1274.

Myrdal, G. (1957) *Rich Lands and Poor: The Road to World Prosperity.* New York: Harper & Brothers.

Ortega, F. and Peri, G. (2013) "The effect of income and immigration policies on international migration." *Migration Studies* 1, pp. 47–74.

Passel, J.S., Cohn, D. and Gonzalez-Barrera, A. (2013) *Population Decline of Unauthorized Immigrants Stalls, May Have Reversed.* Washington, DC: Pew Research Center. Retrieved from: http://www. pewhispanic.org/files/2013/09/Unauthorized-Sept-2013-FINAL.pdf [10 January 2014].

Pedersen, P.J., Pytlikova, M. and Smith, N. (2008) "Selection and network effects: migration flows into OECD countries 1999–2000." *European Economic Review* 52(7), pp. 1160–1186.

Portes, A. and Bach, R.L. (1985) *Latin Journey: Cuban and Mexican Immigrants in the United States.* Berkeley: University of California Press.

Razin, A. and Wahba, J. (2011) "Welfare magnet hypothesis, fiscal burden and immigration skill selectivity." *National Bureau of Economic Research Working Paper* No. 17515. Cambridge, MA: National Bureau of Economic Research.

Reinhold, S. and Thom, K. (2013) "Migration experience and earnings in the Mexican labor market." *Journal of Human Resources* 48(3), pp. 768–820.

Reyes, B.I. (2004). "Changes in trip duration for Mexican immigrants to the United States." *Population Research and Policy Review* 23(3), pp. 235–252.

Simpson, N.B. and Sparber, C. (2013) "The short- and long-run determinants of less-educated immigrant flows into U.S. states." *Southern Economic Journal* 80(2), pp. 414–438.

Statistics Canada (2013) *2011 National Household Survey: Immigration, place of birth, citizenship, ethnic origin, visible minorities, language and religion.* Available at: http://www.statcan.gc.ca/daily-quotidien/ 130508/dq130508b-eng.htm [10 March 2014].

Sun, W. (2013) "The productivity of return migrants: The case of China's 'sea turtles.'" *IZA Journal of Migration* 2.

Tienda, M. (2013) "Multiplying diversity: Family reunification and the regional origins of late-age immigrants, 1981–2009." *IZA Working Paper* No. 2390. Bonn: Institute for the Study of Labor.

Timmer, A.S. and Williamson, J.G. (1998) "Immigration policy prior to the 1930s: Labor markets, policy interactions, and globalization backlash." *Population and Development Review* 24(4), pp. 739–771.

United Nations (2013) "Total international migrant stock." Available at: http://esa.un.org/unmigration/ TIMSA2013/migrantstocks2013.htm?mtotals [9 January 2014].

United Nations Development Programme (UNDP) (2009) *Human Development Report 2009.* New York, NY: United Nations Development Programme.

Warren, R. and Peck, J.M. (1980) "Foreign-born emigration from the United States: 1960 to 1970." *Demography* 17(1), pp. 71–84.

World Bank (2014) "GDP per capita." Available at: http://data.worldbank.org/indicator/NY.GDP. PCAP.CD [20 February 2014].

Yang, D. (2006) "Why do migrants return to poor countries? Evidence from Philippine migrants' responses to exchange rate shocks." *Review of Economics and Statistics* 88(4), pp. 715–735.

Zavodny, M. (1999) "Determinants of recent immigrants' locational choices." *International Migration Review* 33(4), pp. 1014–1030.

Part 2

Immigrant Selection and Assimilation

4   Selection in Immigration

In economic models of the migration decision, cross-country differences in economic conditions play a central role in determining whether people move. The utility- or income-maximization model and the gravity model predict that changes in relative economic conditions lead to changes in migration flows. Chapters 2 and 3 focused on how changes in relative economic conditions affect the number of people who migrate. This chapter focuses on how changes in relative economic conditions affect the composition, or characteristics, of immigrants. Immigrants are unlikely to be perfectly representative of the population in the origin. They may be predominately high skilled or predominately low skilled. They may be disproportionately workers, students, children, stay-at-home spouses or retirees.

Who chooses to migrate is often as important to both origin and destination countries as the number of migrants. Origin and destination countries can have many different perspectives on what characteristics are "desirable" among migrants. These perspectives may or may not conflict. For example, origin countries may be concerned that out-migration of skilled workers will slow economic growth, while destination countries may want to attract skilled workers in order to boost economic growth. Origin countries may want students to go abroad to receive an education but then return home to contribute to the economy. Destination countries may want to attract tuition-paying foreign students and then have them leave so that they do not compete with native-born workers. Alternatively, destination countries may not want to incur the cost of educating foreign students unless they will stay and join the workforce.

The economics of immigration uses selection models to look at immigrants' characteristics. Studies of immigrant selection have focused primarily on the relationship between immigrants' skill levels and returns to skill in the origin and destination. This chapter therefore focuses on skill. However, the model presented in this chapter can be applied to other characteristics as well. The key prediction of the model is that immigrants' characteristics depend on the relative returns to those characteristics. The model can also be applied to return migration, as discussed later in this chapter.

The selection model can explain why not all migrants from an origin country go to the same destination country. People in the same country typically share a culture and language, and they are about the same distance from other countries. So why do some migrants go to one place while others go elsewhere? The selection model developed below predicts that people sort across potential destinations—including the origin—based on their skills and the relative returns to those skills.

The Roy model

The economist George Borjas (1987) developed an influential model of skill selection in immigration. The model is based on a canonical model by Andrew Roy (1951) that examined how self-selection into occupations affects the distribution of income. In Borjas's version of the Roy model, workers earn the average wage in their country plus a random term. The average wage differs across countries, as does the distribution of the random term. In the origin country, the distribution of wages is

$$ln(Wage) = \mu + \varepsilon \tag{4.1}$$

where μ is the average wage and ε is a measure of how much wages vary across individuals relative to the average. (The model examines the natural log of wages because logarithmic functions have nice properties that the model exploits.) People with positive values of ε earn more than the average, while people with negative values of ε earn less than the average. One way to interpret ε is as measuring the return to skill—how much wages increase as skill increases. The model assumes that ε is distributed normally with a mean of 0 and a variance of σ^2. (Borjas makes this assumption because normal distributions also have nice properties that the model exploits.) The larger σ^2 is, or the bigger the variation in ε, the higher the return to skills is in the origin country and the greater income inequality is there. As the variation in income increases, income inequality grows.

If everyone in the origin country migrates to the destination country, their distribution of wages in the destination country is

$$ln\left(\widetilde{Wage}\right) = \tilde{\mu} + \tilde{\varepsilon} \tag{4.2}$$

where $\tilde{\varepsilon}$ is distributed normally with a mean of 0 and a variance of $\tilde{\sigma}^2$ (terms with a tilde ($\sim$) over them refer to the destination country, and terms without it refer to the origin country). Everyone knows μ, $\tilde{\mu}$ and the cost of migrating, and people know their own ε and $\tilde{\varepsilon}$.

The model assumes that ε and $\tilde{\varepsilon}$ are correlated with, or related to, each other, with a correlation coefficient equal to ρ. This correlation coefficient can range from 1 to -1. Bigger numbers in absolute value mean a stronger relationship between earnings in the origin and the destination. If ρ is positive, then people who have higher-than-average earnings in the origin also have higher-than-average earnings in the destination, and people with lower-than-average earnings in the origin have lower-than-average earnings in the destination. This would occur if skills that are valuable in the origin are also valuable in the destination. For example, an engineer in Kenya who has a PhD is likely to earn an above-average wage in Kenya and elsewhere, while a street cleaner from India who has no formal education is likely to earn a below-average wage in India and elsewhere. The more similar two countries are, the higher ρ is likely to be.

If ρ is negative, then people who have higher-than-average earnings in the origin have lower-than-average earnings in the destination. For example, people who are relatively successful in an agricultural economy that rewards physical strength and stamina might be relatively unsuccessful in an industrialized economy that values education. The correlation coefficient may be negative for immigrants moving from some developing countries to industrialized countries.

People choose to migrate if their earnings will be higher in the destination than in the origin, net of migration costs, or if

$$\widetilde{Wage} - Migration\ costs > Wage \tag{4.3}$$

Rearranging equation 4.3, people migrate if

$$\frac{\widetilde{Wage}}{Wage + Migration\ Costs} > 1 \tag{4.4}$$

Another way to express equation 4.4 is by taking the natural log of both sides. People migrate if

$$ln\left(\frac{\widetilde{Wage}}{Wage + Migration\ Costs}\right) > 0 \tag{4.5}$$

Substituting in equations 4.1 and 4.2 and using the properties of log functions, people migrate if, approximately,

$$\tilde{\mu} - \mu - \pi + \tilde{\varepsilon} - \varepsilon > 0 \tag{4.6}$$

where $\pi = Migration\ Costs\,/\,Wage$. (The appendix to this chapter presents the mathematical details.) Borjas calls π a "time-equivalent" measure of migration costs because it is measured relative to the wage in the origin. In his initial version of the model published in 1987, Borjas assumed that migration costs are the same for everyone in an origin country. Later work by Borjas and other economists allows migration costs to vary randomly or to depend on people's skill levels.

With a few assumptions, the model makes several predictions similar to the utility- or income-maximization model developed in Chapter 2. People will be more likely to migrate as the average wage in the destination, $\tilde{\mu}$, increases, and less likely to migrate as the average wage in the origin, μ, increases. People will be less likely to migrate as migration costs, π, increase. In addition, the model has several new insights. People who will earn more than the average in the destination—people with larger $\tilde{\varepsilon}$—are more likely to migrate, and people who earn more than the average in the origin—people with larger ε—are less likely to migrate, all else equal. As the gap between their differences from the averages ($\tilde{\varepsilon} - \varepsilon$) increases, people are more likely to migrate. This means that people who have skills that are rewarded more in the destination than in the origin are more likely to move, all else equal. And as skills become more transferable, or ρ increases, people are more likely to migrate.

The direction of selection

Borjas developed the selection model to examine where immigrants are likely to be in the distributions of wages in the origin and the destination, or the direction of selection. The model assumes that the destination country has higher wages than the origin country ($\tilde{\mu} > \mu + \pi$), but the destination country may have a higher or lower return to skill than the origin country.

In Borjas's model, the return to skill is related to the extent of income inequality—the higher income inequality is, the higher the return to skill is. The extent of income inequality is measured by the variance in wages in each country. When inequality in the origin is greater than inequality in the destination, $\sigma^2 > \tilde{\sigma}^2$. If income inequality is greater in the origin than in the destination, the return to skill is higher in the origin than in the destination. Relative income inequality, or the relative return to skill, affects the direction of selection in the model.

Positive selection occurs when immigrants are from the top part of the skill (and wage) distribution in the origin and the destination. In other words, there is high-skilled emigration from the origin to the destination. Positive selection is sometimes called "brain drain." (Figure 4.1 shows a normal distribution and an example of what positive selection and negative selection look like.) The model predicts that positive selection occurs when skills are transferable, or ρ is high enough, and income inequality is higher in the destination than in the origin. More-skilled people will earn a higher return to their skills in the destination than in the origin and therefore want to move. Meanwhile, less-skilled people will be penalized more for their relatively low skill levels in the destination than in the origin and therefore do not want to move.

If there is positive selection and income inequality increases further in the destination relative to the origin, immigration increases and becomes less positively selected. Intuitively, people who were just below the marginal skill level for migrating now become willing to move. This lowers the average skill level of immigrants. If income inequality instead increases in the origin relative to the destination (but still remains lower in the origin), immigration decreases and becomes even more positively selected.

Conversely, negative selection occurs if immigrants are at the lower end of the skill distribution in the origin and the destination. The model predicts that negative selection occurs when skills are transferable but income inequality is lower in the destination than in the origin. The relatively high return to skill in the origin encourages more-skilled people to remain in the origin and less-skilled people to migrate. Less-skilled people are penalized less in the destination than in the origin for their relatively low skill levels and therefore want to move to the region with a more equal distribution of wages. More-skilled people would receive a smaller premium in the destination for their skills, so they do not migrate, all else equal. If

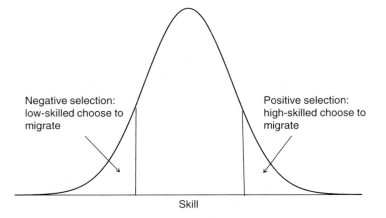

Figure 4.1 The direction of selection in a normal distribution of skill.

income inequality decreases in the origin relative to the destination, immigration increases and becomes less negatively selected. But if income inequality increases further in the origin relative to the destination, immigration decreases and becomes even more negatively selected.

Figure 4.2 shows how the relative return to skill affects the direction of selection. Wages are assumed to increase linearly with skill, and skill is perfectly transferable across countries (or $\rho = 1$). The steepness of the skill–wage profile indicates the return to skill in a country—the steeper the line, the higher the return to skill. In Figure 4.2(a) on the left, the return to skill is higher in the destination than in the origin. The opposite is the case in Figure 4.2(b) on the right.

When the return to skill is higher in the destination than in the origin, people with low skill levels earn more in the origin than in the destination, and people with high skill levels earn more in the destination than in the origin. In Figure 4.2(a), everyone whose skill level is below s^*, the skill level at which the lines cross, stays in the origin, while everyone with a higher skill level migrates. In Figure 4.2(b), everyone whose skill level is below s^* migrates, while everyone with a higher skill level stays.

The effect of changes in the relative return to skill can be seen by pivoting one of the skill–wage lines in either figure while leaving the other line unchanged. For example, an increase in the relative return to skill in the destination causes the dashed skill–wage lines to steepen, as Figure 4.3(a) shows. The skill threshold for migrating versus staying, s^*, then changes, and the number of immigrants changes as a result. If immigrants are positively selected and the relative return to skill in the destination increases, the skill threshold for migrating falls. More people migrate, and migration becomes less selective as a result. Note that the direction of selection changes only if the change in the relative return to skill is so large that the country that previously had the lower return to skill now has the higher return to skill, and vice versa.

The effect of a change in average income in the origin or the destination can be seen by shifting one of the skill–wage lines up or down in either figure while again leaving the other line

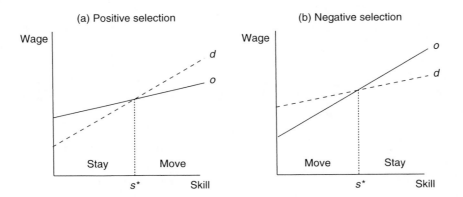

Figure 4.2 Relative returns to skill and the direction of selection.

In (a), positive selection occurs because the return to skill is higher in the destination than in the origin, as indicated by a more steeply sloped skill–wage curve in the destination (the dashed line) than in the origin (the solid line). In (b), negative selection occurs because the return to skill is higher in the origin than in the destination, as indicated by a more steeply sloped skill–wage curve in the origin (the solid line) than in the destination (the dashed line).

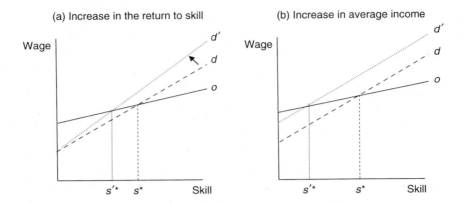

Figure 4.3 The effect of changes in the relative return to skill or average income in the destination.

In (a), an increase in the relative return to skill in the destination decreases the skill threshold for migrating if there is already positive selection. More people migrate, and migration becomes less positively selected. In (b), an increase in the average wage in the destination decreases the skill threshold for migrating.

unchanged. An increase in the average wage in the destination causes the dashed skill–wage line to shift up in Figure 4.3(b), for example. A change in average income does not affect the direction of selection, but it does change the magnitude of immigration and, by changing s^*, the skill level of the marginal immigrant and the average immigrant. If there is already positive selection, the skill threshold for migrating falls and more people migrate. Migration thus becomes less selective in this case, as Figure 4.3(b) shows.

The effect of a change in migration costs can also be seen by shifting one of the lines. For example, an increase in migration costs is effectively a lower wage at all skill levels in the destination, or a downwards shift in the skill–wage line for the destination.

Refugees and selection

Borjas discusses a third type of selection, when immigrants are from the low end of the wage distribution in the origin but are in the upper end of the wage distribution in the destination country. This is particularly likely to happen when ρ is negative. Borjas terms this "refugee sorting" or "inverse sorting" and argues that this case is particularly likely for migration from countries that adopt a Communist or Socialist government that confiscates privately owned assets. When such transitions occurred in Eastern Europe, Cuba and parts of Latin America during the twentieth century, many highly skilled people whose prospects at home worsened migrated. Those migrants typically were successful in the market-oriented economies of their destinations.

However, not all refugees are successful. Many have low skill levels and do poorly in both the origin and the destination. If they are doing well in the origin, they have little reason to flee. Refugees may be negatively selected relative to the destination if they would not migrate absent some adverse event, such as a natural disaster or a civil war. Because their migration is not motivated by potential economic gains, they are unlikely to be selected on characteristics that are valued in the destination. Refugees also may have little choice of destination country but simply flee to the nearest safe country or to a country that will take them, not necessarily the country in which they will be the most successful. Ultimately, the direction of selection among refugees depends on the nature of the refugee-producing event and other idiosyncratic factors (Chin and Cortes, 2014).

Intermediate selection

If migration costs depend on skill, intermediate selection may occur instead of positive or negative selection. Intermediate selection is when immigrants are from the middle of the skill (and wage) distribution. Suppose the return to skill is higher in the origin than in the destination, as in Figure 4.2(b). If all immigrants have the same migration costs, negative selection occurs. But if migration costs decrease as skill increases, intermediate selection may occur instead. Low-skilled people have bigger gains from migrating but also higher migration costs than people with more skill. Low-skilled people therefore may not benefit from migrating. People with intermediate skill levels may benefit from migrating from a country with relatively high inequality because their migration costs are lower than for low-skilled people.

There are several reasons why migration costs might decrease as skill increases. People with low skill levels and hence low incomes may face "cash-in-advance" or liquidity constraints, situations where they cannot save or borrow enough to pay the costs of migrating. Such constraints may not be binding for people with higher skill levels and hence higher incomes. Immigration policies that favor skilled migrants may make migration costs lower for skilled migrants than for unskilled migrants. In addition, migrant networks may increase with skill. Migration costs then would decrease as skill increases since having a bigger migrant network reduces migration costs, all else equal.

If migration costs instead increase with skill, intermediate selection may occur from countries with relatively low inequality. Intermediate selection might occur if an origin country with relative low inequality imposes highly progressive taxes—tax rates that increase with income—on emigrants, for example. In that case, high-skilled, high-income people may stay in order to avoid paying high taxes if they emigrate.

The selection model applies to selection on both observable characteristics and unobservable characteristics. Education and income are examples of observable characteristics. Unobservable characteristics are, by definition, characteristics that datasets do not include since they are not observable or easily quantified by researchers. Ambition and willingness to work hard are examples of unobservable characteristics. Economists usually measure unobservable characteristics by estimating wage models. The residual, or error term, after controlling for observable characteristics serves as a measure of unobservable characteristics. Selection on observable and unobservable characteristics is usually in the same direction, although not always.

Summing up the model

The selection model has two key insights. First, the number of immigrants depends not only on relative incomes in the origin and the destination but also on the variances of those incomes, or the relative return to skill. Second, not just the number of immigrants but also their composition—their skill level—depend on the relative return to skill. In essence, less-skilled people are better off in countries with a lower return to skill and less income inequality, while more-skilled people are better off in countries with a higher return to skill and more income inequality, all else equal.

In both the selection model developed in this chapter and the utility- or income-maximization model developed in Chapter 2, people decide whether to move based on their income in the origin and in the destination. If their income will be higher in the destination, net of migration costs and adjusted for the cost of living, they move. Such models imply that we should observe almost no one living in developed countries. For most people in developing countries, their income would be higher in an industrialized country, even after adjusting for the difference in the cost of living. Why then do we observe so few people migrating from developing countries? Barriers to immigration in developed countries, such as quotas, are one major reason. Liquidity constraints, limited migrant networks and lack of information about the gains to migrating are other reasons. In addition, the indirect, or psychic, costs of migration may be very high.

Measuring income inequality and the return to skill

Economists who apply the selection model to immigration must decide how to measure the return to skill. There are several potential measures. Some studies use a measure of income inequality, such as the Gini index. The Gini index measures how much the distribution of income deviates from a perfectly equal distribution. It ranges from zero, which indicates perfect equality of incomes, to one hundred, which indicates that one person or household receives all of the income in that country. Table 4.1 lists the Gini index for major immigrant-sending or -receiving countries.

Income shares and income ratios are other measures of income inequality. Income shares measure what fraction of total income accrues to a specific portion of the income distribution. For example, a study might use the ratio of the percentage of total income that accrues to the top 25 percent of households to the percentage of total income that accrues to the bottom 25 percent of households as a measure of income inequality. This is the 75/25 income share. Alternatively, a study might use the ratio of income earned by a household at the 75th percentile of the income distribution to income earned by a household at the 25th percentile of the income distribution. This is the 75/25 income ratio. Studies also use other points in the income distribution, such as the 90th percentile and the 10th percentile, to measure income inequality.

Another way to measure the return to skill is to compare the earnings of workers in different skill groups. For example, a study might compare the earnings of workers who have a bachelor's degree and workers who have a high school diploma. (Remember, economics often uses education as a proxy for skill.) This gives the return to a bachelor's degree relative to a high school diploma. Alternatively, a study might compare the earnings of workers in white-collar (office) jobs with the earnings of workers in blue-collar (manual labor) jobs.

Empirical evidence on selection

Globally, immigrants tend to be positively selected from source countries. Figure 4.4 shows emigration rates for adults age 25 and older by country of origin and level of education

Table 4.1 Gini index for 20 major immigrant-sending or -receiving countries

	Gini index
Thailand	53.6
Mexico	48.3
China	47.4
United States	45.0
Philippines	44.8
Russia	42.0
United Kingdom	40.0
India	36.8
Poland	34.1
Bangladesh	33.2
France	32.7
Canada	32.1
Spain	32.0
Italy	31.9
Egypt	30.8
Pakistan	30.6
Australia	30.3
Kazakhstan	28.9
Ukraine	28.2
Germany	27.0

Source: U.S. Central Intelligence Agency (2014) *World Factbook*. Available at: https://www.cia.gov/library/publications/the-world-factbook/rankorder/2172rank.html [19 March 2014].

in 2010. (The data only include emigrants to 20 OECD countries, not all emigrants. Only outliers and countries of particular interest are labeled.) For each country, the log odds of emigration for adults with no schooling, primary school or lower secondary school (primary educated) are plotted on the horizontal axis, and the log odds of emigration for adults with a college education (tertiary educated) are plotted on the vertical axis.[1]

Almost all of the points in Figure 4.4 are above a 45° line from the bottom left corner to the top right corner of the figure. This indicates positive selection—for most countries, people with a college education are more likely to become immigrants than people with a primary education. Out of the 195 countries displayed in Figure 4.4, the emigration rate is higher among tertiary-educated adults than among primary-educated adults for 177 countries. Studies that control for origin- and destination-country characteristics likewise find that immigrants tend to be positively selected (e.g., Grogger and Hanson, 2011).

The United States is one of the few countries below the 45° line, indicating negative selection on education among U.S. natives who emigrate to the other countries in the dataset. Consistent with the model, the United States has more income inequality and higher returns to skill (by the measures discussed earlier) than almost all of the other 19 destination countries included in the data. U.S. natives who move to other destination countries might, of course, be positively selected instead. Anecdotes about young U.S.-born entrepreneurs moving to Asia in search of better opportunities there suggest positive selection in emigration, but little data are available to evaluate the direction of selection in immigration to developing countries.

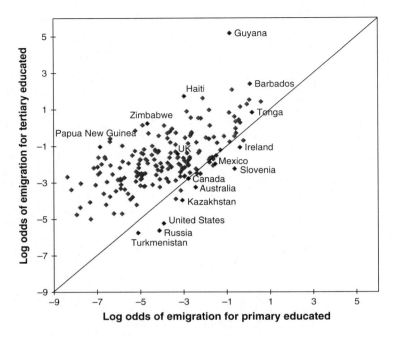

Figure 4.4 Emigration rates for adults by source country and education, 2010.

Source: Emigration rate from Brücker, H., Capuano, S., Marfoulk, A. (2013) "Education, gender and international migration: Insights from a panel-dataset 1980–2010." Available at http://www.iab.de/en/daten/iab-brain-drain-data.aspx [12 December 2013]. The data include adults age 25 and older.

Like the United States, Russia and Turkmenistan have higher returns to skill than most of the twenty OECD destination countries included in the data used here and are below the 45° line in Figure 4.4. Mexico is also below the 45° line, although closer to it than Russia, Turkmenistan and the United States.

It is difficult to use Figure 4.4 to draw clear conclusions about the validity of the selection model. On the one hand, the fact that most immigrants are positively selected seems at odds with the selection model. We should observe a mix, with countries with relatively low returns to skill above the 45° line and countries with relatively high returns to skill below the 45° line. On the other hand, the data combine 20 destination countries, some of which have higher returns to skill than many origin countries and some of which have lower returns to skill. Looking at a single destination country may therefore be more useful.

Figure 4.5 looks at selection among immigrants to a single country, the United States. The horizontal axis in the figure is the ratio of earnings of workers with a tertiary education to workers with only a primary education in 31 countries. This ratio is a proxy for the return to skill. The vertical axis is the natural log of the ratio of the emigration rate to the United States among adults with a tertiary education to the emigration rate among adults with a primary education for those 31 origin countries. The selection model predicts that the figure should show a negative relationship—the more high-skilled workers earn relative to low-skilled workers in the origin country, the lower the emigration rate should be among

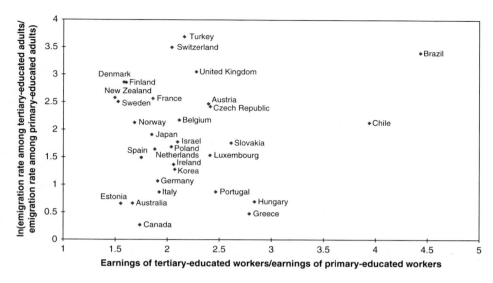

Figure 4.5 Relative earnings and emigration rates to United States for tertiary- and primary-educated adults, by origin country.

Source: Emigration rate from Brücker, H., Capuano, S. and Marfoulk, A. (2013) "Education, gender and international migration: Insights from a panel-dataset 1980-2010." Available at http://www.iab.de/en/daten/iab-brain-drain-data.aspx [12 December 2013]; earnings data from table A6.1 of OECD (2013) *Education at a Glance 2013*. Available at: http://www.oecd.org/edu/eag2013%20(eng)--FINAL%2020%20June%202013.pdf [19 March 2014].

high-skilled workers relative to low-skilled workers. However, this is not the case. Statistically, there is not a relationship between the return to skill and the emigration rate among these origin countries.

Some early research finds results that appear consistent with the selection model. For example, Borjas (1987) analyzes data on male immigrants from 41 countries to the United States. He concludes that male immigrants' wages are negatively related to income inequality in their origin country, as measured by the 90/20 income share. This finding is consistent with the selection model. However, the finding is sensitive to what other variables are included in the model. Deborah Cobb-Clark (1993) applies Borjas's approach to female immigrants from 60 countries to the United States. She similarly finds that immigrants' wages tend to be negatively related to income inequality, as measured by the 95/20 income share. She also finds that immigrants' wages may be negatively related to the return to schooling in their origin country, as measured by the return to completing secondary education (high school). These findings are again consistent with the selection model but sensitive to what other variables are included in the model.

Early studies of the selection model were hampered by data limitations. Testing the selection model requires data on the returns to skill in the origin and in the destination and data on emigration rates by skill level. Early studies had proxies for the rates of return to skill in the origin and destination and data on the characteristics of immigrants, but they lacked data on people who did not migrate. Early studies therefore examined the relationship between the average skill level of immigrants from a country and the relative rate of return to skill. This relationship is not a true test of the selection model because it says nothing about the skills of immigrants relative to the population of the origin country. For example, an immigrant from a developing country might look low skilled compared with a U.S. native or an immigrant from an industrialized country but might be from the top portion of the developing country's skill distribution. Early studies were also limited to examining only one or a handful of destination countries.

In recent years, the Internet and faster computers have allowed researchers to use better data. Frédéric Docquier, Abdeslam Marfouk and colleagues led the way by creating estimates of emigration rates by education from a large number of origin countries to OECD destination countries. Such estimates allow researchers to better test the validity of the selection model. The results provide support for the model, but only under certain conditions.

For example, Michèle Belot and Timothy Hatton (2012) examine the education levels of immigrants from 70 source countries to 21 OECD countries. They find that immigrants tend to be more positively selected in terms of education as the difference in wages between high- and low-educated workers, which proxies for the relative return to skill, widens between the destination and the source country. In other words, as the return to skill increases in the destination relative to the origin, selection becomes more positive. However, they only find this result when they control for the poverty rate in the source country. Belot and Hatton hypothesize that poverty prevents low-skilled people from migrating from countries with high returns to skill.

Jeffrey Grogger and Gordon Hanson (2011) apply the selection model to data on the education levels of immigrants from more than 100 source countries to 15 high-income OECD destination countries. They note that immigrants to the OECD countries they examine are positively selected even though in many cases the model predicts, based on the relative return to skill, that they should be negatively selected. Grogger and Hanson find that bigger differences in the relative return to skill between the destination and the origin decrease immigrant selectivity, the opposite of the model's prediction.[2] They obtain this result using a variety of measures of the relative return to skill. They argue that liquidity constraints—the inability to save or borrow enough to migrate—may explain why low-skilled people do not move even though they would experience the biggest proportional gains from moving. Other research also finds evidence at odds with the Roy model and attributes it to migration costs or barriers to immigration by the low skilled (e.g., Brücker and Defoort, 2009).

There are several additional limitations that apply to both earlier and more recent studies. One is that most available data combine all types of immigrants. Ideally, researchers would have separate data on economic immigrants, refugees and family-based immigrants. The model has a different prediction for refugees than for economic immigrants, and it does not apply well to family-based immigrants who do not plan to work. Data that combine all types of immigrants may appear to not support the model simply because the data combine groups with different predicted effects. Another limitation is that researchers typically do not know immigrants' characteristics prior to migration. Immigrants' earnings in the origin before migrating are usually not known, nor are their education levels prior to migrating. If immigrants acquire education in the destination, it may not be a surprise that immigrants have more education than people who do not migrate.[3]

Evidence on migration costs and other factors

Migration costs and cultural factors shape immigrant selectivity as well. Research typically finds that the bigger the distance between the origin and the destination, the more educated immigrants are. Distance is a proxy for migration costs. Linguistic proximity, or how similar the official languages are in the source and destination countries, is also usually positively related to immigrants' education levels. This suggests that when skills are more transferable, or ρ is higher, immigrants are more positively selected. Interestingly, a historical colonial relationship between a source and a destination country is associated with more negative selectivity. Destination countries often have immigration policies that favor citizens of former colonies, making it easier for low-skilled residents of former colonies to enter. Residents of former colonies also may have bigger networks in the former colonial power, and these networks may enable low-skilled people to migrate.

Research indicates that immigrant selectivity tends to decrease as migrant networks grow. Simone Bertoli and Hillel Rapoport (2013) note that networks create a "swinging door"—the first migrants to push through the door encounter the most resistance, while followers benefit from the lower resistance of a door that is swinging. Bertoli and Rapoport measure networks using the number of earlier immigrants from the same origin to the same destination, and immigrant selectivity using the ratio of college-educated to non-college-educated recent immigrants. Bigger immigrant networks are associated with more negative selection of immigrants in 15 of the 20 destination countries they examine. Two of the countries without a negative relationship between network size and immigrant quality in their study are Australia and Canada, arguably the countries with immigration policies that emphasize skill the most. (The other countries where bigger networks do not lead to more negative selection are Finland, Norway and Spain.) Box 4.1, "The role of networks in Turkish migration," further discusses the relationship between networks and selectivity.

Box 4.1 The role of networks in Turkish migration

Turkey offers an interesting window into the importance of networks in determining the number and characteristics of migrants. Turkey is roughly equidistant from Germany, Luxembourg and Spain. It has no colonial ties to any of those Western European countries, nor is its language similar to the languages spoken in those countries. Germany recruited workers from Turkey during the 1960s and early 1970s. As a result, some 1.2 million Turks lived in Germany in 2000. About 6 percent of them had a tertiary education, and 86 percent had a primary education (the remaining 8 percent had a secondary education). About 194 Turks lived in Luxembourg in 2000; 44 percent of them had a tertiary education, and 26 percent had a primary education. About 1,040 Turks lived in Spain; 33 percent of them had a tertiary education, and 29 percent had a primary education. Michel Beine, Frédéric Docquier and Çağlar Özden (2011) note, "This simple example highlights the striking relationship between migrants' networks and both the size and the skill composition of migration flows" (p. 32).

Evidence on immigration policy

Immigration policy in destination countries is likely to affect the direction and magnitude of selection. Admissions policies that emphasize skills, such as education and ability to speak the destination country's language, are expected to lead to more positive selection among immigrants. Admissions policies that emphasize family ties to residents are expected to lead to more negative selection since such policies increase the importance of networks and allow immigrants who have family ties but not high skill levels to enter.

Immigration policies differ considerably across countries. The United States strongly emphasizes family ties when admitting permanent residents, for example, while Australia and Canada put considerable emphasis on skills. (Chapter 13 discusses U.S. immigration policy in more detail, while Chapter 14 discusses policies elsewhere.) Heather Antecol, Deborah Cobb-Clark and Stephen Trejo (2003) show that immigrants in Australia and Canada have higher levels of English fluency, more education and higher incomes relative to natives than is true of immigrants in the United States. This is consistent with the greater role that skills play in the admissions process for those two countries. But Antecol, Cobb-Clark and Trejo also show that immigrants' English fluency, education and relative incomes are similar across the three countries if immigrants from Latin America are not included in the analysis. Relatively few immigrants from Latin America are admitted to the United States on the basis of skill—they typically are admitted based on family ties or are unauthorized immigrants. The researchers conclude that geography and historical ties between countries appear to play a more important role than skill-based admissions policies in immigrant selectivity across countries.

Countries cannot change their geography, but they can adopt immigration policies that affect immigrant selectivity. For example, in the 1990s Australia increased the emphasis on skills in its immigrant admissions system and began excluding most new immigrants from public assistance programs for the first two years after arrival. Cobb-Clark (2003) shows that after Australia adopted those changes, new immigrants were more fluent in English, had more education and were less likely to be unemployed than earlier immigrants. In addition, Australia's point-based admission system that emphasizes skill appears to break the link between bigger networks and more negative selection. Bertoli and Rapoport's study of networks and selectivity shows that before the country adopted its point system, immigrants to Australia were more negatively selected the bigger their migrant network. After the system was adopted, immigrant selectivity is not related to network size.

Research shows that immigrants are more negatively selected if a destination country does not require a visa for immigrants from an origin country (e.g., Grogger and Hanson, 2011). However, open borders do not necessarily result in negative selection. If two countries are both members of the Schengen area, immigration between them tends to be positively selected.

Research shows that immigrants to destination countries with more generous refugee/asylum policies are more negatively selected from their origin countries (e.g., Grogger and Hanson, 2011). In a number of industrialized countries, refugees tend to earn less initially than natives and other immigrants but experience faster wage growth over time than other immigrants (Chin and Cortes, 2014). These findings are consistent with Borjas's proposition that refugees are negatively selected from the origin country skill distribution but positively selected relative to the destination country skill distribution. However, more evidence on wage growth among refugees relative to natives, not just other immigrants, in various destination countries is needed.

One way to examine the role of immigration policy in selection is to look at how immigrants are selected in the absence of immigration policy. During the late 1800s and early 1900s, the United States imposed few barriers to immigration from Europe. Virtually anyone in good health with the funds to migrate could enter the United States and stay there. Ran Abramitzky, Leah Platt Boustan and Katherine Eriksson (2012, 2013) examine immigrants from Norway to the United States during that time. One-quarter of Norway's population eventually migrated to the United States. Norway had a more unequal income distribution than the United States at the time, so the Roy model predicts negative selection. Historical records indicate that immigrants were indeed negatively selected in terms of family wealth. Norwegians who, because of their birth order or sibling composition, could expect to inherit land were less likely to migrate. In addition, migrants had poorer fathers than non-migrants did.

Today, there are no barriers to immigration to the United States by people born in U.S. territories, such as Puerto Rico. Earnings inequality is higher in Puerto Rico than in the United States, suggesting that Puerto Rico–U.S. migration should be negatively selected. Research shows that this is indeed the case. As of 2000, almost 45 percent of working-age men born in Puerto Rico who had not completed high school had moved to the United States, compared with 30 percent of college graduates (Borjas, 2008). Interestingly, Puerto Rico also experiences inflows from the United States, typically by descendants of earlier Puerto Rico–U.S. migrants. These U.S.–Puerto Rico migrants are positively selected on education, as the Roy model predicts.

The United States also allows unrestricted immigration by citizens of the Federated States of Micronesia (FSM), a set of islands in the western Pacific Ocean. Research shows that FSM–U.S. immigrants have higher education levels than non-migrants (Akee, 2010). Immigrants also tend to be positively selected on earnings. Earnings inequality is higher in FSM than in Hawaii and Guam (the main places FSM migrants go), so this positive selection is counter to the Roy model's prediction. The relative return to skill is thus not the only factor that determines the composition of migration flows.

Table 4.2 Distribution of Mexican residents and immigrants by education in 2000

Years of education	Men		Women	
	Mexican residents	*Mexican immigrants*	*Mexican residents*	*Mexican immigrants*
0–9	69.4	60.1	72.5	62.0
10–11	4.5	5.5	4.0	4.9
12	10.1	21.2	11.2	20.4
13–15	4.7	8.3	4.2	7.9
16+	11.3	5.0	8.0	4.8

Source: Table 2 of Chiquiar, D. and Hanson, G. H. (2005) "International Migration, Self-Selection, and the Distribution of Wages: Evidence from Mexico and the United States." *Journal of Political Economy* 113(2), pp. 239–281.

Selection among Mexico–U.S. immigrants

Economists have devoted considerable attention to the direction of selection among Mexico–U.S. immigrants because of the sizable magnitude of this migration stream. The Roy model predicts that immigrants from Mexico will be negatively selected since Mexico has greater earnings inequality and higher returns to schooling than the United States. However, several studies show that Mexican immigrants tend to be more educated than non-migrants (e.g., Chiquiar and Hanson, 2005; Orrenius and Zavodny, 2005; Caponi, 2011).[4] Table 4.2 shows the distribution of adult Mexicans living in Mexico and in the United States in 2000. The proportions who have at most nine years of education or 16 or more years of education are lower among immigrants than among non-migrants. The opposite is true for intermediate levels of education. The proportion with 12 years of education is about twice as high among immigrants as among non-migrants. Importantly, these data do not include people who migrated before age 21. This pattern is therefore unlikely to be due to Mexican immigrants acquiring education in the United States.

In addition, research shows that Mexico–U.S. immigrants' skill levels would place them in the middle or upper end of Mexico's earnings distribution (Chiquiar and Hanson, 2005). This again suggests that the direction of selection in Mexico–U.S. migration is intermediate or positive, not negative. Despite this evidence of intermediate selection on education, Mexico–U.S. immigrants appear to be negatively selected from Mexico's earnings distribution—they are from the bottom of the earnings distribution there. This suggests that workers who earn less in Mexico than they should given their skill level—workers with a relatively low return to skill—are more likely to migrate (Ambrosini and Peri, 2012; Kaestner and Malamud, 2014). Together, these patterns are consistent with Mexico–U.S. immigrants being negatively selected on unobservable characteristics, whereas intermediate selection occurs on observable characteristics like education.

Barriers to migration by the least skilled may explain why the direction of selection in Mexico–U.S. immigration does not match the model's prediction with regard to observable characteristics. Such barriers include limited networks and liquidity constraints. Research shows that Mexico–U.S. migration is negatively selected from communities with sizable migrant networks but positively selected from communities with small migrant networks (Ibarraran and Lubotsky, 2007; McKenzie and Rapoport, 2010). Less-skilled migrants may rely on friends or family in the United States to help them find jobs and housing there. Skilled migrants, in contrast, may be better able to navigate U.S. job and housing markets on their own. As Mexican migrant networks have grown over time in the United States, immigrants from Mexico are likely to have become more negatively selected. Research indicates this appears to be the case (e.g., Campos-Vazquez and Lara, 2012).

Bigger networks also help potential immigrants borrow from people who have already migrated. This relaxes liquidity constraints that may prevent the poor from migrating. Selection from rural Mexico tends to be more positive than from urban Mexico, in part because of differences in the return to skill but also because of differences in networks and wealth (Fernández-Huertas Moraga, 2013). An anti-poverty program in Mexico named *Oportunidades* that gives money to low-income households leads to more migration by those households, consistent with liquidity constraints (Angelucci, 2013). The additional migration lowers the average skill level among migrants, suggesting that the direction of selection is positive or intermediate.

U.S. border enforcement appears to affect selection among unauthorized Mexican immigrants. Selection becomes more positive when U.S. border enforcement, as measured by total hours worked along the U.S.–Mexico border by U.S. Border Patrol agents, is stricter (Orrenius and Zavodny, 2005). Stricter enforcement raises migration costs because unauthorized immigrants are more likely to need to hire a *coyote*—a smuggler—to help them enter the United States. In terms of Figure 4.2(a), the destination wage line effectively shifts down when migration costs go up. The degree of positive selection then increases, and the number of immigrants falls.

Selection on health

Most economic research on immigrant selection has focused on immigrants' education or earnings, but a few studies have examined selection on health. Studies typically find that immigrants are positively selected on health relative to both non-migrants in the origin and natives in the destination (e.g., Kennedy et al., 2006). This hypothesis is known as the "healthy immigrant effect."

There are several potential explanations for the healthy immigrant effect. First, health tends to be positively related to education and income. Immigrants tend to be positively selected on education relative to non-migrants and must have enough income to bear migration costs, so it is not surprising that immigrants tend to be healthier than non-migrants in the origin. But immigrants also tend to be healthier than natives in the destination, even in destination countries where immigrants have less education and lower incomes, on average, than natives. Immigration policies that screen immigrants on health, income or skill may contribute to the healthy immigrant effect.

Self-selection may also play a role. Characteristics that increase the likelihood a person becomes an immigrant, such as having a low discount rate, may be associated with healthy behaviors. Such behaviors include exercising, eating a healthy diet and not smoking. Immigrants also tend to be relatively young, so adverse health conditions may have not yet manifested for many immigrants. The healthy immigrant effect tends to decrease as duration of residence in the destination increases, as discussed in the next chapter.

Irish immigrants to England are an interesting example of selection and health. As Liam Delaney, Alan Fernihough and James Smith (2013) show, Irish immigrants to England who were born before 1920 or after 1960 tend to be healthier than their counterparts who remained in Ireland and than the English. However, the opposite is true for those who were born between 1920 and 1960. That group of migrants tended to be negatively selected on education as well, and they had experienced relatively high rates of child abuse. This created high psychic costs of staying in Ireland for many of them. Although studies typically emphasize the psychic costs of migrating, it is important to note that some people may face greater psychic costs of staying. The study notes that although these migrants have relatively poor physical and mental health, they probably benefited from the fact that health care quality tended to be higher in England than in Ireland when they migrated.

Selection in return migration

Immigrants who choose to out-migrate from the destination country, either to return to the origin country or to migrate to yet another country, may not be randomly selected from the population of immigrants in the destination. Understanding whether out-migrants are positively or negatively selected is important for several reasons. First, selective out-migration affects the wage profile of an arrival cohort of immigrants over time. An arrival cohort is a group of immigrants who arrive during a certain period, such as 2000 to 2010. If out-migration is positively selected, the average wage among a cohort of immigrants will increase less over time than it would if out-migration was random or negatively selected. As discussed in the next chapter, measuring assimilation—how well immigrants do in the destination country over time—in most datasets requires knowing the direction and extent of selection in return migration.

Selective out-migration affects a number of other outcomes as well. In the destination country, it affects immigration's labor market and fiscal impacts. Positively selected out-migration means that remaining immigrants will compete more with low-skilled natives, and they will pay less in taxes while receiving more in government transfers. The direction of selection in return migration also affects labor market and fiscal impacts in the origin country. Those effects are likely to be the opposite of the effects in the destination country.

Finally, selection in immigration and in return migration can have long-run effects. One channel through which selection matters in the long run is the second and higher generations, or the children and later descendants of immigrants. How well immigrants' children and later descendants do is likely to depend on immigrants' characteristics and success in the destination. Another channel is through political power and fiscal policies. Over time, immigrants may become eligible to vote in the destination. Their preferences regarding taxes, government spending and other government functions and institutions can affect political decisions that in turn affect long-run economic growth.

The Roy model and return migration

Borjas and Bernt Bratsberg (1996) use the Roy model to examine selective out-migration. The model is similar to the model Borjas developed for selection in the initial migration decision but adds the possibility of returning to the origin if wages are higher there than in the destination. This can occur for several reasons. The immigrant could have accumulated skills in the destination that are valued in the origin, boosting her wage there. Alternatively, the immigrant could have misestimated her wage in the destination, and her wage is actually higher in the origin than in the destination. In addition, economic conditions could have unexpectedly improved in the origin, raising the immigrant's wage there if she returns.

Christian Dustmann and Joseph-Simon Görlach (2014) present a version of the model in which a person's lifetime wages are

$$ln(Wage) = \tau(\tilde{\mu} + \tilde{\varepsilon}) + (1 - \tau)(\mu + \varepsilon + \tau k) \tag{4.7}$$

where τ is the fraction of time spent in the destination.[5] (Remember from earlier in this chapter that a person earns the average wage μ plus a random term ε that indicates how much his wage deviates from the average in the origin, and $\tilde{\mu}$ plus $\tilde{\varepsilon}$ in the destination.) The term k represents skills acquired in the destination that are valued in the origin. The bigger k is, the higher a return migrant's wage in the origin; k can be negative if, as a consequence of migrating, return migrants have lost or forgotten skills that are valued in the origin and therefore earn less there.

A worker chooses to migrate from the origin to the destination under two circumstances. First, her wage is expected to be higher in the destination than in the origin after subtracting off migration costs. This is equivalent to

$$\tilde{\mu} + \tilde{\varepsilon} - \textit{Migration Costs} > \mu + \varepsilon \tag{4.8}$$

As before, a person is more likely to migrate as the expected wage in the destination increases, the expected wage in the origin decreases or migration costs decrease. The second reason a worker will migrate is that her wage while she is in the destination plus her wage back in the origin after return migrating, after subtracting off migration costs and return migration costs, is higher than her wage in the origin if she never migrates. This is equivalent to

$$\tau(\tilde{\mu} + \tilde{\varepsilon}) + (1 - \tau)(\mu + \varepsilon + \tau k) - \textit{Migration Costs} - \textit{Return Migration Costs} > \mu + \varepsilon \tag{4.9}$$

Return migration also requires that a person's wage after return migrating is higher than if she stays in the destination, or

$$\mu + \varepsilon + \tau k - \textit{Return Migration Costs} > \tilde{\mu} + \tilde{\varepsilon} \tag{4.10}$$

A person is more likely to return migrate the higher k is, the lower return migration costs are, the higher the average wage in the origin and the lower the average wage in the destination.

Suppose that the returns to skill in the origin and the destination are related, with $\tilde{\varepsilon} = \delta\varepsilon$. The term δ represents the return to skill in the destination relative to the origin. If δ is positive and greater than one, the return to skill is higher in the destination than in the origin. The Roy model then predicts that immigration is positively selected. Ignoring migration costs and return migration costs, equations 4.9 and 4.10 predict that people migrate permanently if

$$\varepsilon > \frac{\mu - \tilde{\mu} + k}{\delta - 1} \tag{4.11}$$

and people never migrate if

$$\varepsilon < \frac{\mu - \tilde{\mu} - k}{\delta - 1} \tag{4.12}$$

People with intermediate values of ε migrate and then return. Thus, the least-skilled people never leave the origin, while the most-skilled people migrate and never return.

Figure 4.6 shows the pattern of selection in migration and return migration if skill, ε, is normally distributed and the relative return to skill is higher in the destination. People with skill below the cutoff given in equation 4.12 never migrate, while people with skill above the cutoff

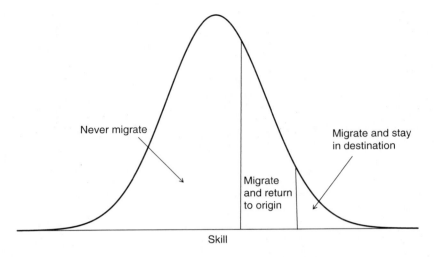

Figure 4.6 The direction of selection in permanent and return migration if the relative return to skill is higher in the destination.

given in equation 4.11 migrate and never return. People in the middle region migrate and then return. Both cutoffs shift to the left as the average wage in the destination, $\tilde{\mu}$, increases and to the right as the average wage in the origin, μ, increases. An increase in the value in the origin of skills acquired abroad, k, widens the intermediate range by causing the lower cutoff to shift to the left and the higher cutoff to shift to the right. More people will migrate and then return because skills acquired abroad are more valuable in the origin. An increase in δ, the relative return to skill in the destination, shrinks the intermediate range by causing the cutoffs to move closer together. Fewer people migrate, but those who do are less likely to return migrate.

If δ is positive and less than one, the return to skill is lower in the destination than in the origin. The Roy model then predicts that immigration is negatively selected. The inequalities in equations 4.11 and 4.12 switch direction. The most-skilled people never migrate. Among migrants, the least skilled remain in the destination while those in the middle region return migrate.

In essence, the model predicts that return migration reinforces the direction of selection in migration. If migration is positively selected, it becomes more positively selected over time as a consequence of return migration. If migration is negatively selected, it becomes more negatively selected over time as a consequence of return migration.

The model also predicts the optimal duration of migration, τ^*, which is

$$\tau^* = \frac{\tilde{\mu} - \mu + (\pi - 1)\varepsilon + k}{2k} \tag{4.13}$$

Equation 4.13 yields several predictions.[6] The optimal duration of migration increases as the average wage in the destination ($\tilde{\mu}$) rises and decreases as the average wage in the origin (μ) rises. If the return to skill is higher in the destination than in the origin ($\delta > 1$), the optimal duration of migration increases as skill, ε, increases. The opposite is true if the return to skill is higher in the origin.

Empirical evidence on selection in return migration

Borjas and Bratsberg examine the validity of the model using average wages and out-migration rates among U.S. immigrants by country of origin. They find that immigrants' average wage increases as the out-migration rate increases if the return to skill—measured using the 90/20 income share—is lower in the origin than in the United States. In this case, the model predicts that selection in initial migration is positive, and selection in return migration is negative. Conversely, average wages decrease as the out-migration rate increases if the return to skill is higher in the origin than in the United States. In this case, the model predicts that selection in initial migration is negative, and selection in return migration is positive. The relationships between average wages and out-migration rates that Borjas and Bratsberg find match the model's prediction that out-migration intensifies the direction of selection. They also find that out-migration rates from the United States increase as origin country GDP rises, which is consistent with the model.

In related research, Bratsberg (1995) finds support for the model among foreign students studying in the United States. The lower the return to skill or income inequality in their home country, the more likely students are to stay in the United States after finishing their studies. Students tend to return if they receive a high return in the origin on their studies. If income inequality is lower in the origin than in the United States, the average wage among highly educated immigrants from that country falls as more foreign students stay in the United States after completing their studies. Conversely, the average wage among highly educated immigrants increases as more foreign students stay in the United States after completing their studies if income inequality is higher in the origin than in the United States. In other words, the least skilled leave if income inequality is lower in the origin, pushing average wages up among those who remain. The most skilled leave if income inequality is higher in the origin, pushing down average wages among those who remain. This result is consistent with the model.

Out-migration from the United States generally appears to be negatively selected. One study finds that out-migrants are negatively selected among foreign-born scientists and engineers in the United States (Borjas, 1989). Another study likewise finds that out-migration from the United States is negatively selected among immigrants as a whole (Lubotsky, 2007). The pattern is different for Sweden and Finland. Migration to those countries is negatively selected on education, while return migration from those countries is positively selected (Rooth and Saarela, 2007). Sweden and Finland have much less income inequality and lower returns to skill than the United States, which may explain this pattern.

The direction of return migration to Mexico from the United States has received considerable attention. Return migration to Mexico from the United States is high—an estimated 31 percent of people who left Mexico for the United States during 2005 to 2010 returned to Mexico by 2010, for example (Campos-Vazquez and Lara, 2012). Researchers have compared return migrants with people who have never migrated and with migrants who have remained in the United States. One study finds positive selection among return migrants relative to never-migrants in 1990 but negative selection for men and intermediate selection for women in 2010 (Campos-Vazquez and Lara, 2012). The change could be due to a decrease in the return to skill in Mexico relative to the United States over time, a decrease in migration costs or an increase in networks that enables less-skilled people to migrate but also leads to them returning. Return migrants appear to be positively selected among the pool of Mexican migrants (Ambrosini and Peri, 2012; Biavaschi, 2012).

Final thoughts on selection

Selection can be measured relative to either the origin or the destination. Origin countries are mainly interested in the characteristics of the people who leave relative to those who stay. Destination countries are mainly interested in the characteristics of immigrants relative to natives and earlier immigrants, not relative to the origin population. Both origin and destination countries care about whether return migrants are positively or negatively selected among immigrants in the destination. The next chapter discusses another way of thinking about immigrant selection: assimilation, or how well immigrants do in the destination, both initially and over time.

Problems and discussion questions

1   Explain how a decrease in the return to skill in the origin affects the direction of selection and the number of immigrants if (a) immigration is positively selected, or (b) immigration is negatively selected. Assume that the return to skill in the destination and migration costs do not change.

2   Explain how a decrease in the average wage in the destination affects selectivity and the number of immigrants if (a) immigration is positively selected, or (b) immigration is negatively selected. Assume that the return to skill in the destination and migration costs do not change.

3   Suppose a destination country adopts a policy that guarantees all residents, including immigrants, a minimum income well above the current lowest income in the origin. How will this affect the direction of selection and the number of immigrants if (a) immigration is positively selected, or (b) immigration is negatively selected? Assume that the earnings distribution in the origin and migration costs do not change.

4   Can a destination country experience both positive and negative selection in immigration at the same time? Why or why not?

5   Can a destination country experience both immigration from an origin country and return migration to that country at the same time? If so, what does that imply about the directions of selection for immigration and return migration?

6   Explain what happens to the number of immigrants, the number of return migrants and selectivity in initial and return migration if the value of skills acquired in the destination declines in the origin country. What happens if instead the return to skill falls in the destination relative to the origin?

7   Income taxes can affect immigrant selection. Suppose the destination country has a more progressive tax structure than the origin country. How would this affect selection?

Notes

1 The log odds ratio of x is $\ln(x/(1-x))$. The motivation for using the log odds ratio here is to better show the dispersion in the data.
2 Grogger and Hanson (2011) do find that absolute differences in income affect who moves. Positive selection is stronger when the absolute reward to skill in the destination relative to the origin is higher. If immigrants move based on absolute, not relative, differences in income and the absolute wage gap between the destination and the origin country is large enough, immigrants could be positively selected even if the rate of return to skill is lower in the destination than in the origin.
3 Some studies therefore only look at immigrants who arrived old enough to be unlikely to have acquired additional education in the destination.
4 However, some research concludes that selection from Mexico is negative, such as Fernández-Huertas Moraga (2011).
5 For simplicity, the model ignores discounting.
6 The optimal duration, τ^*, can be found by taking the first derivative of equation 4.7 with respect to τ, setting it equal to 0 and solving for τ.

Internet resources

Mexico's National Institute of Statistics and Geography (known in Spanish as Instituto Nacional de Estadística y Geografía, or INEGI) conducts a decennial census and other surveys that ask about migration experience. Their website is http://www.inegi.org.mx/.

Suggestions for further reading

Borjas, G.J. (1987) "Self-selection and the earnings of immigrants." *American Economic Review* 77(4), pp. 531–553.
Borjas, G.J. and Bratsberg, B. (1996) "Who leaves? The outmigration of the foreign-born." *Review of Economics and Statistics* 78(1), pp. 165–176.
Dustmann, C. and Görlach, J.S. (2014) "Selective outmigration and the estimation of immigrants' earnings profiles." In: Chiswick, B.R. and Miller, P.W. (eds.) *Handbook of the Economics of International Migration*, vol. 1A. Amsterdam: Elsevier.

References

Abramitzky, R., Boustan, L.P. and Eriksson, K. (2012) "Europe's tired, poor, huddled masses: Self-selection and economic outcomes in the age of mass migration." *American Economic Review* 102(5), pp. 1832–1856.
Abramitzky, R., Boustan, L.P. and Eriksson, K. (2013) "Have the poor always been less likely to migrate? Evidence from inheritance practices during the age of mass migration." *Journal of Development Economics* 102, pp. 2–14.
Akee, R. (2010) "Who leaves? Deciphering immigrant self-selection from a developing country." *Economic Development and Cultural Change* 58(2), pp. 323–344.
Ambrosini, J.W. and Peri, G. (2012) "The determinants and the selection of Mexico-US migrants." *World Economy* 35(2), pp. 111–151.
Angelucci, M. (2013) "Migration and financial constraints: Evidence from Mexico." *IZA Discussion Paper* No. 7726. Bonn: Institute for the Study of Labor.
Antecol, H., Cobb-Clark, D.A. and Trejo, S.J. (2003) "Immigration and the skills of immigrants to Australia, Canada, and the United States." *Journal of Human Resources* 38(1), pp. 192–218.

Beine, M., Docquier, F. and Özden, Ç. (2011) "Diasporas." *Journal of Development Economics* 95(1): 30–41.

Belot, M.V.K. and Hatton, T.J. (2012) "Immigration selection in the OECD." *Scandinavian Journal of Economics* 114(4), pp. 1105–1128.

Bertoli, S. and Rapoport, H. (2013) "Heaven's swing door: Endogenous skills, migration networks and the effectiveness of quality-selective immigration policies." *IZA Discussion Paper* No. 7749. Bonn: Institute for the Study of Labor.

Biavaschi, C. (2012) "Recovering the counterfactual wage distribution with selective return migration." *IZA Discussion Paper* No. 6795. Bonn: Institute for the Study of Labor.

Borjas, G.J. (1987) "Self-selection and the earnings of immigrants," *American Economic Review* 77(4): 531–553.

Borjas, G.J. (1989) "Immigrant and emigrant earnings: A longitudinal study." *Economic Inquiry* 27(1), pp. 21–37.

Borjas, G.J. (2008) "Labor outflows and labor inflows in Puerto Rico." *Journal of Human Capital* 2(1), pp. 32–68.

Borjas, G.J. and Bratsberg, B. (1996) "Who leaves? The outmigration of the foreign-born." *Review of Economics and Statistics* 78(1), pp. 165–176.

Bratsberg, B. (1995) "The incidence of non-return among foreign students in the United States." *Economics of Education Review* 14(4), pp. 373–384.

Brücker, H. and Defoort, C. (2009) "Inequality and the self-selection of international migrants: Theory and new evidence." *International Journal of Manpower* 30(7), pp. 742–764.

Campos-Vazquez, R.M. and Lara, J. (2012) "Self-selection patterns among return migrants: Mexico 1990-2010." *IZA Journal of Migration* 1, 8.

Caponi, V. (2011) "Intergenerational transmission of abilities and self-selection of Mexican immigrants." *International Economic Review* 52(2), pp. 523–547.

Chin, A. and Cortes, K.E. (2014) "The refugee/asylum seeker." In: Chiswick, B.R. and Miller, P.W. (eds.) *Handbook of the Economics of International Migration,* vol. 1A. Amsterdam: Elsevier.

Chiquiar, D. and Hanson, G.H. (2005) "International migration, self-selection, and the distribution of wages: Evidence from Mexico and the United States." *Journal of Political Economy* 113(2), pp. 239–281.

Cobb-Clark, D.A. (1993) "Immigrant selectivity and wages: The evidence for women." *American Economic Review* 83(4), pp. 986–993.

Cobb-Clark, D.A. (2003) "Public policy and the labor market adjustment of new immigrants to Australia." *Journal of Population Economics* 16(4), pp. 655–681.

Delaney, L., Fernihough, A. and Smith, J.P. (2013) "Exporting poor health: The Irish in England." *Demography* 50(6), pp. 2013–2035.

Dustmann, C. and Görlach, J.S. (2014) "Selective outmigration and the estimation of immigrants' earnings profiles." In: Chiswick, B.R. and Miller, P.W. (eds.) *Handbook of the Economics of International Migration,* vol. 1A. Amsterdam: Elsevier.

Fernández-Huertas Moraga, J. (2011) "New evidence on emigrant selection." *Review of Economics and Statistics* 93(1), pp. 72–96.

Fernández-Huertas Moraga, J. (2013) "Understanding different migrant selection patterns in rural and urban Mexico." *Journal of Development Economics* 103, pp. 182–201.

Grogger, J. and Hanson, G.H. (2011) "Income maximization and the selection and sorting of international migrants." *Journal of Development Economics* 95(1), pp. 42–57.

Ibarraran, P. and Lubotsky, D. (2007) "Mexican immigration and self-selection: New evidence from the 2000 Mexican Census." In: Borjas, G.J. (ed.) *Mexican Immigration to the United States.* Chicago: University of Chicago Press.

Kaestner, R. and Malamud, O. (2014) "Self-selection and international migration: New evidence from Mexico." *Review of Economics and Statistics* 96(1), pp. 78–91.

Kennedy, S., McDonald, J.T. and Biddle, N. (2006) "The healthy immigrant effect and immigrant selection: Evidence from four countries." Mimeo, Department of Economics, University of New Brunswick.

Lubotsky, D. (2007) "Chutes or ladders? A longitudinal analysis of immigrant earnings." *Journal of Political Economy* 115(5), pp. 820–867.

McKenzie, D. and Rapoport, H. (2010) "Self-selection patterns in Mexico-U.S. migration: The role of migration networks." *Review of Economics and Statistics* 92(4), pp. 811–821.

Orrenius, P.M. and Zavodny, M. (2005) "Self-selection among undocumented immigrants from Mexico." *Journal of Development Economics* 78(1), pp. 215–240.

Rooth, D. and Saarela, J. (2007) "Selection in migration and return migration: Evidence from micro data." *Economics Letters* 94(1), pp. 90–95.

Roy, A.D. (1951) "Some thoughts on the distribution of earnings." *Oxford Economic Papers* 3(2), pp. 135–146.

Appendix

Logarithmic functions have several properties that are used to move from equations 4.4 to 4.5 to 4.6 in this chapter. Those properties are

$$ln(1) = 0 \tag{A4.1}$$

And

$$ln\left(\frac{x}{y+z}\right) = x - \left(y+z\right) \tag{A4.2}$$

Substituting equations 4.1 and 4.2 into equation 4.5 gives

$$ln\left(\frac{\tilde{\mu} + \tilde{\varepsilon}}{\mu + \varepsilon + Migration\ Costs}\right) > 0 \tag{A4.3}$$

Applying the property in equation A4.2 to equation A4.3 gives

$$\tilde{\mu} + \tilde{\varepsilon} - \left(\mu + \varepsilon + Migration\ Costs\right) > 0 \tag{A4.4}$$

Equation 4.6 rearranges equation A4.4 and substitutes $\pi = Migration\ Costs\,/\,Wage$ for *Migration Costs* (this substitution makes the equation an approximation).

5 Assimilation

Migration changes people's lives. Many migrants learn a new language, get more education, acquire new skills or enter a new occupation. They are likely to earn more than if they had not migrated. They may marry someone different than they would have married if they had not migrated, and they may have a different number of children. Where migrants go plays a central role in shaping these changes. A person from Poland who migrates to Russia is likely to have a different life in many respects than if she had migrated to England, for example.

This chapter examines how immigrants do in the destination, both initially and over time. The focus is on immigrants' labor market outcomes, particularly their earnings. The chapter also discusses a number of other economic outcomes, such as immigrants' participation in public assistance programs and fluency in the destination country's language. In addition, the chapter discusses cultural factors that have economic implications, such as the determinants of who immigrants marry and how many children they have. All of these outcomes are likely to be quite different than they would be if immigrants had never migrated. They also may be quite different for immigrants than for natives.

Economists use the terms "assimilation" and "integration" when comparing immigrants to natives. Economic models typically examine how immigrants' outcomes compare with natives' soon after immigrants arrive and as their duration of residence in the destination increases. If immigrants' outcomes become more similar to natives' over time, immigrants are said to have assimilated or integrated. Although assimilation is usually viewed as desirable, it can be undesirable if immigrants initially do better than natives but experience "downwards assimilation" towards natives as their duration of residence in the destination increases.

Labor market assimilation

Immigrants typically have worse labor market outcomes than natives when they first arrive in the destination and then converge towards natives over time. Most immigrants who are not admitted on the basis of employment need some time to find a job and to get acclimated to the destination country's labor market. Their employment and earnings improve over time as they acquire skills that are valued in the destination, become more fluent in that country's language and create networks that help them find better jobs.

Economists use "age-employment" or "age-earnings" profiles to examine how employment or earnings evolve as people age. Economists also use these profiles to examine how immigrants' employment or earnings evolve as their duration of residence in the destination increases.

People's employment and earnings tend to follow a rainbow-shaped pattern over the course of their lifetime. When people are young, their earnings tend to be low since they enter the labor force with little experience. Young adults also are less likely to be employed, either because they are in school or because employers are reluctant to hire them since they do not have much experience. Over time, their experience and skills increase. This causes their employment and earnings to increase as they age. Eventually, skills deteriorate or people decide to work less. This leads to reductions in employment and earnings as people reach their fifties and sixties.

As an example of this pattern among immigrants, Figure 5.1 shows how employment and average annual earnings change with years since migration among immigrants in the United States in 2010.[1] The fraction of adult immigrants who are employed increases for the first 22 years since migration and then declines. Earnings increase for the first 30 years and then decline. The downward portion of the employment curve likely reflects labor force withdrawal among retired older immigrants. The downward portion of the earnings curve may be due to selective labor force withdrawal among high-income older immigrants who can afford to retire, causing average earnings to be lower among those who continue to work. It may also reflect lower skill levels among older immigrants who have been in the country longer.

Immigrants with low initial earnings may experience faster earnings growth over time. Immigrants who lack skills that are valued in the destination have a lower opportunity cost of investing in skill acquisition in the destination—they forego less in earnings than skilled immigrants while going to school. Immigrants who invest in acquiring human capital that is valued in the destination are likely to have faster earnings growth than other immigrants. Consistent with this, Harriet Duleep and Mark Regets (2013) show that immigrants with lower earnings soon after entering the United States invest more in acquiring human capital in the destination and experience faster earnings growth than immigrants with higher earnings at entry.

Figure 5.1 actually says nothing about how well immigrants do compared with U.S. natives since it only plots employment and earnings for immigrants. Figure 5.2 therefore shows the

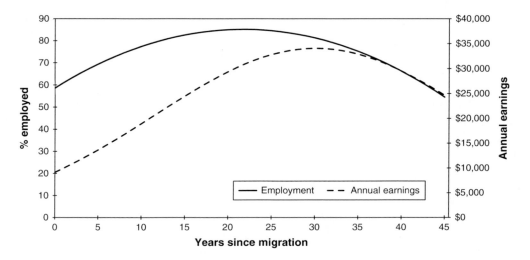

Figure 5.1 Employment and earnings amont U.S. immigrants by years since migration, 2010.

Source: Authors' calculations based on immigrants aged 20 to 65 in 2010 American Community Survey using data from IPUMS (https://usa.ipums.org/usa/).

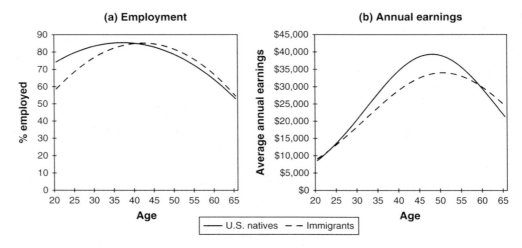

Figure 5.2 Employment and earnings assimilation among U.S. immigrants, 2010.

Source: Authors' calculations based on immigrants aged 20 to 65 in 2010 American Community Survey using data from IPUMS (https://usa.ipums.org/usa/).

same profiles for immigrants as in Figure 5.1 together with the age-employment or age-earnings profile for U.S. natives.[2] Employment increases more rapidly with age for immigrants than for U.S. natives, with immigrants becoming more likely to be employed than U.S. natives by age 40. Immigrants do not overtake U.S. natives in terms of earnings until age 59, however.

Figure 5.2(b) suggests that there is a sizable earnings gap between U.S. natives and immigrants for most of the lifecycle. This pattern was not always the case in the United States. In a seminal study using data from 1970, Barry Chiswick (1978) finds three patterns: Immigrants start off earning less than U.S. natives; immigrants' earnings rise faster than natives'; and immigrants' earnings eventually surpass natives'. Specifically, Chiswick shows that male immigrants earn about 10 percent less than male natives after five years in the United States, the same after about 13 years, 6 percent more after 20 years and 13 percent more after 30 years, all else equal. Chiswick concludes,

> That the foreign born eventually have higher earnings than the native born suggests that they may have more innate ability, are more highly motivated toward labor market success, or self-finance larger investments in post-school training. The higher earnings may therefore be a consequence of a self-selection in migration in favor of high ability, highly motivated workers, and workers with low discount rates for human capital investments.
>
> (pp. 919–920)

Why does the pattern Chiswick observed no longer hold? One reason is that the origin countries of immigrants to the United States have changed over time. Most U.S. immigrants are now from Latin America or Asia; a few decades ago, most immigrants were from Europe. In addition, recent immigrants face a different economic environment than earlier immigrants did. The United States has greater income inequality and higher returns to skill now than in

1970. Meanwhile, recent cohorts of immigrants have lower levels of education relative to U.S. natives than earlier cohorts did, and they have lower levels of English fluency. The implication of these cohort differences for assimilation has been a major research topic in the economics of immigration.

Cohort differences in assimilation

Figures 5.1 and 5.2 are based on cross-sectional data, or data at a single point in time. Inferring assimilation from cross-sectional data requires assuming that recent immigrants will earn the same as earlier immigrants as their duration of residence in the destination increases. But recent arrival cohorts may differ from earlier cohorts. In addition to the reasons noted above, different cohorts may face a different macroeconomic environment upon arrival or in subsequent years that affects their employment and earnings path.

If cohort "quality" has changed over time, cross-sectional data may give a misleading picture of immigrant assimilation. Suppose that each successive cohort of immigrants does worse in the labor market, both initially and over time. Figure 5.3 depicts this situation. Wages increase at the same rate over time for each cohort, but each successive cohort earns less than the previous cohort did at the same number of years since migration. (The figure assumes for simplicity that wages increase linearly.) Cross-sectional data would give the relationship between wages and years since migration indicated by the dotted line. This method clearly overestimates how much wages increase over time for a given cohort. If cohort quality instead increases over time, cross-sectional data would underestimate wage growth.

George Borjas (1985) argues that researchers need repeated cross sections or panel data in order to properly assess assimilation. The decennial U.S. Census is an example of repeated cross-sectional data. Researchers use responses to a Census survey question that asks when

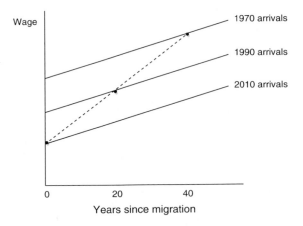

Figure 5.3 Cross-sectional data can give a misleading picture of assimilation.

Suppose earnings increase linearly with years since migration, and each successive cohort earns more than the previous cohort. The true relationship between years since migration and earnings for each cohort is given by the solid lines. Cross-sectional data would indicate a more positive relationship, as indicated by the dotted line.

people born abroad moved to the United States to create cohorts. Researchers then examine how cohorts' outcomes change over time. For example, they examine how immigrants who arrived in the 1960s do in 1970, 1980 and so on. Unlike the decennial Census, panel data—also called longitudinal data—follow specific individuals over time, enabling researchers to get a better estimate of assimilation. Few large-scale panel datasets are publicly available, however, so researchers typically use repeated cross sections to measure assimilation.

Borjas (2013) proposes an empirical model that allows immigrants' initial wages and their wage trajectories to differ across cohorts. It is not possible to separately identify aging, cohort and time period effects for immigrants and natives, so Borjas's model assumes that the time period has the same effect on immigrants and natives. In other words, a recession or economic boom has the same effect on immigrants as it does on natives. Figure 5.4 shows calculations of immigrants' average wages, relative to U.S. natives at the same time, for four arrival cohorts by years since migration based on Borjas's model and decennial U.S. Census data from 1970–2010.

Figure 5.4 shows that earlier cohorts of immigrants appear to have experienced faster assimilation than recent cohorts. Immigrants who arrived during 1965–1969 surpassed U.S. natives after 30 years of residence. Immigrants who arrived during 1975–1979 experienced assimilation but had not yet surpassed U.S. natives at the 30-year mark. Immigrants who arrived during 1985–1989 experienced wage growth during their first 20 years in the United States but earned less soon after arriving than earlier cohorts. They also experienced less wage growth over their first ten years in the United States than earlier cohorts. Immigrants who arrived during 1995–1999 not only experienced less assimilation than earlier immigrants during their first ten years in the United States but actually experienced wage losses relative to U.S. natives—the relative wage line for that cohort is negatively sloped in the figure. Immigrants who arrived during 2005–2009, the most recent cohort of immigrants, are not shown

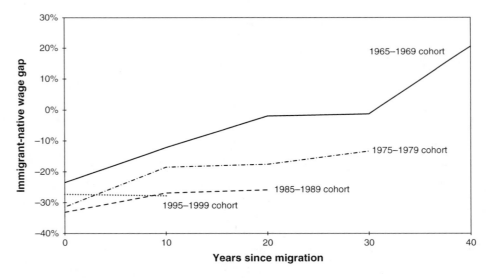

Figure 5.4 Wage gap between immigrants and U.S. natives, by arrival cohort.

Source: Authors' calculations from table 2 of Borjas (2013).

in the figure since they have not yet been in the United States long enough to measure their wage growth. That cohort earned about 33 percent less than U.S. natives soon after arriving, putting them on par with the 1985–1989 arrival cohort soon after they entered.

The data thus suggest that recent cohorts of immigrants do worse soon after arriving and experience slower wage growth, or less assimilation, than earlier cohorts. This seems to contradict the theory that immigrants with lower earnings at entry invest more in acquiring human capital and then experience faster earnings growth over time. However, human capital acquisition in the origin may be a complement to human capital acquisition in the destination (Duleep and Regets, 2013). Immigrants who have more human capital at entry—even if it is not valued in the destination—may find it easier to acquire additional human capital in the destination that is valued there. If recent cohorts of immigrants enter with low levels of human capital, they may not acquire human capital in the destination and therefore may have both low earnings at entry and low earnings over time.

Borjas attributes the decline in immigrants' relative wages across cohorts to a relative decline in their skill levels. Educational attainment has risen over time more slowly among immigrants than among U.S. natives. Figure 5.5 shows the distribution of adult U.S. natives and immigrants by educational attainment during 1980–2010. Immigrants are consistently more likely than U.S. natives to have not completed high school or to have an advanced degree (a master's, professional degree or a PhD) and less likely to have completed high school, some college or a bachelor's degree. Both groups become better educated over time, with the fraction who have not completed high school falling noticeably. However, the decrease is much larger for U.S. natives than for immigrants. The ratio of the fraction of immigrants who have not completed high school to the comparable fraction of natives is 1.4 in 1980 and 3 in 2010.

Borjas notes that the relative decline in immigrants' educational attainment is due to a shift in where immigrants are from. Borjas (1995) states, "The shift in the national origin mix away from the traditional European source countries toward Asian and Latin American countries generates a less 'successful' immigrant flow" (p. 202). Changes in U.S. immigration policy in 1965 led to an increase in immigration from Asia and Latin America, while the share of immigrants from Europe declined. The average education level of immigrants from those new regions, particularly Latin America, tends to be much lower than among immigrants from Europe. A change in immigrants' origin and skill levels that occurred in the United States a century ago gave rise to similar concerns about slower assimilation (see Box 5.1, "Assimilation and cohort effects in the United States a century ago").

Borjas (2013) also attributes part of the decline in immigrants' wage growth across cohorts to recent cohorts of immigrants not becoming as fluent in English as earlier cohorts. Although U.S. immigrants' English tends to improve as their duration of residence increases (as discussed more later in this chapter), rates of English acquisition have slowed across cohorts. Borjas notes that immigrants' English proficiency tends to be lower when there are a large number of immigrants from their origin country in the United States. If there are enough immigrants who speak the same language, there may be less need for immigrants to learn the destination country's language.

Changes in macroeconomic conditions may have contributed to the pattern observed in Figure 5.4. Recent cohorts of U.S. immigrants may have faced a more adverse macroeconomic environment, such as slower GDP growth and a higher unemployment rate, when they

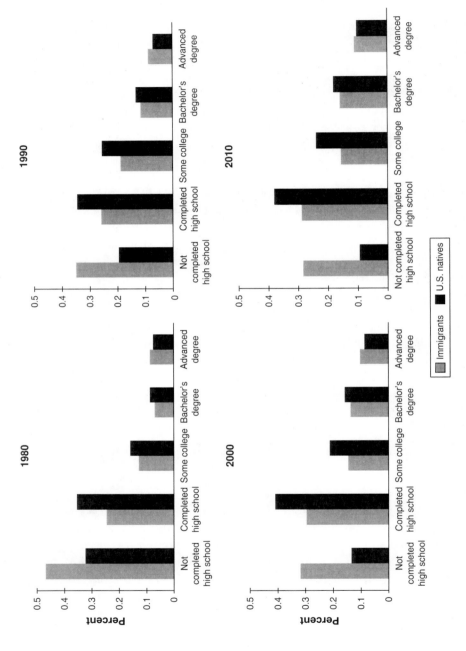

Figure 5.5 Distribution of immigrants and U.S. natives by educational attainment, 1980–2010.

Source: Authors' calculations based on U.S. natives and immigrants aged 25 and older in 1980–2000 Census and 2010 American Community Survey using data from IPUMS (https://usa.ipums.org/usa/).

Box 5.1 Assimilation and cohort effects in the United States a century ago

The United States faced a similar change in immigrants' origins during the late 1800s and early 1900s, when immigrant origins shifted from Northern and Western Europe— mainly Britain and Germany—to Southern and Eastern Europe. At that time, national origin was essentially viewed as the same as race, so immigrants from Southern and Eastern Europe were viewed as being of different races than immigrants from Britain, Germany and Scandinavia. The Immigration Commission of 1907–1911, also known as the Dillingham Commission, issued a report in 1911 that claimed:

> The old and the new immigration differ in many essentials. The former was, from the beginning, largely a movement of settlers who came from the most progressive sections of Europe.... They mingled freely with the native Americans and were quickly assimilated, although a large portion of them, particularly in later years, belonged to non-English-speaking races....
>
> On the other hand, the new immigration has been largely a movement of unskilled laboring men who have come, in large part temporarily, from the less progressive and advanced countries of Europe in response to the call for industrial workers in the eastern and middle western States. They have almost entirely avoided agricultural pursuits, and in cities and industrial communities have congregated together in sections apart from native Americans and the older immigrants to such an extent that assimilation has been slow as compared to that of the earlier non-English-speaking races.
>
> The new immigration as a class is far less intelligent than the old, approximately one-third of all those over 14 years of age when admitted being illiterate. Racially they are for the most part essentially unlike the British, German, and other peoples who came during the period prior to 1880, and generally speaking they are actuated in coming by different ideals, for the old immigration came to be a part of the country, while the new, in a large measure, comes with the intention of profiting, in a pecuniary way, by the superior advantages of the new world and then returning to the old country.
>
> (pp. 13–14)

Much has changed since 1911. We no longer consider Italians and Russians to belong to different races than the English and Germans. And we now know that those immigrants and their descendants assimilated. Of course, circumstances may have changed, and recent cohorts of U.S. immigrants may no longer experience the same upwards trajectory as earlier cohorts. Whether they do is a hotly contested topic in economics and other disciplines.

arrived. Entering under worse macroeconomic conditions may depress earnings at entry and earnings growth over time (Barth, Bratsberg and Raaum, 2004; Bratsberg, Barth and Raaum, 2006). For example, research shows that the adverse effect of entering when the unemployment rate is high persists for at least ten years among immigrants to Sweden (Åslund and

Rooth, 2007). A similar effect occurs among natives—young adults who enter the labor market during an economic downturn earn less years later than young adults who enter the labor market during an economic expansion (Kahn, 2010).

In addition, recent cohorts of immigrants may face a higher rate of return to skill and greater income inequality. An increase in the return to skill will reduce average wages among recent immigrant cohorts if those cohorts have lower average skill levels relative to natives than earlier cohorts did, as is the case in the United States. Research shows that the rise in the return to skill in the United States during the 1980s and early 1990s reduced the earnings of new immigrants relative to U.S. natives by 10 to 15 percentage points (Lubotsky, 2011). Continued increases in the return to skill could contribute to slower earnings growth among those cohorts relative to earlier cohorts.

The U.S. experience does not appear to be universal. A similar decline across cohorts in wages soon after arrival appears to have occurred in Canada, but immigrants' wage growth over time does not appears to have slowed there (Aydemir and Skuterud, 2005). Changes in immigrants' language ability and their distribution across origin countries can explain about one-third of the decline in wages at entry there. Changes in Canadian macroeconomic conditions also contributed to the decline in earnings at arrival. In the United Kingdom, recent cohorts of immigrants appear to earn more soon after arriving than earlier cohorts (Lemos, 2013). Recent cohorts also appear to experience faster wage assimilation toward UK natives.

Research on immigrants in several European countries indicates that immigrants from other European countries or from OECD countries tend to do better in the labor market than other immigrants (e.g., Longva and Raaum, 2003; Algan et al., 2010; Sarvimaki, 2011). Differences remain after controlling for educational attainment, indicating that the wage gaps are not due solely to differences in years of education. Differences in fluency in the destination country language may play a role in the wage gaps.

The fact that immigrants from different regions tend to have different economic outcomes in a destination, both initially and over time, raises an important question: Who is the correct comparison group? Should immigrants' labor market success be evaluated relative to all natives and all earlier immigrants, or relative to natives and earlier immigrants with the same ethnic background? Should immigrants be compared only to natives with similar levels of education or to all natives? There is no single right comparison group. Economists and policymakers should be aware of who a study uses as a comparison group and how using that particular comparison group affects the measurement of immigrants' success.

Gender issues in immigrants' labor market assimilation

In many industrialized countries there are bigger sex differences in immigrants' labor force participation than in natives' labor force participation. In the United States, for example, foreign-born men were more than 23 percentage points more likely than foreign-born women to be in the labor force in 2012, compared with a 10 percentage point gap among U.S. natives (U.S. Bureau of Labor Statistics, 2013). A similar pattern of lower labor force participation among immigrant women than among native-born women holds in many European countries (de la Rica, Glitz and Ortega, 2013).

Gender norms in the origin are a potential reason why immigrant women have a relatively low rate of labor force participation in the destination. Female immigrants in industrialized countries are more likely to work in the destination the higher women's labor force participation rate is in their origin (Antecol, 2000; Bredtmann and Otten, 2014). Immigrant women appear to assimilate toward native-born women's work behavior, but the work behavior of women in the origin still matters over time. When they first enter the United States, for example, immigrant women from countries with high female labor force participation rates and from countries with low rates both work less than U.S.-born women (Blau, Kahn and Papps, 2011). Those from countries with high female labor force participation rates catch up with U.S.-born women after living in the United States for six to ten years. Those from countries with low rates also assimilate towards U.S. natives but never catch up. In addition, a U.S.-born woman married to foreign-born man is less likely to work if the man is from a country with a low female labor force participation rate.

Households may make labor force participation decisions jointly instead of individually. One spouse may work in order to help finance the other spouse's human capital investment. For example, a husband may work to support the family while the wife is in school and then stop working once the wife has finished school and entered the labor force. In the context of immigration, one spouse may work when the family first arrives in order to support the family while the other spouse acquires skills valued in the destination, and then stop working when the other spouse begins working. Evidence for Canada suggests that immigrant women tend to behave this way—their labor force participation actually decreases over time relative to natives (Baker and Benjamin, 1997).[3]

Accounting for return migration

Selective out-migration may bias estimates of assimilation, as noted in Chapter 4. If out-migration is negatively selected, estimates of assimilation will be biased upwards because high-skilled, high-wage immigrants remain in the destination while low-skilled, low-wage immigrants leave. Darren Lubotsky (2007) uses panel data to assess the bias imparted by selective out-migration. He finds that the wage gap between immigrants and U.S. natives closes twice as slowly when using panel data instead of repeated cross sections. In other words, assimilation is one-half as fast when using longitudinal data. The difference between panel and cross-sectional data suggests that low-wage immigrants leave. This negative selection in out-migration creates upwards bias in estimates of assimilation that do not account for selective out-migration.

Negatively selected out-migration from the United States can also bias estimates of assimilation during the early 1900s. Cross-sectional data from 1900–1920 indicate that immigrants initially worked in lower-paid occupations than U.S. natives but experienced rapid assimilation toward natives (Abramitzky, Boustan and Eriksson, 2013). However, panel data from that period indicate that recently arrived immigrants and U.S. natives actually worked in similarly paid occupations, on average, and advanced into higher-paying occupations at the same rate. (Box 5.2, "Ancestry.com and immigration research," further discusses research using historical data.) In addition, immigrants who arrived in the 1890s were less skilled than immigrants who arrived in the 1880s. Estimates that do not account for such cohort effects will overestimate assimilation, as in Figure 5.3.

Box 5.2 Ancestry.com and immigration research

The website Ancestry.com is a treasure trove of historical data for researchers. The website is run by a genealogy company and has a wide array of historical documents posted, including U.S. Census records, ships' passenger lists and U.S. citizenship and naturalization records. The Census records posted on Ancestry.com are a near universe of everyone living in the United States at the time of a decennial Census. People's name, age, birthplace, current place of residence and occupation are available. Some Censuses also ask about education, literacy and what language people speak. (Because of confidentiality restrictions, individual records are publicly available only after 72 years, so 1940 records are the most recent ones that researchers are currently able to use in their entirety. Subsets of more recent data are available with individual identifiers, like name and address, removed.)

Ran Abramitzky, Leah Platt Boustan and Katherine Eriksson use data from Ancestry.com to examine immigrant selection and assimilation. As discussed in Chapter 4, they estimate the returns to migration and selection among migrants by comparing men who migrated from Norway to the United States during the 1800s and early 1900s with their brothers who remained in Norway. They also use U.S. Census data to estimate the extent of assimilation among immigrants from 16 European countries. Using people's names, ages and birthplaces, they track individuals over time in the Census and look at how immigrants' occupations changed as they spent more time in the United States compared with how natives' occupations changed as they aged.

Costanza Biavaschi, Corrado Giulietti and Zahra Siddique use naturalization records to examine whether immigrants who changed their first name to a more "American" name benefited from doing so. An example of "Americanization" is changing from a name like Giovanni to a name like William. About one-third of their sample of men who became naturalized U.S. citizens in New York City in 1930 changed their first names to a more American name. Men who changed their name to a very popular American name, like John, were more likely to move into higher-paying occupations than men who did not. The researchers recognize that the causality might run the other direction: men who move into higher-paying occupations might be more likely to change their names, instead of men who changed their names being more likely to move into higher-paying occupations. To control for the possibility of reverse causality, they use an econometric technique called instrumental variables. The researchers predict how likely men are to change their name based on how complicated their name is. They measure this using the number of points men's names would score in the board game Scrabble. More complicated names are worth more Scrabble points: Zbigniew is worth 22 points, while Sam is worth five points. Men with names worth more Scrabble points were more likely to change their names and were more likely to move into higher-paying occupations.

Immigrant types and assimilation

The basis on which immigrants were admitted to the destination may be related to their assimilation. Duleep and Regets (1996) find that immigrants admitted to the United States on the basis of family ties have lower earnings at entry but experience faster wage growth than employment-based immigrants. Family-based immigrants may have more incentive to invest in human capital acquisition in the destination, and they may have better networks than employment-based immigrants, which facilitates their labor market integration over time. Family-based immigrants may also be more likely to make labor market decisions at the household level instead of at the individual or family level, as their households may include extended relatives. For example, a grandmother may migrate to help care for her grandchildren, which enables her daughter to work.

Refugees are likely to earn less than economic immigrants soon after entering. Since they do not move primarily because of economic gains, refugees may not be a good fit for the labor market in the destination. In the United States, immigrants who are likely to be refugees have lower earnings than economic immigrants soon after entering, but they experience faster wage growth (Cortes, 2004). They also experience faster growth in hours worked. Higher rates of human capital acquisition among refugees contribute to the improvement in their relative outcomes. Refugees may be particularly likely to invest in acquiring destination-specific human capital (skills that are valued only in the destination, not elsewhere) since they are unlikely to return home. (This is also true for permanent immigrants compared with temporary immigrants.) In addition, in many developed countries refugees receive more support than other immigrants from government agencies and other organizations. This support—in the form of transfer payments, language classes and assistance finding jobs, for example—may foster refugees' assimilation.

Unauthorized immigrants typically earn less than other immigrants and experience slower wage growth over time. This is true even after accounting for unauthorized immigrants' relatively low levels of education (e.g., Borjas and Tienda, 1993). Unauthorized immigrants may be less willing than legal immigrants to invest in destination-specific human capital because such investments may not pay off if they are deported. They also may be largely limited to low-skill, low-wage jobs in particular sectors of the economy, such as agriculture, construction and private household services, where more employers are willing to overlook their lack of legal status. Unauthorized immigrants may have less bargaining power in the labor market. They may also have smaller social networks than legal immigrants. All of these factors may reduce unauthorized immigrants' ability to move into better jobs over time unless they are able to obtain legal status.

Participation in public assistance programs

Immigrants' participation in public assistance programs is one of the reasons why immigration tends to be controversial. Because immigrants tend to be poorer than natives in many industrialized countries, they are more likely to qualify for "means-tested" welfare programs, or programs where eligibility depends on income. In the United States, for example, 33 percent of households headed by an immigrant participated in a major means-tested program in 2010–2012, compared with 22 percent of households headed by a native.[4] Another reason why immigrant households are more likely to participate in welfare programs in the United States is that they are more likely than native households to contain children; many welfare programs there are aimed at families with children. However, immigrant households are more likely to receive welfare than native households even after taking such differences into account.

On the other hand, immigrants are more likely than natives to be working age, so they may be less likely to qualify for or receive public assistance in some countries. This appears to be the case among UK immigrants from so-called A-8 countries, the eight Central and Eastern European nations that joined the European Union in 2004. Christian Dustmann, Tommas Frattini and Caroline Hall (2010) show that those immigrants are considerably less likely than UK natives to participate in welfare programs. Among A-8 immigrants who have lived in the United Kingdom for at least a year and therefore are eligible to receive benefits on the same basis as natives, immigrants are 59 percent less likely than natives to receive benefits. The difference is largely due to immigrants' higher probability of working.

If immigrants' labor market outcomes tend to improve as their duration of residence in the destination increases, their participation in public assistance programs should go down as duration increases. However, there are several reasons this may not be the case. First, immigrants may only become eligible for public assistance after a certain number of years of residence. In the United States, for example, most legal immigrants are not eligible for some forms of public assistance until they have been in the country for five years or have become naturalized citizens.

Immigrants' participation in public assistance programs may also increase with their duration of residence because immigrants may learn about those programs over time. Newly arrived immigrants may not know much about public assistance programs, which can have complicated eligibility rules. Over time, immigrant networks may transmit information about public assistance programs (Borjas and Hilton, 1996).

Jorgen Hansen and Magnus Lofstrom (2003) show that immigrants to Sweden are more likely to participate in public assistance programs than natives there. Indeed, they report that social assistance expenditures on immigrants in Sweden equaled expenditures on natives in the mid-1990s even though immigrants comprised only 10 percent of the population. However, immigrants appear to assimilate out of welfare over time: Their participation in social assistance programs decreases as their duration of residence increases. However, it does not decrease fast enough for immigrants to have the same rate of welfare receipt as natives in the long run. Refugees are more likely to receive welfare, but welfare participation rates decline more quickly over time among refugees than among non-refugee immigrants. This may be due to refugees investing more than other immigrants in acquiring human capital in Sweden.

Location choice and enclaves

Immigrants' locations within the destination are likely to change as their duration of residence increases. Immigrants typically first settle in ethnic enclaves—areas with a concentration of people from the same origin—and then move into more integrated areas over time as they become more familiar with the destination country's labor market and language.

Living or working in an enclave offers several advantages for immigrants that are particularly important to recent arrivals. People there are likely to speak the same language as recently arrived immigrants, who may not yet have mastered the language of the destination country. Enclaves can provide a network that can help immigrants find jobs, housing and transportation. Companies owned by earlier immigrants from the same origin often employ recently arrived immigrants in enclaves. Since enclaves contain many people from the same origin, immigrants are likely to face less discrimination there than in the rest of the destination. Enclaves also provide a sense of community and belonging that may be vital to people who have recently moved to a new country.

However, there can be economic downsides to living or working in an enclave. Employment opportunities are likely to be more extensive and higher paying outside of the enclave than inside it. This may limit enclave residents' opportunities for economic advancement. In the United States, for example, enclaves are often located in older urban areas, away from job growth in the suburbs (Cutler, Glaeser and Vigdor, 2008). Living in an enclave may also limit economic advancement by slowing the acquisition of human capital valued in the destination, particularly language skills. Immigrants who live or work primarily with other immigrants from the same origin have less need or opportunity to learn the main language spoken in the destination. They also have less opportunity to create wider social networks that include natives, which may be helpful in finding better jobs.

It is difficult to assess the effect of living in an enclave on immigrants' outcomes, such as their earnings and language skills, because people who live in enclaves may systematically differ from people who live elsewhere. In the United States, immigrants appear to be negatively selected into enclaves—immigrants with less education and less proficiency in English are more likely to live in enclaves. Naïve estimates of the effect of enclaves on immigrants' outcomes therefore may conclude that enclaves have an adverse effect on outcomes simply because the people who choose to live there are negatively selected. Research that corrects for this negative selection finds that living in an enclave tends to boost young adult immigrants' earnings and English ability in the United States (Cutler, Glaeser and Vigdor, 2008). However, this positive effect does not occur for immigrant groups with very low education levels, such as Mexicans and Central Americans. For those groups, living in an enclave appears to worsen already poor outcomes. Enclaves comprised primarily of less-educated immigrants may offer fewer economic opportunities and transmit less human capital than enclaves of more educated groups of immigrants.

Immigrants who would do worse living in the enclave than elsewhere may be less likely to choose to live in the enclave, while immigrants who would do better in the enclave than elsewhere may be more likely to choose to live in the enclave. Such selection makes it difficult to infer the true effect of enclaves on economic outcomes. In order to control for such selection, Per-Anders Edin, Peter Fredriksson and Olof Åslund (2003) examine a "natural experiment" in Sweden, where the government assigns refugees to initial locations. The researchers find that being assigned to live in an enclave is associated with higher earnings among refugees. The gains to living in an enclave are highest among the least educated. The researchers note that this suggests that "enclaves are associated with ethnic networks that primarily benefit the least skilled" (p. 348). Further, the earnings gains to living in an enclave increase with the average income among enclave residents. This suggests that, as in the United States, the "quality" of the network in Sweden matters.

For many immigrants, assimilation occurs in the context of the immigrant community and the broader society of the destination. How earlier immigrants from that origin did in the destination affects the reception that new immigrants receive, which in turns affects how well new immigrants do. Timothy Hatton and Andrew Leigh (2011) argue, "The more established is the tradition of immigration from a particular source, the more integrated that ethnic community will be, and the more easily new immigrants from that source will assimilate into the host labour market" (p. 390). If earlier immigrants from an origin have been successful in the destination, they are in a better position to help new immigrants. In addition, natives then tend to look more favorably on immigrants from that origin, which fosters new immigrants' integration and economic success.

Education

Some people migrate because they want to attend school in the destination, while some other immigrants end up attending school in the destination even though education was not the main reason they moved. Most people who migrate specifically to attend school are in university. About 4.1 million people were enrolled in universities outside their country of citizenship in 2010 (OECD, 2013). Other immigrants who end up attending school in the destination include children who migrate with their parents and people who migrate as adults but realize that there are benefits to obtaining additional education in the destination.

In the United States, average educational attainment rises among immigrant cohorts as their duration of U.S. residence increases. This increase could be due to immigrants going to school in the United States. It could also be due to negative selection on education in return migration. Low-education immigrants may be more likely to leave than high-education immigrants. The demographics of circular migrants may contribute as well: Circular immigrants tend to be agricultural workers with relatively low levels of education. Immigrants who regularly leave the country and later reenter are usually counted as part of the cohort that includes the time of their most recent entry, not their first entry. In addition, rising education levels within immigrant cohorts over time could reflect "grade level inflation," which occurs among cohorts of natives as well—people tend to report higher levels of education as they age even if they have not actually attended more school. Understanding whether educational attainment actually increases among immigrants over time matters because education is closely related to income and other economic outcomes.

Among immigrants, education obtained abroad tends to earn a lower return than education received in the destination. (Economics refers to the increase in earnings associated with an additional year of education—or with having a degree, such as a bachelor's degree—as the "return to education." Typical estimates of the return to education in developed countries are that earnings increase by about 7 to 10 percent for each additional year of education.) Because of this, studies that focus on immigrants' educational attainment typically distinguish between immigrants who arrived as children or young adults and therefore are likely to have attended at least some school in the destination and immigrants who arrived as adults and are unlikely to have attended any school in the destination. Few datasets ask where people obtained their education, making it necessary for economists to infer where education occurred based on the age at which a person migrated and how many years of education she has.

The higher return to education acquired in the destination could be due to differences in the language in which instruction occurred. Instruction conducted in the language spoken in the destination is likely to confer language skills that are valued in the destination independent of the actual content of the instruction. For example, taking a math class taught in German helps an immigrant learn German regardless of whether he is a mathematician or a mechanic.

Education may also be higher quality in industrialized countries than in the developing countries from which many immigrants originate. Consistent with this, research shows that U.S. immigrants from countries with lower student-teacher ratios and higher expenditures per student earn higher returns to education acquired in their origin (Bratsberg and Terrell, 2002). In addition, employers in the destination may not be familiar with educational systems abroad and therefore may discount education obtained elsewhere.

Since education acquired in the destination tends to be more valuable than education acquired in the origin, immigrants have an incentive to go to school in the destination. In the United States, immigrants who are already well educated tend to be the most likely to go to school in the destination. Enrollment rates are lower among immigrant teens than among U.S.-born teens, while immigrants in their twenties and thirties are more likely to be enrolled in school than their U.S.-born peers (Betts and Lofstrom, 2000). The low enrollment rate among immigrant teens is driven by Hispanic immigrants. Many—although not all—Hispanics who arrive in the United States as teens appear to not enroll in school when they arrive. A similar result holds in Canada. Immigrants who arrive there during their teenage years have lower educational attainment as adults than either those who arrive when younger or older (Schaafsma and Sweetman, 2001).

Language

Learning a new language involves costs and benefits. For immigrants, the costs include the direct cost of paying for language classes or other instructional materials plus the opportunity cost of time that could instead be spent working. The benefits include finding a job more easily in the destination and earning more. Immigrants who can speak the language of the destination can also more easily communicate with natives when they shop, interact with their children's schools and go about their daily lives. The difficulty of learning the language of the destination can affect the decision to migrate. As discussed in Chapter 2, migration flows are larger between countries that share a language or use languages that are more linguistically similar.

How well immigrants can speak the language of the destination is typically related to their age at migration.[5] Younger people are usually better able to learn a new language than older people. They also have more opportunities to do so, particularly if they are in school. And since younger immigrants have a longer time to reap the benefits of being proficient in the language of the destination, they have more incentive to learn it.

There are often synergies between education and language acquisition. Highly educated people may find it easier to learn a new language. Speaking the language of the destination facilitates acquiring more education there. In addition, the return to speaking the language of the destination may be bigger for highly educated immigrants. Better-paying jobs may require both more education and greater fluency in the language of the destination. Highly educated immigrants are in a better position to obtain such jobs than less-educated immigrants (because they already meet the education requirement) and therefore have more motivation to learn the language.

Barry Chiswick and Paul Miller (2014) call the determinants of whether immigrants become proficient in the language of the destination the three "E's": exposure to the language of the destination, efficiency in learning the new language and economic incentives for learning the new language. Exposure is higher among immigrants who are still in school and among immigrants who work primarily with natives. Efficiency refers to how difficult it is for an immigrant to learn the language of the destination. This depends on factors such as age at migration, education, ability and the linguistic distance between an immigrant's native language and the language of the destination. For example, English is close to Dutch and Norwegian, while Spanish is close to Italian and Portuguese. The economic incentives for learning the language of the destination are typically biggest for young and highly educated immigrants. Immigrants who expect to stay longer in the destination also have more incentive to learn the language spoken there.

Immigrants' earnings increase with their proficiency in the language of the destination. Research on the United States, for example, finds that a childhood immigrant who speaks English well earns 33 percent more, on average, as an adult than one who speaks English poorly, and one who speaks English very well earns 67 percent more (Bleakley and Chin, 2004). Most of this effect is because childhood immigrants who speak English better also obtained more education. After taking education into account, it is not clear that childhood immigrants who speak better English earn more. Research on all male U.S. immigrants, not just childhood immigrants, finds that immigrants who are proficient in English earn 14 percent more than those who are not, even after taking education into account (Chiswick and Miller, 1995). The positive relationship between proficiency in the language of the destination and earnings is not unique to the United States nor to English-speaking countries. Studies find similar results on the returns to language among immigrants to Australia, Canada (where English and French are spoken), Germany, Israel and the United Kingdom (Chiswick and Miller, 2014).

Immigrants' ability to speak the language of the destination affects other outcomes as well. In the United States, immigrants who speak English better are more likely to marry a U.S. native or an immigrant from a different origin country (Bleakley and Chin, 2010). Their spouses speak English better, earn more and have more education. Immigrants who speak English better are more likely to be divorced, more likely to never marry and have fewer children. They also are less likely to live in ethnic enclaves. Being more proficient in the language spoken in the destination increases assimilation along many dimensions.

The United States does not screen immigrants on their ability to speak or understand English. Indeed, English is not even the official language of the country, although it is the official language in most U.S. states. Immigrants who want to naturalize must take a test on U.S. civics that is given in English (this test is further discussed later in the chapter). Some countries, such as Australia and Canada, include language skills as a criterion used in awarding permanent resident status. In 2006, the Netherlands adopted a unique policy that requires most non-European immigrants to pass an exam on knowledge of the Dutch language and society. Immigrants already living there when the policy was adopted must pass a similar exam in order to be allowed to stay in the country permanently.

Marriage and fertility

Marriages between immigrants and natives both indicate and facilitate immigrants' economic and cultural assimilation into the destination country. The more assimilated immigrants are, the more likely they are to marry a native. Marriages between immigrants and natives are also an indicator of natives' acceptance of immigrants, at least those from a particular national origin group. Meanwhile, marrying a native fosters economic assimilation by improving an immigrant's labor market outcomes and proficiency in the language of the destination. It fosters cultural assimilation as well since an intermarried immigrant becomes more exposed to the destination country's norms. First, some terminology: Marriages between individuals who are in different groups, including immigrants and natives, are termed "intermarriages," "exogamy" or "heterogamy" (the opposites of the last two categories are "endogamy" and "homogamy," marriages between people who are in the same group).

Table 5.1 reports the fraction of immigrants married to a native, and vice versa, for several countries. Immigrants are more likely to be intermarried than natives are. This is not surprising since there are more natives than immigrants in a given country—the "marriage market" for natives and, once they have arrived, immigrants consists primarily of natives. Of course, many adult immigrants are already married before they migrate. Studies on immigrants' marriage patterns therefore often focus on immigrants who were unmarried or young when they migrated.

Immigrants are more likely to marry natives or immigrants from a different origin country if they have been in the destination longer, arrived at a younger age, are more educated, live outside an ethnic enclave or are more proficient in the language of the destination (Furtado and Trejo, 2013). Those factors matter in part because they affect who immigrants meet. For example, immigrants who live outside an ethnic enclave are more likely to meet natives or immigrants from other origin countries. Group size matters as well. If there are fewer people from the same origin in the destination, immigrants are more likely to intermarry. The sex ratio may matter as well. If there are more men than women from the origin in the destination, the men may be more likely than the women to intermarry, and vice versa. However, studies find only weak support for this possibility (Adserà and Ferrer, 2014a).

Intermarriage between immigrants and natives can affect a number of outcomes. It is likely to increase immigrants' proficiency in the language of the destination. Independent of the effect on language proficiency, intermarriage may help immigrants find a better job by broadening

Table 5.1 Intermarriage rates between immigrants and natives

Country	% of immigrants married to a native	% of natives married to an immigrant
Austria	27.1	6.6
Belgium	36.2	6.5
France	37.0	7.0
Germany	28.5	6.8
Greece	17.1	1.6
Netherlands	39.6	5.1
Spain	21.0	3.1
Sweden	34.4	5.4
United Kingdom	31.1	5.1
United States	27.9	4.4

Source: Adserà and Ferrer (2014a).

their social network to include the native-born spouse's family and friends. Xin Meng and Robert Gregory (2005) find that male immigrants in Australia from non-English-speaking countries who marry a native or an immigrant from an English-speaking country earn 20 percent more, on average, than those who marry another immigrant from a non-English-speaking country. Female immigrants earn 46 percent more. Research on the United States indicates that marrying a native boosts immigrants' likelihood of being employed but not their earnings (Kantarevic, 2004; Furtado and Theodoropoulos, 2010).

Immigrants' fertility usually converges toward the fertility of natives in the destination. Migrating can affect fertility behavior through three channels: selection, disruption and adaptation (Adserà and Ferrer, 2014a). The selection channel notes that immigrants can differ systematically from non-migrants (and natives) in ways that are related to their fertility behavior. For example, if female immigrants are positively selected on education, they are likely to have fewer children than non-migrants since highly educated women typically have fewer children regardless of their migration status.

The disruption channel focuses on disruptions due to the migration process. Spouses may be separated as a result of migrating, or women may try to time their fertility to not give birth around the time they plan to move. In addition, there may be a temporary drop in family income around the time of migration, leading to a reduction in fertility then. The disruption channel predicts that there is a temporary decrease in fertility right before and around the time of a move and then a temporary increase after a move to make up for any postponed births.

The adaptation channel is directly related to assimilation. As immigrants integrate into the destination, their fertility behavior begins to resemble that of the native-born population. Since most industrialized countries have lower birth rates than most developing countries, fertility decreases for many immigrants. In addition, the direct cost of raising children and the opportunity cost of women's time are typically higher in industrialized countries than in developing countries. Meanwhile, social norms regarding the desired number of children differ across countries and usually are lower in industrialized countries.

Health

Initially, immigrants tend to be healthier than people who remain in the origin and than natives in the destination. As discussed in Chapter 4, the "healthy immigrant effect" may be largely due to positive selection. As their duration of residence in the destination increases, however, immigrants' health typically worsens and converges toward natives' health (e.g., Antecol and Bedard, 2006). There are a number of potential reasons why immigrants' health deteriorates, on average. Immigrants may adopt natives' unhealthy habits. Immigrants moving from developing to industrialized countries may become more sedentary, eat more processed foods and smoke more, for example. They may experience stress as a result of migrating that worsens their health over time. Immigrants may work in physically strenuous jobs that worsen their health. Better medical care in the destination than in the origin may reveal previously unknown adverse health conditions.

Several factors should lead to better health outcomes among immigrants as their duration of residence in the destination increases. For immigrants moving from developing to industrialized countries, better medical care should improve their health. The higher income that typically accompanies migration and then assimilation should lead to better health outcomes over time given the strong link between income and health. These positive effects do not appear to dominate, however.

Selection in return migration does not appear to contribute to immigrants' downward assimilation with respect to health. Immigrants who are in ill health are more likely to return to their home country. These return migrants may need the help of family and friends in the origin while they are ill. They may feel more comfortable utilizing medical care in their origin than in the destination, or they may be unable to afford medical care in the destination. This negative selection in return migration actually reduces the measured extent of the decline in immigrants' health as their time in the destination increases. Premature deaths by less-healthy immigrants who remain in the destination similarly lead to underestimates of the decline in immigrants' health over time.

Naturalization

One of the most salient indicators of assimilation is becoming a naturalized citizen of the destination country. Naturalization rates vary considerably across countries, as Figure 5.6 shows.

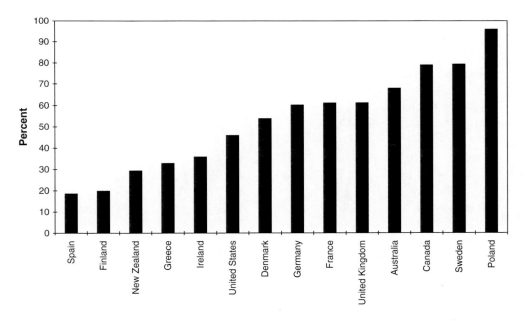

Figure 5.6 Naturalized citizenship rates for immigrants.

Sources: Picot, G., and Hou, F. (2012) "Citizenship acquisition in Canada and the United States: Determinants and economic benefit." In: *Naturalisation: A Passport for the Better Integration of Immigrants?* Paris: OECD; Dronkers, J. and Vink, M. P. (2012) "Explaining access to citizenship in Europe: How citizenship policies affect naturalization rates." *European Union Politics* 13, pp. 390–412; DeVoretz, D.J. (2013) "The economics of immigrant citizenship ascension." In: Constant, A.F. and Zimmermann, K.F. (eds.) *International Handbook on the Economics of Migration*. Cheltenham, UK: Edward Elgar, pp. 470–488.

One reason why the rate varies so much across destination countries is differences in their rules regarding naturalization. These differences include how long immigrants must live there before they can apply for naturalization; how difficult naturalized citizenship is to obtain; how high the fees are; and whether dual citizenship (being a citizen of both the original and new country) is allowed. In the United States, immigrants are usually eligible to apply to become naturalized U.S. citizens five years after receiving legal permanent resident status. Applicants must demonstrate knowledge of U.S. civics and proficiency in English (see Box 5.3, "Can you pass the U.S. citizenship civics test?"). As of late 2013, the application fee was $595. The United States allows dual citizenship.

Naturalization rates also vary because of differences in immigrants' characteristics across destination countries, particularly differences in where immigrants are from. Origin country rules regarding dual citizenship, whether citizens living abroad have to pay taxes and whether citizens can vote in elections while living abroad affect the costs and benefits of becoming a naturalized citizen elsewhere. For example, if a country requires citizens living abroad to pay taxes—like the United States does—emigrants from that country have a greater incentive to become naturalized citizens wherever they are living and renounce their citizenship in the

---

Box 5.3 Can you pass the U.S. citizenship civics test?

There are 100 civics questions on the naturalization test. A U.S. Citizenship and Immigration Services officer asks applicants up to ten of these questions in English. Applicants must orally answer six of the ten questions correctly to pass the civics test. Officers give special consideration to applicants who are 65 years of age or older and who have been living in the United States for at least 25 years. There are 20 specially designated civics questions for such elderly applicants.

Here are some of the questions (and answers):

What is the supreme law of the land? (The Constitution)
The idea of self-government is in the first three words of the Constitution. What are these words? (We the People)
What is the economic system in the United States? (capitalist economy; market economy)
If both the President and the Vice President can no longer serve, who becomes President? (The Speaker of the House of Representatives)
Under the Constitution, some powers belong to the federal government. What is one power of the federal government? (to print money; to declare war; to create an army; to make treaties)
Who wrote the Declaration of Independence? (Thomas Jefferson)
What is the name of the national anthem? (The Star-Spangled Banner)

More than 90 percent of applicants pass the test (U.S. Citizenship and Immigration Services, 2013). But 90 percent of U.S. natives probably can't—one survey indicates that one-third of voting-age U.S. natives cannot answer enough questions correctly to pass the test (Center for the Study of the American Dream, 2012).

origin. For young adults, particularly males, whether citizens are required to serve in the military in the origin (or the destination) for a certain period of time may affect whether they choose to become naturalized citizens. Military service requirements are significant in some countries. In Israel, for example, male citizens are required to serve for three years, and women for two years. Unmarried male migrants who arrive at age 18 or 19 must serve for two and one-half years, and women two years.

Immigrants who have formed more ties in the destination and plan to remain there are more likely to become naturalized citizens. Economic migrants tend to have relatively low naturalization rates since they are more likely to return home. Refugees who are resettled in industrialized countries typically have high naturalization rates since they are unlikely to return home. Family-based migrants' naturalization rates tend to fall in between economic migrants' and refugees'. In industrialized countries, immigrants from other industrialized countries tend to be more likely than immigrants from developing countries to return home and therefore are less likely to become naturalized citizens.

Immigrants who become naturalized citizens tend to have better labor market outcomes than immigrants who do not. In the United States, for example, immigrants who are naturalized citizens earn about 9 percent more than other immigrants (Picot and Hou, 2011). In Canada, the "citizenship premium" is about 5 percent. It is not clear whether becoming a naturalized citizen causes immigrants' labor market outcomes to improve or if immigrants who choose to become naturalized citizens are different from other immigrants. Employers may see naturalized citizens as more committed or more assimilated. Alternatively, immigrants who choose to become naturalized citizens may be positively selected. In addition, people who will reap greater benefits from becoming a naturalized citizen may be the ones who opt to do it. For example, immigrants who can qualify for better jobs if they are a citizen of the destination country may opt to become a naturalized citizen while those who can't, don't. Being a citizen is often required for public sector jobs. Immigrants may also invest more in acquiring destination-specific human capital if they become a naturalized citizen, such as learning the language, and the labor market gains may be returns to that human capital, not to naturalization itself.

Final thoughts on assimilation

Assimilation implies that immigrants become like natives over time. But natives also may change over time in response to immigration. Such changes may lead to convergence, with both immigrants and natives changing and becoming more similar to each other. Alternatively, natives may deliberately try to distinguish themselves from immigrants. Chapters 7 and 8 discuss how such dynamics can play out for natives in the labor market. But first the next chapter examines another aspect of assimilation: how the children of immigrants do.

Problems and discussion questions

1   What are the concerns about using cross-sectional data to measure assimilation?
2   Why might each successive cohort have better labor market outcomes than the previous cohort?

3   Suppose the transferability of skills from an origin to a destination increases. What is likely to happen to immigrants' wages relative to natives' in the destination? What do you think will happen to immigrants' skill acquisition in the destination, and why?

4   How does selection in migration and return migration affect immigrants' assimilation with respect to their health?

5   What factors determine whether immigrants choose to become naturalized citizens in the destination?

Notes

1   The figures are based on a linear regression of employment or log annual earnings (conditional on employment) on age, age squared, years since migration and years since migration squared for immigrants aged 20 to 65 in 2010. Values are then predicted assuming an immigrant arrives at age 20, so that age and years since migration increase together.

2   The figures are based on a linear regression of employment or log annual earnings (conditional on employment) on age, age squared, years since migration and years since migration squared for immigrants aged 20 to 65 in 2010.

3   However, Adserà and Ferrer (2014b) find that this is only true for relatively uneducated immigrant women in Canada. Educated immigrant women appear to experience rising labor force participation and wage assimilation.

4   Major means-tested programs include public health insurance (primarily Medicaid and SCHIP; Medicare is not included), food stamps (SNAP), cash welfare (TANF or SSI) and subsidized housing. Calculations are based on 2011–2013 March Current Population Survey data for benefits received during the previous calendar year using IPUMS data from King et al. (2010).

5   Many countries have multiple common and even official languages, but for simplicity this discussion is written as if the destination has only one language. Studies that examine immigrants' proficiency in the language of the destination in countries with multiple languages, like Canada (English and French), typically look at proficiency in either language.

Internet resources

Information on the Netherlands exam on knowledge of Dutch language and society is available at: http://www.naarnederland.nl/en/the-exam.

The full list of the 100 questions on the U.S. naturalized citizen test is available at: http://www.uscis.gov/sites/default/files/USCIS/Office%20of%20Citizenship/Citizenship%20Resource%20Center%20Site/Publications/100q.pdf.

Suggestions for further reading

Aydemir, A. and Skuterud, M. (2005) "Explaining the deteriorating entry earnings of Canada's immigrant cohorts, 1966-2000." *Canadian Journal of Economics* 38(2), pp. 641–672.

Borjas, G.J. (2013) "The slowdown in the economic assimilation of immigrants: Aging and cohort effects revisited again." *National Bureau of Economic Research Working Paper* No. 19116. Cambridge, MA: National Bureau of Economic Research.

Chiswick, B.R. (1978) "The effect of Americanization on the earnings of foreign-born men." *Journal of Political Economy* 86(5), pp. 897–921

References

Abramitzky, R., Boustan, L.P. and Eriksson, K. (2012) "Europe's tired, poor, huddled masses: Self-selection and economic outcomes in the age of mass migration." *American Economic Review* 102(5), pp. 1832–1856.

Abramitzky, R., Boustan, L.P. and Eriksson, K. (2013) "A nation of immigrants: Assimilation and economic outcomes in the age of mass migration." *National Bureau of Economic Research Working Paper* No. 18011. Cambridge, MA: NBER.

Adserà, A. and Ferrer, A. (2014a) "Immigrants and demography: Marriage, divorce, and fertility." In: Chiswick, B.R. and Miller, P.W. (eds.) *Handbook of the Economics of International Migration*. Amsterdam: Elsevier.

Adserà, A. and Ferrer, A. (2014b) "Labour market progression of Canadian immigrant women." *IZA Discussion Paper* No. 8407. Bonn: Institute for the Study of Labor.

Algan, Y., Dustmann, C., Glitz, A. and Manning, A. (2010) "The economic situation of the first and second-generation immigrants in France, Germany and the United Kingdom." *Economic Journal* 120(542), pp. F4–F30.

Antecol, H. (2000) "An examination of cross-country differences in the gender gap in labor force participation rates." *Labour Economics* 7(4), pp. 409–426.

Antecol, H. and Bedard, K. (2006) "Unhealthy assimilation: Why do immigrants converge to American health status levels?" *Demography* 43(2), pp. 337–360.

Åslund, O. and Rooth, D. (2007) "Do when and where matter? Initial labour market conditions and immigrant earnings." *Economic Journal* 117 (518), pp. 422–448.

Aydemir, A. and Skuterud, M. (2005) "Explaining the deteriorating entry earnings of Canada's immigrant cohorts, 1966-2000." *Canadian Journal of Economics* 38(2), pp. 641–672.

Baker, M. and Benjamin, D. (1997) "The role of the family in immigrants' labor-market activity: An evaluation of alternative explanations." *American Economic Review* 87(4), pp. 705–727.

Barth, E., Bratsberg, B. and Raaum, O. (2004) "Identifying earnings assimilation of immigrants under changing macroeconomic conditions." *Scandinavian Journal of Economics* 106(1), pp. 1–22.

Betts, J.R. and Lofstrom, M. (2000) "The educational attainment of immigrants: Trends and implications." In: Borjas, G.J. (ed.) *Issues in the Economics of Immigration*. Chicago: University of Chicago Press, pp. 51–115.

Biavaschi, C., Giulietti, C. and Siddique, Z. (2013) "The economic payoff of name Americanization." *IZA Discussion Paper* No. 7725 (2013). Bonn: Institute for the Study of Labor.

Blau, F.D., Kahn, L.M. and Papps, K.L. (2011) "Gender, source country characteristics, and labor market assimilation among immigrants." *Review of Economics and Statistics* 93(1), pp. 43–58.

Bleakley, H. and Chin, A. (2004) "Language skills and earnings: Evidence from childhood immigrants." *Review of Economics and Statistics* 86(2), pp. 481–496.

Bleakley, H. and Chin, A. (2010) "Age at arrival, English proficiency, and social assimilation among US immigrants." *American Economic Journal: Applied Economics* 2(1), pp. 165–192.

Borjas, G.J. (1985) "Assimilation, changes in cohort quality, and the earnings of immigrants." *Journal of Labor Economics* 3(4), pp. 463–489.

Borjas, G.J. (1995) "Assimilation and changes in cohort quality revisited: What happened to immigrant earnings in the 1980s?" *Journal of Labor Economics* 13(2), pp. 201–245.

Borjas, G.J. (2013) "The slowdown in the economic assimilation of immigrants: Aging and cohort effects revisited again." *National Bureau of Economic Research Working Paper* No. 19116. Cambridge, MA: National Bureau of Economic Research.

Borjas, G.J. and Hilton, L. (1996). "Immigration and the welfare state: Immigrant participation in means-tested entitlement programs." *Quarterly Journal of Economics* 111(2), pp. 575–604.

Borjas, G.J. and Tienda, M. (1993) "The employment and wages of legalized immigrants." *International Migration Review* 27(4), pp. 712–747.

Bratsberg, B., Barth, E. and Raaum, O. (2006) "Local unemployment and the relative wages of immigrants: Evidence from the Current Population Surveys." *Review of Economics and Statistics* 88(2), pp. 243–263.

Bratsberg, B. and Terrell, D. (2002) "School quality and returns to education of U.S. immigrants." *Economic Inquiry* 40(2), pp. 177–198.

Bredtmann, J. and Otten, S. (2014) "The role of source- and host-country characteristics in female immigrant labor supply." Paper presented at 2014 American Economic Association conference, Philadelphia, PA.

Center for the Study of the American Dream (2012) *As Americans prepare to exercise civic duty this fall, too many remain uninformed.* Cincinnati, OH: Xavier University. Available at: http://www.xavier.edu/americandream/programs/documents/5CivicTestpowerpointfinalPDF.pdf [9 May 2014].

Chiswick, B.R. (1978) "The effect of Americanization on the earnings of foreign-born men." *Journal of Political Economy* 86(5), pp. 897–921.

Chiswick, B.R. and Miller, P.W. (1995) "The endogeneity between language and earnings: International analyses." *Journal of Labor Economics* 13(2), pp. 245–287.

Chiswick, B.R. and Miller, P.W. (2014) "International migration and the economics of language." In: Chiswick, B.R. and Miller, P.W. (eds.) *Handbook on the Economics of International Migration* vol 1A. Amsterdam: Elsevier.

Cortes, K.E. (2004) "Are refugees different from economic immigrants? Some empirical evidence on the heterogeneity of immigrant groups in the United States." *Review of Economics and Statistics* 86(2), pp. 465–480.

Cutler, D.M., Glaeser, E.L. and Vigdor, J.L. (2008) "When are ghettos bad? Lessons from immigrant segregation in the United States." *Journal of Urban Economics* 63(3), pp. 759–774.

de la Rica, S., Glitz, A. and Ortega, F. (2013) "Immigration in Europe: Trends, policies and empirical evidence." *IZA Discussion Paper* No. 7778. Bonn: Institute for the Study of Labor.

Duleep, H. and Regets, M. (1996) "Admission criteria and immigrant earning profiles." *International Migration Review* 30(2), pp. 571–590.

Duleep, H. and Regets, M. (2013) "The elusive concept of immigrant quality: Evidence from 1970–1990." *College of William and Mary Department of Economics Working Paper* No. 138. Williamsburg, VA: College of William and Mary.

Dustmann, C., Frattini, T. and Hall, C. (2010) "Assessing the fiscal costs and benefits of A8 migration to the UK." *Fiscal Studies* 31(1), pp. 1–41.

Edin, P. A., Fredriksson, P. and Åslund, O. (2003) "Ethnic enclaves and the economic success of immigrations: Evidence from a natural experiment." *Quarterly Journal of Economics* 118(1), pp. 329–357.

Furtado, D. and Theodoropoulos, N. (2010) "Why does intermarriage increase immigrant employment? The role of networks." *B.E. Journal of Economic Analysis & Policy* 10(1).

Furtado, D. and Trejo, S.J. (2013) "Interethnic marriages and their economic effects." In: Constant, A.F. and Zimmermann, K.F. (eds.) *International Handbook on the Economics of Migration*. Cheltenham, UK: Edward Elgar, pp. 276–292.

Hansen, J. and Lofstrom, M. (2003) "Immigrant assimilation and welfare participation: Do immigrants assimilate into or out of welfare?" *Journal of Human Resources* 38(1), pp. 74–98.

Hatton, T.J. and Leigh, A. (2011) "Immigrants assimilate as communities, not as individuals." *Journal of Population Economics* 24(2), pp. 389–419.

Immigration Commission (1911) *Reports of the Immigration Commission* vol 1. Washington, DC: Government Printing Office.

Kahn, L. (2010) "The long-term labor market consequences of graduating from college in a bad economy." *Labour Economics* 17(2), pp. 303–316.

Kantarevic, J. (2004) "Interethnic marriages and the economic assimilation of immigrants." *IZA Discussion Paper* No. 1142. Bonn: Institute for the Study of Labor.

King, M., Ruggles, S., Alexander, J.T., Flood, S., Genadek, K., Schroeder, M., Trampe, B. and Vick, R. (2010) Integrated Public Use Microdata Series, Current Population Survey: Version 3.0. [Machine-readable database]. Minneapolis: University of Minnesota.

Lemos, S. (2013) "Immigrant economic assimilation: Evidence from UK longitudinal data between 1978 and 2006." *Labour Economics* 24, pp. 339–353.

Longva, P. and Raaum, O. (2003) "Earnings assimilation of immigrants in Norway: A reappraisal." *Journal of Public Economics* 16(1), pp. 177–193.

Lubotsky, D. (2007) "Chutes or ladders? A longitudinal analysis of immigrant earnings." *Journal of Political Economy* 115(5), pp. 820–867.

Lubotsky, D. (2011) "The effect of changes in the U.S. wage structure on recent immigrants' earnings." *Review of Economics and Statistics* 93(1), pp. 59–71.

Meng, X. and Gregory, R.G. (2005) "Intermarriage and the economic assimilation of immigrants." *Journal of Labor Economics* 23(1), pp. 135–175.

Organization for Economic Cooperation and Development (OECD) (2013) "How many students study abroad?" In: *OECD Factbook 2013: Economic, Environmental and Social Statistics*. Paris: OECD Publishing.

Picot, G. and Hou, F. (2011) "Citizenship acquisition in Canada and the United States: Determinants and economic benefit." In: *Naturalisation: A Passport for the Better Integration of Immigrants?* Paris: OECD, pp. 153–182.

Sarvimaki, M. (2011) "Assimilation to a welfare state: Labor market performance and use of social benefits by immigrants to Finland." *Scandinavian Journal of Economics* 113(3), pp. 665–688.

Schaafsma, J. and Sweetman, A. (2001) "Immigrant earnings: Age at immigration matters." *Canadian Journal of Economics* 34(4), pp. 1066–1099.

U.S. Bureau of Labor Statistics (2013) "Foreign-born workers: labor force characteristics—2012." Available at: http://www.bls.gov/news.release/pdf/forbrn.pdf [12 April 2014].

U.S. Citizenship and Immigration Services (2013) *Applicant performance on the naturalization test.* Washington, DC: U.S. Department of Homeland Security. Available at: http://www.uscis.gov/us-citizenship/naturalization-test/applicant-performance-naturalization-test [9 May 2014].

6   The Second Generation

Immigration is a multigenerational process. Some migrants are accompanied or joined by their children, while others have children in the receiving country. These children and their descendants comprise a significant share of the population of the receiving country. In the United States, more than one in eight U.S. natives has at least one foreign-born parent, and one in four immigrants arrived here as children.[1] How well immigrants' descendants do therefore has major implications for the economy.

In economics, the children of immigrants are called second-generation immigrants. Their parents who migrated are called first-generation immigrants. Children are considered members of the second generation if either or both of their parents are immigrants. If both parents are natives of the destination but at least one grandparent was an immigrant, the children are called the third generation. (Few surveys ask about grandparents' immigrant status, so studies often refer to the third-plus generation.) People who immigrate as children are called the 1.5 generation because in some ways they are more like the first generation while in other ways they are more like the second generation. They have usually spent some of their formative years in the origin and some in the destination. It is worth noting that members of the second generation are not necessarily citizens of the country in which they were born. Whether they are depends on that country's rules regarding citizenship.[2]

Economic research on the second and higher immigrant generations focuses on several issues. Studies examine intergenerational mobility, or how well each subsequent generation of immigrants does compared with the previous one. Studies also examine intergenerational transmission, or whether the characteristics of one generation are replicated in the next generation. Immigrant parents may pass on their characteristics or behaviors to their children. In addition, they may pass on the culture of their origin country.

This chapter first explains how economists measure intergenerational mobility and intergenerational transmission in general, not just with respect to immigrants. The chapter then explores how economists have applied those measures to immigrants. Research has focused primarily on intergenerational issues with regard to immigrants' labor market and education outcomes. There is also some evidence on a number of other interesting issues regarding the second generation, such as their language proficiency, marriage and fertility patterns and ethnic identity. The chapter discusses each of these areas in turn.

Measuring intergenerational mobility

Economists measure intergenerational mobility by examining how later generations do relative to earlier generations. There are many dimensions to intergenerational mobility, including income, wealth, education, occupation and socioeconomic status (or "class"). There are two important types of intergenerational mobility. The first is absolute mobility, which measures whether one generation does better or worse than another generation in levels. Whether children earn more or less than their parents, adjusting for inflation, is a measure of absolute mobility. Absolute mobility can be measured using data on average values for each generation or using data that matches family members across generations. An example of the former is looking at average years of education completed among the parents' generation and among their children's generation. An example of the latter is looking at what percentage of children have completed more years of education than their own parents have.

The second type of mobility is relative mobility, which compares each generation's position in the distribution. For example, comparing where children and their parents are in the distribution of income measures relative mobility in terms of income. Unlike absolute mobility, relative mobility is a "zero-sum game"—if someone moves up in the distribution, someone else must move down. Like absolute mobility, relative mobility can be measured using data on average values for each generation or using data that matches family members across generations. Both absolute and relative mobility can be measured in terms of direction (up or down) and magnitude (by how much).

One common way of measuring relative mobility is a transition matrix. A transition matrix shows the probability of people in one generation being in a higher, lower or the same place in the distribution than people in another generation. Figure 6.1 shows a hypothetical transition matrix for parents and their children. In the figure, the income distribution is divided into quintiles, or fifths; a transition matrix can use any number of quantiles (equally spaced

		Child's position in income distribution				
		Bottom quintile	Second quintile	Middle quintile	Fourth quintile	Top quintile
Father's position in income distribution	Bottom quintile	p_{11}	p_{12}	p_{13}	p_{14}	p_{15}
	Second quintile	p_{21}	p_{22}	p_{23}	p_{24}	p_{25}
	Middle quintile	p_{31}	p_{32}	p_{33}	p_{34}	p_{35}
	Fourth quintile	p_{41}	p_{42}	p_{43}	p_{44}	p_{45}
	Top quintile	p_{51}	p_{52}	p_{53}	p_{54}	p_{55}

Figure 6.1 Hypothetical transition matrix.

intervals). Each row contains one-fifth of the income distribution for parents, and each column contains one-fifth of the income distribution for children. Each cell in the matrix has an entry p_{ij}, where i indicates the parents' quintile and j indicates the child's quintile. For example, p_{23} is the probability that parents with income in the second quintile will have a child with income in the third, or middle, quintile. It is also the percentage of children with parents in the second quintile who end up in the third quintile. Each row or each column adds up to one (or 100 percent). Cells on the diagonal are people who do not experience any mobility. Cells above the diagonal are people who experience upward mobility, while cells below the diagonal are people who experience downward mobility.

Intergenerational transmission and intergenerational elasticities

Intergenerational elasticities are another way that economists measure intergenerational mobility. Intergenerational elasticities measure how closely related outcomes are across generations, or how much earlier generations transmit outcomes to later generations. The typical model that economists use to measure intergenerational transmission from generation t to generation $t+1$ is

$$\textit{Outcome in generation } t+1 = \alpha + \beta \textit{ Outcome in generation } t + \varepsilon \qquad (6.1)$$

Outcome is some economic variable, such as absolute income or relative income. The left-hand side of the equation is the values of the outcome for people in generation $t+1$. The right-hand side of the equation is the values of the outcome for people in generation t. The term α is a constant. The term β is the intergenerational elasticity, or how much the outcome is transmitted across generations.[3] If $\beta = 1$, there is complete intergenerational transmission—children's outcomes are exactly like their parents' outcomes. (If $\beta = 1$, everyone is on the diagonal in the transition matrix.) If $\beta = 0$, there is no intergeneration transmission—children's outcomes are not related at all to their parents' outcomes. Higher values of β thus indicate more intergenerational transmission and less intergenerational mobility. Lower values of β indicate less intergenerational transmission and more intergenerational mobility. The term ε is the residual, which captures all other factors besides outcomes in generation t that affect outcomes in generation $t+1$.

Measuring intergenerational mobility requires considerable data. Most studies use longitudinal data, or data over time, in order to measure different generations at the same age. Studies that use cross-sectional data, or data at a point in time, risk capturing lifecycle differences due to age. For example, parents may earn more than their children simply because they are older and have more years of labor market experience, or they may earn less because they are retired. However, collecting longitudinal data takes more time and is more expensive than collecting cross-sectional data. In addition, differences in macroeconomic conditions and other factors over time can complicate the interpretation of longitudinal data. For example, some people may have entered the labor market during a recession, whereas others entered the labor market during a boom. As discussed later in this chapter, the data issues are even more complicated when measuring intergenerational mobility among immigrants.

Studies of intergenerational mobility among immigrants typically focus on comparing the first and the second generation of immigrants, or migrants and their children. Some studies also examine later generations in traditional immigrant destinations, like Australia, Canada, New Zealand and the United States, where large-scale immigration has occurred long enough that the third and higher generations have reached adulthood. This chapter is particularly U.S.-focused since there are many studies of the second and higher generations in the United States because of its large and long-standing immigrant population.

Intergenerational mobility among immigrants in the labor market

The extent of intergenerational mobility in the labor market depends on a number of factors. Many of these factors are country-specific. Labor market institutions, such as the extent of unions and the level of the minimum wage, and the level of inequality in a country affect intergenerational mobility there. The structure of a country's educational system also affects intergenerational mobility there. The tremendous differences in such factors across countries make it difficult to generalize about intergenerational mobility. Cross-country differences in where immigrants are from make it even harder to generalize about intergenerational mobility among immigrants.

In the United States, the second generation tends to do better in the labor market than the first generation. Intergenerational progress does not necessarily continue with the third-plus generation, however. Table 6.1 shows the incomes of first- and second-generation male immigrants relative to the third-plus generation in the United States by year.[4] Generations can be followed along the diagonal in the table. In 1950, first-generation immigrant men earned about the same as third-plus-generation men (actually 0.3 percent more, but the difference is not significant), taking into account differences in age, education and state of residence. Their sons, who comprise much of the second generation in 1970, did better—they earned 7.3 percent more than third-plus-generation men. In other words, the second generation did better, relative to the third-plus generation, than the first generation did.

A similar pattern holds in more recent data. In 1970, first-generation immigrant men earned 6.7 percent less than third-plus-generation men. Their sons again did better, earning 2 percent more than third-plus-generation men in 1994–1996. In 1994–1996, the first generation earned substantially less than the third-plus generation—more than 25 percent less. In

Table 6.1 Average income gap relative to third-plus generation, by year in the United States

Year	1st generation	2nd generation
1950	0.3%	3.6%
1970	−6.7%	7.3%
1994–1996	−25.3%	2.0%
2011–2013	−23.7%	−2.4%

Note: Calculations based on men aged 25 to 64 for years indicated, controlling for age, education and state of residence, using 1950 and 1970 Census and 1994–1996 and 2011–2013 March Current Population Survey data from King et al. (2010).

2011–2013, the most recent period available, the second generation earned 2.4 percent less than the third-plus generation.

The results in Table 6.1 are consistent with George Borjas's contention, as discussed in Chapter 5, that U.S. immigrant cohort quality has declined over time. The first generation did worse, relative to the third-plus generation, in 1970 than in 1950, and in 1994–1996 than in 1970. The results also suggest that this decline in quality persisted into the second generation. The second generation did less well in 1994–1996 than in 1970, and it did worse in 2011–2013 than in 1994–1996.

There are several potential reasons for this decline. As discussed in Chapter 5, the distribution of U.S. immigrants across origin countries has changed over time. More U.S. immigrants are now from relatively poorer, less-educated countries. Immigrants from those countries may have fewer resources to help the second generation succeed. In addition, the racial and ethnic makeup of immigrants has changed. Immigrants and their descendants may face racial or ethnic discrimination in the United States. (However, social conceptions of race and ethnicity have changed over time as well—as Chapter 5 discussed, earlier cohorts of immigrants from Italy and Russia were not considered "white.") Recent cohorts of immigrants and their descendants also face a different macroeconomic environment than earlier cohorts. In particular, the return to skill has increased in the United States. If the first and second generations are less skilled than the third-plus generation, the income gaps between the generations will widen as the return to skill increases.

There are several reasons why the second generation earns more than the first generation in the United States. The second generation tends to be better educated than the first generation. In addition to having more years of education, the second generation received their education in the United States. Much of the first generation received their education in their origin country. The second generation therefore is more likely to be fluent in English. They are also better informed about opportunities in the U.S. labor market. The second generation has broader social networks and is less likely than the first generation to live in ethnic enclaves.

Where the second generation's parents are from matters. Borjas (1993) shows that a member of the second generation in the United States earns more if his parents are from a country with higher output, less income inequality or English as an official language. Earnings for a member of the second generation are also higher if his parents are from a country further from the United States. The same patterns hold for earnings among the first generation. The finding for income inequality in the parents' origin relates back to the selection model developed in Chapter 4: the higher income inequality—a proxy for the return to skill—is in the origin relative to the destination, the more negatively selected immigrants will be, all else equal. The direction of selection among the first generation thus appears to carry over to the second generation.

In the United States, upward mobility in earnings appears to be smaller from the second generation to the third-plus generation than from the first to the second. The smaller gains in the labor market may reflect smaller gains in education and skills. The second and the third-plus generations receive their education in the same country, whereas the first and the second generations typically receive their education in different countries. The second and third-plus generations therefore are more similar than the first and second generations, leaving less room for upward mobility in the labor market. First-generation immigrant parents may also offer a benefit to their children that sociologists call "immigrant optimism." They may have attitudes that promote successful outcomes in the next generation, such as pushing their children to do

Box 6.1 Tiger mothers and the second generation

In 2011, Yale Law School professor Amy Chua ignited a firestorm with publication of her book *Battle Hymn of the Tiger Mother*. The book recounted how she raised her two daughters with an emphasis on strict discipline and academic success. She required her daughters to spend many hours each week studying and practicing the violin or piano. They were not allowed to watch TV, play computer games, have playdates, attend sleepovers, earn a grade less than an A or play any other musical instrument. She argued that this "tiger mother" way of raising children leads to self confidence and success.

Research on time use shows that U.S. teens with immigrant parents use their time differently than those with native-born parents. Teens with foreign-born parents spend more time at school and more time studying than teens with U.S.-born parents (U.S. Bureau of Labor Statistics, 2012). Teens with U.S.-born parents spend more time engaging in paid work outside the home than teens with foreign-born parents.

There are substantial differences by race and ethnicity in how U.S. teens spend their time. The average non-Hispanic white high school student in the United States reports spending 5½ hours per week studying (Ramey, 2011). Black students spend an average of about 3½ hours per week, and Hispanic students 4½ hours. The average Asian student, in contrast, spends 13 hours per week studying. And this number averages in vacations! Contrary to Amy Chua's parenting practices, Asian high school students in the United States spend more time playing computer games than other U.S. teens, on average, and they do not spend more time practicing musical instruments. They spend less time working, socializing and playing sports than their peers.

When they get to college, Asian students in the United States continue to spend more time studying than their peers. The average Asian college student spends more than 15 hours per week studying, versus about ten for non-Hispanic whites and even less for blacks and Hispanics (Ramey, 2011).

In the United States, Asian mothers spend more time engaged in educational activities with their children than other mothers (Ramey, 2011). The tiger mother phenomenon thus appears to not be limited to Amy Chua. But it's worth noting that she writes that her tiger mother technique ultimately backfired with her younger daughter, and she had to change her parenting style.

well in school and in the labor market. Related to this, the box "Tiger mothers and the second generation" discusses differences in how children in the United States spend their time.

Data from Sweden present a considerably different picture of intergenerational progress in the labor market. Mats Hammarstedt (2009) uses data on first-generation immigrants in 1968 and 1970, second-generation immigrants in 1980 and 1985, and third-generation immigrants in 1999, 2001 and 2003. He compares their earnings with the earnings of fourth-plus generation Swedes at the same point in time. The results indicate a clear decline in relative earnings across immigrant generations—the first generation earns more than fourth-plus-generation Swedes, the second generation earns about the same and the third generation earns less. This pattern holds for males and females. Hammarstedt notes that early immigrants to Sweden were positively selected and entered a strong labor market. Their descendants have faced tougher macroeconomic conditions. The differences in intergeneration progress in Sweden versus the United States illustrate the importance of institutional context and the difficulty in generalizing across countries.

Transition matrices in Switzerland

As discussed earlier, economists sometimes measure relative mobility using a transition matrix. Figure 6.2 shows transition matrices for Switzerland using cross-sectional data from 1991. More than 20 percent of Swiss residents are not Swiss citizens, and immigration has accounted for most of the country's population growth since the 1960s (Bauer, 2006). The left-hand side of the figure gives a transition matrix for immigrants (between immigrant fathers and foreign- or Swiss-born sons) while the right-hand side gives a transition matrix for natives (Swiss-born fathers and sons). In general, there is less intergenerational mobility among immigrants than among natives in Switzerland. For example, among fathers in the bottom quartile of the income distribution, about 45 percent of immigrants' sons are in the bottom quartile, compared with 37 percent of natives' sons. (Intergenerational studies often focus on fathers and sons since men were historically much more likely than women to be in the labor market.)

Intergenerational transmission

As discussed earlier, one way that economists examine intergenerational mobility is by looking at the relationship between parents' outcomes and their children's outcomes, or the extent of intergenerational transmission. This requires data that match family members across generations. Datasets with this information are uncommon and usually have a small number of observations. This makes it difficult to examine intergenerational transmission among immigrants, who are already a small share of the population in most countries. Some studies therefore use data on averages within origin-country groups by immigrant generation. These studies

| | | Son's position in income distribution | | | | | | | |
| | | Immigrants | | | | Natives | | | |
		Bottom quartile	Second quartile	Third quartile	Top quartile	Bottom quartile	Second quartile	Third quartile	Top quartile
Father's position in income distribution	Bottom quartile	45	28	17	10	37	25	20	17
	Second quartile	30	29	26	15	29	29	22	21
	Third quartile	12	29	25	34	17	27	30	26
	Top quartile	13	14	32	41	15	18	30	37

Figure 6.2 Transition matrices for natives and immigrants in Switzerland.

Source: Adapted from Bauer (2006). Some numbers are adjusted slightly so that rows and columns sum to 100 percent.

examine the relationship between the average outcome among first-generation immigrant men from a particular origin country and the average outcome among second-generation men (and perhaps women) whose father is from that country.

The model these studies estimate is similar to equation 6.1. It is

$$Outcome\ in\ 2nd\ generation_o = \alpha + \beta\ Outcome\ in\ 1st\ generation_o + \varepsilon_o \tag{6.2}$$

where *Outcome* represents education, earnings or another variable of interest. On the left-hand side of the equation is the average value of this outcome for people in the second generation whose fathers are from country o. On the right-hand side of the equation is the average value of the outcome for men in the first generation from country o. As in equation 6.1, β is the intergenerational elasticity, or how much the outcome is transmitted across generations. Higher values of β mean more intergenerational transmission and less intergenerational mobility. In the context of immigrants, higher values of β mean less intergenerational assimilation.

David Card, John DiNardo and Eugena Estes (2000) use U.S. data from 1940, 1970 and 1994–1996 to examine intergenerational transmission of earnings and education from fathers in the first generation to sons and daughters in the second generation. They estimate equation 6.2 using data on 34 countries (or country groups) for 1940 and 1970, and 33 countries (or country groups) for 1970 and 1994–1996. Table 6.2 shows some of their estimates of β. For example, the intergenerational elasticity of average earnings from the 1940s first generation to 1970s second-generation males is 0.44, and 0.21 to second-generation females. The intergenerational transmission of earnings increases across cohorts, particularly for females. The authors conclude:

> There are strong links between the education and earnings of immigrant fathers and the outcomes of their native-born children. Countries with higher immigrant earnings (such as Germany and the United Kingdom) have higher second-generation earnings, while countries with lower immigrant earnings (notably Mexico) have lower second-generation earnings.
>
> (pp. 252–253)

Francine Blau and co-authors (2013) use a similar approach to examine intergenerational transmission in education and labor supply from the first generation to the second generation in the United States. Unlike most studies, they look at both men and women in the first generation, not just men. They find that average educational attainment among first-generation male immigrants from the father's origin country is transmitted to sons and daughters in the second generation. Average education among male or female immigrants from the mother's origin country is not transmitted, nor is average education among female immigrants from

Table 6.2 Intergenerational transmission of earnings and education

Time periods	Men		Women	
	Earnings	Education	Earnings	Education
1940 and 1970	0.44	0.41	0.21	0.47
1970 and 1994–1996	0.62	0.43	0.50	0.42

Source: Adapted from Card, D., DiNardo, J. and Estes, E. (2000).

the father's origin country. Something about fathers thus appears to matter more than mothers for education, and this is true for both sons and daughters. However, they find that labor supply among female immigrants from both the mother's and the father's origin countries is transmitted to daughters, while labor supply among male immigrants from both the mother's and the father's origin countries is transmitted to sons. This suggests that the first generation transmits beliefs about gender roles to the second generation.

One interpretation of intergenerational transmission among origin-country groups is that immigrants from the same country share "ethnic capital." Borjas (1992) argues, "The skills of the next generation depend not only on parental inputs, but also on the average quality of the ethnic environment in which parents make their investments, or 'ethnic capital'" (p. 124). There may be externalities within origin-country groups that affect educational attainment and labor market outcomes in the second and higher generations. In addition, racial and ethnic minorities may face discrimination. The presence of ethnic capital slows the process of assimilation. This is advantageous to immigrants if their ethnic capital includes high levels of education and good labor market outcomes, but disadvantageous if it includes low levels of education and poor labor market outcomes.

Issues in measuring intergenerational mobility among immigrants

Measuring intergenerational mobility among immigrants raises several issues. First, researchers need to be careful if using cross-sectional data to measure intergenerational immigrant mobility. As Chapter 5 discussed, cross-sectional data can give a misleading picture of assimilation among the first generation if there are changes in cohort quality or the macroeconomic environment. Similar lessons apply for measuring intergenerational mobility among immigrants. A naïve strategy might be to compare first- and second-generation immigrants using cross-sectional data from, say, 2010. The problem is that people in the second generation in 2010 are not necessarily the children of people in the first generation in 2010. The first generation includes people who just arrived in the receiving country and have not yet had children there. The first generation does not include people who have died but whose children are still alive. It also does not include people who have returned to their origin country, perhaps to retire there, but whose children have stayed in the destination country.

If cohort quality is decreasing over time, naïve comparisons using data from a single cross section may be upward biased. In other words, such comparisons may indicate more upward mobility than actually occurred. Suppose a study uses data from a single cross section to examine educational attainment among first- and second-generation adults, and educational attainment has fallen across immigrant cohorts. The first generation includes both the more-educated, earlier cohorts and the less-educated, recent cohorts. The second generation includes only the adult children of the more-educated, earlier cohorts (since the less-educated, recent cohorts' children who are born in the destination are not yet adults). If there is any intergenerational transmission of educational attainment, the children of the more-educated, earlier cohorts will have more education than the children of the less-educated, recent cohorts, on average. Not including the latter group in the second generation—since they are not yet adults—biases the second generation's education upward. Further, within the first generation, a larger fraction of the more-educated, earlier cohorts may have died since they are likely to be older than the less-educated, recent cohorts. This will bias the first generation's education downwards. Both biases cause mobility in education to look more positive than it really is.

Comparisons using data from repeated cross sections can give a more accurate picture of intergenerational mobility. Data from repeated cross sections can be used to measure the first generation at a point in time and then the second generation at another point in time, typically 20 to 30 years later. For example, a study might examine first-generation immigrants in 1990 and second-generation immigrants in 2015. The second generation is then likely to be largely comprised of the children of the first generation. Researchers can restrict the age range of the first and second generations to make it even more likely that the second generation is largely the children of the first generation. Data that enable researchers to connect parents and children are ideal for tracking intergenerational mobility, but such data are uncommon, particularly in studies related to immigration.

Return migration can affect intergenerational mobility and its measurement. If return migration is negatively selected, the first generation that remains in the destination will have higher earnings, education and other outcomes than if no return migration occurred or return migration was random. If return migrants' children remain in the destination instead of accompanying their parents, intergenerational mobility will be biased upward in data from a single cross section. Data from repeated cross sections that measure the first generation before return migrants leave will be unbiased, however. If return migrants' children (and any later generations) accompany them when they leave, estimates of intergenerational mobility are unbiased in data from a single cross section—it is as if those families had never migrated. But data from repeated cross sections will give biased results if the data include the first generation (who have not yet return migrated) but miss the second generation. In short, it is difficult to measure intergenerational mobility accurately.

Intergenerational mobility in education

In most industrialized countries, the second generation is considerably more educated than the first generation. Table 6.3 shows the percentages of the first, second and third-plus generations that have not completed secondary school and the percentages that have at least attended college for selected countries. The data illustrate considerable diversity across countries. Nonetheless, several patterns emerge. In most countries, the second generation is more likely than the first generation to have completed secondary school—the percentage who have not completed secondary school declines across generations in most countries. Ireland, Spain and the United Kingdom are exceptions.

The second generation is also more likely than the first generation to have completed college in most countries. Germany and Sweden are exceptions. The second generation, particularly the portion with only one immigrant parent instead of two, is also more likely to have attended college than the third-plus generation in most countries. Sweden is again an exception.

Overall, there is no clear pattern in Table 6.3 as to whether the second or the third-plus generation is more likely to have completed secondary school. There is also no clear pattern as to whether the second generation is more likely to have completed secondary school

Table 6.3 Educational attainment by immigrant generation

Country	% not completed secondary school				% attended college			
	1st gen.	2nd gen.		3rd+ gen.	1st gen.	2nd gen.		3rd+ gen.
		1 immigrant parent	2 immigrant parents			1 immigrant parent	2 immigrant parents	
Canada	23	19	14	24	45	44	50	37
France	43	24	26	23	26	35	29	31
Germany	34	—	19	8	27	28	14	27
Ireland	16	19	—	28	47	47	53	34
Netherlands	37	24	29	22	27	35	29	35
Spain	40	33	55	43	24	40	21	35
Sweden	29	14	15	13	35	32	28	34
Switzerland	27	6	7	5	35	39	34	36
United Kingdom	20	20	22	25	34	43	45	33
United States	31	5	11	10	34	45	45	40

Source: Adapted from Sweetman, A. and van Ours, J.C. (2014).

or attended college if one or both parents are immigrants. The clearest result that emerges from Table 6.3 is thus that the second generation tends to be more educated than the first generation.

Table 6.3 is based on data at a single point in time for each country. As discussed earlier, using a single cross section can give a misleading picture of intergenerational progress. Table 6.4 therefore reports education measures for the various immigrant generations at several different points in time in the United States. Not surprisingly, educational attainment has increased over time. Within each generation, the fraction that has not completed high school has decreased over time, and the fraction that has at least attended college has increased over time.

Table 6.4 also suggests considerable intergenerational educational progress. For example, 76 percent of first-generation immigrants had not completed high school in 1950, whereas only 34 to 46 percent of the second generation—their children—had not completed high school in 1970. In 1994–1996, only 12 percent of the third generation—their grandchildren—had not completed high school. The pattern for the fraction attending college likewise indicates intergenerational progress.

Looking at any single year in Table 6.4, the third-plus generation does not appear to be much more educated than the second generation. For example, 41 percent of the third-plus generation has not completed high school in 1970, compared with 34 to 46 percent of the second generation. Likewise, 25 percent of the third-plus generation has at least attended college in 1970, compared with 21 to 30 percent of the second generation. A similar pattern holds for many countries in Table 6.3, indicating that this pattern is not unique to the United States. It also does not appear to be a recent phenomenon—a similar pattern holds in all four time periods included in Table 6.4. Using data from a single cross section thus suggests that educational progress stops after the second generation. However, the third-plus generation

Table 6.4 Educational attainment by immigrant generation, United States

Year	% not completed secondary school				% attended college			
	1st gen.	2nd gen.		3rd+ gen.	1st gen.	2nd gen.		3rd+ gen.
		1 immigrant parent	*2 immigrant parents*			*1 immigrant parent*	*2 immigrant parents*	
1950	76	56	63	62	9	18	14	16
1970	51	34	46	41	24	30	21	25
1994–1996	42	10	12	12	35	59	58	52
2011–2013	37	6	9	7	36	70	68	63

Source: Calculations based on adults aged 25 to 64 using 1950 and 1970 Census and 1994–1996 and 2011–2013 March Current Population Survey data from Ruggles et al. (2010) and King et al. (2010).

does make educational gains relative to the second generation about 20 years earlier. The difference in the results illustrates the pitfalls of using a single cross section instead of repeated cross sections to measure intergenerational progress.

Performance on standardized tests offers another perspective on educational progress and assimilation across immigrant generations. Scores on reading and math exams among the second generation are strongly related to education levels among the first generation (Dustmann, Frattini and Lanzana, 2012). In countries where immigrant parents tend to be well educated, such as Australia and Canada, the second generation tends to do at least as well as the third-plus generation on exams. But in countries where immigrant parents tend to have relatively low levels of education, such as Denmark, Germany, Norway and Sweden, the second generation does worse than the third-plus generation on exams.

Several factors play a role in how well the second generation does in terms of education. Parental education is a key determinant. Highly educated parents have highly educated children, on average. As Table 6.2 indicates, intergenerational transmission of education is strong in the United States. This is the result of a number of factors, including parental resources, ability and emphasis on education.

The structure of a country's educational system may matter as well. Systems that are more open and inclusive may do better at integrating immigrants' children than closed systems that track children from a relatively young age. Whether funding and curriculum are the same across schools within a country may affect intergenerational mobility and transmission of education, particularly if immigrants are concentrated in ethnic enclaves. The pace of assimilation among the second generation likely accelerates once they reach school age and interact more with their peers and less with their family. School systems that provide more opportunity for interaction between the various immigrant generations likely foster more rapid integration.

Whether immigrants expect to remain in the destination country may affect not only their own educational investments but also their children's. As discussed in Chapter 5, immigrants who expect to remain in the destination country have more incentive to invest in acquiring destination-specific skills. They also have more incentive to invest in their children's acquisition of destination-specific skills (Dustmann, 2008). One of many factors that influences whether immigrant parents intend to remain in the destination is whether their children are citizens of that country. After Germany began issuing citizenship to children born in Germany to long-time legal residents, immigrant parents there became more involved in the community and more likely to speak German (Avitabile, Clots-Figueras and Masella, 2013). Such changes are likely to lead to better outcomes not only for the parents but also for the second generation and beyond.

Language proficiency

Not surprisingly, proficiency in the language of the destination is higher among the second generation than among the first generation. The typical pattern is that first-generation immigrant parents speak their native language to their children, who become proficient in speaking that language but not in reading and, particularly, writing it. Because they attend school in the destination, most of the second generation becomes proficient in the language of the destination even if it is not spoken at home. The third generation typically has at most limited proficiency in the first generation's native language and is fluent in the language of the destination.

Table 6.5 reports the fraction of children in the United States ages 5 to 17 living with both parents who speak a language other than English at home in 1980–2010.[5] If the child is an immigrant, the odds are very high that the child speaks a language other than English at home—between 75 and 82 percent of such children speak a language other than English at home. If the child was born in the United States and only one parent is an immigrant, the child is quite likely to speak only English at home. Only 26 to 40 percent of such children speak a language other than English at home. But if both parents are immigrants, the child is almost as likely as a foreign-born child to speak a language other than English at home. If both parents are born in the United States, the child is very unlikely to speak a language other than English at home. Less than 5 percent of third-plus-generation children speak a language other than English at home.

The fact that a child speaks a language other than English at home does not mean that the child is not proficient in English. In 2010, fewer than one in ten children who are themselves immigrants—members of the 1.5 generation—do not speak English at least well. Among second-generation children, less than 5 percent do not speak English at least well. Of course, it should be noted that this measure of English proficiency is reported by an adult in the

Table 6.5 Percentage of children in the United States who speak a language other than English at home

Year	1st gen.	2nd gen.		3rd+ gen.
		1 immigrant parent	2 immigrant parents	
1980	75.3	25.8	68.7	4.3
1990	87.7	30.8	78.7	4.6
2000	85.5	36.2	82.5	4.6
2010	81.8	40.1	81.3	4.7

Source: Calculations based on children aged 5 to 17 who live with both parents using 1980–2000 Census or 2010 American Community Survey data by Ruggles et al. (2010).

household, and immigrant parents may overestimate their children's ability to speak the language of the destination. However, other measures, such as scores on reading exams, also indicate that the vast majority of the second and higher generations are proficient in the language of the destination by the time they finish school.

How well their parents speak the language of the destination plays an important role in determining how well children in the second generation speak that language. However, Hoyt Bleakley and Aimee Chin (2008) show that, in the United States, the effect of parents' proficiency in English on children's proficiency weakens as children age and appears to no longer matter by age 12. However, immigrant parents' ability to speak English does affect some outcomes among older second-generation youth. Bleakley and Chin show that immigrant parents' ability to speak English affects whether their children drop out of high school and whether their children are in the usual grade for their age. These effects only hold among parents from poor countries. If parents are from high-income countries, parental proficiency in English does not affect educational outcomes among the second generation.

The second and higher generations are more likely to speak a language other than the language of the destination if they live in an ethnic enclave. Living in an enclave does not necessarily mean that the second and higher generations do not become proficient in the language of the destination, however. In addition, being able to speak more than one language can lead to economic advantages. Bilingualism is associated with cognitive advantages, and bilinguals tend to complete more education than monolinguals, particularly when parental education and income are taken into account. However, bilinguals generally do not earn more than monolinguals in the United States after their higher educational attainment is taken into account (e.g., Fry and Lowell, 2003). One exception is that nurses in the United States who are bilingual in Spanish and English earn up to 7 percent more than nurses who only speak English (Kalist, 2005).

Marriage and fertility

As discussed in Chapter 5, intermarriage is an important indicator of assimilation because it implies both that immigrants are integrating with natives and that natives accept immigrants. In the United States, first-generation immigrants are more likely to be married to another first-generation immigrant than to a native, while natives are much more likely to be married to another native than to an immigrant. Members of the second generation fall somewhere in between. In 1994–1996, three of five adults in the second generation were married to a native, while about one in five were married to another member of the second generation (Card, DiNardo and Estes, 2000). (The other one in five were married to a first-generation immigrant.) In couples where both spouses are second-generation immigrants, both spouses' fathers are typically from the same country.

Age at marriage is related to whether second-generation immigrants marry within their ethnic group (Furtado and Trejo, 2013). People who marry younger are more likely to marry within their ethnic group. This could be due to greater influence of parental preferences on younger adults. It also could be due to exposure—younger people may have had less opportunity to meet people outside their ethnic group.

The size and composition of the ethnic group appears to affect whether second-generation immigrants marry within their ethnic group. People tend to marry not only within their ethnic group but also within their education group. Economists call this pattern "assortative mating." For example, second-generation Italians tend to marry other second-generation Italians, and college graduates tend to marry other college graduates. However, if the number of potential spouses within the same education and ethnic group is small, people are more likely to marry outside at least one of the groups. Research on the United States indicates that the second and higher generations increasingly prioritize marrying within their education group over marrying within their ethnic group (Kalmijn, 1993; Furtado and Theodoropoulos, 2011).

Fertility rates among the second generation are positively related to fertility rates among the first generation. If first-generation immigrant women from a given country have a higher fertility rate, second-generation immigrant women whose mothers are from that country will also typically have a higher fertility rate. The fertility rate among second-generation immigrant women is also positively related to the fertility rate among first-generation immigrant women from their father's country. Blau and her colleagues (2013) document this pattern in the United States and suggest that it is due at least in part to intergenerational transmission of gender roles. They find an intergenerational elasticity of fertility of 0.4 from first- to second-generation immigrants in the United States.

Fertility rates among the second generation also are positively related to fertility rates in the first generation's country of origin. The higher the birth rate in her mother's origin country, the more children a second-generation woman living in the United States typically has (Fernández and Fogli, 2009). Gender roles and other cultural attitudes that influence fertility in the origin country thus appear to be transmitted to the second generation in the destination country.

Ethnic identity

The more generations removed a person is from his immigrant ancestors, the less that person tends to identify with those ancestors' origin countries. Since ties to those origin countries typically grow weaker with each successive generation, it may come as no surprise that many people in the third or fourth generation do not base their ethnic identity on their grandparents' or great-grandparents' origin. More surprisingly, some people in the second generation do not base their ethnic identity on their parents' origin. Most surprisingly of all, not everyone in the first generation bases his identity on his origin.

Table 6.6 reports estimated ethnic attrition rates for select groups of Hispanics and Asians in the United States. Brian Duncan and Stephen Trejo (2012) calculated these based on country of birth for the first generation, and parents' country of birth for the second generation. The fraction of the first generation that does not report belonging to the ethnic group corresponding to their country of birth (e.g., Indian for someone born in India) ranges from 1.1 to 8.5 percent. Of course, some of these people may not actually belong to that ethnic group, such as people of French ancestry who were born in India and subsequently immigrated to the United States. Nonetheless, the estimated ethnic attrition rates are surprisingly high for the first generation.

The estimated ethnic attrition rates are much higher for the second generation than for the first. One key reason for this is intermarriage. If two parents are from different origin countries or different ethnic groups, their children must choose whether to identify with only one, both or neither of those origin countries or ethnic groups. The three columns on the right of

Table 6.6 Ethnic attrition rates in the United States, by immigrant generation

Country	1st gen.	2nd gen.		
		Both parents born in country	*Only father born in country*	*Only mother born in country*
China	1.8	4.6	27.4	42.5
Cuba	2.2	5.2	31.4	31.6
Dominican Republic	10.1	11.7	23.2	23.5
El Salvador	3.1	23.6	88.1	83.8
India	8.5	14.5	68.7	84.1
Japan	3.4	2.3	26.7	41.6
Korea	1.7	2.6	42.0	31.5
Mexico	1.1	2.1	8.3	10.2
Philippines	4.1	4.8	31.3	51.1

Source: Based on Figures 1 and 2 of Duncan and Trejo (2012).

Table 6.6 show the ethnic attrition rate if people report that both parents are from a given country, the father only or the mother only. Ethnic attrition rates are much lower if both parents are from the same country. There is no clear pattern in whether the second generation is more likely to self-identify with the mother's ethnic group or the father's ethnic group if the mother and father are from different countries.

Parents who are particularly concerned with passing their ethnic identity to their children are more likely to marry within their ethnic group and to require their children to engage in activities that reinforce that identity. The role of intermarriage in ethnic identification is therefore more complicated than it may initially appear. People who are willing to marry someone not from their ethnic group may attach less importance to being part of that ethnic group and pass that along to their children regardless of who they marry.

People change their racial or ethnic identity over time. Research indicates that almost 6 million people in the United States reported a different race or ethnicity in 2010 than in 2000 (Liebler et al., 2014). The most common change was reporting being Hispanic and "some other race" in 2000, and being Hispanic and white in 2010. (The U.S. Census has separate questions for race and Hispanic ethnicity). Self-identity may change as immigrants assimilate, or it may change in response to broader social forces, like how a group is perceived.

People may deliberately choose to not identify with their ancestors' ethnic group. This is particularly true if that ethnic group is viewed unfavorably or has relatively poor outcomes. If someone has a choice of ethnic groups to identify with, they may choose to identify with the group that has the best outcomes. Alternatively, people with the best outcomes may not have the same ethnic self-identity as people with the same ethnic origins but worse outcomes. People's self-identity may be systematically related to their outcomes. For example, research shows that third-generation Mexican teens living in the United States are 25 percent more likely to be high school dropouts if their parents identify them as Mexican than if they do not (Duncan and Trejo, 2011). In other words, among U.S. families with Mexican grandparents, parents whose children finish high school are less likely to report that they are Mexican than those whose children do not finish high school. Self-identification as Mexican appears to be negatively selected on education. Self-identification as Asian appears to be positively selected on education, in contrast (Duncan and Trejo, 2012).

Selection in ethnic self-identification can bias measures of intergenerational assimilation. Suppose two second-generation immigrants both have a mother from Ireland and a father from India. If the more successful member of the second generation self-identifies as Indian while the less successful one self-identifies as Irish, measured intergenerational progress will be slower than actual progress for the Irish, and faster for Indians.

Final thoughts on the second generation

As more people become immigrants around the world, the second and higher generations will grow as well. In the long run, immigrants and their descendants become part of a country, and the country becomes them as well. Traditional immigrant destinations—Australia, Canada, New Zealand and the United States—have sizable second generations that generally do better than their immigrant parents in terms of education and earnings (Sweetman and van Ours, 2014). Many European countries switched from being immigrant-sending nations to being immigrant-receiving nations within the last few decades, and the long-term performance of the second generation there is as yet unknown. The reception that the first and higher generations face depends in part on how immigration affects the economy, the topic to which this book turns in the next chapter.

Problems and discussion questions

1   Examine the data in Table 6.7 on UK immigrants by ethnicity and generation. The data are from the British Labour Force Survey for the period 1993–2007. The data are the percentage difference in hourly wages between immigrant/ethnic groups and second-plus generation whites. The estimates were calculated by Yann Algan et al. (2010) and take education and potential experience into account. What patterns do you see in the data? Do the data suggest intergenerational progress? How does the fact that these data are (essentially) from a single cross section affect your interpretation of them?

Table 6.7 Average income gap relative to native-born whites, by ethnicity in the United Kingdom

Ethnic group	Men		Women	
	1st gen.	*2nd+ gen.*	*1st gen.*	*2nd+ gen.*
White	−3.4%	−	−5.5%	−
Indian	−26.9%	−4.7%	−23.6%	−5.1%
Pakistani	−34.2%	−11.0%	−21.3%	−3.9%
Black African	−43.5%	−30.1%	−31.8%	−17.6%
Black Caribbean	−21.6%	−12.8%	−8.7%	−2.9%
Bangladeshi	−55.3%	−12.9%	−21.4%	−3.8%
Chinese	−27.4%	−9.4%	−17.3%	−2.3%

Note: Adapted from Algan et al. (2010).

2 Explain how positive selection in return migration is likely to bias estimates of inter-generational progress if the second generation remains in the destination country and a study uses data from a single cross section. Are the results biased if a study uses data from repeated cross sections?

3 Some studies indicate that first-generation blacks from the Caribbean or Africa do better in terms of earnings than their U.S.-born children relative to U.S.-born whites. What does this suggest about the direction of assimilation? What mechanisms might underlie this?

4 Bleakley and Chin show that, among poor families in the United States, second-generation children are more likely to drop out of high school if their parents do not speak English well. In higher-income families, there is no relationship between parents' English profi-ciency and whether the second generation drops out of high school. What might explain this difference?

5 What are some examples of activities that parents require their children to do in hopes of reinforcing their ethnic identity? When does economics predict that parents will be more likely to do this, and what types of parents does it predict are more likely to do this?

Notes

1 Calculations based on March 2013 Current Population Survey IPUMS data from King et al. (2010).

2 In *jus soli* countries, such as the United States and Canada, second-generation immigrants are native-born citizens. In *jus sanguinis* countries, second-generation immigrants are not native-born citizens unless they receive citizenship because one of their parents was a citizen. For example, a child born in India to a father who is an Indian citizen and a mother who is, say, a Ukrainian citizen is a native-born Indian citizen. If neither of the child's parents is an Indian citizen, the child is not a native-born Indian citizen. In some *jus sanguinis* countries, second-generation immigrants who are born there can become naturalized citizens as adults by meeting certain conditions, such as passing a test demon-strating their knowledge of the country's language and culture.

3 If the outcome measures on the left- and right-hand side of the equation are in logs, β gives the per-centage change in the left-hand-side variable for a 1 percent change in the right-hand-side variable. It is therefore called an elasticity. If the outcome measures are in levels instead of logs, β can be trans-formed into an elasticity by multiplying it by the ratio of the mean of the right-hand-side variable to the mean of the left-hand-side variable.

4 The years shown were chosen because the decennial Census stopped asking about parents' birthplace in 1980 and the Current Population Survey did not begin asking about it until 1994. Estimates are based on regressions of log wage and salary income on age (as a quartic), dummy variables for 4 of 5 education categories, dummy variables for being in the first or second generation and state fixed effects. People born in U.S. territories and possessions are not included.

5 After the decennial Census stopped asking about parents' place of birth in 1980, the only way to link across generations is to examine children young enough to be living with their parents. The Current Population Survey, which has asked about parents' place of birth since 1994, does not ask about language.

Internet resources

The New York Times has an interactive map that shows how different immigrant groups settled across the United States and when, available at http://www.nytimes.com/interactive/2009/03/10/us/20090310-immigration-explorer.html?exampleSessionId=1236781879280&exampleUserLabel=nytimes.

The UK's Office for National Statistics has maps of the distribution of different ethnic groups across England and Wales, available at http://www.ons.gov.uk/ons/interactive/census-map-2-1---ethnicity/index.html.

The Urban Institute's Children of Immigrants data tool generates charts and tables about the children of immigrants in the United States, available at http://datatool.urban.org/charts/datatool/pages.cfm.

Suggestions for further reading

Borjas, G.J. (1993) "The intergenerational mobility of immigrants." *Journal of Labor Economics* 11(1), pp. 113–35.

Sweetman, A. and van Ours, J.C. (2014) "Immigration: What about the children and grandchildren?" In: Chiswick, B.R. and Miller, P.W. (eds.) *Handbook of the Economics of International Migration.* Amsterdam: Elsevier.

References

Algan, Y., Dustmann, C., Glitz, A. and Manning, A. (2010) "The economic situation of first and second-generation immigrants in France, Germany and the United Kingdom." *Economic Journal* 120(542), pp. F4–F30.

Avitabile, C., Clots-Figueras, I. and Masella, P. (2013) "The effect of birthright citizenship on parental integration outcomes." *Journal of Law and Economics* 56(3), pp. 777–810.

Bauer, P. (2006) "The intergenerational transmission of income in Switzerland: A comparison between natives and immigrants." *University of Basel Faculty of Business and Economics Working Paper* 2006-1. Basel: University of Basel.

Blau, F.D., Kahn, L.M., Liu, A.Y.H. and Papps, K.L. (2013) "The transmission of women's fertility, human capital, and work orientation across immigrant generations." *Journal of Population Economics* 26(2), pp. 405–535.

Bleakley, H. and Chin, A. (2008) "What holds back the second generation? The intergenerational transmission of language capital among immigrants." *Journal of Human Resources* 43(2), pp. 267–298.

Borjas, G.J. (1992) "Ethnic capital and intergenerational mobility." *Quarterly Journal of Economics* 107(1), pp. 123–150.

Borjas, G.J. (1993) "The intergenerational mobility of immigrants." *Journal of Labor Economics* 11(1), pp. 113–135.

Card, D., DiNardo, J. and Estes, E. (2000) "The more things change: Immigrants and the children of immigrants in the 1940s, the 1970s, and the 1990s." In: Borjas, G.J. (ed.) *Issues in the Economics of Immigration.* Chicago: University of Chicago Press, pp. 227–269.

Chua, A. (2011) *Battle Hymn of the Tiger Mother.* New York: Penguin Press.

Duncan, B. and Trejo, S.J. (2011) "Intermarriage and the intergenerational transmission of ethnic identity and human capital for Mexican Americans." *Journal of Labor Economics* 29(2), pp. 195–227.

Duncan, B. and Trejo, S.J. (2012) "The complexity of immigrant generations: Implications for assessing the socioeconomic integration of Hispanics and Asians." *IZA Discussion Paper* No. 6276. Bonn: Institute for the Study of Labor.

Dustmann, C. (2008) "Return migration, investment in children, and intergenerational mobility: Comparing sons of foreign- and native-born fathers." *Journal of Human Resources* 43(2), pp. 299–324.

Dustmann, C., Frattini, T. and Lanzana, G. (2012) "Education of second-generation immigrants." *Economic Policy* 27(69), pp. 143–185.

Fernández, R. and Fogli, A. (2009) "Culture: An empirical investigation of beliefs, work, and fertility." *American Economic Journal: Macroeconomics* 1(1), pp. 146–177.

Fry, R. and Lowell, B.L. (2003) "The value of bilingualism in the U.S. labor market." *Industrial and Labor Relations Review* 57(1), pp. 128–140.

Furtado, D. and Theodoropoulos, N. (2011) "Interethnic marriage: A choice between ethnic and educational similarities." *Journal of Population Economics* 24(4), pp. 1257–1279.

Furtado, D. and Trejo, S.J. (2013) "Interethnic marriages and their economic effects." In: Constant, A.F. and Zimmermann, K.F. (eds.) *International Handbook on the Economics of Migration*. Cheltenham, UK: Edward Elgar, pp. 276–292.

Hammarstedt, M. (2009) "Intergenerational mobility and the earnings position of first-, second-, and third-generation immigrants." *Kyklos* 62(2), pp. 275–292.

Kalist, D.E. (2005) "Registered nurses and the value of bilingualism." *Industrial and Labor Relations Review* 59(1), pp. 101–118.

Kalmijn, M. (1993) "Spouse selection among the children of European immigrants: A comparison of marriage cohorts in the 1960 Census." *International Migration Review* 27(1), pp. 51–78.

King, M., Ruggles, S., Alexander, J.T., Flood, S., Genadek, K., Schroeder, M.B., Trampe, B. and Vick, R. (2010). *Integrated Public Use Microdata Series, Current Population Survey: Version 3.0*. [Machine-readable database]. Minneapolis: University of Minnesota.

Liebler, C.A., Rastogi, S., Fernandez, L.E., Noon, J.M. and Ennis, S.R. (2014) "America's churning races: Race and ethnic response changes between Census 2000 and Census 2010." Paper presented at Population Association of America conference, Boston, MA.

Ramey, V. (2011). "Is there a tiger mother effect? Time use across ethnic groups." *Economics in Action*, issue 4. San Diego: University of California, San Diego Department of Economics. Available at: http://economics.ucsd.edu/economicsinaction/issue-4/tiger-mother.php [21 May 2014].

Ruggles, S., Alexander, J.T., Genadek, K., Goeken, R., Schroeder, M.B. and Sobek, M. (2010) *Integrated Public Use Microdata Series: Version 5.0*. [Machine-readable database]. Minneapolis: University of Minnesota.

Sweetman, A. and van Ours, J.C. (2014). "Immigration: What about the children and grandchildren?" In: Chiswick, B.R. and Miller, P.W. (eds.) *Handbook of the Economics of International Migration*. Amsterdam: Elsevier.

U.S. Bureau of Labor Statistics (2012). "Time use of youths of immigrant and native-born parents, 2003–2010." Available at: http://www.bls.gov/opub/ted/2012/ted_20120712.htm [21 May 2014].

Part 3

Labor Market Effects of Immigration

7 Labor Market Effects of Immigration: Theory

Immigration affects both the countries that immigrants leave and the countries where immigrants go. This chapter examines how immigration affects the labor market in the destination country from a theoretical perspective. The chapter focuses on how immigration affects natives' wages and employment. Concern that immigration has a negative effect on native-born workers often dominates discussions about immigration policy, making this one of the most important topics in the economics of immigration.

The effect of immigration on natives' labor market outcomes depends critically on how substitutable or complementary immigrants and natives are in the labor market. If immigrants are substitutable for natives, foreign-born workers can replace native-born workers. Consider, for example, mushroom pickers in Ireland. An influx of Polish immigrants who are willing and able to pick mushrooms could adversely affect Irish natives who work as mushroom pickers since the skills required to pick mushrooms are not unique to natives. Being able to pick mushrooms does not require any specific education or language proficiency, for example. The increase in the number of workers will tend to push wages down for mushroom pickers. In addition, immigrants may be willing to supply their labor at lower prices (wages) than natives to mushroom growers. If so, then mushroom growers will be inclined to hire immigrants instead of natives in order to lower their production costs. In this case, immigrants will replace native-born workers. As a result, employment of natives falls, and wages fall for mushroom pickers. However, total employment of natives plus immigrants may not change—indeed, it is likely to increase since wages are lower.

Immigrants and natives could be complements in production instead of substitutes. Consider an IT firm in the United States that requires both managers and computer programmers in order to produce video games. Managers and computer programmers work together—they are complements in the production process. The United States attracts large numbers of computer programmers from India. For simplicity, assume that all managers are U.S. natives and all computer programmers are immigrants from India. Depending on the extent of the complementarities, an increase in the number of Indian immigrants could actually increase U.S. natives' employment and wages. An increase in the supply of computer programmers would lower their wages and hence lower firms' production costs. Firms might then expand output, which requires hiring more computer programmers and more managers. As demand for managers increases, their wages rise. In this case, immigration can benefit natives who are complements to immigrants in the production process.

This chapter discusses the conditions under which each of the above cases—substitutes or complements—occurs. Using the neoclassical model explained in Chapter 1, this chapter highlights the key assumptions in labor demand and supply that determine whether immigrants have a positive or negative labor market effect on natives. This chapter focuses on theoretical predictions, and the next chapter (Chapter 8) discusses empirical findings on the labor market impact of immigration in the destination country. In the chapter, we use graphical representations of the immigration model (and its various assumptions), while the appendix to this chapter includes details about mathematical representations of the model for interested readers.

Immigration model

Recall the basic model of immigration from Chapter 1 that graphed labor demand and supply for the destination (*D*) and origin (*O*) countries. Figure 7.1 combines the labor market graphs for the destination and the origin into one graph. The left-hand-side vertical axis represents wages in the destination country, and the right-hand-side vertical axis represents wages in the origin country. The number of workers in the destination is measured from left to right on the horizontal axis, and the number of workers in the origin is measured from right to left. The total number of workers across the two countries is *L*, the length of the horizontal axis. In each country, there is a demand for labor that is based on the value of workers' output. The demand for labor is higher in the destination country than in the origin country, as indicated

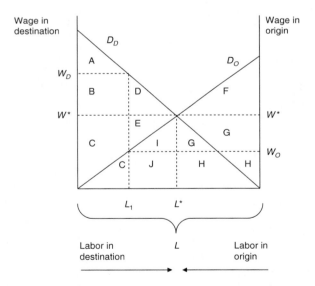

Figure 7.1 Welfare effects of immigration in the destination and the origin.

Before immigration, there are L_1 workers earning W_D in the destination and $L–L_1$ workers earning W_O in the origin. Immigration occurs until workers in both countries earn W^*, resulting in L^* workers in the destination and $L–L^*$ workers in the origin. Native-born workers in the destination lose area B after immigration. Native-born workers in the origin gain area G after immigration. Immigrants earn the sum of areas E, I and J.

by the higher vertical intercept for D_D than for D_O. This reflects higher productivity among workers in the destination. In both countries, quantity of labor demanded increases as the wage decreases. This reflects diminishing marginal productivity of labor, or each additional worker hired is less productive than the previous worker when other inputs to production are fixed.[1] For now, the model assumes that other inputs to production are held fixed (or constant) in order to isolate the relationship between native- and foreign-born workers. (This assumption is relaxed later in the chapter.) Although the demand curve may seem upward sloping for the origin country in Figure 7.1, it still represents the inverse relationship between wages and labor demand since it is "flipped," or a "mirror image" of most demand curve depictions, because the horizontal axis is measured from right to left for the origin country.

The supply of labor is assumed to not depend on the wage and is perfectly inelastic (a vertical line). This assumption is made for simplicity, but the general results of the model carry through if the labor supply curves are upward sloping (as discussed in the next section). Before immigration occurs, natives of each country supply all of the labor in that country. The pre-immigration labor market equilibrium in the destination is L_1 workers and wage W_D in Figure 7.1, and $L_O = L - L_1$ workers and wage W_O in the origin.

Focus on pre-immigration wages for a moment. In Figure 7.1, before immigration occurs the wage is lower in the origin country than in the destination country. Workers in the origin country have an incentive to move to the destination country because wages are higher there. Suppose that workers in the destination and the origin are perfect substitutes. A native-born worker in the destination is interchangeable with an immigrant worker from the origin. As migration occurs, the number of workers in the destination increases, and the number of workers in the origin decreases.

In the case of open migration, workers move until wages equalize between the two countries. This occurs at the point where labor supply (L^*) intersects labor demand in each country. Workers move until wages are the same in the two countries, so $W_D = W_O = W^*$ in equilibrium. This occurs at L^* workers in the destination and $L - L^*$ workers in the origin in Figure 7.1. The number of immigrant workers is $L^* - L_1$. The wage in the destination falls from W_D to W^*. Because labor supply is perfectly inelastic, all native-born workers in the destination are willing to work at the lower wage, W^*. Meanwhile, the wage in the origin country rises from W_O to W^* as migration occurs. (Of course, this is a theoretical model and we have assumed that there are no barriers to migration here. In reality, wage equalization has not occurred across many regions, especially across developed and developing countries.)

In this model, immigration creates winners and losers. Immigrants earn higher wages and are clearly better off: immigrant workers gain the areas E and I from migration (in Figure 7.1); prior to immigration they earned area J (in the origin country), and after immigration they earn E + I + J. (That area represents wages per worker times the number of immigrant workers.) Native-born workers in the destination are worse off because they earn less (their wages go from W_D to W^*). Before immigration, native-born workers earn B + C. After immigration, they earn only area C. Native-born workers thus lose B due to immigration. Before immigration, other factors of production in the destination (such as capital owners) earn area A. After immigration, they earn A + B + D. Immigration thus transfers area B from native-born workers to other factors of production, and it creates a net gain of D in the destination country. Area D is called the immigration surplus.

Table 7.1 Winners and losers from immigration

Group	Without immigration	With immigration	Gain (or loss)
Immigrants	J	J + E + I	E + I
Destination country:			
Competing workers	B + C	C	−B
Other factors of production	A	A + B + D	B + D
Origin country:			
Competing workers	H	H + G	G
Other factors of production	F + G + I	F	−(G + I)
Net gain due to immigration			D + E

Welfare gains and losses accruing to different groups in Figure 7.1.

Wages in the origin country increase due to the outflow of workers. Before immigration, competing workers in the origin country (workers who do not eventually migrate) earned area H. After immigration, those workers earn G + H. The workers who remain thus gain G. Before immigration, other factors of production in the origin earn F + G + I. After immigration, other factors earn only area F. Table 7.1 summarizes the winners and losers due to immigration. Overall, the winners win more than the losers lose. Adding up the gains and losses from Table 7.1, the net gain from immigration is the area D + E. The gains from immigration (which accrue to the immigrants themselves, workers in the origin and other factors of production in the destination) outweigh the costs of immigration (the losses to native-born workers in the destination and other factors of production in the origin).

This model is a simplified version of how immigration affects labor markets. Immigration can have different effects on natives' wages and employment, depending on the assumptions made about labor demand and supply. As the discussion at the beginning of the chapter suggested, immigration can raise or lower natives' wages, depending on whether immigrants and natives are complements or substitutes in the production process. The assumption in Figure 7.1 is that immigrants and natives are perfect substitutes in production—they substitute one-for-one with each other. In addition, the model assumes that immigrants can easily and costlessly move from one region to another. The next section relaxes this assumption by allowing for migration costs.

Immigration model with costs

The model illustrated in Figure 7.1 is the case of costless migration, when workers are free to move across borders without incurring migration costs or facing immigration restrictions. Of course, that is not the case in the real world. Migration costs can be significant. Explicit costs include travel costs and visa fees associated with a move, while implicit costs include psychic costs or cultural adjustments that people experience when they move away from their family and friends. Immigrants may incur costs associated with learning a new language and searching for a new job. The model in Figure 7.1 can be extended to include migration costs.

Assume that migration costs are constant and denoted by the parameter $C > 0$. If workers in the origin migrate to the destination, they must incur these migration costs. When migration costs are added to the model, the net gain to migration is smaller. Figure 7.2 graphs the basic immigration model with migration costs C. Equilibrium occurs when the net gain to migration (after migration costs) equals the return to staying in the origin. In equilibrium, workers migrate until $W_D^{**} - C = W_O^{**}$, which occurs at L^{**} in the graph. Fewer workers find it optimal to migrate compared to the case with no migration costs—only $L^{**} - L_1$ workers migrate (instead of $L^* - L_1$ workers, as in Figure 7.1). Wages adjust, but not as much as in the free migration case (when $C = 0$). Notice that in the destination, wages still fall when migration occurs (from W_D to W_D^{**}), but not as much as in the free migration case (W^*). Thus, the wage effects of immigration on natives are smaller when migration costs exist. A desire to protect natives' wages can motivate governments to restrict migrant flows. In fact, governments could charge sufficiently high migration fees to prevent legal immigration altogether.

The immigration surplus is smaller when there are migration costs. The gains to immigrants are smaller as well. With migration costs, there is a deadweight loss, or loss of economic efficiency, compared with free migration. The deadweight loss due to migration costs is the shaded area in Figure 7.2. Part of the deadweight loss is gains that would have accrued to other factors of production in the destination, and part of it is gains that would have accrued to immigrants. Theoretically, the world would be better off if there were no migration costs or immigration restrictions—the welfare gains would be bigger.

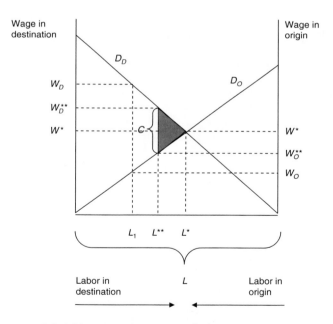

Figure 7.2 Adding migration costs to the basic immigration model.

Each immigrant incurs a fixed cost equal to C. In equilibrium, workers migrate until $W_D^{**} - C = W_O^{**}$, which occurs at L^{**}. The shaded area is the loss in social welfare due to migration costs compared with costless migration.

Upward-sloping labor supply when immigrants and natives are perfect substitutes

So far, the model has assumed that labor supply in both the destination and the origin is perfectly inelastic, which means that workers will work at any wage. Assume instead that labor supply has some elasticity—some workers are no longer willing to work if wages fall. If labor supply has some elasticity, the labor supply curve slopes up instead of being vertical. An upward-sloping labor supply curve is more realistic.[2]

Figure 7.3 graphs the labor market in the destination country when immigrants and natives are perfect substitutes. Notice that the labor supply curve is upward sloping. Immigration causes the labor supply curve to shift to the right, from S to S'. Wages fall from W_D to W_D'. Total employment increases from L_D to L_D'. However, with an upward-sloped labor supply curve, employment of natives falls from L_D to L_N because only L_N natives are willing to work at the new, lower wage W_D'. The number of immigrant workers is $L_D' - L_N$. The number of immigrant workers is equal to the rightward shift of the labor supply curve.

The key difference between an upward-sloping labor supply curve and the perfectly inelastic case is whether workers are willing to work at any wage. As immigration increases the supply of labor, there is downward pressure on wages. If labor supply is not perfectly inelastic, not all natives are willing to work at the new, lower wage. Some natives decide not to work at the lower wage, and employment of natives falls. Note that this has nothing to do with unemployment. Rather, it implies that even in a model of full employment, some native workers simply decide to exit the labor market altogether because the wage is too low to entice them to work. In the perfectly inelastic case, all native-born workers are willing to work at the lower wage, so immigration does not lead to a change in the number of natives employed.

The elasticity of labor supply has welfare implications. With a perfectly inelastic (vertical) labor supply curve, the immigration surplus is area C + F + G in Figure 7.4. If labor supply

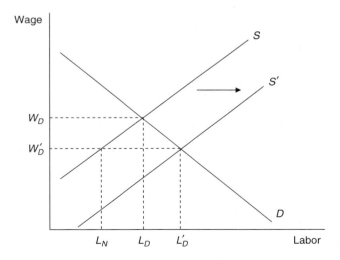

Figure 7.3 Effects of immigration in the destination with upward-sloping labor supply.

Immigration causes the supply of labor to shift to the right. The wage falls from W_D to W_D'. The number of natives employed falls from L_D to L_N. The number of immigrants employed is $L_D' - L_N$.

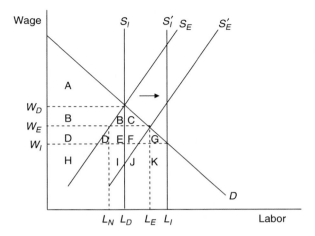

Figure 7.4 Welfare effects of immigration in the destination.

S_I and S_I' are perfectly inelastic labor supply before and after immigration, respectively. S_E and S_E' are labor supply with some elasticity before and after immigration, respectively. In either case, immigration causes the wage to fall from W_D to W_D'. Employment of natives is unchanged at L_D if labor supply is perfectly inelastic. Employment of natives falls from L_D to L_E if labor supply has some elasticity.

has some elasticity, the immigration surplus is just area C. Other factors of production in the destination earn A + B + C + D + E + F + G after immigration if labor supply is perfectly inelastic, and just A + B + C if labor supply has some elasticity. If labor supply is perfectly inelastic, immigrants earn J + K; they earn E + F + I + J if labor supply has some elasticity. If labor supply has some elasticity, some natives (LD − LN) exit the labor force and the wage falls to WE in response to immigration. If labor supply is perfectly inelastic, LD natives remain employed, but at wage WI after immigration. If labor supply is perfectly inelastic, the welfare loss to native-born workers is B + D + E. If labor supply has some elasticity, the welfare loss to native-born workers is B + E.

Labor demand

In addition to increasing labor supply, immigrants buy goods and services in the destination country. This increases aggregate demand. (Aggregate demand is the value of all final goods and services purchased in an economy in a given year.) Firms increase production to meet this increase in aggregate demand. Firms hire more workers, leading to an increase in labor demand. Labor demand increases because it is what economists call a "derived demand"—it depends on the demand for products (or final goods and services), which has increased because of immigration. As demand for products increases, output prices increase. This makes it profitable for firms to hire more workers. As a result, immigration increases total output, or GDP.

Figure 7.5 shows the effect of an increase in labor demand due to immigration in a destination country that has an upward-sloping labor supply curve. Notice that the shift in labor demand is smaller than the shift in labor supply. The increase in labor demand offsets some of the effects of the increase in labor supply on the wage. The wage still falls in this case, but it

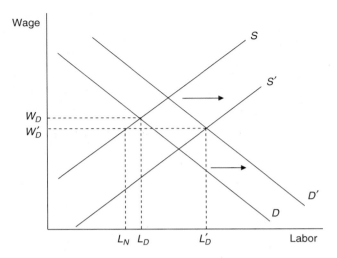

Figure 7.5 Effects of immigration that increases labor demand and labor supply.

Immigration increases both labor supply and labor demand, but the increase in labor demand is assumed to be smaller than the increase in labor supply. The wage falls from W_D to W_D'. The number of employed natives falls from L_D to L_N.

does not fall as much as it did in Figure 7.3 when only the labor supply curve shifted to the right. In addition, the loss in natives' employment $(L_D - L_N)$ is smaller as a result of the increase in labor demand.

The increase in demand mitigates the adverse effects of the increase in labor supply on natives' wages and employment.

In Figure 7.5, immigration increases labor supply more than labor demand. However, if immigrants do not work, immigration may actually increase labor demand more than labor supply. For example, immigrants might be retirees moving to a country with a better climate and more amenities. Alternatively, immigrants could be investors instead of workers. In this case, natives' wages and employment could actually increase due to immigration! If the effect on labor demand is similar to the effect on labor supply (the sizes of the shifts are similar), then immigration might have no effect on natives' wages or employment. This may explain why researchers often find small, if any, effects of immigration on natives' wages. There are many confounding factors that affect labor supply and demand. The effect of immigration on wages and employment is therefore truly an empirical question, which Chapter 8 covers.

Upward-sloping labor supply when immigrants and natives are complements

Thus far, the model has assumed that immigrants and natives are perfect substitutes in production. It is easy to imagine that immigrants and natives are not perfectly interchangeable. An immigrant may not be able to do work done by a native, and vice versa. Perhaps the skills that immigrants have are inherently different from natives' skills. Instead of being substitutes,

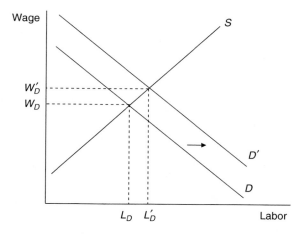

Figure 7.6 Effects of immigration when immigrants and natives are complements.

Immigration increases demand for workers who are complements to immigrants in production. The increase in labor demand causes the wage to rise from W_D to W_D' and the number of employed natives to rise from L_D to L_D'.

immigrants and natives may be complements in production. In this case, they do not compete in the same labor market. Instead, immigrants and natives work together to produce output. If more of one group is hired, labor demand for the other group increases. Consider the example of computer programmers earlier in this chapter. As the number of computer programmers (immigrants) increases, the firm needs more managers (natives). Thus, the demand for native-born workers increases. Or in the case of mushroom pickers, an increase in immigrant workers may help some native-born workers, such as managers or grocers.

Figure 7.6 shows the labor market effects of immigration on complementary workers. Since natives and immigrants do not compete with one another in the labor market, immigration does not change labor supply for the complementary input in the destination. Instead, immigration increases the demand for native-born workers. An increase in the demand for native-born workers (by itself) leads to an increase in natives' wages and employment. Meanwhile, the labor market for native-born workers who are substitutable with immigrants looks like Figure 7.3, and natives' wages and employment fall in that labor market. In the long run, some natives may retrain in order to move from a labor market where they are perfect substitutes for immigrants to a labor market where they are complements (or imperfect substitutes) for immigrants, which would increase labor supply in that labor market as well.

Unskilled and skilled labor

So far, the model has not differentiated workers by skill level. In reality, workers differ in their skill levels, and more-skilled workers are more productive than less-skilled workers. Because they are more productive, more-skilled workers earn higher wages than less-skilled workers. In equilibrium, the wage is equal to the marginal productivity of labor. That is, the equilibrium wage is equal to the value of the additional output of the last worker hired. Under diminishing marginal returns, an increase in the supply of less-skilled workers will reduce less-skilled workers' wages and raise the relative wages of more-skilled workers. Conversely, an increase in the supply of more-skilled workers will reduce more-skilled workers' wages and raise the relative wages of less-skilled workers.

Differentiating workers by skill level can have important implications for the labor market effects of immigration. If the majority of immigrants in a country are less skilled, they will compete with less-skilled natives and reduce their wages. Meanwhile, more-skilled natives will benefit if more-skilled and less-skilled workers are complements in production (they may also benefit in other ways, such as lower prices, as discussed in Chapter 9).

For simplicity, assume that there are only two skill levels: skilled and unskilled. Figure 7.7 plots the relative demand and supply of skilled to unskilled labor. S represents the number of skilled workers and U the number of unskilled workers. The horizontal axis is the relative number of skilled workers to unskilled workers, or S/U. The vertical axis is the relative wage of skilled workers to unskilled workers, or W_S/W_U. The labor demand and supply curves represent relative demand and supply of skilled workers to unskilled workers. (For simplicity, the figure assumes that the relative supply of labor is perfectly inelastic.) The relative wage reflects the return to being skilled compared with being unskilled, often called the skill premium or the return to skill. For example, a skill premium of 1.85 indicates that skilled workers (e.g., those with a college degree) earn 85 percent more than unskilled workers (e.g., those with a high school degree), or almost twice as much. In the United States in 2012, the college-high school skill premium was 1.85.[3]

If the destination receives an influx of skilled workers from abroad, the relative supply of skilled workers in the destination country will increase. Notice that the model assumes that skilled natives and skilled immigrants are perfect substitutes in production. This will result in

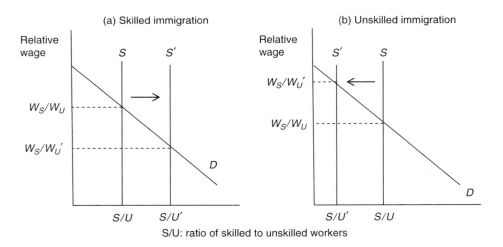

Figure 7.7 Effects of immigration with skilled and unskilled workers.

In (a), an increase in the ratio of skilled to unskilled workers due to skilled immigration reduces the relative wage of skilled to unskilled workers. In (b), a decrease in the ratio of skilled to unskilled workers due to unskilled immigration raises the relative wage of skilled to unskilled workers.

Box 7.1 Manual and communication tasks

In a seminal paper, Giovanni Peri and Chad Sparber (2009) extend the concept of unskilled and skilled workers to examine an additional dimension of complementarities between immigrant and native workers. They classify workers into two types: those who do manual tasks, and those who do tasks that require more communication. Using data from 2003 to 2008, Sparber (2011) documents that U.S. natives are more likely to hold jobs that require communication skills, while immigrants are more likely to hold jobs that require manual labor. Natives have a comparative advantage in jobs that require communication skills, while immigrants have a comparative advantage in jobs that require manual labor. In fact, Peri and Sparber (2009) show that natives will move to different jobs in response to immigration. This movement reduces the adverse effects of immigration on natives. For example, immigration causes natives—who have a better understanding of local networks, rules, customs and language—to pursue jobs requiring interactive tasks, while immigrants more often specialize in jobs that require manual tasks (and hence are relatively unskilled).

Figure 7.8 plots the relative demand for communication skills (C) versus the relative demand for manual tasks (M) based on the Peri-Sparber model. The same methodology applies to the relative supply curve. The vertical axis is the relative wage, and the horizontal axis is the relative quantity of labor. The supply curve represents a weighted average of immigrants and natives. (Here there is some elasticity to relative labor supply—some workers can move across types of jobs based on the relative wage.) The equilibrium relative wage is W_C/W_M, which corresponds to the equilibrium relative number of workers C/M.

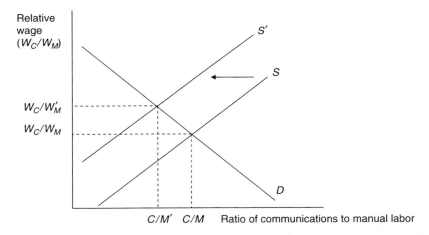

Figure 7.8 Effect of immigration on relative supply and demand for communication versus manual skills.

If natives are concentrated in jobs requiring communication skills and immigrants are concentrated in jobs requiring manual skills, immigration causes the relative supply of communications to manual labor to shift to the left. The wage of communications workers increases relative to the wage of manual laborers.

> If the native-born labor force increases, then the labor supply curve shifts to the right because there is an increase in the supply of communication skills relative to manual skills. If the number of immigrants increases, then the relative supply curve shifts to the left because there is an increase in the relative supply of manual skills.
>
> In Peri and Sparber's model, immigration shifts the relative supply curve to the left, as in Figure 7.8. The ratio of communication workers to manual laborers decreases. As a result, the relative wages of communication to manual workers increase. Therefore, if natives have a comparative advantage in communication skills, immigration will increase the average wage among natives by increasing the relative wage in communications jobs. However, there are winners and losers. In this case, natives in jobs with manual tasks have lower wages and less employment because of immigration.

a rightward shift of the relative labor supply curve, as in Figure 7.7(a). The relative wage falls, while the ratio of skilled to unskilled workers increases. The fall in the relative wage could be due to a decrease in the wages of skilled workers or an increase in the wages of unskilled workers, depending on the production process. Either way, the skill premium falls when skilled immigrants move to the destination country.

Conversely, suppose unskilled immigrants move to the destination. This would decrease the relative supply of skilled workers, leading to a leftward shift in the relative supply curve, as in Figure 7.7(b). The result is a higher skill premium and a decrease in the ratio of skilled to unskilled workers. Again, either the wages of skilled workers could increase or the wages of unskilled workers could decrease, depending on the production process.

The skill premium (the ratio of skilled to unskilled wages) is one way to measure income inequality in a particular country. As the skill premium rises, the gap between skilled wages and unskilled wages increases, leading to more income inequality. An increase in the number of less-skilled immigrants working in a country could increase the skill premium.

Elasticity of substitution between different types of workers

Economic theory indicates that the effect of immigration on natives' wages could be positive or negative. The effect depends in part on the elasticity of substitution between natives and immigrants. Suppose there are three levels in the production process. In the first (innermost) level, young inexperienced workers combine with older experienced workers to produce output. This level has an elasticity of substitution across experience groups, which measures the extent to which young workers are substitutable for older workers. The elasticity would be close to zero if younger and older workers (within an education group) are not easily substitutable, and it would be very large if they are easily substitutable. The second, or middle, level of the production process combines workers in different education groups. In this level, the elasticity of substitution across education groups measures how easy it is to substitute workers in one education group for workers in another education group (such as workers with a high school diploma for workers with a bachelor's degree). The third, or outermost, level of the production process combines labor and capital. This level concerns the elasticity of substitution between labor and capital.

In order for a researcher to measure the effects of immigration on natives' wages in this model, the researcher has to know the three elasticities of substitution. The three levels of the production are embedded in a nested production function with a constant elasticity of substitution (CES). The CES production function has become the standard production function in recent studies that try to measure how immigration affects natives' wages. The next chapter discusses the results of such studies.

Physical capital

So far, the model has ignored the role of physical capital in the production process. Most production functions include physical capital (K) as an important input to production. Physical capital refers to the infrastructure and equipment used in production; it does not include financial capital. Including physical capital in the production function yields an important relationship between capital and labor, regardless of whether immigrants and natives are complements or substitutes for each other in the production function.

Typically, economists assume that capital is fixed in the short run. That is, firms cannot change their amounts of infrastructure and equipment over a short time horizon. The models in Figures 7.1 through 7.8 assumed that physical capital is fixed and does not change. However, over time firms can add more infrastructure and purchase more equipment to use in the production process, which will affect workers' productivity. For example, if a new piece of equipment is purchased, workers will be more productive if capital and labor are complements, which increases labor demand.

The link between immigration and capital in the long run is unclear. Immigrants may bring capital with them, thereby increasing the stock of capital in the destination. But this is not usually the case, with the exception of immigrants who move for investment purposes. Alternatively, the firm may decide to increase its physical capital (in order to increase production capacity, for example). In either case, the relationship between labor and capital in the production process is important. If labor and capital are complements in production, immigration will encourage firms to increase their capital stock.[4] Importantly, the firm will adjust labor and capital until the ratio of the marginal product of labor (MPL) to the marginal product of capital (MPK) equals the ratio of the wage (w) to the rental rate (r) on capital (i.e., the price of physical capital), or

$$\frac{MPL}{MPK} = \frac{w}{r} \tag{7.1}$$

The ratio of marginal products—which is called the marginal rate of technical substitution—reflects the relative productivity of labor to capital. In order to minimize costs and maximize profits, firms will choose their mix of capital and labor such that the above equality holds. If immigration reduces wages, the ratio of capital to labor must be adjusted to keep this relationship in balance. If labor and capital are complements, both labor and capital will rise as firms scale up their operations.

Many economists believe that physical capital and skilled workers are usually complementary to each other in the production process, while physical capital and unskilled workers are

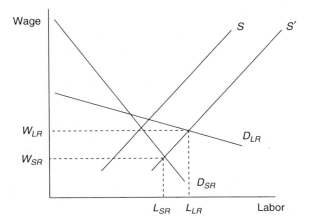

Figure 7.9 Labor demand is more elastic as physical capital adjusts in the long run.

In the short run, physical capital is fixed. Over time, physical capital adjusts. This causes labor demand to become more elastic and the labor demand curve to become flatter. The decrease in wages as a result of immigration is therefore smaller in the long run ($W_{LR} > W_{SR}$).

more substitutable for each other. The idea of capital-skill complementarity is simple. For production processes that require more physical capital (automated manufacturing plants, for example), firms need workers with more skills to operate and maintain the physical capital.[5] Meanwhile, physical capital may replace unskilled workers by doing repetitive tasks at a lower cost. Thus, the use of more advanced technology in the production process, which has led to more investment in physical capital, has reduced the demand for unskilled workers and increased the demand for skilled workers. This has implications for immigration. If immigrants to a particular country are primarily unskilled and substitutes for unskilled natives, then capital-skill complementarity will further deteriorate unskilled natives' wages. However, if immigrants are relatively skilled, then immigration can help meet the increased demand for skilled workers in the economy.

Over time, the stock of physical capital adjusts in response to the increase in labor supply due to immigration. This causes labor demand to become more elastic. That is, the labor demand curve becomes flatter. Figure 7.9 illustrates the effect of immigration (a rightward shift in labor supply) with short- and long-run labor demand curves. A flatter labor demand curve leads to a smaller change in the wage in response to the increase in labor supply. As is evident in Figure 7.9, the adverse effects of immigration on natives' wages are smaller in the long run than in the short run. Thus, the offsetting response of physical capital dampens (and possibly even fully offsets) the adverse effect of immigration on natives' wages.

Open versus closed economy

The model so far has assumed that there are two countries: the origin and the destination. The model initially assumed that labor could migrate freely between the two countries. In

Figure 7.1, wages in the destination were initially higher than in the origin. Once migration occurred, wages equalized between the destination and the origin (to $W*$), and the incentive to migrate disappeared. That is, equilibrium occurred when $W_D = W_O = W*$. This is called factor price equalization and is a common feature of international trade models when there are no costs of trade. The factor (or input) is labor. Factor price equalization states that the prices of identical factors of production, such as wages, will be equalized across countries as a result of international trade. If wages are equalized across countries, there is no incentive to migrate.

In an open economy model, labor, capital and goods and services can move across borders. Figure 7.10 shows the three components of international mobility. To be classified as an open economy, countries must allow for the mobility of goods and services (international trade), labor (migration) and capital (foreign investment) across borders.

In an open economy model, each country is endowed with an initial amount of labor and capital. Countries produce goods and services in which they have a comparative advantage based on their endowments. For example, if a country is abundant in labor (such as China), it should produce labor-intensive goods, such as clothing. Alternatively, if capital is abundant (as in Japan), then the country should produce capital-intensive goods, such as automobiles and computers.

The endowments of each country and the production functions for goods and services dictate how immigration affects natives' wages and employment. If immigration causes an increase in labor supply in a country already endowed with a lot of labor, the country can export more of the labor-intensive good. Natives' wages may remain unchanged in equilibrium even though labor supply has increased because the country can export the extra output it produces.

However, if countries cannot export goods and services freely to other countries (due to tariffs or quotas, for example), an increase in labor supply due to immigration could result in lower wages for natives. In this case, the model is a closed economy in that goods and services cannot freely move across countries. The extent to which a country is closed or open in terms of trade in goods and services and capital mobility will influence how immigration affects the labor market outcomes of natives. The production function matters as well, since it determines whether immigrants are complements or substitutes for natives and whether capital is

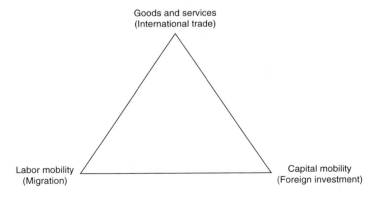

Figure 7.10 Three components of international mobility.

a substitute or complement for labor. As this chapter has made clear, how immigration affects natives' labor market outcomes depends in large part on the production function.

Final thoughts on the empirical labor market effects

How immigration affects natives in the labor market depends critically on how different types of labor are related to one another. Under some production functions, immigration adversely affects natives' wages. Under other production functions, immigration can have a positive effect. Economists must assume the nature of the production function—they cannot see it. Which assumptions are the most realistic is a heated debate among economists that has real-world implications. When setting immigration policy for a country, policymakers would like to know whether immigration hurts or helps natives' wages and employment. In order to resolve this debate, economists have turned to data to estimate how immigration affects natives in the labor market, using theory as their guide. The next chapter presents recent findings on the topic and sheds some light on the difficulties in measuring these effects.

Problems and discussion questions

1   Show using Figure 7.2 how large migration costs have to be for no migration to occur in equilibrium. What happens to natives' wages in this case?

2   Using Figure 7.1, show the labor market effects of an increase in labor demand in the destination country. What would lead to an increase in labor demand in the destination? Show the new equilibrium and explain the impact of the demand shift on the welfare of immigrants and natives in both the destination and the origin.

3   Suppose the United States experiences an increase in relative demand for skilled labor. Using the relative supply model of Figure 7.7, show how much the ratio of skilled to unskilled labor supply would have to increase to keep relative wages constant. What immigration policies could help meet the rise in relative demand for skilled labor?

4   Suppose the South Korean government tightens border security, making it more difficult for North Koreans immigrants to enter South Korea. Illustrate the effects on the immigration model. Show the effects on: wages in North and South Korea, the number of immigrants and the number of workers in each country. North Korean immigrants will experience welfare reductions due to increased border security. Show this welfare loss on your graph and label it "Loss." In addition, South Korean natives will experience welfare gains due to increased border security. Show this welfare gain on your graph and label it "Gain." Show the deadweight loss associated with increased border security. Label this area "DWL."

5   Now suppose South Korea had not increased border security (that is, we are back at the initial equilibrium). Instead, suppose South Korea enters a severe recession (which does not directly affect North Korea's economy). Draw separate labor market diagrams for North and South Korea (assuming perfectly inelastic labor supply in both countries), and analyze the effects of the recession on North Korean immigration. Illustrate the effects of a prolonged recession in South Korea on wages in North and South Korea and the equilibrium number of immigrants.

Notes

1 If physical capital is fixed, adding more workers to a firm will reduce their marginal productivity because the same amount of physical capital has to be shared among more workers, making each worker less productive.
2 A change in wages has two effects: an income effect and a substitution effect. The income effect causes people to work less when their wage increases. The higher wage allows them to achieve their target level of income with fewer hours of work. The substitution effect causes people to work more when their wage increases. The higher wage raises the opportunity cost of leisure (not working), leading people to substitute work for leisure. An upward-sloping supply curve arises when the substitution effect dominates the income effect.
3 http://www.census.gov/hhes/www/cpstables/032013/perinc/pinc03_000.htm (based on median earnings of people ages 25 and older) [20 July 2014].
4 Strictly speaking, this assumes that labor and capital are what economists call "gross complements" in production. A decrease in the price of one causes an increase in demand for the other.
5 The seminal paper on capital-skill complementarity is Krusell et al. (2000). Lewis (2013) discusses the role of capital-skill complementarity when analyzing the effects of immigration.

Suggestions for further reading

Krugman, P., Obstfeld, M. and Melitz, M. (2011) *International Economics: Theory and Policy, 9th Edition.* Boston: Pearson Education.

References

Borjas, G.J. (2013) "The analytics of the wage effect of immigration." *IZA Journal of Migration* 2(1), 22.
Card, D. (2009) "Immigration and inequality." *American Economic Review Papers & Proceedings* 99(2), pp. 1–21.
Krusell, P., Ohanian, L.E., Ríos–Rull, J.V. and Violante, G.L. (2000) "Capital–skill complementarity and inequality: A macroeconomic analysis." *Econometrica* 68(5), pp. 1029–1053.
Lewis, E. (2013) "Immigration and production technology." *Annual Review of Economics* 5(1), pp. 165–191.
Ottaviano, G.I. and Peri, G. (2012) "Rethinking the effect of immigration on wages." *Journal of the European Economic Association* 10(1), pp. 152–197.
Peri, G. and Sparber, C. (2009) "Task specialization, immigration and wages." *American Economic Journal: Applied Economics* 1(3), pp. 135–169.
Sparber, C. (2011) "Immigration and the employment opportunities of native workers." Mimeo, Colgate University.

Appendix

Analyzing how immigration affects the labor market requires making assumptions about the production process. This appendix explains in a more mathematical way some of the types of production functions that economists use.

Production function

The production function is a mathematical expression that relates inputs to output. The functional form of the production function tells how the inputs are related to one another (i.e., whether they are substitutes or complements). Economists make assumptions about whether inputs are substitutes or complements (i.e., imperfect substitutes) when they choose a functional form for the production function.

Natives and immigrants as perfect substitutes

If native- and foreign-born workers are perfectly substitutable in production, the production function could take the following form:

$$Y = A(L)^{\alpha} \tag{A7.1}$$

where L is the total number of workers in the destination, which includes natives (L_N) and immigrant workers (M) and $0 \leq \alpha \leq 1$. That is, $L = L_N + M$. The production function yields a functional form for labor demand. The demand for labor is derived using the concept of the marginal product of labor (MPL). The marginal product of labor is the additional output that an additional unit of labor produces. In other words, the marginal product of labor is the change in output if one more worker is hired.[1]

Using equation A7.1 and some simple calculus (not shown), the marginal product of labor in the destination is

$$MPL = \alpha A(L)^{\alpha-1} \tag{A7.2}$$

Importantly, in equilibrium, wages equal the value of the marginal product of labor. This makes sense: Wages should reflect how much the worker is producing at the margin. For example, if the worker yields an additional 20 units of output for the firm, the worker should be paid a wage that is equivalent to those 20 units of output. If the worker is paid less than that amount, he may not be willing to work for the firm. If the worker is paid more than that amount, the firm may find it unprofitable to employ that worker. Thus, in equilibrium, wages are exactly equal to the marginal product of labor. For values of α between zero and one, the marginal product of labor is decreasing in labor, thereby exhibiting diminishing marginal returns. The wages of natives in the destination are therefore

$$W = \alpha A(L)^{\alpha-1} \tag{A7.3}$$

Since natives and immigrants are perfectly substitutable, wages for natives and immigrants are exactly the same in the destination. An important property emerges from equation A7.3. As the number of total workers (L) in the destination increases, natives' wages fall. Equation A7.4 can be rewritten as

$$W = \alpha A \left(\frac{1}{L}\right)^{1-\alpha} \tag{A7.4}$$

Since $A > 0$ and L is in the denominator, an increase in L causes wages to fall. This result stems from the assumption that the Law of Diminishing Returns holds, and is reflected in the choice of the production function. The intuition is as follows: as more and more workers are added to the production process, the additional output produced falls since the additional workers are less productive than the workers already hired. In terms of compensation, since each additional worker adds less additional output, firms will pay workers lower wages. In this case, when immigrants and natives are perfectly substitutable, an increase in either the native-born workforce or the number of immigrants would lead to a reduction in natives' (and immigrants') wages.

Thus, in a standard production function in which native- and foreign-born workers are perfectly interchangeable, immigration causes natives' wages to fall.

Natives and immigrants as imperfect substitutes

Suppose output depends on the number of native-born workers (L_N) and the number of immigrant workers (M), but they are imperfect substitutes in production. An example of a production function in the destination is

$$Y = AL_N^\alpha M^\beta \tag{A7.5}$$

where $0 \leq \alpha, \beta \leq 1$. Notice that if $\alpha = \beta$, then equation A7.5 simplifies to equation A7.1 since $L = L_N + M$. (You may have seen a similar production function with labor (L) and capital (K). This is called a Cobb-Douglas production function.) Using equation A7.5, the wages of native-born workers in the destination are

$$W_{L_N} = \alpha A L_N^{\alpha-1} M^\beta \tag{A7.6}$$

Notice once again that the Law of Diminishing Returns holds: as the number of native-born workers (L_N) increases, natives' wages fall. However, equation A7.6 delivers another important result: as the number of immigrants increases, natives' wages increase. According to equation A7.6, an increase in the number of immigrants increases the marginal product of native-born workers, which is represented as a rightward shift in labor demand for native-born workers. (In a model with just K and L, this is analogous to an increase in capital causing labor productivity to rise.) As a result, natives' wages increase. This arises from the production function, which here assumes that natives and immigrants are imperfect substitutes.

Then immigrants' wages are

$$W_M = \beta A L_N^\alpha M^{\beta-1} \tag{A7.7}$$

Notice that an increase in the number of immigrants (M) lowers immigrants' wages. In effect, immigrants are competing with themselves for jobs, and having more immigrants puts downward pressures on their own wages. This point is often neglected in discussions about the labor market effects of immigration—the primary effect is usually felt by other immigrants, not natives.

Unskilled and skilled labor

So far, the production function has not differentiated workers by skill level. Workers differ in their skills. In the neoclassical model, workers are paid according to their skill; wages in equilibrium are equal to the value of the marginal product of labor. Workers who have not completed high school (unskilled workers) earn much less than those with a college degree (skilled workers). The production function in equation A7.5 can be extended to consider the role of unskilled and skilled labor:

$$Y = AU^{\alpha}S^{\beta} \tag{A7.8}$$

where U represents the number of unskilled workers and S the number of skilled workers. This yields unskilled and skilled wages (W_U, W_S):

$$W_U = \alpha A U^{\alpha-1} S^{\beta}, \tag{A7.9}$$

and

$$W_S = \beta A U^{\alpha} S^{\beta-1} \tag{A7.10}$$

Again, there are diminishing returns: An increase in the number of unskilled workers (U) will lower unskilled workers' wages but raise skilled workers' wages. Conversely, an increase in the number of skilled workers (S) will lower skilled workers' wages but raise workers' unskilled wages. Therefore, an increase in the number of unskilled immigrants in a country will increase wages for skilled natives. Alternatively, an increase in the number of skilled immigrants in a country will increase wages for unskilled natives.

Physical capital

Most specifications of a production function include physical capital (K) as an important input to production. The Cobb-Douglas production function with capital and labor looks like

$$Y = A(L_N + M)^{\alpha} K^{\gamma} \tag{A7.11}$$

where L_N is number of native-born workers, M is the number of immigrant workers and K is the stock of physical capital in the destination country (and $\gamma \geq 0$). Note that once again immigrants and natives are assumed to be perfect substitutes in production. Wages of natives and immigrants in the destination are

$$W = \alpha A(L_N + M)^{\alpha-1} K^{\gamma} \tag{A7.12}$$

The Law of Diminishing Returns holds yet again: as the number of immigrants (M) increases, wages fall. In addition, an increase in capital stock will increase wages.

Elasticity of substitution between different types of workers

Immigrants and natives may have some degree of substitutability for each other but not be perfectly substitutable. To account for cases like this, economists have developed the constant elasticity of substitution (CES) production function. A CES production function takes the form

$$Y = A\left[\mu L_N^\sigma + (1-\mu) M^\sigma\right]^{\frac{1}{\sigma}},$$ (A7.13)

where Y represents output in the destination country, L_N is the number of native-born workers, M is the number of immigrant workers, μ is the share of income from native-born workers and $\frac{1}{1-\sigma}$ is the elasticity of substitution between immigrants and natives. The elasticity of substitution reflects the ease with which firms can substitute immigrants for natives in the production process. The higher the elasticity is, the more substitutable immigrants are for natives. When σ equals zero, the elasticity of substitution is one. When σ equals one, immigrants and natives are perfect substitutes in production.

The CES production function gives the following function for natives' wages:

$$W_{L_N} = A\left[\mu L_N^\sigma + (1-\mu) M^\sigma\right]^{\frac{1-\sigma}{\sigma}} \mu L_N^{\sigma-1}$$ (A7.14)

The complexity of equation A7.14 is due to various cross effects between different types of labor. Based on equation A7.14, an increase in the number of immigrants (M) would cause an increase in natives' wages when σ is less than 0 (when the elasticity of substitution is relatively small).[2] However, when σ is positive, so that the elasticity of substitution is relatively large, an increase in the number of immigrants would reduce natives' wages. The value of σ is important in determining the impact of immigration on natives' wages.

Recent research analyzes an even more complex production function that differentiates workers by skill and nativity. This production function includes unskilled natives, unskilled immigrants, skilled natives and skilled immigrants using a nested CES production function (e.g., Card, 2009; Ottaviano and Peri, 2012; Borjas, 2013). This specification assumes that natives and immigrants are imperfect substitutes within a skill group. In this setting, the cross effects are more complex: Unskilled natives can interact with unskilled immigrants differently than skilled natives interact with skilled immigrants. The wage effects of immigration become more complicated. The adverse labor market effects of immigration on natives' wages become smaller when differentiating by skill levels in addition to nativity.

Notes

1 For students who are comfortable with calculus, this is equivalent to taking the first derivative of the production function.
2 To show this mathematically, take the derivative of equation A7.14 with respect to M.

8   Labor Market Effects of Immigration: Evidence

One of the most hotly debated issues in the economics of immigration is how immigration affects the labor market outcomes of natives in the destination country. Indeed, how immigration affects natives' wages is one of the most studied topics in the economics of immigration. Many people believe that immigration adversely affects native-born workers. Fears that immigrants take jobs from native-born workers and depress wages have been widely expressed in the media. In the United Kingdom, for example, almost 40 percent of the population agrees that immigration lowers wages (Dustmann, Glitz and Frattini, 2008). Despite the prevalence of such concerns, the evidence is less conclusive.

Theoretical models are critical to understanding the expected impact of immigration policy. As Chapter 7 explained, basic neoclassical theory predicts that immigration will put downward pressure on wages and employment of substitutable, or competing, natives in the short run. However, immigration should boost labor market outcomes among natives who are complements to immigrants. The canonical labor supply and demand approach to immigration indicates that there are winners—immigrants themselves, firms that hire them and native-born workers who complement them—and there are losers—native-born workers who compete with immigrants.

In more complex theoretical frameworks, the impact of immigration on wages is a function of a number of factors, such as differences in workers' skills, the speed of capital adjustment, the response of firms in terms of their production technology and output mix and the time period under study. These models can give ambiguous predictions regarding winners and losers. Theoretical models often predict different outcomes under different assumptions. To resolve this ambiguity, economists turn to data to test the underlying assumptions and predictions of theoretical models.

Surveys of empirical research conclude that the evidence indicates, on balance, that immigration has had a small negative effect or no effect at all on average wages among natives in the United States and Europe (Friedberg and Hunt, 1995; Longhi, Nijkamp and Poot, 2005, 2008; Dustmann et al., 2008; Kerr and Kerr, 2011; Peri, 2014). However, there is a wide range of estimated effects, from sizable negative effects to positive ones. One reason for the wide range is that different studies use different methods, each of which has limitations. Studies also examine different countries and different time periods, making it difficult to compare their results. Nonetheless, the balance of studies suggests that immigration has had a minimal impact on natives' wages.

Some economists interpret the lack of strong evidence of a negative wage effect as indicating that native-born workers are insulated from immigration. Immigrants may be absorbed into the workforce through responses by firms, native-born workers themselves or other adjustment channels. Other economists focus on the results of recent simulations that are heavily based on economic theory. As discussed later in this chapter, some of these studies tend to find more negative impacts, including a significant decrease in wages among workers who compete most directly with immigrants.

This chapter explains the four main methodologies that economists use to estimate the labor market effects of immigration: spatial correlation, natural experiments, skill cells and structural estimation. The focus is on how immigration affects natives' wages and employment. The chapter then discusses evidence on other effects, such as the possibility of skills and occupational upgrading; changes in production technology and the output mix; and productivity gains from immigration.

Brief review of theory

The predicted effect of immigration on native-born workers hinges on how substitutable immigrants are for natives. In the extreme, immigrants and native-born workers are perfect substitutes. Immigration increases labor supply. Absent an offsetting increase in labor demand, the equilibrium wage falls. Some natives may not be willing to work at the new, lower wage. If so, employment of natives falls even though total employment increases (as shown in Figure 7.3). Native-born workers are worse off: they earn less, and fewer of them may be employed as well.

For native-born workers who are complements to immigrants, immigration leads to an increase in labor demand. As a result, their wages and employment increase (as shown in Figure 7.6). Overall, basic neoclassical theory predicts that immigration lowers the wages of substitutable native-born workers, improves labor market outcomes for complementary native-born workers, increases the income of owners of capital and increases national income (GDP). However, in reality there may be other adjustments, and the effect of immigration on labor market outcomes may be more complex.

Empirical approaches

Studies that estimate the impact of immigration on labor market outcomes must address a number of empirical issues. The most important issue is endogeneity. Immigration does not occur in a vacuum. Immigrants typically choose when and where to migrate based on their well-being. Economic immigrants, particularly those who plan to work, often choose their destination based on economic opportunities. Immigrants may choose to go to places where jobs are plentiful and wages are rising. It may then appear that immigration does not have a negative effect on natives' wages and employment since natives have good economic opportunities in those places as well. However, natives' wages and employment might have been even higher absent immigration. Endogeneity or reverse causality biases estimates of the causal relationship between immigration and labor market outcomes—it makes estimates inaccurate. In some cases, the bias can be quite severe.

To further complicate matters, natives may choose to move away from (or not move to) places that are receiving immigrants. For example, did increased immigration in California in the 1980s and 1990s deter competing U.S. workers from moving there? If some natives leave or don't come when immigrants arrive, it will be harder to detect negative labor market effects. Offsetting migration by natives is an additional potential source of bias.

Another empirical challenge is to correctly categorize which immigrants and natives are substitutes in the production process and which are complements. In order to examine how immigrants affect natives, economists need to know which immigrants and which natives to examine. For example, are high school graduates substitutable for high school dropouts? Are immigrants with college degrees substitutable for natives with college degrees? After all, they may speak different languages, have a different quality of education, work in different occupations and so on. Combining substitutable and complementary workers in the same analysis may cancel out the effects and lead to the mistaken conclusion that immigration does not affect natives' labor market outcomes.

Lastly, firms may make adjustments in response to immigration in terms of their location choices, product mix, use of capital and scale of operations. For example, firms may move to areas or expand operations where there is an abundant supply of labor and greater demand for their products. Furthermore, in areas with sizable immigrant populations, firms may switch to more labor-intensive production processes and shift the goods and services they produce to ones that are more labor intensive. Empirical work that does not address these adjustment channels may reach inaccurate estimates of the effect of immigration and overestimate or underestimate the impact of immigration on natives.

To tackle these problems, empirical economists who study immigration have used four main methodological approaches: spatial correlation, natural experiments, skill cells and factor proportions models. In the spatial correlation approach, changes in wages and employment in areas experiencing large immigrant inflows are compared with changes in wages and employment in areas experiencing small immigrant inflows. The natural experiment approach also studies areas, but economists exploit plausibly exogenous variation in immigrant inflows due to laws, policies or events. In the skill cells approach, the labor market is divided into skill groups, and the change in immigrant inflows to skill groups is compared with the change in wages within those skill groups. Lastly, factor proportions models use structural techniques to examine labor markets. Economists estimate the elasticity of substitution between immigrants and natives and the responsiveness of wages to changes in labor supply and then simulate how immigration affects natives' wages and employment.

Approach #1: Spatial correlation

The spatial correlation approach examines the correlation, or relationship, between the number of immigrants in an area and the labor market outcomes of natives in that area. Because economists use data on multiple areas and compare across them, this approach is also sometimes called the cross-area approach. To date, the majority of empirical studies in the economics of immigration utilize the spatial correlation approach. Most of these studies focus on wage effects. The basic hypothesis these studies test is whether areas with more immigrants have lower wages than areas with fewer immigrants. The number of immigrants is typically measured as a fraction of the population or the workforce and is called the "immigrant share." The evidence in these studies is mixed, but most studies find evidence of only a small negative relationship between the immigrant share and natives' wages or even no relationship at all (Friedberg and Hunt, 1995; Smith and Edmonston, 1997).

The earliest studies using the spatial correlation approach use a single year of data, called a cross section. Figure 8.1 shows an example of the approach based on U.S. data from 2013. Each data point represents a metropolitan area. The horizontal axis is the immigrant share, and the vertical axis is average hourly earnings among natives. The underlying data are based on adults ages 18 to 64 who have at most completed high school, or less-educated adults. The line is the best linear fit for the data. Interestingly, it is slightly upward sloping. This suggests that the relationship between the immigrant share and natives' wages is, if anything, positive.[1] But a positive relationship could reflect many other factors, such as the tendency of immigrants to go to relatively high-wage areas.

Concerns that a single cross section, like Figure 8.1, reflects unobservable differences across areas, like higher wages in areas that attract immigrants, motivate studies to use multiple years of data. These studies examine the relationship between the change in the immigrant share and the change in wages within areas. Looking at changes implicitly controls for the fact that wages tend to be consistently higher in cities with high immigrant shares. This technique allows economists to see if immigrant inflows—the change in the immigrant share—have a negative effect on wage growth—the change in wages. Joseph Altonji and David Card (1991) use this approach to examine the effect of immigration on less-skilled natives using data for 120 U.S. metropolitan areas in 1970 and 1980, for example. They find no negative effect

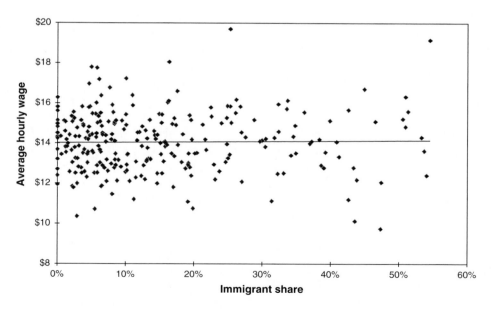

Figure 8.1 The relationship between the immigrant share and less-skilled natives' wages, 2013.

Source: Authors' calculations from the 2013 Current Population Survey Merged Outgoing Rotations Groups.

of immigration on less-skilled U.S. natives' wages or employment. Studies using the spatial correlation approach also find little evidence of adverse effects in Australia (Addison and Worswick, 2002) and a number of European countries (Brücker et al., 2002).

The main strength of the spatial correlation approach is that it is straightforward. Researchers find a region that experienced immigrant inflows and look to see what happened in that labor market and then compare it to what happened in nearby or similar regions. Researchers use regression analysis to estimate the impact of an increase in the immigrant share on wages or employment, holding other variables constant. There is typically only one parameter of interest, namely the elasticity of wages or employment with respect to immigration, and most statistical packages can produce output that is easy to interpret.

There are several potential problems with the spatial correlations approach, however, that researchers and policymakers need to consider. First, it assumes that changes in the immigrant share are exogenous, or that immigration is a supply "shock" to the labor market. In other words, it assumes that immigrants' location choice is not endogenous—immigrants do not choose their location based on changes in wages or employment. This is a strong assumption. Economists address this concern with a technique called instrumental variables, which requires finding a variable correlated with immigration but not directly related to the strength of the labor market in the destination.

Good instrumental variables are difficult to find. Most researchers use historical immigration patterns to predict contemporaneous patterns. This approach, sometimes referred to as the "shift share approach," exploits the tendency of new immigrants to locate in ethnic enclaves, areas where immigrants of the same nationality already reside.[2] However, if the economic conditions that attracted immigrants historically persist over time and continue to attract new immigrants, the shift share approach is biased as well. Other studies use variables related to politics or the weather as instruments for immigration flows. Such variables are not directly tied to the strength of the labor market in the destination. Some examples include identifying spatial variation in communist coups in Nepal; measuring rainfall at the origin area in Indonesia; and assessing access to paved roads and highways in Mexico (Bansak and Chezum, 2009; Kleemans and Magruder, 2011; Basu and Pearlman, 2013).

The second weakness of the spatial correlation approach is that it assumes that natives do not respond to immigration by moving out of an area. If out-migration by natives offsets in-migration by immigrants, the labor market effect of immigration is underestimated. The labor supply curve shifts to the right as immigrants move in and then back to the left as natives move out (see Figure 8.2). Further, labor market outcomes in other, comparison areas worsen as natives move there, even if they do not receive migrants from foreign countries.

Economists disagree on how much natives "vote with their feet" and move away from areas with large immigrant populations or inflows. In the United States, George Borjas (2006) estimates that the response by native-born workers can offset wage effects by 40 to 60 percent, whereas David Card and John DiNardo (2000) do not find evidence of a large response. Studies of European countries also do not find evidence of out-migration by natives in response to in-migration by immigrants (Hunt, 1992; Pischke and Velling, 1997).

The third weakness of the spatial correlation approach is its assumption that industries and occupations remain fixed in areas experiencing immigration. This may not be the case if new

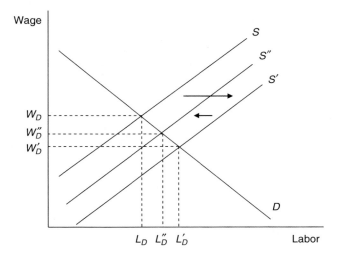

Figure 8.2 Effect of out-migration in response to immigration.

In-migration causes the labor supply curve to shift from S to S'. Out-migration by natives causes the labor supply curve to shift from S' to S''. The fall in the equilibrium wage is smaller as a result of out-migration.

firms enter those areas or existing firms change their product mix or production technology in response to immigration. Such responses would attenuate estimates of the negative wage effects from immigration.

A final problem is small sample sizes. The spatial correlation approach compares regions, such as states or metropolitan areas. Even large-scale surveys may not have samples large enough at the regional level to detect meaningful relationships between variables (Aydemir and Borjas, 2011). Indeed, this problem is evident in Figure 8.1, in which 14 out of 265 metropolitan areas have an immigrant share equal to zero. It is not the case that these areas do not have any less-skilled immigrants but rather that the survey did not have a large enough sample size to have captured any less-skilled immigrants in those areas.

Approach #2: Natural experiments

The natural experiment approach is oftentimes a variant of the spatial correlation approach. For example, economists might examine differences in immigrant shares and wages between an area that experienced an immigration shock—an exogenous inflow of immigrants—and an area that did not experience that shock. The optimal experiment would be to randomly assign immigrants to one location but not another and then observe changes in labor market outcomes in both locations. Since this is typically not feasible, economists try to find specific events or occurrences in the real world where immigration shifted labor supply in a plausibly exogenous fashion. Such "natural experiments" are typically caused by law, policy or an unusual event. The area experiencing the exogenous immigrant inflow is called the "treatment group." Researchers then find a plausible "control group," or an area that is similar to the treatment group in all ways except for the immigrant inflow. The control group shows what would have happened to wages or employment in the absence of the immigrant inflow.

The estimation technique typically used to examine a natural, or quasi-, experiment is the difference-in-differences estimator. Economists estimate the change—or difference—in an outcome, such as the average wage, in the treatment group before and after the immigrant inflow. This difference is compared with the difference in the control group. This second difference helps economists control for other factors, such as changes in economic conditions or in demographics over time. The difference-in-differences estimator, called D-in-D, applied to wages, for example, is

$$D\text{-}in\text{-}D = \left(Wage_{Treatment}^{After} - Wage_{Treatment}^{Before}\right) - \left(Wage_{Control}^{After} - Wage_{Control}^{Before}\right) \tag{8.1}$$

where the subscript indicates the area (treatment or control) and the superscript indicates the time (before or after the immigrant influx).

Studies that use the natural experiment approach find limited evidence of an adverse effect of immigration on natives' labor market outcomes. The seminal work using this approach is David Card's (1990) examination of the Mariel Boatlift. In 1980, Cuba's president, Fidel Castro, suddenly and temporarily allowed people to leave from the port of Mariel for the United States. About 125,000 Cubans, who were later called the *Marielitos*, moved by boat from Cuba to Miami, Florida. This event meets many of the qualities of a natural experiment. It was unexpected, and Cuban migrants moved to Miami because it is the U.S. city closest to Cuba, not because it had a particularly strong economy.

Card examines what happened to unemployment rates in Miami compared with four other U.S. cities. Table 8.1 shows the difference-in-difference estimator for whites and blacks. The unemployment rate among whites in Miami fell by 1.2 percentage points between 1979 and 1981. For blacks, it rose by 1.3 percentage points. However, in the comparison cities the comparable changes were a drop of 0.1 percentage points and an increase of 2.3 percentage points, respectively. If these comparison cities represent what would have happened in Miami in the absence of the immigration shock, the evidence

Table 8.1 Unemployment rates before and after the Mariel Boatlift

	Before (1979)	After (1981)	Difference
Miami:			
Whites	5.1	3.9	−1.2
Blacks	8.3	9.6	1.3
Control group cities:			
Whites	4.4	4.3	−0.1
Blacks	10.3	12.6	2.3
Difference:			
Whites	0.7	−0.4	−1.1
Blacks	−2.0	−3.0	−1.0

Source: Card (1990).

points towards a relative decline in the unemployment rate of 1.1 percentage points among whites and 1.0 percentage points among blacks. In other words, if anything, it seems as if the supply of new workers put downward pressure on unemployment rates, thus improving employment outcomes for natives. Card also shows that there was little effect on wages.

Why was there so little impact? Card suggests that the Miami labor market was able to absorb the *Marielitos* because of two possible factors. The *Marielitos* may have displaced other immigrants and natives who would have moved to Miami in the early 1980s had the Mariel Boatlift not occurred. In addition, firms may have responded to the influx by shifting their production techniques toward using more low-skilled labor, and firms that utilized low-skilled workers may have moved to Miami.

In another novel and influential work using the natural experiment approach, Jennifer Hunt (1992) examines the impact of the repatriation of approximately 900,000 people from Algeria to France after Algeria became independent in 1962. Repatriation is when people return to their place of origin or citizenship. Hunt concludes that the repatriation had little impact on unemployment or wages in France.

In a third important study, Rachel Friedberg (2001) examines mass migration into Israel between 1990 and 1994. People of Jewish ancestry and their spouses are able to migrate to Israel under the country's Law of Return. After Mikhail Gorbachev opened the borders of the USSR and allowed Soviet Jews to leave the country for Israel, the population of Israel grew by 12 percent between 1990 and 1994. Friedberg finds little evidence of an adverse impact on Israeli natives.

The natural experiment technique has several strengths. The first is that it is computationally straightforward. Difference-in-differences estimates can be computed easily. Second, this approach aims to avoid endogeneity by exploiting exogenous sources of variation. This approach tells a story and gives economists, policymakers and students the opportunity to make a convincing argument as to why the labor supply shift is truly exogenous.

Although this approach has benefits, it also has limitations. The first is that the natural experiment may not be truly exogenous. If this is the case, the results of difference-in-differences estimates may be biased. Finding a true natural experiment is quite difficult. If government policy creates the variation in labor market outcomes, the timing of the policy enactment, implementation and impact are not always clear. Policy does not occur in a vacuum. Policymakers, immigrants and natives may anticipate what will happen and react in advance. This is particularly true if there is a lengthy debate over legislation before it is enacted.

Second, it is difficult to find a valid control group. The labor supply shift may not be the only response to immigration. There may also be variations in supply and demand across regions that create confounding results. Joshua Angrist and Alan Krueger (1999) demonstrate this with regard to the Mariel Boatlift. In 1994, another Cuban boatlift was redirected to Guantanamo, Cuba, instead of reaching Miami. Using a natural experiment approach similar to Card's, they found that the unemployment rate among blacks rose by 6.3 percentage points in Miami between 1993 and 1995 compared with the control group cities. If the control group is valid, the difference-in-differences estimate should be zero since no boatlift occurred. This suggests that other factors affected the treatment and control groups differently. Similar differences could have existed in 1979 and 1981 as well.

Third, all of the concerns about the spatial correlations approach apply when natural experiments are used to make cross-area comparisons. Offsetting movements by natives or firms may occur. Firms may change their production techniques or output mix. Small sample sizes may not be able to detect the effect of immigration.

Approach #3: Skill cells

Studies using the spatial correlation and natural experiments approaches tend to find zero or small adverse effects of immigration on natives' labor market outcomes. Given the large magnitude of immigrant inflows examined, this seems to contradict the basic neoclassical model. However, those two approaches are vulnerable to the problems outlined earlier. Those problems motivate the third and fourth approaches: skill cells, and factor proportions models. In particular, the skill cells and factor proportions approaches can be applied at the national level. This addresses concerns that the responses of native-born workers and firms to an immigrant influx in a particular region diffuse the costs and benefits of immigration across an entire country. The skill cells and factor proportions approaches also attempt to focus on workers who are believed to be closely substitutable for one another in order to avoid capturing substitutabilities and complementarities that cancel each other out.

In an important study using the skill cells approach, Borjas (2003) uses skill groups defined by education and experience at the national level to examine the impact of immigration. He focuses on relative supply shifts within skill groups. In essence, the approach exploits the fact that the distribution of immigrants across age and education groups is different from the distribution of natives. Immigration therefore increases labor supply more in some skill groups than in other skill groups. In the United States, which Borjas analyzes, immigrants tend to be younger than natives, and immigrants are concentrated at the top and bottom of the education distribution. The basic neoclassical model predicts that natives' wages should fall in education and experience groups, or skill cells, where immigration inflows are concentrated. All told, Borjas's analysis has 40 skill cells (five education by eight experience groups). The underlying assumption is that immigrants and natives are substitutable within those 40 skill cells.

Figure 8.3 shows an example of the skill cells approach based on Borjas's study.[3] Each data point in the figure represents an education-experience cell. The horizontal axis measures the change in the immigrant share over a ten-year period. The vertical axis measures the change in natives' real log weekly earnings over the same ten-year period.[4] The line is the best linear fit for the data points in the figure. The negative slope of the line indicates that wages fell as the immigrant share increased.[5]

Using this approach, Borjas finds evidence of a sizable negative impact of immigration on natives' wages. His estimates indicate that a 10 percent increase in labor supply due to immigration leads to 3 to 4 percent decline in male U.S. natives' average weekly earnings. The effect is even larger for U.S.-born men who did not complete high school—the estimates suggest that immigration caused a 9 percent drop in those workers' earnings between 1980 and 2000. Thus, Borjas's national-level skill cells results suggest that the effect of immigration on wages is more negative than regional-level estimates from the spatial correlation and natural experiments approaches suggest. Interestingly, Borjas does not find evidence of a negative effect on the earnings of college-educated U.S. natives using the skill cells approach. In addition,

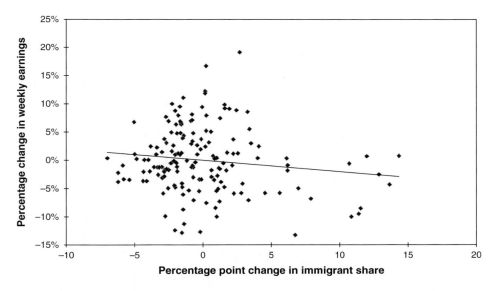

Figure 8.3 The relationship between the immigrant share and wages in the skills cells approach, 1960–2000.

Source: Authors' calculations based on data from Borjas (2014).

the skill cells approach indicates that immigration does not affect natives' employment, as measured by the fraction of weeks worked by the average working-age adult.

Similar national-level skill cells studies reveal negative effects in Canada, Germany and Norway. In Canada, a country with policies favoring skilled immigrants, the relationship between the immigrant share and wages is negative, with a 10 percent increase in the immigrant share reducing wages by 3.5 percent (Aydemir and Borjas, 2007). Studies of the influx of immigrants into Germany find a smaller but still negative impact of increased immigrant shares on wages at the national level, with a 10 percent increase in the immigrant share reducing wages by about 1 percent (Bonin, 2005; Steinhardt, 2011). In Norway, which experienced a large immigrant influx over the past few decades, a 10 percent increase in the immigrant share reduces wages by 2.7 percent (Bratsberg et al., 2014).

Studies have also applied the skill cells approach to regional data. Borjas (2003) also examines the education and experience groups at the state level, with up to 2000 cells per year. He continues to find that increases in the immigrant share reduce natives' earnings, but the estimated effects are about one-half to one-third the size of the national-level estimates. This suggests that "spatial arbitrage"—offsetting movements by natives and firms in response to immigration—cuts the national estimate of the impact of immigration by one-half to two-thirds. Pia Orrenius and Madeline Zavodny (2007) create skill cells by occupation and metropolitan area. They find evidence that immigration has hurt the wages of workers in manual labor occupations but not the wages of workers in service or professional occupations.

The main benefit of the skill cells approach is that, by dividing workers into groups, it may better focus on natives and immigrants who are substitutable for each other. The fact that it tends to find more negative results, particularly for low-skilled workers, suggests that this is the case. It can be performed at the national or regional level. However, it requires assuming that natives do not change their skill levels in response to immigration. This is reasonable in the short run but perhaps not in the long run. Like the spatial correlation approach, it requires assuming that immigrant inflows are exogenous or finding a good instrument to use to control for endogeneity bias. However, endogeneity is far less of a concern at the national level than at the regional level. Another limitation is that the skill cells approach does not account for possible complementarities between cells. For example, immigration by young workers who have not completed high school may boost the wages of middle-aged natives who have completed college, but the skill cells approach will not attribute those positive effects to immigration.

Approach #4: Factor proportions models (structural estimates)

The spatial correlation, natural experiments and skill cells approaches are called "reduced form" approaches. In essence, economists decide on a linear relationship (like the best fit lines in Figures 8.1 and 8.3) to estimate and then turn to the data. These approaches impose very little structure on the equation that economists estimate. Over the past decade, there has been a renewed interest in using structural methods to estimate the labor market impact of immigration. Researchers estimate or simulate a series of equations that build on key theoretical relationships. The set of equations is structural in that it specifies the structure of the labor market, or how different groups of workers interact with each other in the production process. These interactions are called cross effects.

In order to estimate cross effects, researchers need to make assumptions about the production process in order to make the estimation tractable, or possible given the data available. The intuition behind this approach is the following. The economist picks a production function, which specifies how many types of labor there are and how those types interact with each other and with capital. The production function has elasticities of substitution between the various types of labor and capital built into it. The economist then assumes that workers are paid the value of their marginal product of labor and estimates or simulates a complete set of cross effects. Although the assumption that workers earn the value of their marginal product is standard, there is considerable disagreement about how many types of labor there are and what the various elasticities of substitution should be. Those assumptions have huge consequences for the estimated effects of immigration.

In an important study using this approach, Borjas (2003) assumes that the functional form of the production process is a three-level nested constant elasticity of substitution (CES) production function. As discussed in Chapter 7, the three levels are the elasticity of substitution across experience groups within an education group; the elasticity of substitution across education groups; and the elasticity of substitution between capital and labor. Assuming that there are only three levels makes the model tractable, or computable. Once these elasticities are computed, the next step is to simulate how immigration affects the wage structure. Studies using these models usually simulate the impact of historical immigrant inflows. These simulations are typically conducted for both the short run and the long run. The capital stock is held constant in the short run, but in the long run the capital stock can change in response to changes in labor supply or wages.

A key feature of factor proportions models is the extent of substitution (or complementarity) between different groups of workers. Estimates of elasticities of substitution vary widely. This leads to a wide variety of wage effects in factor proportions models. Using high elasticities of substitution across education and experience groups, Borjas (2014) concludes that the magnitude of immigration that the United States experienced during 1990 to 2010 caused the average wage of high school dropouts to fall by 6.2 percent in the short run and 3.1 percent in the long run. For college graduates, the simulated wage effect is a 3.2 percent decline in the short run and 0.1 percent decline in the long run.

Gianmarco Ottaviano and Giovanni Peri (2012) challenge the assumption that immigrants and natives are highly substitutable even within education and experience groups. To do so, they introduce a fourth level of nesting to allow for complementarities (or imperfect substitution) between immigrants and natives within cells. They find evidence of complementarities in this framework as seen by an increase in the wages of natives within a skill cell in response to an influx of immigrants. Meanwhile, Borjas, Jeffrey Grogger and Gordon Hanson (2012) report opposing results. Their results indicate that there is significant substitutability between immigrants and natives within a skill cell.

Other studies have pointed out the importance of treating high school graduates and high school dropouts as different education groups versus pooling them together. Card (2009), for example, suggests adding yet another level of nesting to the theoretical model to account for the fact that not all skill groups are equally substitutable. In particular, he argues that high school dropouts are highly substitutable for high school graduates. If true, immigration of less-skilled workers to the United States has had a much smaller effect on labor supply than if high school dropouts are not highly substitutable for graduates. Most U.S. natives have graduated from high school, but many immigrants have not. Pooling these education groups reduces the relative magnitude of the immigrant influx. Determining the elasticity of substitution between high school dropouts and graduates is difficult. Results are sensitive to the specifications used and to the assumptions made about the relative demand for the two groups. As a result, it is unclear what elasticity factor proportions models should use for these key groups of workers.

The main strength of factor proportions models is that they are strongly rooted in economic theory. However, this strong theoretical underpinning is also their biggest limitation. The results of these models depend critically on the assumptions made about the substitutability of different groups of workers. As noted above, there is considerable debate regarding the elasticities of substitution used to generate wage effects. These models present simulations of the impact of immigration—they are only as good as the assumptions that the economist makes. Factor proportions models tend to be sensitive to the form of the production function, which the economist must assume. Most models assume a form of the production function that requires the long-run effect on average wages to be zero.[6]

Other channels of labor market adjustment

Immigration may affect other labor market outcomes besides natives' wages and employment. These include the possibilities that natives change jobs and firms change their production technology or output mix. In addition, immigration may lead to the adoption of new technologies.

These possibilities may account for the failure of many studies to find negative wage and employment effects. These margins of adjustment can attenuate the adverse effect of immigration on natives' wages and employment and are typically assumed to occur only in the long run.

Job upgrading by natives

One possible reason for the limited evidence of a negative effect of immigration on natives' wages is that immigrants may not be perfect or even close substitutes with natives. A number of studies suggest that immigrants and natives are only imperfect substitutes within skill groups. One reason for this imperfect substitutability may be differences in language ability. When immigrants first arrive, they may not have the language skills of natives, even within education groups. Because they have a comparative advantage in communication-related tasks, natives may shift into jobs that reward language skills. These jobs may be higher paying than the jobs that natives previously held.

Using data from the U.S. Department of Labor that categorizes the abilities needed for each occupation, Peri and Chad Sparber (2009) categorize occupations into those that focus on manual skills and those that focus on communication skills. They find that an increase in immigration to the United States leads natives with a high school degree or less education to shift from manual-intensive occupations into communication-intensive occupations. As shown in Figure 8.4, less-skilled immigrants are disproportionately represented in manual-intensive occupations, and less-skilled U.S. natives in communication-intensive occupations. Further, they find that manual- and communication-intensive occupations appear to be complements. Immigration therefore boosts labor demand for communication-intensive occupations, raising wages in those occupations. Peri and Sparber show that less-educated natives dramatically

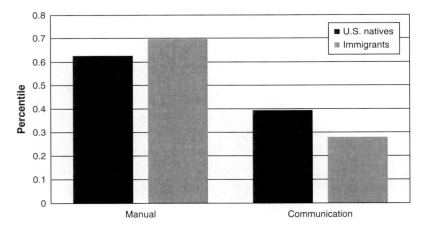

Figure 8.4 Intensity of manual and communication skills among less-skilled U.S. natives and immigrants, 2003–2008.

Source: Based on Sparber (2011). Shown are the average manual and communication intensities of occupations held by U.S. natives and immigrants who have at most a high school diploma, relative to the average intensities of all U.S. workers.

reduce their wage losses from immigration by specializing in communication-intensive occupations.

Similarly, Ottaviano and Peri (2012) develop a CES-type framework that allows for skill upgrading and specialization. They find that immigration to the United States between 1990 and 2006 reduced the wages of U.S. natives without a high school degree between 0.6 and 1.7 percent. Meanwhile, U.S. natives overall saw their wages increase by 0.6 percent because of immigration. These estimates are more positive than those found by earlier studies using the factor proportions approach. Ottaviano and Peri also find that when high-skilled immigrants, such as scientists and engineers, enter the United States, college-educated natives are more likely to move into managerial occupations.

Changes in input and output mix

Immigration may also affect how and what a firm produces. If there is an influx of immigrants, firms may shift to more labor-intensive production methods. Ethan Lewis (2011) finds that U.S. manufacturing firms added automation technology more slowly in areas where immigration caused the relative supply of high school dropouts to grow more quickly. This capital-labor adjustment attenuated the adverse effect of immigrant inflows on wages.

Firms may also change their output mix toward more labor-intensive goods and services in response to immigrant inflows. Immigration of less-skilled workers may have slowed the movement of labor-intensive jobs overseas, a movement often called "offshoring" (Ottaviano, Peri and Wright, 2013). An example is the immigrant-intensive garment industries in Los Angeles, California, and New York City remaining in the United States instead of moving completely offshore. Changes in output mix may even create jobs for natives who are complementary to immigrant inflows. However, economic research to date finds little evidence of sizable changes in output mix in response to immigration (Lewis, 2013).

Productivity gains

There are numerous production technologies available to produce the same goods and services. When there is an influx of immigrants, firms may adjust their technologies in response to the increased labor supply. If new immigrant arrivals are relatively unskilled, firms may adopt manual-intensive technology. If low-skilled labor and capital are substitutes, firms will substitute low-skilled labor for capital if immigrant inflows are predominately low skilled, as discussed above. But if new arrivals are high-skilled, firms may adopt more capital if high-skilled labor and capital are complements. Because the capital may make workers more productive, workers may see their wages increase. In addition, high-skilled immigrants may bring capital with them, further increasing the stock of capital in the destination and boosting wages among complementary native-born workers. Studies typically find that the adverse impact of immigration is smaller among high-skilled natives than among less-skilled natives and even zero or positive, perhaps because of such complementarities.

Immigration, particularly of high-skilled workers, may lead to increases in productivity. In addition to increasing capital, which increases productivity, high-skilled immigrant inflows may lead to innovation. If immigrants invent new technologies or bring new ideas from their home countries, productivity may increase in the destination. Studies suggest that immigration of high-skilled workers, particularly those in technical fields, leads to increases in productivity (e.g., Hunt and Gauthier-Loiselle, 2010; Kerr and Lincoln, 2010; Peri, 2012; Peri, Shih and Sparber 2014). In the long run, higher productivity is the only way that wages can increase.

Effects on previous immigrants

The most adverse labor market impact of immigration appears to fall on earlier immigrants, not on natives. Studies that reach differing conclusions about the effect of immigration on natives agree that immigration has had a sizable negative effect on earlier immigrants. Ottaviano and Peri (2012) conclude that during 1990 to 2006 immigrant inflows to the United States reduced the wages of earlier immigrants by about 6.7 percent. Borjas (2014) concludes that immigrant inflows during 1990 to 2010 reduced the wages of earlier immigrants by about 4.4 percent. It makes sense that previous immigrants are the group most affected by immigrant inflows. New immigrants are typically more substitutable for earlier immigrants than for natives. They are more likely to have similar education levels and quality, work in the same occupations, speak the same language, live in the same regions within the destination country and so on.

Concluding thoughts

It does not appear that there is a single right answer regarding the labor market effects of immigration on natives in the destination. Workers who are most similar to immigrants may lose, while those who are most different may gain. Empirical evidence on the wage effect for the average native-born worker—the topic most intensively studied and discussed by economists—appears to be inconclusive at best. As a result, this is an ongoing area for research, with new findings appearing regularly. In addition, studies are examining alternative adjustment mechanisms, such as changes in production technologies and output mix.

To summarize, although many studies find that immigration does not appear to have had negative labor market effects on natives in the destination, some studies do find evidence that certain groups, such as high school dropouts and previous immigrants, have seen their wages fall because of immigration. Studies that use the spatial correlation and natural experiments approaches tend to find smaller, if any, negative effects on wages and employment of native-born workers. Studies that use the skill cells approach or factor proportions models tend to find more evidence of detrimental effects, although there are exceptions. The labor market effects of immigration thus remain open to debate.

Problems and discussion questions

1   Suppose natives do not move to areas experiencing immigrant inflows. How does this affect the accuracy of estimated labor market effects using each of the four approaches described in this chapter?
2   Are all native-born workers likely to be equally affected by immigration? Why or why not?
3   How are firms likely to respond to immigration of high-skilled workers?

4   Describe the spatial correlation approach to measuring the effect of immigration. What are its advantages and disadvantages?

5   Think of another natural experiment regarding immigrant inflows. Why is it likely to be a good natural experiment, and what criticisms might it face?

Notes

1 The slope of the line is 0.232, with a standard error of 0.688 in an ordinary least squares regression. The slope therefore is not significantly different from zero.
2 The "shift share methodology" pioneered by Card (2001) hinges on the assumption that immigrants tend to move to and live where other immigrants from the same country already reside (immigration enclaves). The outcome of this approach is to decompose the current share of immigrants in a particular region (MSA) into a predicted share based on past immigration rates and a residual share. Card calls the predicted component the supply push component and uses this as an instrumental variable in his analysis. Many studies have followed suit.
3 Unlike figure II in Borjas (2003), Figure 8.3 uses data for both sexes and the regression line is not based on weighted data. The data represent 40 education-experience cells for four 10-year periods each during 1960 to 2000, for a total of 160 data points.
4 The difference in log wages is approximately the percentage change, or growth, of the wage.
5 The slope of the line is −0.0020, with a standard error of 0.0012 in an ordinary least squares regression.
6 Most studies assume a Cobb-Douglas production function and that the rate of return to capital is constant in the long run. This requires that the average wage be constant in the long run as well. In addition, the change in the average wage in the short run with a Cobb-Douglas production function must be capital's share of income times the magnitude of the shift in labor supply. Further, the nested CES model requires that the relative wage effects for different groups of workers be the same in the short and the long run.

Internet resources

The U.S. Bureau of Labor Statistics releases data annually on the labor force characteristics of U.S.- and foreign-born workers, including their earnings, education and distribution across occupations. http://www.bls.gov/news.release/forbrn.toc.htm

Suggestions for further reading

Peri, G. (2014) "Do immigrant workers depress the wages of native workers?" *IZA World of Labor* 42. Available at: http://wol.iza.org/articles/do-immigrant-workers-depress-the-wages-of-native-workers.pdf [10 June 2014].

References

Addison, T. and Worswick, C. (2002) "The impact of immigration on the earnings of natives: Evidence from Australian micro data." *Economic Record* 78(240), pp. 68–78.

Altonji, J.G. and Card, D. (1991) "The effects of immigration on the labor market outcomes of less-skilled natives." In: Abowd, J.M. and Freeman, R.B. (eds.) *Immigration, Trade, and the Labor Market*. Chicago: University of Chicago Press, pp. 201–234.

Angrist, J.D. and Krueger, A.B. (1999) "Empirical strategies in labor economics." In: Ashenfelter, O.C. and Card, D. (eds.) *Handbook of Labor Economics* vol. 3A, pp. 1277–1366. Amsterdam: North-Holland.

Aydemir, A. and Borjas, G.J. (2007) "Cross-country variation in the impact of international migration: Canada, Mexico, and the United States." *Journal of the European Economic Association* 5(4), pp. 663–708.

Aydemir, A. and Borjas, G.J. (2011) "Attenuation bias in measuring the wage impact of immigration." *Journal of Labor Economics* 29(1), pp. 69–112.

Bansak, C. and Chezum, B. (2009) "How do remittances affect human capital formation of school-age boys and girls?" *American Economic Review Papers & Proceedings* 99(2), pp. 145–148.

Basu, S. and Pearlman, S. (2013) "Violence and migration: Evidence from Mexico's drug war." Mimeo, Vassar College.

Bonin, H. (2005) "Wage and employment effects of immigration to Germany: Evidence from a skill group approach." *IZA Discussion Paper* No. 1875. Bonn: Institute for the Study of Labor.

Borjas, G.J. (2003) "The labor demand curve is downward sloping: Reexamining the impact of immigration on the labor market." *Quarterly Journal of Economics* 118(4), pp. 1335–1374.

Borjas, G.J. (2006) "Native-born internal migration and the labor market impact of immigration." *Journal of Human Resources* 41(2), pp. 221–258.

Borjas, G.J. (2014) *Immigration Economics.* Boston: Harvard University Press.

Borjas, G.J., Grogger, J. and Hanson, G.H. (2012) "Comment: On estimating elasticities of substitution." *Journal of the European Economic Association* 10(1), pp. 198–210.

Bratsberg, B., Raaum, O., Røed, M. and Schøne, P. (2014) "Immigration wage impacts by origin." *Scandinavian Journal of Economics* 116(2), 356–393.

Brücker, H., Epstein, G.S., McCormick, B., Saint-Paul, G., Venturini, A. and Zimmermann, K.F. (2002) *Managing Migration in the European Welfare State: Immigration Policy and the Welfare System.* Oxford: Oxford University Press.

Card, D. (1990) "The impact of the Mariel boatlift on the Miami labor market." *Industrial and Labor Relations Review* 43 (January), pp. 245–257.

Card, D. (2001) "Immigrant inflows, native outflows and the local labor market impacts of higher immigration." *Journal of Labor Economics* 19 (January), pp. 22–64.

Card, D. (2009) "Immigration and inequality." *American Economic Review Papers & Proceedings* 99(2), pp. 1–21.

Card, D. and DiNardo, J.E. (2000) "Do immigrant inflows lead to native-born outflows?" *American Economic Review Papers & Proceedings* 90(2), pp. 360–367.

Dustmann, C., Glitz, A. and Frattini, T. (2008) "The labour market impact of immigration." *Oxford Review of Economic Policy* 24(3), pp. 477–494.

Friedberg, R.M. (2001) "The impact of mass migration on the Israeli labor market." *Quarterly Journal of Economics* 116(4), pp. 1373–1408.

Friedberg, R.M. and Hunt, J. (1995) "The impact of immigrants on host country wages, employment and growth." *Journal of Economic Perspectives* 9(2), pp. 23–44.

Hunt, J. (1992) "The impact of the 1962 repatriates from Algeria on the French labor market." *Industrial and Labor Relations Review* 9(2), pp. 556–572.

Hunt, J. and Gauthier-Loiselle, M. (2010) "How much does immigration boost innovation?" *American Economic Journal: Macroeconomics* 2(2), pp. 31–56.

Kerr, S.P. and Kerr, W.R. (2011) "Economic impacts of immigration: A survey." *Finnish Economic Papers* 24(1), pp. 1–32.

Kerr, W.R. and Lincoln, W.F. (2010) "The supply side of innovation: H-1B visa reforms and U.S. ethnic innovation." *Journal of Labor Economics* 29(3), pp. 473–508.

Kleemans, M. and Magruder, J. (2011) "Labor market changes in response to immigration: Evidence from internal migration driven by weather shocks in Indonesia." Mimeo, Yale University.

Lewis, E. (2011) "Immigration, skill mix, and capital skill complementarity." *Quarterly Journal of Economics* 126(2), pp. 1029–1069.

Lewis, E. (2013) "Immigration and production technology." *Annual Review of Economics* 5, pp. 165–191.

Longhi, S., Nijkamp, P. and Poot, J. (2005) "A meta-analytic assessment of the effect of immigration on wages." *Journal of Economic Surveys* 19(3), pp. 451–477.

Longhi, S., Nijkamp, P. and Poot, J. (2008) "Meta-analysis of empirical evidence on the labour market impacts of immigration." *IZA Discussion Paper* No. 3418. Bonn: Institute for the Study of Labor.

Orrenius, P. M. and Zavodny, M. (2007) "Does immigration affect wages? A look at occupation-level evidence." *Labour Economics* 14(5), pp. 757–773.

Ottaviano, G. and Peri, G. (2012) "Rethinking the effect of immigration on wages." *Journal of the European Economic Association* 10(1), pp. 152–197.

Ottaviano, G., Peri, G. and Wright, G. (2013) "Immigration, offshoring and American jobs." *American Economic Review* 103(5), pp. 1925–1959.

Peri, G. (2012) "The effect of immigration on productivity: Evidence from U.S. states." *Review of Economics and Statistics* 94(1), pp. 348–358.

Peri, G. (2014) "Do immigrant workers depress the wages of native workers?" *IZA World of Labor* 42. Available at: http://wol.iza.org/articles/do-immigrant-workers-depress-the-wages-of-native-workers.pdf [10 June 2014].

Peri, G., Shih, K.Y. and Sparber, C. (2014) "Foreign STEM workers and native wages and employment in U.S. cities." *National Bureau of Economic Research Working Paper* No. 20093. Cambridge, MA: National Bureau of Economic Research.

Peri, G. and Sparber, C. (2009) "Task specialization, immigration, and wages." *American Economic Journal: Applied Economics* 1, pp. 135–169.

Pischke, J.S. and Velling, J. (1997) "Employment effects of immigration to Germany: An analysis based on local labor markets." *Review of Economics and Statistics* 79(4), pp. 594–604.

Smith, J. P. and Edmonston, B. (eds.) (1997) *The New Americans: Economic, Demographic, and Fiscal Effects of Immigration.* Washington, DC: National Academies Press.

Sparber, C. (2011) "Immigration and the Employment Opportunities of Native Workers." Mimeo, Colgate University.

Steinhardt, M.F. (2011) "The wage impact of immigration in Germany: New evidence for skill groups and occupations." *BE Journal of Economic Analysis and Policy* 11(1), pp. 1935–1682.

Part 4

Other Effects of Immigration

9 Effects on Other Markets in the Destination

The previous two chapters discussed how immigration affects the labor market in the destination country, specifically, how immigration affects the wages and employment of natives in theory and in practice. This chapter considers other effects of immigration on domestic markets. Immigration increases the number of consumers in the destination, which leads to higher demand for goods and services. In addition, immigration adds to the local labor supply and increases the supply of certain products in an area. These effects translate into competing effects on prices: an increase in demand will lead to higher prices, while an increase in supply will cause prices to fall.

In the case of housing markets, the evidence indicates that the demand effect wins out, and immigration leads to higher housing prices. Immigration does appear to lead to lower prices for some other immigrant-intensive goods and services, however. Immigrants can add to product variety in a local area by creating goods and services that would not otherwise be offered. In addition, immigration may promote international trade and financial investment by improving information flows across countries. Finally, immigration may have macroeconomic effects by affecting physical capital, output and consumption in the destination country.

Housing

Economic theory tells us that as the number of consumers of a good increases, the price of that good increases. This holds for housing: an increase in the number of households in an area will raise the demand for housing. This will result in a rightward shift in the demand for housing and hence a price increase, as shown in Figure 9.1(a). Note that the figure assumes that the supply of housing is relatively inelastic, which is certainly true for areas where vacant land is scarce, such as parts of London. The rightward shift in demand causes prices to rise from P to P'. The equilibrium quantity of housing will increase as well (from Q to Q').

The elasticity of housing supply varies tremendously across regions and states. If housing supply is more elastic in an area, then an increase in housing demand will have less effect on housing prices, as shown in Figure 9.1(b). Either way, an increase in the number of home buyers or renters due to immigration will cause housing prices to increase. The extent of the effect depends on how many immigrants move into a region and how elastic (or inelastic) the supply of housing is in that region. Thus, the impact of immigrants to the local housing market really depends on the local situation. In areas with inelastic supply (such as San Francisco), an

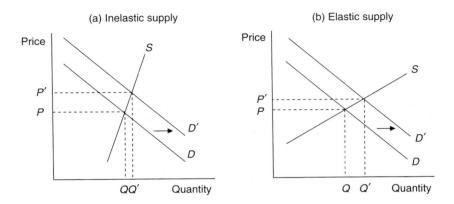

Figure 9.1 Effects of immigration on the housing market.

In (a), the supply of housing is inelastic. An increase in the demand for housing causes the price of housing to increase sizably, from *P* to *P'*. In (b), the supply of housing is elastic. An increase in the demand for housing causes a smaller increase in prices.

influx of immigrants will lead to significantly higher housing prices. In areas with more elastic supply (such as Phoenix or Atlanta), an influx of immigrants will have a smaller positive effect on housing prices.

Higher housing prices have good and bad effects. On the positive side, they raise the value of people's homes. For many households that are homeowners, their house is a large portion of their overall wealth. Thus, higher housing prices can have positive effects on household wealth. However, higher housing prices make it more expensive for households to purchase a house or rent, and immigrants may crowd out some natives from the housing market. That is, by making houses more expensive, fewer households can afford to buy or rent housing, particularly low- and middle-income households. The majority of the adverse effects of higher housing prices are felt by households with lower incomes. Once again, there are winners and losers with migration, but now the benefits and costs are in terms of housing prices.

Immigrants could potentially affect housing prices through another mechanism. An increase in immigration to a region could lead to out-migration by natives. Natives may prefer not to live near ethnic enclaves, or they move away from areas where there is increased competition for jobs. Housing demand would still increase due to immigration (as long as emigration does not completely offset immigration), but the net effect would be smaller since some natives leave the area, as shown in Figure 9.2. The resulting effect on housing prices would be dampened. Again, how much prices rise depends on how elastic the supply of housing is in that region.

If immigration and out-migration by natives are of similar magnitudes, immigration may have no effect on housing prices. This discussion shows how difficult it can be to tease out the effect of immigration since it may be offset by other effects. Economists therefore have to carefully analyze the various mechanisms that may be at play.

Economists have examined whether housing prices increase in response to immigrant inflows. Albert Saiz (2007) tests this hypothesis with U.S. data and finds that an immigrant

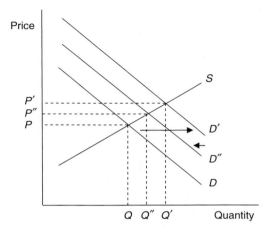

Figure 9.2 Housing market in the destination when natives respond to immigration by moving out of the area.

Immigration increases the demand for housing from *D* to *D'*. However, if some natives leave the area, the demand for housing may shift back part of the way (to *D''*). The resulting house prices (*P''*) are higher than without migration (*P*), but lower if there was no out-migration of natives (*P'*).

inflow equal to 1 percent of the population of a large "gateway" U.S. city leads to a 1 percent increase in rental and house prices in that city. Gateway cities are cities that historically attracted a relatively large share of new immigrants, such as Los Angeles and New York City. This effect is sizeable compared with the labor market effects discussed in Chapter 8. In fact, Saiz points out that the positive effect of housing prices appears to be an order of magnitude bigger than the negative effect on wages. In addition, Saiz's analysis indicates that immigrants do not displace natives one-for-one: although some natives may migrate out of an area in response to the immigrant inflow, the overall positive effect on housing prices suggests that immigration increases housing demand and prices.

Research on Spain also finds that immigration affects housing prices. Libertad Gonzalez and Francesc Ortega (2013) investigate whether the housing market boom in Spain between 1998 and 2008 was due in part to the large inflow of immigrants the country experienced during that period. The foreign-born population in Spain rose from 0.5 million to 5 million in ten years! At the same time, house prices increased 175 percent. Gonzalez and Ortega find that immigrant flows are at least part of the story behind the housing market bubble in Spain. Their analysis concludes that the immigrant inflows, which increased the working-age population by about 1.5 percent annually, led to an annual increase in housing prices of 2 percent. This effect is even bigger than Saiz's estimate for the United States. In fact, Gonzalez and Ortega claim that immigrant inflows explain why the housing boom was larger in Spain than in other parts of the European Union and in the United States.

Other economists have studied how immigrants affect the cultural diversity of a city. Gianmarco Ottaviano and Giovanni Peri (2006) measure the economic value that immigrants bring to U.S. cities. They find that immigration raised the average rental prices that U.S.

natives paid in major cities during 1970 to 1990; immigration also raised the average wage of natives, according to their study. Unlike Saiz, who argues that immigrants raise house prices by increasing housing demand, Ottaviano and Peri suggest that immigrants raise housing values because they bring cultural diversity, which some natives value, and higher wages.

Prices of goods and services

Immigrant workers contribute to the supply of goods and services. As discussed in Chapters 7 and 8, immigration may put downward pressure on wages. Lower labor costs may translate into lower prices for goods and services, particularly in sectors of the economy in which immigrant workers are concentrated.

For example, consider the landscaping industry in the United States. Approximately 30 percent of workers in this industry are low-skilled immigrants (Cortes, 2008). Immigration may have reduced labor costs in this sector, leading to an increase in the supply of landscaping services. Figure 9.3 shows the effect of immigration on the market for landscaping services. The price of landscaping services falls in response to the rightward shift in the supply curve.

This is also true for other industries in which immigrants represent a significant share of the labor force, such as housekeeping, babysitting and dry cleaning. All of these sectors are nontradeable services. Nontradeable services are services that are not traded in international markets. The country cannot import the service from abroad and therefore has to produce it using the local labor force. Nontradeable goods and services face less competition, and less competition can cause prices to be higher. However, if the labor force includes lots of immigrants who are working locally in these industries, that can help to keep prices down.

This is exactly what Patricia Cortes (2008) finds when examining U.S. price data during 1980 to 2000. Service industries, such as landscaping, in which low-skilled immigrants comprise a sizable share of the labor force, are classified as immigrant-intensive services. Cortes finds that a 10 percent increase in the share of low-skilled immigrants in the labor force causes a 2 percent decrease in the prices of immigrant-intensive services. Her estimates suggest that

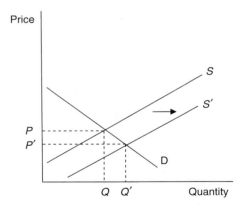

Figure 9.3 Market for landscaping services with immigration.

Immigration leads to a rightward shift in the supply curve for landscaping services. The price of landscaping services falls from P to P'.

U.S. immigrant inflows during 1980 to 2000 reduced the price of immigrant-intensive services by at least 9 to 11 percent in the average U.S. city.

Lower prices are a good thing for consumers. Undoubtedly, lots of families have benefited from lower prices for landscaping and babysitting. In fact, studies suggest that lower daycare costs due to immigration have encouraged more high-skilled female natives to work (Furtado and Hock, 2008; Cortes and Tessada, 2011). Cortes finds that high-skilled U.S. natives have benefited the most from the price decreases because they spend more on these types of services. Low-skilled natives benefit less since they consume less of these services. Meanwhile, low-skilled natives are more likely than high-skilled natives to compete with low-skilled immigrants in the labor market. Low-skilled natives are therefore more likely hurt by immigration through lower wages. Notice that in Figure 9.3, the demand for landscaping services does not increase as a result of more immigration. It is not likely that many low-skilled immigrants would use landscaping services given their relatively low incomes. Therefore, more immigration of low-skilled workers would not lead to an increase in the demand for landscaping workers that could offset the negative wage effect of the increase in labor supply.

Immigrants do increase the demand for certain goods and services, which can put upward pressure on prices. In addition to housing, immigrants increase the demand for many different types of necessities (such as food) and wants (such as cell phones), which can make those goods and services more expensive. Overall, immigration can have important distributional consequences on natives' purchasing power: An increase in immigration of low-skilled workers would favor high-skilled natives by reducing the prices of services they purchase but hurt low-skilled natives by reducing their purchasing power via higher prices on some goods and services and lower wages.

Product diversity

Have you ever walked through an immigrant community, like Chinatown in London or San Francisco, or Little Italy in New York City or Buenos Aires? If so, you would notice that consumers can obtain goods and services there that are difficult to find elsewhere in the country. Immigrant communities add to the variety and diversity of products in a country. Think about the wonderful mix of ethnic food that consumers can find in New York City and London. The majority of the ethnic food produced in those cities is produced by immigrants. Not only do immigrants add to the variety of food, but they add to the quality. In fact, as the size of the immigrant population increases in an area, both the quantity and the quality of ethnic food increase. Many would argue that large immigrant cities have some of the best restaurants in the world, and it is due to the diversity of food that immigrants bring with them to their destination.

Immigrants have a comparative advantage in the production of ethnic goods. A comparative advantage is when an individual or group can perform an economic activity at a lower opportunity cost than other individuals or groups. In this case, immigrants can make food from their home country at a lower cost and higher quality because they have the skills and knowledge to do so. Ethnic restaurants are another good example of nontradeable goods and services since they are locally produced. While the public has long viewed this type of diversity as an important effect of immigration, economists have only recently started to quantify these effects.

Immigrants can affect product diversity (or product variety) in the destination in two ways. First, they form part of the consumer base and increase the demand for ethnic goods. For example, they may want to buy certain types of rice or seasonings in the destination. The increase in the demand for these goods and services is shown in Figure 9.4. This increased demand for ethnic goods will encourage producers to supply these goods, and they then become available to native consumers. Second, immigrants are often suppliers of ethnic goods, as in the case of ethnic restaurants. Figure 9.4 also shows an increase in the supply of ethnic food. By consuming and producing ethnic food, immigrants increase both the quantity and quality of the food. This leads to more options, or "consumption variety," for natives.

The overall impact of immigration on the prices of ethnic goods and services depends on which effect dominates, demand or supply. As shown in Figure 9.4, if the increases in the demand and supply of ethnic food due to immigration are of the same magnitude (leading to equivalent rightward shifts), then the net effect on prices is zero. However, if the supply shift is larger, then the net effect on prices would be negative (it would be positive if the demand shift is larger). No matter what, an increase in immigration will lead to more ethnic food in equilibrium, as shown in Figure 9.4.

Ottaviano and Peri (2006) study the increase in consumption variety due to immigration and show that immigrants create more ethnic diversity in some local goods and services. As they state, "Who can deny that Italian restaurants, French beauty shops, German breweries, Belgian chocolate stores, Russian ballets, Chinese markets, and Indian tea houses all constitute valuable consumption amenities that would be inaccessible to Americans were it not for their foreign-born residents?" (p. 10). If natives prefer more variety and diversity in their consumption, then immigration improves the overall welfare of natives.

Francesca Mazzolari and David Neumark (2012) examine these effects in California, focusing on restaurants and retail industries. In terms of ethnic restaurants (which are nontradeable and immigrant-intensive, as discussed above), Mazzolari and Neumark find that an increase in the immigrant share in an area leads to an increase in share of ethnic restaurants in that area.

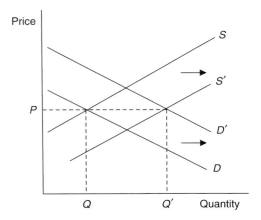

Figure 9.4 Market for ethnic food with immigration.

Immigration increases the supply and demand for ethnic food. If the increases in demand and supply are the same magnitude, then the price remains at *P*.

Their analysis suggests that the supply effect is larger than the demand effect, although both channels appear to be important in the market for ethnic restaurants.

However, the results are not the same for the retail sector. Mazzolari and Neumark find that there is less diversity in the retail sector as a result of immigration. Retail industries are much less immigrant-intensive than restaurants in that immigrants represent a smaller share of the workforce. In addition, immigrants tend to have lower incomes and to be more sensitive to prices than natives. Immigration therefore increases demand for big-box retailers, such as Walmart and Home Depot, which tend to have lower prices than smaller, stand-alone retailers. As a result, areas in California with relatively large immigrant populations have fewer small establishments, more big-box retailers and less overall diversity in retail stores.

In sum, immigration affects both the supply and demand for nontradeable goods and services. Which effect dominates determines how immigration affects the prices of goods and services. The evidence suggests that immigration decreases prices and increases product variety in some immigrant-intensive sectors, including the restaurant industry, day care, housekeeping and landscaping. However, immigration can have negative effects on product diversity for retail stores, which rely less on immigrant labor.

International trade

The last two sections suggested that the tradability of a good or service determines how that good or service is impacted by immigration. This section builds on this idea and considers how immigration affects international trade and the implications for consumers in the destination country.

Exports are goods and services produced domestically and sold abroad to foreigners. Imports are goods and services produced abroad and sold domestically. Net exports are the difference between exports and imports. A country that is a net exporter has a higher value of exports than imports in a given period and runs a trade surplus. A country that is a net importer imports more than it exports and runs a trade deficit. The United States currently has a trade deficit of about $45 billion, while China has a trade surplus close to $20 billion.[1] If exports are constant, an increase in imports leads to a reduction in net exports.

Immigrants can be both consumers and producers of internationally-traded goods and services and thereby affect a country's exports and imports. As consumers, immigrants are likely to want goods and services from their origin country. Immigration therefore may lead to an increase in imports. In a comprehensive study analyzing immigration in OECD countries in the year 2000, Peter Egger, Doug Nelson and Maximilian von Ehrlich (2012) examine the effect of immigration on imports. Their hypothesis is that immigration enhances migrant networks, which reduce transactions costs of trade. Thus, having more immigrants from a specific country should increase imports from that country. They find that imports are positively affected by the number of immigrants until there are about 4,000 immigrants from a specific country of origin. After that point, there is no relationship between imports and immigration.

Other economists have studied how immigration affects exports. Immigrants can be producers of goods and services in the destination country, and many of those goods and services may be exported back to the origin country, where the immigrants have connections. As such, immigration could boost exports. In Spain, an increase in the number of immigrants living in a province leads to an increase in trade with those immigrants' country of origin (Peri and Requena-Silvente, 2010). A similar effect holds for U.S. states: an increase in the immigrant population in a U.S. state leads to an increase in that state's exports to the country of origin (Herander and Saavedra, 2005). In both cases, the effects are quantitatively important.

If immigration positively affects both exports and imports, as suggested above, the effect on net exports depends on which effect is bigger. If exports respond more to immigration than imports, then the net effect on the trade balance is positive. But if the reverse occurs and imports respond more to immigration than exports, then net exports fall. Using data on Canada, Keith Head and John Ries (1998) find that immigration has a larger effect on imports. Thus, increases in the number of immigrants in a country may actually reduce net exports and worsen the trade balance.

Besides affecting the volume of trade across borders, immigration affects product variety, as discussed earlier. Today, consumers around the world can purchase a much greater variety of products than they used to, and much of the increased variety is due to international trade between countries. The variety of imported products in the United States increased by a factor of three between 1971 and 2001 (Broda and Weinstein, 2006). Bo Chen and David Jacks (2012) have found that approximately one-quarter of the growth in product variety in Canada during 1988 to 2006 was due to immigration during that period. They argue that immigrants are in a unique position since they have better knowledge of the variety of goods available, better access to global markets, better ability to predict market conditions and a better understanding of the regulatory environment back home. Chen and Jacks find that the increase in product variety due to immigration led to welfare gains for Canadian natives.

The link between immigration and international trade is important but complicated since immigration potentially affects both exports and imports. The net effect depends on the magnitudes of these effects, which likely vary over time and across countries. That is, the trade position of a country may be more or less responsive to its immigrants. That responsiveness may depend on the number of immigrants in that country and the composition of those immigrants in terms of their age, years of residence in the duration, skill levels and so on. Either way, immigrants may be both consumers and producers of goods and services. In addition, immigration likely lowers the transactions costs of buying and selling goods abroad and hence facilitates more international trade.

Financial markets

As with international trade of goods and services, immigration may facilitate financial flows across countries. Imagine high-skilled Chinese immigrants working in Australia. These Chinese immigrants have knowledge of financial institutions in both China and Australia. They may consider investing in Australia through financial markets. In addition, the presence of high-skilled Chinese workers in Australia may attract other Chinese financial investors who learn about opportunities in Australia from their compatriots who work there. The flow of workers from China to Australia may increase financial flows from China to Australia.

It is well known in the financial world that financial investors exhibit "home bias." Home bias in financial markets means that investors prefer to invest in their home country because of information problems abroad, even if returns are potentially higher abroad. For example, investors may not understand or trust regulations and laws in other countries, and this may result in a preference towards home-country investments. If the information problems are severe, which is the case when countries are quite different from one another in terms of financial institutions, regulations and political situations, then financial capital may not flow efficiently between countries. Studies show that information problems reduce the flow of financial capital across countries. However, these information problems have diminished over time as a result of innovations in information technology (IT) and decreases in the cost of international telecommunications. Still, given the sizable difference in asset returns across countries, there should be even more international mobility of financial capital than is observed in the data.

The existence of information problems across countries may create a role for immigration to boost international financial flows. More immigration between countries should reduce these information problems, promoting more international financial investment. Maurice Kugler, Oren Levintal and Hillel Rapoport (2013) study the effect of immigration on financial flows between a large set of countries during 1990 to 2000. They find that immigration has important positive effects on bilateral financial flows between countries, and the largest effects occur in countries in which information problems are the most acute. Their results indicate that high-skilled immigrants and long-term bonds drive the effects of immigration on international financial flows.

Immigrant networks may also affect foreign direct investment by lowering the risk associated with investing abroad. Hisham Foad (2012) finds that immigration is positively correlated with foreign direct investment in U.S. states. A state with a larger immigrant network has more foreign-owned affiliates open each year. In addition, high-skilled immigrant communities attract more foreign direct investment.

This area of research is still preliminary, but it suggests that immigration can help promote the flow of financial capital across countries, much like it promotes the flow of goods and services across countries.

Physical capital investment

As discussed in Chapter 7, including physical capital in the production function has implications for the wage effects of immigration. Physical capital is typically assumed to be constant in the short run, so immigration is assumed to not affect physical capital in the short run. In the long run, physical capital can be adjusted, so firms may respond over time to an influx of immigrants by changing their stock of physical capital.

Immigration may affect the demand or supply of physical capital. If immigrants bring capital with them, then the supply of physical capital may increase with immigration. Alternatively, the demand for physical capital may change in response to an immigrant-induced increase in labor supply. The direction of the effect on the demand for capital depends on the relationship between labor and capital in the production process. If labor and capital are complements in production, an increase in labor supply will encourage firms to acquire more capital. However, if firms can substitute physical capital for labor, then an increase in workers (via immigration) may reduce the demand for physical capital. The firm will adjust labor and capital until the marginal rate of technical substitution equals the ratio of wages to rental rates on capital, as discussed in Chapter 7.

The specification of the production function has important implications for how immigration affects capital investment. In the case of a Cobb-Douglas production function with physical capital and labor (as in equation A7.11 in the appendix to Chapter 7), an increase in the number of workers causes the marginal productivity of capital to increase. When immigration increases the number of workers, firms will have an incentive to invest in more capital. This effect is larger when immigration consists of high-skilled workers who bring skills and expertise with them and when there are capital–skill complementarities in the production process. However, other specifications of the production function may yield different results. For example, if firms can substitute between physical capital and labor, then an increase in the number of workers will reduce the demand for physical capital.

Peri (2012) studies the effects of immigration on physical capital using U.S. data for 1960 to 2006. He finds that in the long run (defined as ten years), immigration did not have a significant effect on capital intensity—the ratio of physical capital to output—in U.S. states. This result is consistent with employment, capital and output all growing at approximately the same rate. If capital and output were growing at similar rates, then the ratio of capital to output (e.g., capital intensity) remained constant over time.

Technology and innovation

An important channel through which immigration increases aggregate output is total factor productivity (TFP). In a typical production function, TFP measures the overall effectiveness of the other inputs to production. In a simple production function with capital and labor as inputs, TFP could include technological innovation in IT services and the intensity of research and development (R&D) since these factors are not directly captured by labor and physical capital. That is, TFP is the residual output that is not explained by the other inputs to production. TFP cannot be measured directly. It must be imputed by specifying a production function and then attributing to it the amount of output that is not attributable to other inputs.

Peri (2012) finds that immigration had a significant, positive effect on TFP growth in U.S. states between 1960 and 2006. His results indicate that states with larger-than-average inflows of immigrants experienced faster output growth per worker, and this was entirely due to higher TFP growth. Much of the TFP growth occurred because immigrants and natives specialized in different types of tasks in the labor force (as discussed in Chapters 7 and 8).

Immigration can also affect the level of innovation within a firm or industry.[2] For example, if the number of high-skilled immigrant workers who possess certain knowledge not readily available within the domestic workforce increases, firms or industries could experience innovation that would have beneficial effects on productivity and output. These effects are often described as "knowledge spillovers," in which natives learn and benefit from immigrants who have more or different knowledge or innovative ideas. A common way to measure innovation is to track the number of patents over time. Patents grant inventors intellectual property rights over their invention or idea; patent holders have monopoly rights for a certain amount of time. Jennifer Hunt and Marjolaine Gauthier-Loiselle (2010) indicate that a 1 percentage point increase in the population share of immigrant college graduates in the United States results in a 15 percent increase in patents per capita. Using different U.S. data, William Kerr and William Lincoln (2010) show that increases in the number of immigrant scientists and engineers admitted to the United States on H-1B visas lead to more patents among workers with Indian and Chinese last names. (For more details about the H-1B visa program, see Chapter 13.) In fact, about 12 percent of all patents in the United States are issued to people with Indian or Chinese last names! Importantly, both studies do not find evidence that immigrants crowd out U.S. natives in terms of patents. In fact, both studies suggest positive spillovers onto U.S. natives' patent activity.

Another study by Hunt (2011) focuses on innovation by immigrant college graduates who enter the United States on different types of visas. She finds that immigrants who enter on temporary worker visas or student/trainee visas outperform U.S.-born college graduates in terms of wages, patents and publishing. As Hunt explains, part of the reason for this pattern is that these immigrants are more likely to have majored in a scientific or technical field and to have a graduate degree. Meanwhile, immigrants who enter as legal permanent residents tend to perform similarly to U.S. natives. Thus, immigrants who come to the United States to work or train are more innovative than those who come for other reasons (such as family reunification).

In addition, immigrants tend to be entrepreneurial. Hunt (2011) finds that "immigrants are more likely than natives to start a company with more than 10 workers, suggesting that immigrants have a niche in start-ups based on technical knowledge from master's and doctoral degrees" (p. 422). Entrepreneurial spirit encourages the development of new goods and services and can boost employment among natives. As Hunt (2011) states, "U.S. total factor productivity benefits from the presence of creative, inventive, and entrepreneurial immigrants in the United States" (p. 419).

Income

The basic immigration model first laid out in Chapter 1 shows that immigration leads to an increase in national income that economists term the immigration surplus. As discussed in Chapter 7, that model assumes that there are no migration costs and immigrants and natives are perfect substitutes in production. The immigration surplus arises from the fact that immigration reduces wages, which encourages firms to hire more workers and increase output. Although that model is a good starting point, it does not include other ways that immigration affects the destination, many of them discussed in this chapter. Figure 9.5 displays the mechanisms discussed so far: housing, prices of products, product variety, international trade, financial markets, capital, and innovation and productivity.

Some of these mechanisms are difficult to quantify. One approach to quantifying the effect of immigration on national income is to bypass the various mechanisms and directly measure how immigration affects national income. Ortega and Peri (2014) find that the share of immigrants in the population has a large positive effect on long-run income per capita among a large sample of rich and poor countries in 2000. That is, a country with more immigrants has higher income per capita. They find, using instrumental variables to control for endogeneity, that a 10 percentage-point difference in the share of foreign born is associated with differences in income per person by a factor near two (equivalent to a 100 percent increase in per capita income). Their estimates imply that if Japan, which has an immigrant share of about 1 percent, increased its immigrant share to 11 percent, its income per capita would double in the long run.

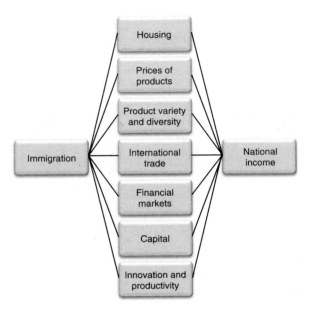

Figure 9.5 Various channels of how immigration affects national income.

Income inequality

Immigration can affect the distribution of income, or income inequality. As Chapter 4 discussed, there are several ways to measure income inequality, including the Gini index, income shares and relative earnings of workers in different skill groups. As Chapter 7 discussed, low-skilled immigration will tend to increase the relative wages of high-skilled workers and increase the skill premium, while high-skilled immigration will tend to decrease the relative wages of high-skilled workers and decrease the skill premium.

Income inequality has risen in many developed countries since the late 1970s, most notably in the United States and United Kingdom. A number of factors are often given as reasons for rising income inequality. Potential institutional factors include falling union membership, declining minimum wages and adoption of less progressive tax structures. Another potential factor is an increase in the demand for high-skilled labor combined with a decrease in the demand for low-skilled labor as a result of skill-biased technical change (SBTC), or changes in the production function that favor high-skilled workers. Greater international trade may also have contributed to rising income inequality by reducing the demand for low-skilled labor in developed countries. Many low-skilled labor-intensive goods can be produced more cheaply abroad, leading to lower low-skilled wages in developed countries.

Immigration may contribute to income inequality. An inflow of low-skilled immigrants that reduces low-skilled wages would increase income inequality. An inflow of high-skilled immigrants that drives down high-skilled wages would reduce income inequality. (Which one occurs depends on the relative return to skill, as discussed in Chapter 4.) Martin Kahanec and Klaus Zimmermann (2011) find that immigration tends to decrease income inequality in western European countries. Specifically, they show that the college-educated population share in OECD countries is positively related to the immigrant population share, and the college-educated population share, in turn, is negatively related to the Gini index. In other words, by increasing the relative size of the college-educated population, immigration has put downwards pressure on inequality in much of Western Europe. Research specific to the United States shows that immigration has had very little effect on wage inequality there (Card, 2009).

Growth accounting

Immigration can also have a long-run effect on output growth. Economists often do growth accounting exercises to determine the primary sources of growth in an economy. The production function tells us how inputs combine to produce output. It is expressed as

$$Y = Af(L, K) \tag{9.1}$$

where A is total factor productivity, L is the number of workers, K is the stock of physical capital and f is the production function that relates labor and capital to output. For output to grow, an input to production (labor or capital) or TFP has to grow. We can rewrite equation 9.1 in terms of growth rates (or percent changes) as

$$\%\Delta Y = \%\Delta A + a_L \%\Delta L + a_K \%\Delta K \tag{9.2}$$

where a_L and a_K represent the elasticity of output with respect to labor and capital, respectively. (Notice that the elasticity of output with respect to TFP equals one. The appendix to this chapter gives an example using a Cobb-Douglas production function.) The elasticities for labor and capital (a_L, a_K) are assumed to be between zero and one and must be estimated using data. For example, if $a_L = 0.7$, then a 1 percent increase in labor will cause a 0.7 percent increase in output. It is important to note that when talking about growth rates of countries, a 1 percent increase in output (GDP) is relatively large. Consider the U.S. economy, with GDP close to $17 trillion; a 1 percent increase in U.S. GDP for one year is $170 billion! Countries that are less wealthy tend to grow at higher rates.

Equation 9.2 is called the growth accounting equation. TFP growth has a one-to-one effect on output growth. For example, a 2 percent increase in TFP will lead to a 2 percent increase in output (holding capital and labor fixed). This is not true for capital and labor: Labor's contribution to output growth consists of multiplying the elasticity of output with respect to labor by the growth rate in labor. Since this elasticity is less than one, a 1 percent increase in labor will lead to output increasing by less than 1 percent. The same is true for capital.

For developed countries such as the United States, the elasticity of output with respect to labor is approximately 0.7. If immigration creates growth in the labor supply (which is usually the case), then immigration will positively affect output growth (holding TFP and capital constant). For example, if labor supply increases by 1 percent in the United States due to immigration (which is 1.55 million workers given a labor force of 155 million), then U.S. GDP would increase by 0.7 percent, or $119 billion (again, assuming no growth in TFP and capital).

Researchers have found little to no effect of immigration on capital, but there is evidence of positive effects on TFP (Peri, 2012), suggesting that immigration could actually increase GDP through both the labor supply and TFP channels.

The Solow model

The canonical model for considering the growth effects in an economy is the Solow growth model. The Solow growth model is an example of an exogenous growth model where the source of growth is exogenous to, or outside, the model. Growth models are able to tell us how countries grow over the long term (think decades instead of years). In the Solow model, output is measured in per capita terms and depends on the capital–labor ratio. Recall from Chapter 7 that capital evolves over time. Over very long periods of time, the capital stock will reach a steady state such that there is no further adjustment of capital. The model below examines the effect of immigration on this steady-state equilibrium.

The aggregate production function in the Solow model is expressed in per-worker notation. Total output is again expressed as

$$Y = Af(L, K) \tag{9.3}$$

where A is TFP and $f(L, K)$ is the production function. If there are constant returns to scale, we can divide both sides of the equation by the number of workers, L. In per-worker notation, this yields

$$y = Af(k) \tag{9.4}$$

where $y = Y/L$ and $k = K/L$. If the production function has the usual properties (such as diminishing marginal returns to capital), then graphically it looks like Figure 9.6. As shown in the figure, y is increasing in k but at a decreasing rate.

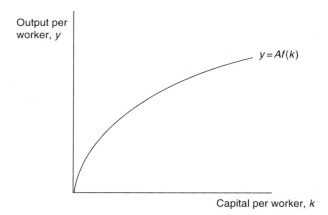

Figure 9.6 Solow growth model.

The mathematical derivation of the Solow growth model is complicated (and can be found in most intermediate macroeconomics textbooks), so we provide only its graphical representation here. Central to the model is that the demand for physical capital, investment per worker (expressed as i), equals the supply of physical capital, or savings per worker (expressed as s). Per-worker savings is the fraction of total income that is saved, or

$$s = \lambda y = \lambda Af(k) \tag{9.5}$$

where λ is the savings rate, or the marginal propensity to save. Notice in Figure 9.7 that per-capita savings takes the same general shape as the production function but is lower since the savings rate λ is a value between zero and one. For example, $\lambda = 0.3$ indicates that the savings rate is 30 percent.

Meanwhile, investment per worker (i) consists of two components: the population growth rate (n), and the depreciation rate of physical capital (d). Specifically,

$$i = (n + d)k \tag{9.6}$$

which increases linearly with k. Thus, Figure 9.7 plots the investment line as a straight line with a slope equal to $n + d$. As with the savings rate, the population growth and depreciation rates are values between zero and one.

The model is in equilibrium when savings equals investment, or $s = i$. In Figure 9.7 the intersection of i and s occurs at k^*, which is the steady-state capital–labor ratio. Countries are moving towards this steady state. The steady-state capital–labor ratio is called the Golden Rule level of capital if it maximizes consumption per worker.

In the Solow growth model, higher population growth will affect investment. Specifically, a higher population growth rate (n) will make the investment line steeper (but it still originates

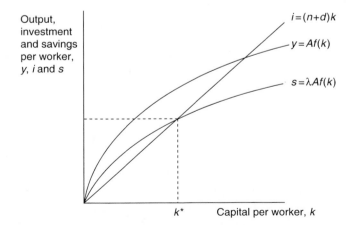

Figure 9.7 Solow growth model steady state.

The steady-state level of capital per worker, k^*, occurs where investment per worker equals savings per worker.

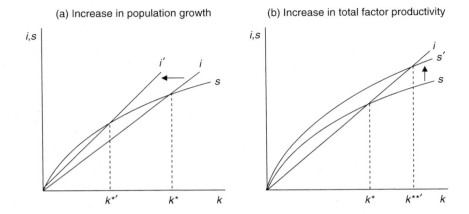

Figure 9.8 Solow growth model with population growth and TFP increase.

In (a), the investment line, *i*, pivots to the left as population growth increases, so that $k*$ decreases to $k*'$. In (b), the savings line, *s*, shifts up as total factor productivity increases, so $k*$ increases to $k**'$.

at the origin). This is shown in Figure 9.8(a) as the movement from *i* to *i'*. A steeper investment line will lower the steady-state value of $k*$ to $k*'$. The intuition is as follows: With higher population growth, the same capital stock has to be shared among more workers. Thus, the capital–labor ratio (*k*) falls. As the capital–labor ratio falls, output per worker (*y*) falls. Thus, faster population growth will lower output per worker. If immigration causes faster population growth in a country (which is most often the case), then immigration will reduce output and steady-state consumption per capita in that country.

Our discussion above suggests that immigration positively affects TFP through innovation and entrepreneurship. If this is the case, the Solow growth model delivers the following result: an increase in TFP will shift the production function upward by increasing the parameter *A*. An increase in *A* raises output per worker (*y*) and hence savings per worker (*s*). This is shown in Figure 9.8(b) as the shift from *s* to *s'*. An upward shift in *s* raises the steady state from $k*$ to $k**'$. Therefore, the Solow growth model suggests that if immigration increases TFP, then immigration can increase the capital–labor ratio, output growth and consumption per capita in the long run.

Final thoughts

Immigration has important but complicated effects on an economy. This chapter highlighted some of the markets in the destination that are directly affected by immigrants, including housing, financial markets, international trade and physical capital. In many cases, immigrants can have competing effects: they may increase the demand for a good or service, but they may also increase the supply. The net effect on prices depends on the relative magnitudes of these competing effects. In most cases, immigration leads to more production of goods and services in an economy and a greater variety of products offered. At the macroeconomic level, immigration can increase the amount of physical and financial capital in an economy and boost innovation and productivity. If the productivity effects are big enough, the net effect of immigration on the long-run growth rate should be positive. The next chapter considers the fiscal effects of immigration on the destination.

Problems and discussion questions

1   Using Google Maps, figure out the location of Chinatown in San Francisco. Count the number of Chinese restaurants in that area and print out the map. Discuss the reasons why Chinese restaurants are geographically distributed in this way. What are the costs and benefits of large concentrations of ethnic restaurants in major U.S. cities?

2   Saiz (2007) finds that an influx of immigrants in a gateway U.S. city increases rental and house prices in that city. Choose what you believe to be a gateway city (why might it be a gateway city?) and find the median house price and immigrant share of the population. Then calculate the effect of an immigrant inflow equal to 1 percent of the population on house prices according to Saiz's results.

3   Egger, Nelson and von Ehrlich (2012) find that immigration from a source country positively affects imports from that country until the immigrant stock from that source country reaches 4,000. After that point, additional immigrants from that source country do not appear to affect imports. Explain why this might be the case using the information about migrant networks provided in this chapter.

4   Give an example of immigration increasing exports to the source country and an example of immigration increasing imports from the source country. In each case, what is the effect on GDP in the destination country?

5   Economists have found that immigration can increase productivity and stimulate innovation. How might a firm benefit from the ideas of immigrant workers? Find an example of a patent or business created by immigrants that has contributed to the destination country's economy.

6   Pick a destination country. Using United Nations data (links below), find the foreign-born stock as a percentage of the total population in that country in 2013. Ortega and Peri (2014) find that a 10 percentage-point difference in the immigrant share leads to a 100 percent increase in income per person (on average). Using this estimate, how much would per capita GDP increase if that country increased their immigrant share by 0.1 percentage points? 1 percentage point? 10 percentage points?

Notes

1   Federal Reserve Economic Data, Federal Reserve Bank of St. Louis. Available at: http://research.stlouisfed.org/fred2/ [3 September 2014].
2   For a good discussion of how innovation and entrepreneurship due to immigration affects productivity, see Lewis (2013).

Internet resources

UN data on the migrants stock by sex and age are available at http://esa.un.org/unmigration/TIMSA2013/migrantstocks2013.htm.
UN data on GDP are available at http://unstats.un.org/unsd/snaama/selcountry.asp.

References

Broda, C. and Weinstein, D.E. (2006) "Globalization and the gains from variety." *Quarterly Journal of Economics* 121(2), pp. 541–585.

Card, D. (2009) "Immigration and inequality." *American Economic Review Papers & Proceedings* 99(2), pp. 1–21.

Chen, B. and Jacks, D. (2012) "Trade, variety, and immigration." *Economics Letters* 117(1), pp. 243–246.

Cortes, P. (2008) "The effect of low-skilled immigration on US prices: Evidence from CPI data." *Journal of Political Economy* 116(3), pp. 381–422.

Cortes, P. and Tessada, J. (2011) "Low-skilled immigration and the labor supply of highly skilled women." *American Economic Journal: Applied Economics* 3(3), pp. 88–123.

Egger, P., Nelson, D. and von Ehrlich, M. (2012) "Migration and trade." *World Economy* 35(2), pp. 216–241.

Foad, H. (2012) "FDI and immigration: A regional analysis." *Annals of Regional Science* 49(1), pp. 237–259.

Furtado, D. and Hock, H. (2008) "Immigrant labor, child care services, and the work fertility trade-off in the United States." *IZA Discussion Paper* No. 3506. Bonn: Institute for the Study of Labor.

Gonzalez, L. and Ortega, F. (2013) "Immigration and housing booms: Evidence from Spain." *Journal of Regional Science* 53(1), pp. 37–59.

Head, K. and Ries, J. (1998) "Immigration and trade creation: Econometric evidence from Canada." *Canadian Journal of Economics* 31(1), pp. 47–62.

Herander, M. and Saavedra, L.A (2005) "Exports and the structure of immigrant-based networks: The role of geographic proximity." *Review of Economics and Statistics* 87(2), pp. 323–335.

Hunt, J. (2011) "Which immigrants are most innovative and entrepreneurial? Distinctions by entry visa." *Journal of Labor Economics* 29(3), pp. 417–457.

Hunt, J. and Gauthier-Loiselle, M. (2010) "How much does immigration boost innovation?" *American Economic Journal: Macroeconomics* 2(2), pp. 31–56.

Kahanec, M. and Zimmermann, K.F. (2011) "International migration, ethnicity and economic inequality." In: Salverda, W., Nolan, B. and Smeeding, T.M. (eds.) *The Oxford Handbook of Economic Inequality*. Oxford: Oxford University Press, pp. 455–490.

Kerr, W.R. and Lincoln, W.F. (2010) "The supply side of innovation: H-1B visa reforms and U.S. ethnic invention." *Journal of Labor Economics* 28(3), pp. 427–508.

Kugler, M., Levintal, O. and Rapoport, H. (2013) "Migration and cross-border financial flows." *IZA Discussion Paper* No. 7548. Bonn: Institute for the Study of Labor.

Lewis, E. (2013) "Immigration and production technology." *Annual Review of Economics* 5:1, pp. 165–191.

Mazzolari, F. and Neumark, D. (2012) "Immigration and product diversity." *Journal of Population Economics* 25(3), pp. 1107–1137.

Ortega, F. and Peri, G. (2014) "Openness and income: The roles of trade and migration." *Journal of International Economics* 92(2), pp. 231–251.

Ottaviano, G.P. and Peri, G. (2006) "The economic value of cultural diversity: Evidence from US cities." *Journal of Economic Geography* 6(1), pp. 9–44.

Peri, G. (2012) "The effect of immigration on productivity: Evidence from US states." *Review of Economics and Statistics* 94(1), pp. 348–358.

Peri, G. and Requena-Silvente, F. (2010) "The trade creation effect of immigrants: Evidence from the remarkable case of Spain." *Canadian Journal of Economics* 43(4), pp.1433–1459.

Saiz, A. (2007) "Immigration and housing rents in American cities." *Journal of Urban Economics*, 61(2), pp. 345–371.

Appendix

We can use the Cobb-Douglas production function from the appendix to Chapter 7 in our growth accounting. If natives and immigrants are perfect substitutes, the production function is

$$Y = A(L_N + M)^\alpha K^\gamma \tag{A9.1}$$

where A is total factor productivity, L_N is the number of native-born workers, M is the number of immigrant workers, K is the stock of physical capital in the destination country and $\alpha, \gamma \geq 0$. If the production function exhibits constant returns to scale, then $\alpha + \gamma = 1$.

Under constant returns to scale, we can manipulate equation A9.1 to rewrite it in terms of percentage changes:

$$\%\Delta Y = \%\Delta A + \alpha\%\Delta L_N + \alpha\%\Delta M + \gamma\%\Delta K \tag{A9.2}$$

Notice that in the Cobb-Douglas specification, the elasticities—the percentage change in output for a 1 percent change in an input—are the exponents for labor and capital. For example, if the number of immigrant workers (M) increases by 1 percent, output (Y) increases by α percent. If natives and immigrants are perfect substitutes (as shown here), these elasticities are the same for natives and immigrants. (This would not be the case if they were imperfect substitutes or complements.) Thus, as more immigrants enter a country ($\%\Delta M > 0$), output increases ($\%\Delta Y > 0$).

10 Fiscal Effects

One major concern regarding immigration worldwide is the impact on federal, state and local governments. The net fiscal impact of immigration—the difference between tax revenues from immigrants and the cost of publicly funded services received by immigrants—on receiving countries is the subject of considerable debate. Estimates vary within and across countries and over time. Concerns mainly center on the impacts of less-skilled and undocumented immigrants. The most-cited concerns are that these immigrants "do not contribute their fair share" or that "they are getting something for nothing." Highly skilled immigrants, who generally pay more in taxes than they receive in government-funded services, are less controversial from a fiscal standpoint.

Estimating the fiscal impact of immigrants is important for a number of reasons. Policymakers need estimates of short- and long-run fiscal effects of immigration in order to determine under which scenarios immigrants will be net fiscal contributors and under which scenarios they will be a net fiscal drain. Understanding the mechanics behind the fiscal impact of immigration can help policymakers target and alleviate other fiscal imbalances. For example, policymakers in countries with aging populations may aim to increase immigration in order to offset future labor and pension shortages. Understanding immigrants' usage of public services and publicizing these figures may affect public perceptions, which in turn have the potential to shape immigration policy. Surveys show that opinions about immigrants are tied closely to perceptions about their fiscal impact (OECD, 2013).

Many factors contribute to the fiscal impact of immigration, such as immigrants' age at arrival, their reasons for migrating (economic vs. humanitarian and family reunification migrants), their skill levels, the generosity of publicly funded services and the structure of the tax system. These factors all tie to the most important determinant: immigrants' employment outcomes. Although there is a wide range of fiscal effects by demographic characteristics and regions, most estimates of the net fiscal impact of immigration are relatively small, especially in comparison to most developed countries' fiscal imbalances. Studies of 27 OECD countries report minor fiscal effects of immigration, with the net fiscal impact rarely exceeding 0.5 percent of GDP (OECD, 2013).

This chapter discusses several important aspects of the fiscal effect, sometimes referred to as the taxpayer effect, of immigration. Methodological and measurement issues are presented first, followed by current estimates of the fiscal effect for the United States and other OECD countries under various assumptions and measurement methods. The chapter concludes with an in-depth discussion of immigrants' participation in four government-funded programs in the United States: welfare, education, health care and Social Security.

Measuring the fiscal impact

Measuring the fiscal impact of immigration accurately can be quite complicated. Two main methods are used. The first is the static accounting method. This method calculates tax revenues from the immigrant population minus expenses during a particular time period (usually a fiscal year). The second method is dynamic modeling. This method can be further separated into net transfer profile-based projections and the generational accounting method. Dynamic modeling takes into account long-run considerations, such as the fiscal impact of immigrants' descendants. It may also include the impact of immigration on economic growth, which in turn affects tax revenues.

Fiscal costs and benefits

When computing the fiscal effect of immigration, economists must decide which revenues and expenses to include and how to estimate them. Government transfers and publicly funded services received by immigrants are clearly costs, but some other services, such as public goods, are more difficult to quantify. (Public goods are goods that are both non-excludable and non-rivalrous, or people cannot be effectively excluded from using them and use by one person does not reduce other people's ability to use them.)

On the cost side for the government, the most straightforward transfers are cash welfare and government-funded retirement benefit programs (like Social Security in the United States), while the most direct public services are public education and health care. In the United States, public schools are required to provide K-12 education and medical providers to provide emergency medical care regardless of people's legal status. The cost of these services can be substantial, particularly for states and cities near the U.S.–Mexico border. In some countries, the government pays for language training for school-aged children and adult migrants. The cost of this integration-related service can be sizable for the first few years after immigrants arrive. In addition, analyses of the fiscal impact of immigration may count expenses incurred for active labor market policies, such as job training programs, for immigrants. The number of categories of publicly funded programs can be quite extensive, and they are a key component of any estimate of the fiscal impact of immigration.[1]

Studies make various assumptions regarding how immigration affects the provision and cost of public goods. For pure public goods, such as national defense, immigration may actually decrease the cost per capita since these fixed costs are now spread over a larger population.[2] This is not the case for congestible public goods, however. Congestible public goods need to be provided in greater numbers as the size of the population increases—these goods become congested as more people use them, so the government must provide more of them as immigration occurs. Such goods include roads and other infrastructure, law enforcement and labor market programs.

On the revenue side, many immigrants pay taxes tied to employment, such as income and payroll taxes. Various levels of government also impose numerous taxes tied to daily living. These include sales taxes, property taxes, value-added taxes, fuel, liquor, tobacco and excise taxes.

When using any of the methodologies described in this chapter, there are a number of assumptions and decisions that must be made. First, the unit of analysis must be determined. This entails deciding whether the focus is on the household, individual, cohort or generation and whether it is at the national or regional level. In addition, economists must decide whether children born in the destination country to immigrant parents should be included in the analysis and whether education is a cost or an investment. Second, assumptions must be made regarding unauthorized immigrants' contribution to fiscal coffers and use of government-funded services. Researchers must estimate the number of unauthorized immigrants and decide whether they have different usage or take-up rates than legal immigrants. Third, economists must posit the impact of immigration on public goods, as mentioned above. Fourth, economists must make assumptions regarding various cohorts of immigrants and their benefits usage and contribution rates since cohorts may differ in terms of educational attainment, age, language ability and reason for migrating. Fifth, for dynamic methodologies in particular, projections are needed for the future population sizes of native-born individuals and immigrants. Dynamic methodologies also need to make assumptions about the future of government spending, tax policies and other economic indicators.

Static accounting method

In the static accounting method, economists calculate the difference between taxes and other contributions made by immigrants (credits) and fiscal transfers made to immigrants (debits). This calculation is typically done for a fiscal year and is the most straightforward and direct way to measure the fiscal impact of immigration. Usually, the credits are immigrants' tax payments, and the debits are government expenditures on immigrants. The advantages of this method are that it is relatively simple and relies on only a few assumptions. The main weakness of the static accounting method is that it does not account for longer-run considerations, such as immigrant lifecycle effects, the impact of their descendants or indirect effects on natives' wages and employment.

The most widely referenced study for the United States that uses this method (and also a dynamic method discussed later) is part of a 1997 study by the National Research Council (NRC). The NRC study makes a number of assumptions, most notably constraining all changes to be budget neutral (Smith and Edmonston, 1997). Any increase in expenditures must be balanced out by an increase in taxes. The annual fiscal effect of immigrants on a typical native is then approximated by

$$NAFI_N = -\Delta T_N \tag{10.1}$$

where $NAFI_N$ is the net annual fiscal impact of immigration on natives and ΔT_N is the change in taxes paid by native-born residents because of new immigration. If $NAFI_N$ is positive, the average native's taxes fall. If $NAFI_N$ is negative, the average native's taxes rise.

In this method, revenues are based mainly on taxes paid by current natives, current immigrants and businesses. The number of natives is represented by N, and the number of immigrants by M. T_N and T_M are the average tax rates for native-born and migrant households, respectively. A is a measure of other revenues on a per-native basis, such as taxes paid by businesses. The expense side includes the cost of government services provided to natives and migrants. The per-person cost of government services is represented by E_N for natives and E_M for migrants. Additional expenses are represented by X_N, which captures the cost of all other government spending on a per-native basis. The following equality must hold in any given year:

$$T_N N + T_M M + A_N N \equiv E_N N + E_M M + X_N N \tag{10.2}$$

Equation 10.2 represents the government's budget constraint. To address possible changes in immigration or government policy, the budget constraint can be shown in terms of flows of new migrants (ΔM) and changes in taxes and spending for immigrants and natives on a per-native basis:

$$-\Delta T_N = (T_M - E_M)(\Delta M / N) + (\Delta T_M - \Delta E_M)(M / N) + (\Delta A_N - \Delta X_N) \tag{10.3}$$

The left-hand side of equation 10.3 shows the effect on the average native's taxes for all changes that may have occurred as a result of immigration. Again, if the left-hand side is negative ($-\Delta T_N < 0$), this means that new immigrants are a fiscal burden on current residents. Conversely, if the left-hand side is positive, then new immigrants provide fiscal benefits. If $\Delta T_N = 0$, new immigrants are fiscally neutral, or have no net fiscal effect.

Immigration's impact is separated into three components on the right-hand side of equation 10.3. The first term, $(T_M - E_M)(\Delta M / N)$, shows the impact on native residents (N) if new immigrants (ΔM) are similar to previous immigrants. If government spending on immigrants is more than immigrants pay in taxes ($T_M - E_M < 0$), immigrants will increase the tax burden on natives, and the first term will be negative. The opposite is true if previous immigrants provide a net fiscal benefit and new immigrants continue to do so. In other words, the first term assumes that new immigrants pay and use services at the same rate as previous immigrants. However, this may not be the case. The second term, $(\Delta T_M - \Delta E_M)(M / N)$, allows for this possibility.

The second term shows the effect of changes due to differences in the demographic characteristics of new immigrants. If new immigrants are less skilled and require more services or pay less in taxes than previous immigrants, $\Delta T_M - \Delta E_M$ is likely to be negative, which increases the tax burden on natives. More specifically, ΔT_M would be negative if new immigrants pay less in taxes, and ΔE_M would be positive if new immigrants receive more in publicly funded services. If new immigrants are more skilled, the opposite would occur.

The last term, $\Delta A_N - \Delta X_N$, addresses other revenues and spending obligations that immigration may affect. For example, if the fiscal impact is estimated at the state level, a state may receive federal aid to assist its new immigrant population. This additional revenue would be captured in ΔA_N. At the federal level, new immigrants may start businesses that contribute tax revenues (ΔA_N) or create additional government expenses (ΔX_N).

Dynamic modeling

Dynamic modeling takes the age profiles of immigrants and the impact of their descendants into consideration. There are two main dynamic models: net transfer profile-based projections, and the generational accounting method.

The method behind net transfer profile projections is to augment the static models with projections of tax revenues and government benefits usage in the future. The end result of such studies is to compute the net present value (NPV) of contributions by each additional immigrant, taking into account various demographic characteristics and age profiles. For example, an immigrant's net fiscal contribution can be calculated by education, sex, age of arrival, legal status and country of origin, and the calculation can include descendants. The 1997 NRC report uses this method, and its results for the United States are discussed later in this chapter. Economists have also used this method to assess the fiscal impact of immigration in several OECD countries, including Germany, the Netherlands and Sweden.

To arrive at overall NPV estimates, researchers first produce age profiles of the annual fiscal impact of immigrants at a point in time (cross-sectional age profiles). These age profiles are typically presented graphically and can be split into three age groups: childhood, working age and retirement. Assessments of the costs, benefits and net impact of each age group of immigrants are the building blocks for NPV calculations. As shown in the top panel of Figure 10.1,

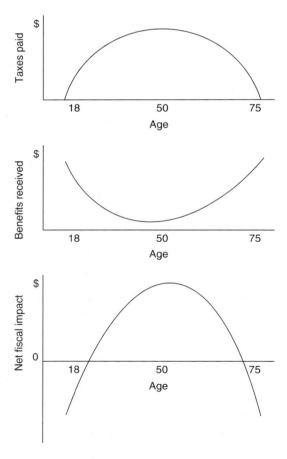

Figure 10.1 Age profiles of taxes paid, benefits received and net fiscal impact.

taxes paid by immigrants (and natives) tend to form an inverted U-shaped pattern. Taxes paid tend to start at zero for the young who are in school, rise with age as people move through working age and peak in the mid-fifties. After that, income and taxes tend to fall as people transition into retirement. For benefits received, shown in the middle panel, the opposite pattern occurs. Receipt of government benefits tends to be higher among the young who are in school and the elderly who are in retirement. Putting these costs and benefits together requires subtracting the middle panel from the top panel. The resulting net fiscal impact is also an inverted-U shape, as shown in the bottom panel. In this case, however, there are negative values as the benefits received by the young and the old outstrip their tax contributions. In other words, the net fiscal effect (taxes minus benefits) is negative during the childhood and retirement phases of the lifecycle.

The next step for NPV calculations is to construct longitudinal age profiles that show the fiscal impact as a person (often called a "representative agent") moves through the lifecycle. Longitudinal age profiles are more complicated to compute than cross-sectional age profiles because tax policies, the generosity of benefits, productivity and other economic factors may change as immigrant cohorts age. Specifically, researchers need to make assumptions about fiscal policy, debt/GDP ratios, the real interest rate, the generosity of benefits to immigrants, the taxes paid by immigrants, the costs of education and the likelihood of return migration by immigrants and descendants over their lifetimes. Regarding fiscal deficits (when government spending exceeds tax revenues and the government's debt increases), researchers typically assume that the debt-to-GDP ratio will ultimately stabilize at some point in the future. As countries hit their debt limits, they may need to increase taxes and cut spending, and research-ers need to make assumptions about these changes. Another complicating factor in comput-ing the fiscal impact of immigration is that GDP will likely grow as a result of immigration. This occurs because of the immigration surplus, complementarities between immigrants and natives and higher productivity and innovation in the receiving country as a result of immigra-tion. (Chapters 7 and 8 discuss the theory and evidence regarding these effects.) Holding all else constant, if this gain is large enough, policymakers could reduce the tax rate while still hitting debt targets.

The last step in net transfer profile projections produces the NPV estimates by summing up all the discounted impacts of an immigrant estimated in the longitudinal age profiles. This discounting requires assuming an interest rate. Researchers often use the govern-ment's borrowing rate. Discounting gives more weight, or importance, to fiscal effects closer to the present and less weight to the future. Using the assumptions above plus other demographic assumptions regarding family structure and assimilation of immigrants and their descendants, the researcher arrives at the estimated NPV of an immigrant's fiscal impact.

The second dynamic model is the generational accounting (GA) method, introduced by Alan Auerbach, Jagadeesh Gokhale and Laurence Kotlikoff (1991). Policymakers can use this method to assess whether a government's current path of taxes and transfers is sus-tainable. The GA method involves an intertemporal budget constraint. The intertemporal budget constraint puts the typical budget constraint, where spending is limited by income, into a multi-period and dynamic context. The intertemporal budget constraint requires that the tax payments made by immigrants and natives over their lifetimes and those of all future generations cover current and future government spending, including any past government indebtedness. Either current or future generations ultimately must pay for fiscal deficits.

GA models can be used to assess the impact of changes in the size of the immigrant population on the current generation or future generations. The end result of this method is to quantify a generational account, or a fiscal balance, for a particular generation under various assumptions. To make these calculations, economists must estimate or project the size of the current and future population, economic growth, taxes and transfers corresponding to the attributes of the population, government debt, interest rates and any likely policy changes (Auerbach and Oreopoulos, 1999). The Congressional Budget Office (CBO) makes many projections like this for the United States. [3]

The government's inter-temporal budget constraint with immigration is

$$\sum_{s=0}^{D}\left(N_{t,t-s}+M_{t,t-s}\right)+\sum_{s=1}^{\infty}(1+r)^{-(s-t)}\left(N_{t,t+s}+M_{t,t+s}\right)=\sum_{s=t}^{\infty}G_{s}(1+r)^{-(s-t)}-W_{t} \qquad (10.4)$$

The left-hand side of equation 10.4 represents the present value of all taxes paid by current and future generations. The right-hand side is the present value of government expenditures and current indebtedness. Specifically, N represents the NPV of taxes paid by natives, and M represents the NPV of taxes paid by immigrants. The first term on the left-hand side shows taxes paid by the current generation, which is born at time $t-s$ and has a lifespan of D years. The second term sums all future generations, where s is the number of years after t that an individual is born. On the right-hand side, the first term is the present value of government spending, where r represents the real interest rate and G represents government spending. The last term, W, is government net worth or wealth, which is the difference between the government's assets and debt.

Researchers can use this framework to determine whether immigration contributes to fiscal stress or alleviates it on a generational basis. Using an intertemporal model avoids the pitfalls of examining a certain cohort of immigrants at a point in time. Different populations will have different impacts on taxpayers at different points in their lifetime. For example, if immigrants in a country are mostly working age, the deficit may fall in the short run because of their tax contributions. However, when those immigrants eventually retire and receive benefits, such as publicly funded pensions, they will boost government spending and the deficit. If another country receives a large share of school-age immigrants, it will need to fund their education in the short run. However, in the longer run those immigrants are likely to pay more in taxes than they cost in government spending.

Estimates of the fiscal impact of immigration

Numerous studies have estimated the fiscal effects of immigration using the static and dynamic methods explained above. The main findings of major studies are summarized below. The methodology and assumptions used can result in large variations in estimates.

United States

The most comprehensive analysis of the fiscal impact of immigration in the United States was conducted by the National Research Council (NRC) in 1997. This study includes estimates using both the static accounting method and a dynamic model.

The NRC study does not include national estimates using the static accounting method, but it does present estimates of the annual fiscal effect of immigration for California and New Jersey, two states with large immigrant populations. The study finds a negative fiscal impact at the state and local levels in both states. The negative state-level fiscal impact is three times larger in California than in New Jersey. This difference is attributed to the large differences in immigrants' skills and educational attainment across the two states. Table 10.1 presents the main findings of the study. Expenditures are broken down into K-12 education, government transfers and all other expenditures. Revenues are broken down into property tax, income tax, sales tax and all other revenues. Since the fiscal budgets must balance at the local and state levels (because of

Table 10.1 Local and state expenditures, revenues and average fiscal balance per household (1996 dollars): New Jersey and California

	New Jersey			California		
	All	Natives	Immigrants	All	Natives	Immigrants
Expenditures						
Local:						
K-12 education	2273	2162	2985	974	768	1581
All other	868	807	1251	4549	4522	4627
Total	3141	2969	4326	5523	5290	6208
State:						
K-12 education	1625	1585	1878	1537	1212	2496
Transfers to households	502	496	530	817	594	1474
All other	588	566	738	780	704	1003
Total	2715	2647	3146	3134	2510	4973
Revenues						
Local:						
Property tax	2949	2921	3126	1059	1092	965
All other	192	192	188	4464	4481	4412
Total	3141	3113	3314	5523	5573	5377
State:						
Income tax	1515	1526	1446	1738	1964	1070
Sales tax	582	586	562	688	727	570
All other	618	623	576	708	714	701
Total	2715	2735	2584	3134	3405	2341
Average fiscal balance						
Local	$\equiv 0$	144	−922	$\equiv 0$	283	−831
State	$\equiv 0$	88	−562	$\equiv 0$	895	−2632
Total	$\equiv 0$	232	−1484	$\equiv 0$	1178	−3463

Source: Smith and Edmonston (1997).

balanced budget requirements there), total revenues must equal total expenses at those levels. For New Jersey, the average household receives and pays $3,141 for services at the local level and $2,715 at the state level, both of which are predominantly for K-12 education (all figures are in 1996 dollars). In California, these figures are $5,523 and $3,134, respectively.

The bottom line of the NRC study is that there is a fiscal redistribution from native-born households to immigrants. In New Jersey, immigrant-headed households imposed an average fiscal cost of $922 at the local level and $562 at the state level. This translates into an additional $144 tax bill at the local level and $88 at the state level, or $232 in total, for each household headed by a U.S. native. In California, the redistribution is estimated to be even larger, with a fiscal cost of $831 at the local level and $2,632 at the state level per immigrant household. This translates into a total fiscal burden of $1,178 per native-born household in California. Larger family sizes and relatively low incomes among immigrant households in California resulted in greater use of educational services, greater receipt of government transfers and smaller state tax payments there than in New Jersey.

Table 10.2 reports fiscal estimates at the federal level for native- and immigrant-headed households in California. The average native-born household pays $2,722 more in federal taxes than it receives in federally funded services and transfers. The average immigrant-headed household, in contrast, pays $2,682 less in taxes than it receives in federally funded services and transfers. These estimates include expenditures on national defense. If defense is treated as a pure public good and not included, the average immigrant-headed household in California makes a net contribution of $127 at the federal level.

The 1997 NRC report has other key findings. First, fiscal burdens stem from low tax revenues received from low-wage earners rather than from high rates of receipt of social services. Second, state and local governments bear the costs while the federal government reaps benefits, at least while immigrants are young and healthy. Immigrants lower the per capita costs of public goods such as national defense and interest on government debt but increase congestion costs on public goods such as roads, sewers, law enforcement, libraries, and airports. Pure public goods tend to be provided by the federal government, while congestible public goods tend to be provided by state and local governments. Third, the children of immigrants tend to be upwardly mobile. This last point has important implications for dynamic estimates, which are discussed later in this chapter.

A more recent study by the OECD (2013) uses the static accounting method to compute an updated aggregate measure for the United States. That analysis concludes that both native- and foreign-born households are net fiscal contributors. However, households

Table 10.2 Federal state expenditures, revenues and average fiscal balance per household (1996 dollars): California

	All	*Natives*	*Immigrants*
Expenditures	13,549	13,625	13,326
Revenues	14,896	16,347	10,644
Average fiscal balance	1,347	2,722	−2,682

Source: Smith and Edmonston (1997).

headed by a U.S. native make a larger net fiscal contribution than households headed by an immigrant. These results diverge from the results in the NRC study. Much of the divergence appears to be due to differences in the categories of taxes and benefits included in the two studies. The NRC study focuses on the state and local level, where immigrants typically impose the largest costs, while the OECD study focuses on the federal level, where immigrants tend to be net contributors when not including defense spending. Policymakers relying on such studies need to use caution and understand all of the assumptions underlying the estimates.

Several studies focus on the impact of undocumented immigrants on government budgets. Although undocumented immigrants are not eligible for most public assistance programs, state and local governments incur costs related to education, health care and law enforcement.

Media reports often suggest that undocumented immigrants create severe hardships to local areas by filling up emergency rooms and schools. Most studies confirm that unauthorized immigrants receive more in services than they pay in taxes at the state and local level. However, this fiscal burden tends to be localized in major immigrant-receiving states and cities, and estimates suggest that its magnitude is actually relatively small. The CBO (2007) surveyed 29 studies of the impact of unauthorized immigrants on state and local budgets. Overall, the studies confirm that states incur net fiscal costs from unauthorized immigrants, but these costs are typically less than 5 percent of total government expenditures. Net expenditures ranged from millions of dollars for small states to billions of dollars for California, the state with the largest number of unauthorized immigrants. Even in jurisdictions with large fiscal burdens in California, spending on unauthorized immigrants was less than 10 percent of total spending on government services.

Estimates of the net economic impact—as opposed to the net fiscal impact—of immigration should incorporate any economic gains (and losses) as well as net fiscal costs. In Texas, a report prepared by the state comptroller estimates that unauthorized immigrants paid $424 million more in revenue than was spent at the state level to provide education, health care and law enforcement to unauthorized immigrants in fiscal year 2005 (Strayhorn, 2006). The report also concludes that local governments incurred net costs of $1.4 billion in 2005 to provide health care and law enforcement. Education was the largest expense at the state level, and health care was the largest expense at the local level. Without the 1.4 to 1.6 million undocumented workers, however, the state's GDP would have been $17.7 billion, or 2.1 percent, smaller.

Legalizing undocumented immigrants affects their net fiscal position. A legalization program, or amnesty, for unauthorized immigrants can lead to higher tax revenues, but it also may lead to greater eligibility for government benefits. The net impact is thus theoretically uncertain. The CBO (2013) estimated that a legalization program included in a bill passed by the U.S. Senate in 2013 would have led to larger increases in federal spending than in tax revenues, suggesting that legalization programs increase the fiscal burden of immigrants in the United States. Most of the increase in federal spending was due to health care.

As discussed above, static estimates are only a snapshot and cannot be used to predict the future since they do not include changes in demographics, fiscal policy or immigration policy.

Dynamic models can be used to evaluate various assumptions and scenarios. The NRC study includes a dynamic analysis, which concludes:

> The average fiscal impact of immigrants under the baseline assumptions is positive in part because they tend to arrive at young working ages, in part because their descendants are expected to have higher skills and incomes, in part because they pay taxes for some items, such as national defense and interest on the federal debt, for which they do not impose costs, and in part because they will help to pay the public costs of the aging baby-boom generations.
>
> (Smith and Edmonston, 1997: 353)

The main results of the dynamic analysis are NPV calculations of the fiscal impact of an additional immigrant and his descendants over 300 years.[4] Table 10.3 summarizes the results. The main finding is that the average immigrant makes a positive fiscal contribution. This is due to the immigrants' descendants, who are assumed to assimilate quickly. The average net fiscal impact of an immigrant is $80,000 per immigrant (all figures are in 1996 dollars). Not surprisingly, the largest positive impact is $198,000 for an immigrant with more than a high school degree, including descendants. For those just with a high school degree, the estimate is a $51,000 fiscal gain. For immigrants without a high school degree, the average impact is a $13,000 fiscal loss.

The second and third rows of Table 10.3 decompose the overall impact into the separate impacts of an immigrant and his descendants. Not including descendants, the average immigrant creates a fiscal cost of $3,000. The cost rises to $89,000 for an immigrant without a high school degree. Although there is large variation in the NPV impacts of immigrants themselves by educational attainment, the fiscal impact of their descendants is positive, large and relatively similar across parental education groups. These estimates reflect assimilation by immigrants' children and later descendants.

The study also looks at NPVs by age at arrival and finds that immigrants who arrive at a younger age make larger net contributions. The NPV of the fiscal impact peaks for immigrants who arrive between ages 10 and 25 and then reaches a trough for those who arrive in their late sixties, when the impact is a large negative number. Meanwhile, the NPV for immigrants' descendants is positive regardless of immigrants' age at arrival.

In addition to a number of robustness checks, the study estimates the impact of an additional 100,000 immigrants entering the United States per year on the average citizen. It concludes there would be only a minimal fiscal effect. The overall effect would be a fiscal benefit of $30 per U.S. resident, which includes an increase of $40 at the federal level and a decrease of $10 at the state level. Thus, the NRC report concludes that, despite concerns over the fiscal

Table 10.3 Average net fiscal impact of an immigrant (1996 dollars)

	Overall	*Less than high school graduate*	*High school graduate*	*College and higher*
Immigrants and their descendants	80,000	−13,000	51,000	198,000
Immigrants	−3,000	−89,000	−31,000	105,000
Descendants	83000	76,000	82,000	93,000

Source: Smith and Edmonston (1997).

burden imposed by immigrants, "Our calculations suggest that immigrants may instead, on average, and in the long run, have a positive fiscal impact" (p. 352).

OECD countries

Across OECD countries, estimates suggest that the fiscal impact of immigration is small in terms of GDP (OECD, 2013). Further, the average fiscal impact is around zero. The OECD report notes, "Immigrants tend to have a less favourable net fiscal position than the native-born, but this is almost exclusively driven by the fact that immigrant households contribute on average less in terms of taxes and social security contributions than the native-born and not by a higher dependence on benefits" (p. 2).

Table 10.4 reports results for OECD countries using the static accounting method. Recall that this method is not forward-looking, relies on a number of assumptions and reflects past migration flows rather than current or future flows. In the OECD study, the unit of analysis is the household. Households are categorized as native born, mixed or migrant households based

Table 10.4 Net fiscal contribution by migration status, 2007–2009 average (in euros, PPP adjusted)

Country	Native	Mixed	Migrant
Switzerland	14,968	21,437	14,549
Iceland	12,272	17,558	9,292
Luxembourg	−1,228	7,232	9,178
Italy	3,980	12,126	9,148
United States	8,534	17,158	8,274
Greece	5,008	10,511	7,728
Spain	3,107	9,830	7,496
Belgium	9,159	16,830	5,560
Canada	7,552	15,494	5,167
Norway	5,055	20,366	4,505
Portugal	950	9,799	4,479
United Kingdom	2,604	11,954	3,029
Slovenia	4,450	2,368	3,006
Netherlands	9,940	21,303	2,544
Denmark	7,362	17,713	2,368
Austria	3,375	6,443	2,353
Australia	3,776	8,353	2,303
Hungary	1,081	1,915	1,864
Finland	5,706	12,265	1,314
Sweden	6,815	−13,473	896
Estonia	4,514	5,877	−2
Czech Republic	3,474	1,116	−184
Ireland	2,487	6,511	−1,274
France	2,407	9,131	−1,451
Slovak Republic	2,148	752	−2,171
Germany	5,875	−4,453	−5,622
Poland	291	−4,630	−5,691

Source: Organization for Economic Cooperation and Development (2013).

on the nativity of up to two household heads. The household heads are native born in native-born households; one is native born and the other foreign born in mixed households; and the heads are foreign born in migrant households. The estimates are based on data for the period 2007 to 2009 and are expressed in a common currency (the euro) and adjusted for purchasing power parity (PPP). Also, estimates typically exclude migrants with less than one year of residency. This may understate the positive impact of immigration since recent or temporary immigrants often come to work and are therefore net fiscal contributors.

As shown the last column of Table 10.4, estimates of the net fiscal contribution of the average migrant household vary considerably across countries. The estimates for migrant households are positive in 20 of the 27 countries. The largest net fiscal contribution is about 15,000 euros per migrant household in Switzerland, while the most negative estimate is –5,691 euros in Poland. Most of the countries with negative numbers for migrants have older immigrant populations who receive pensions, while Ireland was suffering from a deep financial crisis during the period under study (2007–2009). Notice that the net fiscal contribution is negative for native-born and mixed households in a few countries as well.

Net fiscal contributions tend to be smaller for immigrants than for natives. According to the OECD study, this gap is not explained by differences in age or educational attainment. Instead, the main factor underlying the gap between immigrants' and natives' fiscal effects is employment, which can explain about one-half of the gap. Immigrants are less likely than natives to be employed in most of the countries where natives make a larger fiscal contribution than immigrants. There are some places where immigrants contribute more than natives, such as Greece, Italy, Portugal and Spain, largely due to high employment rates among recent immigrants. Mixed households tend to have positive net contributions and often out-contribute native-born households. One reason for this pattern is that mixed households, by definition, are comprised of two adults, whereas native-born and migrant households can be comprised of single adults.

In most of the 27 countries in the OECD study, immigrants pay less than natives in taxes and receive less in transfers. Table 10.5 shows average contributions paid and benefits received by households' migrant status in each of the countries. The least generous countries, not surprisingly, in terms of benefits are those facing the worst fiscal crises—Greece, Iceland, Italy, Portugal and Spain. At the other extreme, migrant households receive more than native-born households in benefits in France and Germany. Native-born and migrant households alike make large fiscal contributions in Luxembourg and Switzerland, but migrant households' contributions exceed natives' there.

In addition to the comprehensive OECD (2013) report, numerous country-level studies give static estimates of the fiscal impact of immigration. Immigrants have a positive fiscal effect in Australia and New Zealand, both countries with point-based admissions systems (Slack et al., 2007). Meanwhile, immigrants have a negative fiscal effect in Canada, which also has a point-based system (Grubel, 2005; Grubel and Grady, 2011; Javdani and Pendakur, 2011). Immigrants are a net fiscal drain in Denmark and Sweden, which tend to have generous welfare programs (Ekberg, 1999; Wadensjö, 2000; Gerdes and Wadensjö, 2006; Wadensjö, 2007). In the United Kingdom, immigrants tend to be net fiscal contributors during periods of economic growth, whereas they impose fiscal costs during economic downturns (Gott and Johnston, 2002; Sriskandarajah, Cooley and Reed, 2005).

Results based on dynamic models are mixed across European countries. For Sweden, estimates of the projected fiscal impact of immigration between 2006 and 2050 range from

Table 10.5 Fiscal contributions paid and benefits received by household migration status, 2007–2009 average (in euros, PPP adjusted)

Contributions paid				Benefits received			
Country	Native	Mixed	Migrant	Country	Native	Mixed	Migrant
Luxembourg	20,043	23,732	20,463	Germany	9,498	18,629	13,727
Switzerland	19,858	26,353	20,149	France	10,952	12,193	11,412
Belgium	18,856	25,611	13,707	Luxembourg	21,270	16,500	11,285
US	15,527	22,844	13,145	Sweden	10,226	10,999	10,109
Netherlands	21,175	32,576	12,415	Austria	13,330	15,022	9,980
Iceland	18,972	23,117	12,380	Netherlands	11,236	11,273	9,871
Norway	17,382	31,613	12,368	Denmark	10,211	8,715	8,673
Austria	16,705	21,465	12,334	Ireland	12,014	10,063	8,583
Italy	15,346	19,552	12,310	Belgium	9,697	8,781	8,147
Canada	12,959	21,160	11,518	Poland	5,178	10,483	8,009
Denmark	17,574	26,428	11,041	Norway	12,327	11,246	7,863
Sweden	17,041	24,472	11,005	UK	8,899	9,036	7,774
UK	11,503	20,990	10,803	Finland	9,482	7,706	7,628
Slovenia	13,316	14,096	10,491	Slovenia	8,866	11,728	7,485
Spain	10,518	14,820	10,057	Canada	5,407	5,666	6,351
France	13,359	21,324	9,961	Switzerland	4,889	4,917	5,601
Greece	13,246	16,068	9,476	Australia	4,700	3,961	5,144
Finland	15,188	19,970	8,942	Czech Rep	4,990	6,965	5,100
Portugal	8,024	13,854	8,320	US	6,993	5,687	4,871
Germany	15,373	14,176	8,094	Hungary	5,450	6,551	4,779
Australia	8,476	12,314	7,447	Slovak Rep	4,003	6,123	4,610
Ireland	9,527	16,574	7,309	Estonia	3,014	3,501	3,992
Hungary	6,531	8,466	6,643	Portugal	7,074	4,055	3,841
Czech Rep	8,465	8,095	4,914	Italy	11,366	7,426	3,162
Estonia	7,528	9,378	3,990	Iceland	6,701	5,559	3,087
Slovak Rep	6,151	6,876	2,439	Spain	7,412	4,990	2,561
Poland	5,470	5,853	2,319	Greece	8,238	5,557	1,748

Source: Organization for Economic Cooperation and Development (2013).

−1.6 percent of GDP to +1.3 percent of GDP, depending on the assumptions made about new immigrants' employment rates and the level of public spending (Ekberg, 2011). In The Netherlands, the NPV of fiscal effects is considerably more positive (or less negative) for an immigrant who arrives at age 25 instead of as a child; the most negative estimate is −96,000 euros, and the most positive estimate is 45,000 euros (Roodenburg, Euwals and ter Rele, 2003). Two studies of Germany find positive fiscal impacts over the typical migrant's lifetime (Bonin, Raffelhüschen and Walliser, 2000; Kirdar, 2010).

U.S. immigrants' participation in government-funded programs

In the United States, individual states have considerable leeway to set eligibility rules and benefit levels for many publicly funded programs. This is particularly true with respect to immigrants in the post-1996 welfare reform era. Furthermore, states have implemented a variety of policies regarding immigrants' access to education, the labor market, businesses licenses and driver's licenses, among others. Most of these policies focus on unauthorized immigrants. This section discusses immigrants' fiscal effect through the lens of their participation in four major government-funded programs and services in the United States: welfare, education, health care and Social Security.

Welfare

Welfare in the United States typically refers to means-tested benefits, either cash or in-kind, made to eligible low-income individuals. Prior to 1996, the main cash welfare program was Aid to Families with Dependent Children (AFDC). In 1996, that program was transformed and renamed Temporary Assistance for Needy Families (TANF). AFDC and TANF are only available to families with minor children. Other cash transfer programs include: the Earned Income Tax Credit (EITC), which acts as a negative income tax for the working poor; Supplemental Security Income (SSI) for the disabled and elderly; and, in some states, General Assistance (GA) programs for poor people who do not qualify for other programs. Major in-kind welfare programs include food stamps (called the Supplemental Nutrition Assistance Program, or SNAP); public housing or housing subsidies (called Section-8 vouchers); and free or subsidized health insurance (Medicaid and the State Children's Health Insurance Program, or SCHIP). Social Security and Medicare are programs for the elderly and are not considered welfare since eligibility is based on age, not income.

Rapid growth in the low-skilled immigrant population during the 1970s and 1980s in the United States raised concerns that the country was becoming a welfare magnet (e.g., Bartel, 1989; Borjas, 1999). Some studies of the pre-1996 era conclude that immigrants are more likely than U.S. natives to participate in welfare programs (e.g., Blau, 1984; Borjas and Hilton, 1996). Although undocumented migrants are not eligible for public assistance programs other than emergency medical care, the growing size of this population created concerns among policymakers about the future fiscal costs of this group of immigrants and their U.S.-born children.

As a result, parts of the 1996 Personal Responsibility and Work Opportunity Reconciliation Act (PRWORA)—commonly referred to as welfare reform—aimed to reduce immigrants' use of government-provided services. Specifically, the law states that "aliens within the Nation's borders [should] not depend on public resources to meet their needs" (U.S. Congress 1996, Section 1601, Chapter 14). Although states were given flexibility in defining eligibility rules and allowed to offset some of the restrictions, the law contained the following provisions regarding immigrants' use of social services: most non-citizens who arrived before August 22, 1996, lost eligibility for Supplemental Security Income (SSI), food stamps and Medicaid; non-citizens arriving after August 22, 1996, are ineligible for most types of public assistance during the first five years after arrival; and non-citizens arriving after August 22, 1996, are subject to stricter eligibility requirements because their sponsors' income and assets are counted along with their own income and assets if they apply for public assistance during their first ten years in the United States.

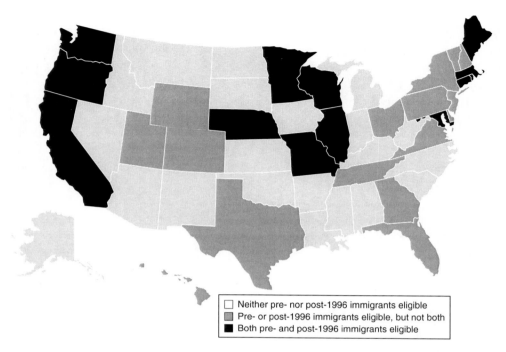

Figure 10.2 Immigrants' eligibility for welfare programs after 1996.

Source: Based on Borjas (2002).

Figure 10.2 shows states' response to the immigrant provisions in PRWORA. Some states continued to allow most immigrants to participate in programs on the same eligibility basis as U.S. natives. Specifically, some offered food stamps and SSI to immigrants who arrived before 1996 and TANF, Medicaid or SSI to immigrants who arrived after 1996. Those states are shown in the darkest color in the map. The lightest-colored states in the map offered neither, while states in the middle color extended eligibility to one or the other group but not both. In general, states with larger immigrant populations were more likely to extend eligibility to immigrants.

After 1996, welfare participation among immigrant households fell more precipitously than among native-born households. George Borjas (2002) attributes the decline to trends in welfare participation rates in California. Other research indicates that conditional on being eligible, immigrants are less likely to participate in public assistance programs, or less likely to "take up" benefits, than U.S. natives after 1996 (Fix, Capps and Kaushal, 2009; Bitler and Hoynes, 2013). These studies suggest "chilling effects" due to immigrants' confusion regarding their eligibility for welfare programs. Further, tougher immigration enforcement, as measured by apprehensions of unauthorized immigrants for removal from the country, reduces immigrants' participation in Medicaid (Watson, 2014).

The 1997 NRC study did not include the effects of welfare reform since those effects were not yet fully known. It estimated that PRWORA would cause the NPV of the average immigrant's fiscal impact to rise by about $8,000.

Education

In the United States, education is primarily funded by state and local governments, not by the federal government. Education is the largest expense for U.S. state and local budgets. It therefore is not surprising that the cost of educating foreign-born children and the children of foreign-born parents is a significant fiscal cost to state and local governments. About one-fifth of school-aged children in the United States are immigrants or the children of an immigrant (Capps et al., 2005). Only a small minority of these children are unauthorized immigrants. Many of the children of both legal and illegal immigrants are U.S. citizens since they were born in the United States. Since 1982, all children residing in the United States are entitled to receive free publicly funded K-12 education, regardless of immigration status.

Educational expenditures on children and young adults are not only a cost but also a significant investment. Children eventually join the workforce and pay taxes. The more education they receive, the higher their eventual earnings typically are and therefore the more they eventually pay in taxes. The education-related fiscal impact of immigration is therefore quite different in the short run than in the long run. Another issue is that the states and cities that disproportionately experience the front-loaded costs of educating immigrants may not be the same locations that eventually receive the benefits if immigrants move as they age.

One particular concern regarding immigrant children and the children of immigrants is the cost of providing bilingual or English as a second language education. The cost of educating students who do not speak English fluently is 20 to 40 percent more than it is for native-born students (CBO, 2007). However, spending on bilingual education represents only 2 percent of total spending at the K-12 level and has been stable over time despite the rise in the immigrant population in the United States (Griswold, 2012).

Whether immigrant children and the children of immigrants continue on to higher education and who pays for their education is the subject of debate, especially for illegal immigrant children. (Chapter 13 discusses the debate about whether to allow unauthorized immigrant youth to pay in-state tuition at public colleges and universities in the United States.) The private and public benefits of higher education are clearly documented. Higher education not only results in higher earnings and lower unemployment but can improve quality of life in other ways as well. For example, people with higher levels of education tend to live healthier lives, have better access to health care and have higher rates of employer-provided health insurance coverage. As earnings rise, so do taxes paid to state, local and federal governments.

Health care

The cost of health care for immigrants is another topic of considerable debate in the fiscal realm. Immigrants tend to be healthier and use less health care than U.S. natives. However, immigrants are less likely to have health insurance, and much of the cost of the health care they receive is funded by taxpayers. Despite this, estimates suggest that increases in the costs of health care in the United States are not due to immigration and that immigrant-related health care costs are not a large share of overall government spending.

Immigrants tend to use less health care than U.S. natives since they tend to be younger and healthier. One way to look at the age distribution of immigrants and natives is the dependency ratio, which is the ratio of working-age people to retirement-age people. When working age is defined as ages 18 to 64, the dependency ratio is estimated at 6.5 to 1 for immigrants, compared with 4.7 to 1 for U.S. natives (Zallman et al., 2013). For undocumented immigrants, the ratio is estimated to be even higher at 12.4 to 1. In other words, there are more working-age people relative to retirement-age people among the foreign-born population than among the native-born population.

Immigrants tend to be much healthier when they arrive because many of them migrate to work, are in their prime working years and have healthier lifestyles. Studies that compare health-related behavior and outcomes show that immigrants have healthier habits in terms of smoking, drinking, consuming unhealthy foods and being obese (Wallace et al., 2012). Not surprisingly, immigrants are therefore less likely than their native-born counterparts to experience serious health problems, such as diabetes, hypertension, heart disease and asthma (Pylypchuk and Hudson, 2009).

Immigrants also tend to use less health care, especially undocumented immigrants, in part because they are more likely to be uninsured. While only about 14 percent of U.S. natives were uninsured in 2010, 34 percent of all immigrants and 59 percent of undocumented immigrants were (DeNavas-Walt, Proctor and Smith, 2011; Batalova and Lee, 2012). Not having health insurance results in greater reliance on emergency rooms or publicly funded clinics for health care, a lower rate of preventative care and less access to regular health care providers (Rodriguez, Bustamante and Ang, 2009).

The federal government requires health care facilities to provide health care in life-threatening circumstances to everyone regardless of immigration or legal status and ability to pay. This results in uncompensated care for providers. It falls on state and local governments to cover much of these expenses. Certain jurisdictions, especially along the U.S.–Mexico border, face sizable costs. Nonetheless, these costs tend to be a small share of total spending.

At the national level, studies suggest that immigrants impose fewer costs on the health care system than native-born residents and pay more into the system through payroll taxes than they receive in services. Immigrants accounted for 8.5 percent of nationwide health care spending in 2000 but were 13 percent of the total population (RAND, 2006). Undocumented immigrants accounted for 1.5 percent of health care spending but were 3.2 percent of the population. During the period 2002 to 2009, undocumented immigrants contributed about $115.2 billion more to Medicare than they received in services (Zallman et al., 2013). Similarly, immigrants paid in $33.1 billion into the Hospital Insurance fund in 2009 but were only responsible for $19.3 billion in expenses (Zallman et al., 2013). Immigrants generated a total surplus in that fund of $115.2 billion during 2002 to 2009. Meanwhile, U.S. natives accumulated a deficit of $28.1 billion during that period.

Social Security

Social Security is the government-funded retirement program for the elderly in the United States. All legal workers and some undocumented immigrants working under stolen or made-up Social Security numbers contribute to Social Security through employer- and employee-paid payroll taxes. This deduction appears on paychecks as the Federal Insurance Contributions Act (FICA) tax. The FICA tax actually includes two separate taxes with different tax rates: Social Security and Medicare. As of 2014, the tax rate for Social Security is 6.2 percent of earnings paid by both the employer and the employee, or 12.4 percent total. There is a maximum taxable amount of earnings, which was $117,000 in 2014. For Medicare, the tax rate is 1.45 percent of earnings paid by both the employer and the employee, or 2.9 percent total. There is no earnings limit on the Medicare tax.

Many undocumented workers use false or fraudulently obtained Social Security numbers (SSNs) to satisfy employment eligibility verification requirements during the hiring process. Employers then use these numbers to withhold federal, state and local income and payroll taxes for employees. Some undocumented workers instead use Individual Tax Identification Numbers issued by the IRS to file tax returns, make payments and apply for refunds. The Social Security Administration estimates that about one-half of undocumented workers pay Social Security taxes (Feinleib and Warner, 2005). Other studies estimate that between 50 and 75 percent of unauthorized immigrants pay federal, state and local taxes (CBO, 2007).

Given that many immigrants, authorized and unauthorized, will not receive Social Security benefits, immigrants contribute to the solvency of the Social Security system. The Social Security Administration (SSA) estimated in 2011 that an increase of 300,000 immigrants per year would extend the solvency of the system by about one year (Griswold, 2012). In fiscal year 2010, the SSA also calculated that unauthorized immigrants contributed about $13 billion in payroll taxes but received only $1 billion in benefits (Goss et al., 2013). Most unauthorized immigrants will never receive benefits based on the contributions they make. Contributions that cannot be matched with a worker because an invalid SSN was used go into the Earnings Suspense File, which totals in the hundreds of billions of dollars.

Final thoughts on fiscal effects

Assessing the impact of immigrants on government accounts is complicated. There are many ways to calculate fiscal impacts, and all methods require that researchers make considerable assumptions. Although estimates vary widely, some patterns do emerge. First, in most countries the fiscal impact of immigration appears to be rather small as a share of overall economic output. Studies that look at the impact in a given year—the static accounting method—typically find an impact between −1 to +1 percent of GDP. Second, immigrants' labor market success affects their fiscal impact. In countries with relatively skilled immigrants admitted on the basis of employment qualifications, such as Australia and New Zealand (although not Canada), immigrants add to government coffers. Countries with sizable humanitarian immigrant populations experience smaller fiscal gains or even losses from immigration. Third, immigrants' age at arrival matters. Countries experience the biggest gains when immigrants, not surprisingly, work more years and therefore contribute more in taxes. Fourth, assimilation by immigrants' children can help alleviate fiscal imbalances, particularly for government-funded retirement benefit programs, in destination countries.

The next chapter shifts the focus from destination countries to source countries, where immigration also has fiscal, labor market and other effects.

Problems and discussion questions

1 What are the fiscal costs and benefits of immigration? At what level of government (federal, state or local) do they occur?
2 Why might unauthorized immigration be a net plus to the U.S. Social Security system?
3 Do immigrants strain the welfare system in the United States? In Europe? Why or why not?
4 What policies have countries implemented to reduce the fiscal costs associated with low-skilled immigrants? What other policies could they implement?
5 Explain the difference between the static and dynamic methods. Which one is more likely to indicate that immigrants are a fiscal cost if immigrants arrive at age 5? At age 25? At age 65? Why the differences?

Notes

1 For example, the National Research Council's study of the fiscal impact of immigrants in New Jersey includes nearly 30 categories of expenses (Smith and Edmonston, 1997). The services provided by the local government include: government administration, courts, police and fire protection services, public works, welfare and public health, recreation and conservation, libraries, vocational education, community colleges and K-12 education. At the state level, expenditures include: government administration, public safety and criminal justice, health, community development, transportation, environmental management, employment training, educational administration and state aid for K-12, higher education, state spending on Medicaid, AFDC and SSI, general state welfare assistance, pharmaceutical assistance for the elderly and disabled, municipal aid to local governments and property tax reimbursements.
2 Other pure public goods may include expenditures on veterans, research and development and the repayment of preexisting public debt.
3 The CBO's budget projections can be found at https://www.cbo.gov/topics/budget/budget-projections.
4 The extensive assumptions include: (1) starting in 2016, the debt/GDP ratio is held constant; (2) budgetary adjustments are done through a combination of higher taxes and lower spending; (3) the real interest rate is 3 percent; (4) immigrants continue to receive benefits as they did in 1994–1995; (5) taxes for immigrants follow the cross-sectional pattern for the first ten years and then become fixed to the age-specific tax payments of natives;(6) immigrants who arrive after age 55 get OASDHI benefits; (7) 30 percent of immigrants return home and bring their young children with them, and 16 percent of second-generation immigrants emigrate with their parents;(8) bilingual education costs raise total educational costs for immigrant and second-generation children by 22 percent.

Internet resources

The OECD's International Migration Statistics includes data on immigrants by citizenship, age, occupation, duration of stay, occupation, field of study and labor status, available at http://www.oecd-ilibrary.org/social-issues-migration-health/data/oecd-international-migration-statistics_mig-data-en.

Suggestions for further reading

Smith, J.P. and Edmonston, B. (eds.) (1997) *The New Americans: Economic, Demographic, and Fiscal Effects of Immigration*. Washington, DC: National Academies Press.
Storesletten, K. (2000) "Sustaining fiscal policy through immigration." *Journal of Political Economy* 108(2), pp. 300–323.

References

Auerbach, A.J., Gokhale, J. and Kotlikoff, L.J. (1991) "Generational accounts: A meaningful alternative to deficit accounting." In: Bradford, D. (ed.) *Tax Policy and the Economy* vol 5. Cambridge, MA: MIT Press.

Auerbach, A.J. and Oreopoulos, P. (1999) "Analyzing the fiscal impact of US immigration." *American Economic Review* 89(2), 176–180.

Bartel, A.P. (1989) "Where do the new U.S. immigrants live?" *Journal of Labor Economics* 7(4), pp. 371–91.

Batalova, J. and Lee, A. (2012) "Frequently requested statistics on immigrants and immigration in the United States." Washington, DC: Migration Policy Institute. Available at: http://www.migrationpolicy.org/article/frequently-requested-statistics-immigrants-and-immigration-united-states-0/ [20 September 2014].

Bitler, M.P. and Hoynes, H.W. (2013) "Immigrants, welfare reform, and the U.S. safety net." In: Card, D. and Raphael, S. (eds.) *Immigration, Poverty, and Socioeconomic Inequality*. New York: Russell Sage Foundation, pp. 315–380.

Blau, F.D. (1984) "The use of transfer payments by immigrants." *Industrial and Labor Relations Review* 37(2), pp. 222–239.

Bonin, H., Raffelhüschen, B. and Walliser, J. (2000) "Can immigration alleviate the demographic burden?" *FinanzArchiv* 57(1), pp. 1–21.

Borjas, G.J. (1999) "Immigration and welfare magnets." *Journal of Labor Economics* 17(4), pp. 607–637.

Borjas, G.J. (2002) "Welfare reform and immigrant participation in welfare programs." *International Migration Review* 36(4), pp. 1093–1123.

Borjas, G.J. and Hilton, L. (1996) "Immigration and the welfare state: Immigrant participation in means-tested entitlement programs." *Quarterly Journal of Economics* 111(2), pp. 575–604.

Capps, R., Fix, M., Murray, J., Ost, J., Passel, J.S. and Herwantoro, S. (2005) "The new demography of America's schools: Immigration and the No Child Left Behind Act." Washington, DC: Urban Institute. Available at: http://www.urban.org/UploadedPDF/311230_new_demography.pdf [20 September 2014].

Congressional Budget Office (CBO) (2007) "The impact of unauthorized immigrants on the budgets of state and local governments." Washington, DC: Congressional Budget Office. Available at http://www.cbo.gov/publication/41645 [20 September 2014].

Congressional Budget Office (CBO) (2013) "Cost estimate: S. 744, Border Security, Economic Opportunity, and Immigration Modernization Act." Washington, DC: Congressional Budget Office. Available at: http://www.cbo.gov/publication/44225 [10 September 2014].

DeNavas-Walt, C., Proctor, B.D. and Smith, J.C. (2011) "Income, poverty, and health insurance coverage in the United States: 2010." U.S. Bureau of the Census Report P60-239. Washington, DC: U.S. Bureau of the Census. Available at: http://www.census.gov/prod/2011pubs/p60-239.pdf [20 September 2014].

Ekberg, J. (1999) "Immigration and the public sector: Income effects for the native population in Sweden." *Journal of Population Economics* 12(3), pp. 411–430.

Ekberg, J. (2011) "Will future immigration to Sweden make it easier to finance the welfare system?" *Journal of Population Economics* 27(1), pp. 103–124.

Feinleib, J. and Warner, D. (2005) "The impact of immigration on Social Security and the national economy." Washington, DC: Social Security Advisory Board. Available at: http://www.ssab.gov/documents/immig_issue_brief_final_version_000.pdf [20 September 2014].

Fix, M., Capps, R. and Kaushal, N. (2009) "Immigrants and welfare: Overview." In: Fix, M.J. (ed.) *Immigrants and Welfare: The Impact of Welfare Reform on America's Newcomers*. New York: Russell Sage Foundation, pp. 1–36.

Gerdes, C. and Wadensjö, E. (2006) "Immigration and the welfare state: Some Danish experiences." *Academy for Migration Studies in Denmark (AMID) Working Paper* No. 60/2006. Copenhagen: Academy for Migration Studies in Denmark.

Goss, S., Wade, A., Skirvin, J.P., Morris, M., Bye, K.M. and Huston, D. (2013) "Effects of unauthorized immigration on the actuarial status of the Social Security Trust Funds." *Actuarial Note* No. 151. Baltimore, MD: Social Security Administration.

Gott, C. and Johnston, K. (2002) "The migrant population in the UK: Fiscal effects." *Research, Development and Statistics Directorate (RDS) Occasional Paper* No. 77. London: Research, Development and Statistics Directorate.

Griswold, D. (2012) "Immigration and the welfare state." *Cato Journal* 32(1), pp. 159–74.

Grubel, H. (2005) "Immigration and the welfare state in Canada: Growing conflicts, constructive solutions." *Fraser Institute Public Policy Sources* No. 84. Vancouver: Fraser Institute.

Grubel, H. and Grady, P. (2011) "Immigration and the Canadian welfare state 2011." Studies in Immigration and Refugee Policy, Fraser Institute. Vancouver: Fraser Institute.

Javdani, M. and Pendakur, K. (2011) "Fiscal transfers to immigrants in Canada." *Metropolis British Colombia Working Paper Series* No. 11-08. Vancouver: Metropolis British Colombia.

Kirdar, M. (2010) "Estimating the impact of immigrants on the host country social security system when return migration is an endogenous choice." *IZA Discussion Paper* No. 4894. Bonn: Institute for the Study of Labor.

Organization for Economic Cooperation and Development (OECD) (2013) *International Migration Outlook 2013*. Paris: OECD Publishing.

Pylypchuk, Y. and Hudson, J. (2009) "Immigrants and the use of preventative care in the United States." *Health Economics* 18(7), pp. 783–806.

Rand Corporation (RAND) (2006) "Rand study shows relatively little public money spent providing health care to undocumented immigrants." Santa Monica, CA: Rand Corporation. Available at: http://www.rand.org/news/press/2006/11/14.html [20 April 2014].

Rodriguez, M.A., Bustamante, A.V. and Ang, A. (2009) "Perceived quality of care, receipt of preventive care, and usual source of health care among undocumented and other Latinos." *Society of General Internal Medicine* 24(3), pp. 508–513.

Roodenburg, H., Euwals, R. and ter Rele, H. (2003) "Immigration and the Dutch economy." The Hague, Netherlands: CPB Netherlands Bureau for Economic Policy Analysis. Available at: http://www.cpb.nl/node/10221 [20 September 2014].

Slack, A., Wu, J. and Nana, G. (2007) "Fiscal impacts of immigration 2005/06." Economic Impacts of Immigration Working Paper Series. Wellington, New Zealand: Department of Labour.

Smith, J.P. and Edmonston, B. (eds.) (1997) *The New Americans: Economic, Demographic, and Fiscal Effects of Immigration*. Washington, DC: National Academies Press.

Sriskandarajah, D., Cooley, L. and Reed, H. (2005) "Paying their way: The fiscal contribution of immigrants in the UK." London: Institute for Public Policy Research. Available at: http://www.ippr.org/assets/media/images/media/files/publication/2011/05/Paying%20Their%20Way_1352.pdf [20 September 2014].

Strayhorn, C.K. (2006) "Undocumented immigrants in Texas: A financial analysis of the impact to the state budget and economy." Special Report (December). Austin, TX: Office of the Comptroller.

Wadensjö, E. (2000) "Immigration, the labour market, and public finances in Denmark." *Swedish Economic Policy Review* 7, pp. 59–83.

Wadensjö, E. (2007) "Immigration and net transfers within the public sector in Denmark." *European Journal of Political Economy* 23(2), pp. 472–485.

Wallace, S.P., Torres, J., Sadegh-Nobari, T., Pourat, N. and Brown, E.R. (2012) "Undocumented immigrants and health care reform." Mimeo, UCLA Center for Health Policy Research.

Available at: http://healthpolicy.ucla.edu/publications/Documents/PDF/undocumentedreport-aug2013.pdf [20 September 2014].

Watson, T. (2014) "Inside the refrigerator: Immigration enforcement and chilling effects in Medicaid participation." *American Economic Journal: Economic Policy* 6(3), pp. 313–338.

Zallman, L., Woolhandler, S., Himmelstein, D., Bor, D. and McCormick, D. (2013) "Immigrants contributed an estimated $115.2 billion more to the Medicare trust fund than they took out in 2002–09." *Health Affairs* 32(6), pp. 1153–60.

11 Effects on Source Countries

Although the number of international migrants continues to rise in absolute terms, the share of the world population who are migrants has remained steady at around 3 percent over the past 50 years. Nonetheless, there have been considerable shifts in migrants' demographic characteristics and their source and destination countries. Most notably, a greater share of migrants move from middle-income countries to high-income countries, and how far migrants move has increased. In addition, the education levels of immigrants have risen.

Researchers point to increased ability to finance migration costs and a significant drop in those costs as the main causes of these shifts. Rising wages in populous former low-income countries have increased migration from middle- to high-income countries. In particular, China and India gained middle-income status, and more of their citizens became able to bear migration costs.[1] In addition, in the late 1970s China became more willing to allow its citizens to leave. Meanwhile, migration costs have fallen, in part due to bigger migrant networks in receiving countries and greater interconnectedness through advances in information technology. The increased prevalence of ethnic enclaves and diasporas has lowered the information costs of migration and thereby increased their force as a "pull" factor. Migrant networks enable potential emigrants to more accurately evaluate economic opportunities in distant countries. Near-universal mobile phones have increased the flow of information and money to source countries, which in turn has the potential to boost emigration and economic development there.

Migrants are increasingly likely to be highly educated, in part because of rising education levels in most source countries, and to choose high-income destination countries. According to Cecily Defoort (2008), the share of migrants in the six largest OECD countries—Australia, Canada, France, Germany, the United Kingdom and the United States—with a tertiary, or college, education rose four-fold between 1975 and 2000. The number of tertiary-educated immigrants in OECD countries then increased by another 70 percent between 2000 and 2013 (United Nations and OECD, 2013).

Higher incomes in destination countries remain the main draw for economic migrants. Workers in high-income countries earn wages that are a multiple of those in middle-income countries (International Labour Organization, 2013). The possibility of earning more attracts high- and low-skilled immigrants alike. High-skilled migrants are also lured by non-pecuniary benefits available in high-income countries, such as better work environments, opportunities to conduct research with colleagues who are leaders in their field and more potential for career advancement.

The effects of emigration on the sending country are the focus of this chapter. To begin, emigration affects the labor market in the source country, with implications for workers and owners of other factors of production who remain there. If migrants are disproportionately high-skilled workers, emigration may adversely affect the living standards of those left behind. However, an outflow of high-skilled workers may actually increase human capital in the source country via increased transfer of knowledge from abroad and return migration. Relatedly, migrants often send funds, or remittances, to family members. As this chapter discusses, these remittances can have important economic effects. Lastly, the chapter explores how migration can affect political, economic and social institutions in the source country.

Labor market consequences of emigration for the source country

Migration has labor market implications in both sending and receiving countries. For the sending country, migration by workers decreases labor supply there. As shown in Figure 11.1, this shifts the labor supply curve to the left. (To simplify the analysis, the figure shows the supply curve as vertical, or perfectly inelastic, and assumes that all workers are identical, or there is only one skill level.)

For example, suppose workers in Poland are considering moving to the United Kingdom. This would occur if wages are higher in the United Kingdom, which is true for most workers. (Higher wages in the United Kingdom could be due to a number of factors, including higher

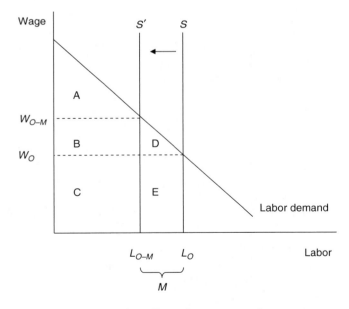

Figure 11.1 Labor market effects of migration in the source country.

Before immigration L_O workers are employed in the origin at wage W_O. After migration, L_{O-M} workers are employed there at wage W_{O-M}.

product demand due to higher incomes there or higher productivity of workers due to differences in the capital stock or technology.) As workers migrate from Poland to the United Kingdom, labor supply decreases in Poland. Wages rise among workers who remain there. In Figure 11.1, wages rise from W_O to W_{O-M}.

Although immigration creates a net welfare gain globally and in the destination, as discussed in Chapter 7, the model indicates that there are welfare losses in the source country. Before migration, workers earn the areas represented by C + E in Figure 11.1. The owners of other factors of production earn the areas represented by A+ B + D. After M workers leave, the remaining workers, L_{O-M}, earn B + C. It appears that workers lose area E while gaining area B, but keep in mind that area E was earned by workers who leave. Area E is therefore not a loss to workers who remain in the source country. Owners of the other factors of production receive only area A after migration. Migration thus leads to a transfer of area B to workers from owners of other factors of production. It also leads to a social welfare loss equal to area D. (Again, area E does not count since it represents income lost by workers who move and then earn even higher incomes.) Thus, the sending country suffers on net in this model, while the world as a whole gains.

Studies indicate that migration does indeed lead to higher wages for those left behind. Using the simple theoretical framework presented above, Prachi Mishra (2007) examines the labor market impact of out-migration from Mexico. She finds that out-migration leads to higher wages there. Specifically, a 10 percent decrease in the number of Mexican workers in a schooling and experience skill group increases the average wage in that skill group by about 4 percent.

Emigration and human capital: brain drain or brain gain?

Beyond its impact on the labor market, emigration may have implications for the source country if it is disproportionately comprised of high-skilled workers. As noted above, this is a real concern for some countries since globally a disproportionate share of migrants is highly educated. When the consequences are perceived as negative, the emigration of highly-skilled workers is often called "brain drain." Originally, the term brain drain was used by the British Royal Society to describe the exodus of scientists and technology workers from the United Kingdom to the United States and Canada in the 1950s and 1960s (Gibson and McKenzie, 2011). Nowadays, the term is often used more broadly to encompass not only high-skilled migration from one developed country to another but also from developing to developed countries and from rural to urban areas within countries. In the past, policymakers typically aimed to stem the outflow or recover the perceived costs of high-skilled emigration. However, recent evidence links high-skilled emigration to positive outcomes in the source country. These benefits have been called "brain gain." Specifically, brain gain results when the remaining members of the sending country benefit from high-skilled emigration.

Studying high-skilled emigration is important because it is part of a broader discussion of the costs and benefits of immigration in global economies. International mobility of workers can create sizable global benefits. Estimates of the net gains from more open borders for all workers are in the trillions of dollars (Clemens, 2011). The gains from removing barriers to migration appear to be more than twice as large as the gains from removing barriers to trade and capital flows. Increased migration of high-skilled workers in particular can increase economic growth and innovation in destination countries, as discussed in Chapter 9.

The implications of high-skilled migration for sending countries are less clear. On the one hand, migration of high-skilled workers may create negative externalities, shortages in certain occupations, problematic shifts in complementarities and fiscal shortfalls for those left behind. Governments in particular worry about squandering scarce resources on educating and training workers who then leave. Governments of developing countries also worry that emigration may exacerbate a shortage of health care workers. On the other hand, strong networks of migrants abroad and return migration may benefit source countries through better access to capital, technology and ideas. Whether high-skilled migration is a boon or a curse for sending countries is thus both a theoretical and an empirical question.

The extent of high-skilled emigration

Economists and demographers have developed several measures to gauge the extent of high-skilled emigration.[2] The most common indicator is the emigration rate of highly educated individuals, such as the fraction of the population with a tertiary education who leave. Another measure is the emigration rate among PhD holders. This measure focuses on workers who are typically involved in research and development (R&D), innovation, patents and other key sources of productivity growth. A third measure is the number or fraction of physicians abroad. Early concerns about brain drain in developing countries focused on the possibility that emigration led to shortages of medical professionals in source countries, particularly in Africa, motivating use of this measure.

Using the first measure, Herbert Brücker, Stella Capuano and Abdeslam Marfouk created emigration rates by country of origin, gender and educational level using data on 20 OECD destination countries.[3] Table 11.1 presents some their estimates for 2010. Specifically, the table presents emigration rates overall and by education attainment for the ten richest countries and the ten poorest countries with populations over one million.[4] Emigration rates are defined as the total number of migrants from the source country divided by the number of migrants plus the number of residents in the source country.

There are several notable patterns in Table 11.1. First, emigration occurs from both rich and poor countries. Indeed, emigration is higher from some rich countries than from some poor countries. Second, emigration rates tend to increase as education increases. Third, emigration of the highly educated tends to be much greater for poor countries than for rich countries. For example, more than one-third of high-skilled people have left Eritrea, Malawi, Mozambique and the Republic of Congo, while Zimbabwe has the highest emigration rate of high-skilled workers, 56 percent, in the table.

Other studies confirm these patterns across countries. The average emigration rate of people with a tertiary education is 7.3 percent in developing countries, with a range from 5.4 percent in larger countries to 13 percent in sub-Saharan African countries to 45 percent in small developing island nations (Docquier, Lohest and Marfouk, 2007). These rates are actually underestimates because they only include a subset of relatively developed destination countries; the same is true for the estimates presented in Table 11.1. As of 2000, Cape Verde, Grenada, Guyana, Haiti, Jamaica, Palau, Saint Kitts and Nevis, Saint Vincent and the

Table 11.1 Emigration rates (per 100 population) by education for richest and poorest countries, 2010

Country	Overall	Education level		
		Low	Middle	High
World	1.91	1.40	1.29	5.31
Richest:				
Qatar	0.18	0.07	0.08	0.68
Singapore	3.28	1.82	1.20	10.30
Norway	3.81	3.34	2.97	5.33
United States	0.46	1.94	0.27	0.53
Hong Kong	9.56	5.78	3.23	30.02
Switzerland	4.51	2.77	3.19	10.59
Canada	3.62	5.86	1.74	5.85
Australia	2.12	7.98	0.81	3.75
Austria	5.65	4.92	3.67	14.35
Netherlands	5.16	8.09	2.66	9.62
Poorest:				
Mali	1.40	0.94	6.63	12.57
Mozambique	1.47	0.53	14.83	46.37
Malawi	0.34	0.17	0.20	35.97
Niger	0.08	0.03	0.33	3.32
Zimbabwe	2.10	0.93	0.61	55.83
Eritrea	2.63	0.98	4.19	42.64
Liberia	3.65	0.71	5.19	20.24
Republic of the Congo	3.41	2.32	2.10	36.33
Burundi	0.35	0.10	1.28	16.51
Central African Republic	0.55	0.26	0.76	10.12

Source: Based on data from http://www.iab.de/en/daten/iab-brain-drain-data.aspx [3 June 2014]. Calculations are based on immigrants in twenty OECD destination countries.

Grenadines, Seychelles, Trinidad and Tobago and Tonga all had high-skilled emigration rates above 75 percent. Frédéric Docquier and Hillel Rapoport (2012b) attribute these high rates to the countries' small size, high poverty rates and (for some) proximity to the United States.

Over time, the absolute number of high-skilled migrants has increased. However, skill levels are increasing in sending countries as well, leaving the high-skilled emigration rate fairly steady. Sub-Saharan Africa appears to be an exception, however. Growth in educational attainment in source countries there has not kept up with increases in out-migration by the highly skilled (Defoort, 2008).

Although it is commonly believed that high-skilled emigration is concentrated among doctors and nurses, there is actually significant diversity in the occupations and industries of educated emigrants. In the United States and Canada, the share of high-skilled immigrants who are medical professionals is actually relatively low at 13 percent and 6 percent, respectively (Gibson and McKenzie, 2011). Nonetheless, some countries suffer severe health professional shortages as a result of emigration (Docquier and Rapoport, 2012b). In Grenada, Dominica,

Fiji, Ireland, Jamaica, Liberia and Saint Lucia, for example, more than 40 percent of physicians have emigrated (Bhargava and Docquier, 2008). Nonetheless, the number of health care professionals who have left some countries, particularly in sub-Saharan Africa, is so small relative to needs there that it effectively does not matter (Clemens, 2007).[5]

Researchers have documented several determinants of high-skilled emigration. Political instability, low average human capital, small populations and religious fractionalization in source countries are push factors for educated migrants (Docquier, Lohest and Marfouk, 2007). The number of high-skilled emigrants is similar for men and women, but this translates into a higher emigration rate among high-skilled women given global gender disparities in education (Docquier and Rapoport, 2012a). The "feminization" of migration gives rise to concerns about future economic growth in developing source countries since a higher level of education among women tends to be linked to lower fertility, higher labor productivity and faster economic growth in those countries (Docquier and Rapoport, 2012b).

Two other patterns have been observed among high-skilled emigrants. The first is that highly educated workers tend to agglomerate in urban areas (Clemens, 2009). The second is that high-skilled migration is correlated with low-skilled migration since high-skilled migrants may bring low-skilled family members with them (Gibson and McKenzie, 2011). In addition, networks in the receiving country may reduce migration costs for both high- and low-skilled migrants alike, while better opportunities may attract both groups.

Theories of brain drain and brain gain

Traditional models of high-skilled emigration predict negative consequences for economic growth in sending countries. In these models, high-skilled immigration results in increased global inequality, with rich countries getting richer and poor countries getting poorer. The models treat education as exogenous, or coming from outside the model, and do not allow education levels in source countries to change in response to emigration. This research was pioneered by Jagdish Bhagwati and Koichi Hamada (1974).[6]

Later models, first developed in the 1990s, are more optimistic. These models recognize that emigration may lead people left behind in the source country to increase their own human capital in an effort to themselves migrate. In addition, source countries may benefit from emigrants returning to follow entrepreneurial pursuits, boosting productivity through information diffusion or increasing investment through remittances. There are four main channels through which brain gain may occur: the human capital channel, the productivity channel, the transfer channel and the institutional channel.

The human capital channel allows the level of educational attainment to depend in part on migration prospects. The prospect of migrating to a country with a higher return to education can motivate people in the sending country to acquire more education. If only a fraction of these people actually migrate, education levels rise in the sending country over time. However, if potential migrants would move to a country with a lower return to education, such as Mexicans migrating to the United States, increased prospects of migrating may reduce the incentive to acquire education. Models that allow human capital to be endogenized, or depend on migration prospects, give ambiguous predictions for the impact of emigration on education levels in the source country (Docquier and Rapoport, 2012b).

Several case studies suggest that the human capital channel leads to an increase in education in source countries. In Fiji, Indo-Fijians invested in education in order to migrate to Australia, New Zealand or Canada after a 1987 military coup created an unstable environment for the Indian minority group. Given that those destinations have skills-based point systems, Indo-Fijians needed to acquire high levels of schooling to be able to migrate there. The rate of emigration among tertiary-educated Indo-Fijians rose, but education levels among the remaining population and returning migrants rose as well (Chand and Clemens, 2008). In Nepal, soldiers are recruited into the British Army as part of the special Gurkha brigade. In order to qualify, Nepalese soldiers must complete a certain level of schooling. An increase in the education cutoff led to a higher likelihood that Nepalese completed primary and secondary education (Shrestha, 2011). Surveys of teachers and students in Ghana, Micronesia, New Zealand, Papua New Guinea and Tonga indicate that students change what they study and teachers change what courses they offer in response to increased emigration (Gibson and McKenzie, 2012). In particular, teachers add foreign languages, teach tolerance of different perspectives and add global botany into their curriculum.

At the country level, studies also find evidence of a positive impact of emigration on human capital attainment in the sending country. Michel Beine, Docquier and Rapoport (2008) examine the impact of high-skilled emigration on educational attainment in 127 developing countries. They find that a doubling of emigration among the highly educated is associated with a 5 percent increase in the proportion of the population with a tertiary education in the source country in the short run, and a 22.5 percent increase in the long run. These numbers suggest a substantial increase in educational attainment in response to high-skilled emigration, particularly in the long run. Using these estimated elasticities, Docquier and Rapoport (2012b) identify winners (those experiencing brain gain) and losers (those experiencing brain drain). Losers include small and medium-sized countries with emigration rates above 50 percent, such as islands in the Caribbean and Pacific. The winners are large countries, such as Brazil, China and India.

In the productivity channel, high-skilled emigrants abroad can return flows of income, investment and expertise or move back to the source country themselves. These flows have a positive impact on total factor productivity (TFP). Enclaves in the receiving country diffuse technology to the sending country and increase TFP there. For most developing countries, adoption of technologies developed abroad, not home-grown innovation, is the main driver of technological progress. Network externalities between migrants abroad and the remaining residents in a sending country can enhance the sending country's adoption of new technologies. In pursuit of such gains, some countries encourage high-skilled emigration and have programs to facilitate training for migration. These countries include China, Cuba, India, the Philippines, Sri Lanka and Vietnam (World Bank, 2006). Countries with large diasporas, such as China, India and the Philippines, have experienced considerable growth in information technology, trade, investment, technology transfers and knowledge circulation as a result of high-skilled emigration (Saxenian, 1999, 2002; Opiniano and Castro, 2006).

The transfer channel links emigration to remittances. Remittances relax households' budget constraints and allow households to increase consumption, investment or savings or to pay off loans. If the funds are used for education, remittances may increase human capital formation and thereby ultimately boost economic growth in the home country. (Remittances are discussed more later in this chapter.)

Lastly, the institutional channel allows for feedback onto political, economic and social institutions in the home country. Better institutions may result in higher TFP. Furthermore, links between diasporas and the home country may boost the economy in the home country via increased trade and foreign direct investment. (Theory and empirical evidence on this channel are discussed later in this chapter.)

Growth accounting

The growth accounting technique from Chapter 9 can be used to analyze the effects of emigration on the source country. Recall that the growth accounting equation is

$$\%\Delta Y = \%\Delta A + a_L\%\Delta L + a_K\%\Delta K \tag{11.1}$$

where Y is output, A is TFP, L is number of workers, K is the stock of physical capital and a_L and a_K represent the elasticity of output with respect to labor and capital, respectively. For output to grow, an input to production (labor or capital) or TFP must grow.

In the simplest case, the reduction in the labor force in the source country means $\%\Delta L < 0$ and hence reduces output growth. However, if emigrants send remittances back to their source country, as posited by the transfer channel, then the capital stock may grow, or $\%\Delta K > 0$. This would contribute to faster growth in output. In addition, transmission of technologies or knowledge may occur when highly educated migrants move abroad and share newly acquired knowledge with their home country, as posited by the productivity channel. If so, TFP grows in the source country, or $\%\Delta A > 0$. The net effect would depend on the relative sizes of the elasticities of output with respect to capital and labor and the relative magnitude of the changes. If a_L is relatively small and a_K relatively big, the net effect of emigration could be positive for the source country. However, if the reverse holds, then emigration may act as a drag on output growth in the source country.

Policy issues and responses to high-skilled emigration

High-skilled emigration receives considerable attention in part because of its relevance for policymakers. When a highly skilled worker leaves, there may be fiscal implications if the source country's government has incurred the majority of the costs for training and educating the worker. The success of policies that tax or limit emigration rests on numerous assumptions and requires information on a wide range of effects in both sending and receiving countries. One well-known proposal, introduced by Bhagwati and Hamada (1974), is a Pigovian tax on high-skilled emigration, or a "tax on brains," to compensate origin countries. Quantifying the magnitude of these costs in order to set the tax is difficult. Further, policymakers have had limited success in imposing taxes or other fees on emigrants. For example, some governments offer student loans to citizens studying abroad and forgive the loan if a citizen returns. Less than 10 percent of these loans were repaid in Brazil, Venezuela and Kenya in the 1980s, and there have been sizable defaults among New Zealand emigrants (Albrecht and Ziderman, 1991).

Some countries aim to make return migration attractive to high-skilled emigrants. For example, India has invested in infrastructure to lure information technology workers to return home. China has attempted to stem its outflow and encourage return migration by creating world-class educational institutions. France and the United Kingdom have tried to increase salaries and employment opportunities at home. The openness of the economies of Ireland, South Korea and Taiwan is another way to attract return migrants as well as investment from abroad (Cervantes and Guellec, 2002).

Remittances

Remittances are income received by households from family members abroad, sent as cash or in-kind transfers. Remittances may flow through formal or informal channels. Formal channels include money wiring services, such as Western Union and Money Gram, and financial institutions, such as banks and credit unions. Informal channels include family or friends returning home who bring money or goods back with them and networks of individuals who operate as money brokers in both the destination and source countries. These brokers are sometimes called *hawala* or *hundi* in South Asia and *padala* in the Philippines (Yang, 2011). Informal channels work on the honor system and are largely reliant on family connections.

Remittances are substantial. For many countries, remittances greatly dwarf foreign aid, and for some countries remittances equal or even exceed the level of foreign direct investment. The most widely used data on remittances are compiled by the World Bank. Figure 11.2 presents the World Bank's estimates of annual global remittances since 1970.[7] Total remittances have grown (in real terms) from slightly under $2 billion in 1970 to over $500 billion in 2013. Remittances fell slightly in 2009 as a result of the global financial crisis but otherwise have

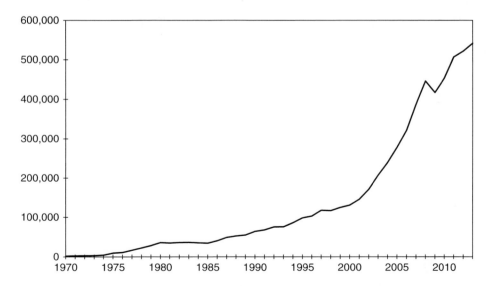

Figure 11.2 Total worldwide remittances, 1970–2013 (in millions, 2013 U.S. dollars).

Source: Based on http://siteresources.worldbank.org/INTPROSPECTS/Resources/334934-1288990760745/RemittanceData_Inflows_Apr2014.xls [10 August 2014].

increased steadily over time. One should be cautious, however, when examining the time trend as some of the growth may be due to better accounting and increased use of formal channels.

The United States is the number one source country for international remittances, accounting for nearly one-fourth of remittances sent worldwide. Table 11.2 lists the top 25 recipient countries in 2013. India is at the top, with about $70 billion in remittances. China ranks second, receiving about $60 billion. Interestingly, several industrialized countries are on the list, including the United States. How can the United States be both the world's largest source of remittances and one of the world's largest recipients of remittances? It has the world's greatest number of immigrants, but it also has enough citizens working overseas and sending funds back to the United States to be on the list. The last column in Table 11.2 gives remittances as a share of GDP. For most of the countries, remittances are a small share of GDP. For the United States, remittances are less than one-tenth of 1 percent of GDP.

The list is strikingly different when looking at the top remittance-receiving countries by share of GDP. Table 11.3 lists those countries. Tajikistan comes out on top, with remittances accounting for more than one-half of GDP. Nine countries receive over 20 percent of their GDP in remittances.

Table 11.2 Top 25 remittance-receiving countries by level of remittances, 2013

Country	In US$ million	As a share of GDP (%)
India	69,969	3.7
China	60,000	0.7
Philippines	25,351	9.8
France	22,863	0.8
Mexico	22,282	2.0
Nigeria	21,000	7.9
Egypt	17,469	7.5
Pakistan	14,626	6.1
Germany	14,496	0.4
Bangladesh	13,776	12.2
Vietnam	11,000	7.1
Belgium	10,566	2.1
Spain	10,133	0.7
Ukraine	9,633	4.8
South Korea	8,765	0.8
Indonesia	7,614	0.8
Italy	7,536	0.4
Lebanon	7,200	16.1
Poland	7,157	1.4
Russia	6,862	0.3
United States	6,703	0.0
Sri Lanka	6,690	10.1
Morocco	6,619	6.8
Thailand	5,555	1.3
Guatemala	5,399	10.0

Source: Based on http://siteresources.worldbank.org/INTPROSPECTS/Resources/ 334934-1288990760745/RemittanceData_Inflows_Apr2014.xls [10 August 2014].

Table 11.3 Top 25 remittance-receiving countries by share of GDP, 2013

Country	In US$ million	As a share of GDP (%)
Tajikistan	3,960	51.9
Kyrgyz Republic	2,290	31.4
Nepal	5,210	24.7
Moldova	1,981	24.6
Samoa	155	23.5
Lesotho	520	22.6
Armenia	2,436	21.4
Haiti	1,696	20.6
Liberia	383	20.4
Kosovo	1,125	17.0
Guyana	493	16.5
El Salvador	4,210	16.5
Lebanon	7,200	16.1
Honduras	3,124	15.8
Gambia	181	15.4
Jamaica	2,277	14.5
Tonga	61	12.6
Bangladesh	13,776	12.2
Jordan	3,680	11.4
Senegal	1,652	11.4
Georgia	2,056	11.2
Bosnia and Herzegovina	1,896	10.8
Sri Lanka	6,690	10.1
Guatemala	5,399	10.0
Philippines	25,351	9.8

Source: Based on http://siteresources.worldbank.org/INTPROSPECTS/
Resources/334934-1288990760745/RemittanceData_Inflows_Apr2014.xls
[10 August 2014].

Remittances make up a large share of the income of migrant workers, according to Dean Yang (2011). For example, Mexican migrants surveyed primarily in Mexico report that they send home 31 percent of their U.S. earnings. Salvadorans working in Washington, DC, report that remittances are 38 percent of their income. Senegalese working in Spain send one-half of their earnings back to Senegal, while Senegalese working in France send back 11 percent of their income.

Remittances are typically small amounts sent frequently. In a sample of Salvadoran immigrants in Washington, DC, for example, the average amount per transaction is $200 to $300, with about one-fourth at $100 or less (Yang, 2011). Migrants remit small amounts frequently for several reasons. Sending small amounts frequently may help the sender save and act as a means of self-control over the temptation to spend the money. It may be a way for migrants and recipients to reduce their losses if they are robbed. It may also help the sender maintain more control over how the recipient allocates the funds—a migrant who is unhappy with how remittances are being used can threaten to stop sending funds more effectively if he is sending them frequently. In addition, migrants may spread their remittances across recipients by sending smaller amounts to multiple people instead of one larger amount to one person.

Remittances are sent typically electronically and incur a fee. Fees can be fixed, a percentage of the transaction amount or a fixed fee plus a percentage. Globally, remittance fees average almost 9 percent of the amount sent (World Bank, 2010). Among Tongan immigrants in New Zealand, the estimated elasticity of remittance transfers with respect to the fixed portion of the fee is $-.22$, or a 1 percent decrease in the fee is associated with a 0.22 percent increase in the amount sent (Gibson, McKenzie and Rohorua, 2006). Among Salvadoran immigrants in Washington, DC, reductions in fees lead to more frequent remittances, which ultimately increases the amount sent per month (Aycinena, Martinez and Yang, 2010). A \$1 decrease in fees leads to migrants sending \$25 more a month there, a strikingly large effect.

Reforms such as increasing competition in money transmission markets or providing migrants with more information on the relative cost of different money transmission services can have a large impact on remittances. Technological innovations, such as mobile banking, can change how migrant families send, receive and use remittances. Mobile banking—using cell phones to conduct financial transactions—can lower transactions costs and help alleviate the shortage of financial institutions that remittance-receiving families in rural areas often face. Mobile banking has already changed the way financial transactions are conducted in developing countries. One of the most widely used forms of mobile banking for remittances is the M-PESA system, as discussed in the box "M-PESA and remittances." Migrants themselves may also face difficulties accessing financial markets. This problem is particularly acute for unauthorized immigrants, who may lack the necessary documents to open a bank account. Mexican migrants in the United States with access to banks are more likely to save and bring back larger amounts of money to Mexico (Amuedo-Dorantes and Bansak, 2006).

Box 11.1 M-PESA and remittances

M-PESA is a mobile banking system run by Kenyan telecom provider Safaricom that allows users to make payments and transfers using their mobile phones. It was introduced in 2007 to reduce the costs of transferring funds from one individual to another. It has attracted worldwide attention for fostering dramatic growth of cell phone-facilitated payments and remittances within Kenya and has spread to other developing countries, including Afghanistan, Romania and Tanzania. In countries where money transfers from urban to rural regions occur frequently, M-PESA provides a service that is secure, convenient and low cost. As of 2013, M-PESA had 17 million active users, including 40 percent of the Kenyan population, and averaged \$320 million in flows every month.

Economists have found that M-PESA has affected remittances. By lowering transactions costs and making transfers easily accessible and safe, mobile banking tends to increase the frequency that migrants send remittances (Morawczynski and Pickens, 2009; Mbiti and Weil, 2011). The amount sent per transaction decreases, but total remittances per month or year increase. Indeed, the income of rural recipients in Kenya rose up to 30 percent after they began using M-PESA (Morawczynski and Pickens, 2009). The rise of mobile banking has also decreased use of informal channels and increased demand for other banking products. However, the availability of M-PESA also seems to reduce migrants' need to return home and may lead to weaker ties to family members in the source country. In the long run, this may ultimately lead to fewer remittances.

Reasons for remitting

Understanding the motivations for remittances is critical to understanding how remittances affect economic outcomes. Economists have identified a number of reasons why migrants send remittances. Altruism models posit that migrants' desire to help family left behind is a strong and common motivation for remittances. The consumption smoothing model posits that migration takes place to diversify household earnings and ensure a steady source of income. In the target saving model, migration occurs in order to accumulate financial assets or fund a specific investment or purchase. Migrants may also plan to return and then open a small business, buy a plot of land for farming or build a house. Migrating to an area with higher-paying jobs helps migrants accumulate the required savings to undertake these relatively large expenses. Target savers are likely to be temporary immigrants. They are also less apt to make investments in the destination, more frugal in their consumption there and likely to remit and carry large sums home.

Migrants may also remit for insurance purposes. The decision to migrate may involve uncertainty, such as how quickly a migrant can find a job and, for an unauthorized immigrant, whether she will be deported. Sending money back can mean having some savings and a warmer welcome if a migrant returns. Another financial motivation for remittances is to repay migration costs. Migration entails an upfront cost, which may be financed through borrowing. Remittances may be necessary to repay the loan. These motivations are not mutually exclusive— any combination of them may apply to a particular migrant, and different motivations are likely to be more common among different groups of migrants.

Evidence on the impact of remittances

Research on the effects of remittances has looked at both macroeconomic effects and microeconomic effects. Macroeconomic effects include the effects on economic growth, exchange rates and capital accumulation. Microeconomic effects include the effects on households' spending and investment patterns and their poverty rate.

Remittances and economic growth

As the growth accounting framework indicates, economic growth can occur via increases in labor, capital or TFP. When migrants send money home, remittances that are saved may lead to an increase in capital. If remittances are used to fund human capital accumulation, then labor (which encompasses both quantity and "quality" of workers) or TFP may increase. However, if remittances enable family left behind to stop working, remittances may reduce labor and thereby act as a drag on output growth. The net effect of remittances on economic growth is thus not necessarily positive.

Further, remittances may reduce GDP through an increase in the exchange rate. If remittances are large enough, they may cause the country's currency to appreciate in value, which in turn may reduce exports. A massive inflow of foreign currency that leads to real exchange rate appreciation and a loss of international competitiveness, which then lead to a decline in the production of manufactured and other tradable goods, is called "Dutch disease." The possibility of Dutch disease is a substantial concern for developing countries whose economies rely heavily on exports. Research suggests this has occurred in El Salvador (Acosta, Lartey and Mandelman, 2009).

Growth may be enhanced, however, through increased tax revenues on goods and services that are purchased with remittances. This assumes, of course, that governments put those tax revenues toward productive uses. Governments may also try to tax remittances directly, although few do so in practice. The Philippines abandoned its tax on remittances in 2010. However, some countries, such as Ethiopia, Pakistan and Venezuela, implicitly tax remittances by forcing the funds to be converted into the local currency at uncompetitive exchange rates.

The causal linkage between economic growth and remittances can run in either direction. Remittances may affect economic growth, and economic growth may affect remittances. Family members may be more likely to migrate and send money home during periods of weak economic growth. This would make remittances counter-cyclical and reduce estimates of the effect of remittances on economic growth that do not account for the effect of economic growth on remittances.

Studies have not reached a consensus on how remittances affect economic growth. Not only are there many channels through which remittances can affect growth, but the effect may be country- and time-specific (Chami et al., 2008). The impact may depend on the state of monetary and fiscal policy in the country receiving the remittances. In addition, studies use different methodologies, making it hard to compare their results.

Remittances and poverty

The majority of studies find that remittances are a key driver in moving people out of poverty and subsistence production in developing countries. In a study of 71 developing countries, Richard Adams and John Page (2005) find that a 10 percent increase in remittances per capita results in a 3.5 percent decline in the share of people living in poverty, defined as living on less than $1 per day. They conclude that "both international migration and remittances significantly reduce the level, depth, and severity of poverty in the developing world" (p. 1645).

Remittances spent on consumption tend to be spent on necessities, not on luxury or status items. In Mexico, for example, 80 percent of remittances are spent on food, clothing, health care, transportation, education and housing expenses (Coronado, 2004). A study finds that households in Albania that receive international remittances spend more at the margin on durable goods and utilities but less on food compared with households that do not receive any remittances (Costaldo and Reilly, 2007).

Remittances and development

At the microeconomic level, remittances can foster economic development if households spend them on investment activities such as acquiring more education, starting a small business or investing in agricultural technology. Evidence on whether remittances boost education is mixed, and the impact can vary within a population (Acosta, Fajnzylber and Lopez, 2007). For example, in El Salvador young girls and boys are more likely to be in school in households receiving remittances (Acosta, 2006). In Nepal, remittances increase the probability that children are in school, but girls benefit less than boys (Bansak and Chezum, 2009).

Evidence is clearer that remittances lead to increased investments in small businesses. Remittances are positively linked to the value of invested capital in small enterprises in Mexico and Pakistan, for example (Woodruff, 2007; Nenova, Niang and Ahmad, 2009). In Bangladesh, agricultural households that engage in international migration are more likely to invest in high-yield seed technology (Mendola, 2008). High-yield seed has a higher output, on average, but also has a greater variance in output. International migration serves as an insurance mechanism for these households, unlike households that are not insured via migration and remittances and therefore fall back on relatively low-yield, lower-variance seed.

Impacts on political, economic and social institutions

Emigration can be a powerful force for change in the origin country. It can affect economic growth and development there, both directly and via remittances. It can also lead to changes in political, economic and social institutions that have broad and potentially long-lasting effects. Xiaoyang Li and John McHale (2009) identify four channels through which emigration can affect institutions. The absence channel is how the loss of people, particularly those who are relatively well educated, affects institutions. The prospect channel is how the possibility of emigrating leads to changes in institutions. The diaspora channel is how emigrants affect institutions in the origin country. The return channel is how return migrants affect political, economic and social institutions.

While emigration may lead to institutional change, it is important to remember that institutions may push people to leave in the first place. People living in countries with corrupt political institutions, ineffective economic institutions or repressive social institutions may be more likely to leave. Researchers therefore need to think carefully about endogeneity and the timing of changes in institutions when examining possible causal linkages between emigration and institutions.

Impact on political institutions

Under the absence channel, the loss of people can reduce pressure for political change, particularly if would-be leaders or people who are discontented leave. Under the prospect channel, the possibility of leaving can empower potential emigrants to advocate for changes in political institutions. In addition, people may want the government to provide more education so that they can leave. Diasporas and return migrants may advocate for political changes. Through exposure to a new environment abroad, migrants may acquire new ideas about how governments should be structured and how they should function.

The diaspora and return channels have been the primary focus of empirical research. Studies suggest that migrants who are exposed to democratic societies abroad export some form of democracy back home. For example, a study of migrants from Cape Verde, which has the highest emigration rate in Africa, finds that emigrants who are exposed to democratic governments exert pressure on political accountability in their home country (Batista, Lacuesta and Vicente, 2012). For example, households with a family member abroad are more likely to take part in lobbying for greater accountability. Similarly, Senegalese migrants in France and the United States strongly encourage their family members back home to increase their political engagement by engaging in activities like voting (Collier, 2013).

A study of return migrants to Mali finds ample evidence of effects on political institutions. Lisa Chauvet and Marion Mercier (2014) look at migrants who returned home after spending time in democratic countries. They find that return migrants are more likely to vote than non-migrants. Other people living in close vicinity to return migrants are also more likely to vote. Finally, and perhaps most remarkably, it is the less educated who tend to copy the new political behavior displayed by return migrants. As migrants return with new political norms, they influence the political culture in their surrounding regions, which has the potential to affect governance.

Another issue pertaining to governance and emigration is whether emigration followed by return migration increases the supply of good leaders. Leaders who were educated abroad may be more likely to foster democratic governance. President Sirleaf of Liberia and President Conde of Guinea, the country's first democratic president, are examples. However, counter examples abound as well, such as President Mugabe of Zimbabwe, who heads a notoriously mismanaged government. A study of 932 politicians in developing countries indicates that, on average, democracy increases more under leaders who were educated abroad (Mercier, 2013). More generally, a study of 183 countries over the period 1960 to 2005 shows that foreign-educated people promote democracy in their home countries, provided they received their education in a democratic country (Spilimbergo, 2009).

Impact on economic institutions

The absence channel predicts that emigration, particularly by the highly skilled, has an adverse impact on economic institutions by reducing the supply of people who might design and staff key institutions, such as banks, the legal system and universities. Further, the absence of highly skilled people may reduce demand for productivity- and growth-enhancing reforms to the economic system (Li and McHale, 2009). The prospect channel notes that the possibility of leaving can induce changes in human capital, either positively or negatively, which in turn affects economic growth. Diasporas and return migrants are often a source of new ideas that benefit the economy, and they may transfer technologies that enhance economic growth. In addition, diasporas and return migrants may promote international trade and foreign direct investment.

Empirical work suggests that emigrants abroad are able to enhance international trade by creating trust in the legal system and understanding the language, culture, values, and practices in both the host and origin countries. Providing information to foreign investors reduces communication barriers and increases the incentive to invest in the migrants' origin country. Research shows that high-skilled emigration increases foreign direct investment (Kugler and Rapoport, 2007). This effect even extends beyond the origin country—research indicates that pairs of countries with more ethnic Chinese residents tend to trade more with each other (Rauch and Trindade, 2002).

Impact on social institutions

Emigration can affect social institutions as well. Living abroad can affect people's attitudes and expectations regarding social norms. For example, research shows that emigration to countries with low levels of gender discrimination promotes gender equality in social institutions in the origin, while emigration to countries with high levels of discrimination has the opposite effect (Ferrant and Tuccio, 2014). The effect occurs regardless of emigrants' gender. Migration can also challenge traditional gender roles when the absence of one spouse causes the other spouse to take on that person's responsibilities. For example, women left behind may become the de facto head of household, in charge of allocating resources and making decisions, while men left behind may need to assume responsibility for running the household and taking care of children. In addition, migration can change intergenerational dynamics. Children may need to take on additional responsibilities if a parent leaves, and elderly parents who expected to live with their adult children may not be able to do so if their children emigrate. Migration also affects fertility. A 1 percent decrease in the fertility rate to which migrants are exposed reduces home country fertility by 0.3 to 0.4 percent (Beine, Docquier and Schiff, 2013).

Final thoughts on source countries

Emigration, and more recently high-skilled migration, presents challenges and opportunities for source countries due to the fact that there are winners and losers. Universal policy recommendations are difficult because of the diversity of migration patterns—policy recommendations depend on the skill levels of migrants, the size of migrant networks in the destination, the sectors affected, the amounts of trade and investment and the size of the source country, among other factors. To further complicate matters, conclusions regarding government policies are hard to make given the scarcity of data and research on the topic. We have much to learn about the impact of emigration and remittances on economic growth, development and institutions.

Problems and discussion questions

1 Why would high- and low-skilled immigration be positively related? Negatively related?
2 How can international migration increase human capital levels in sending countries? Explain the various channels.
3 What are the benefits of high-skilled migration to the sending country?
4 What are the main reasons people send remittances? What factors are likely to influence how much they remit and their reasons for sending funds home?
5 Think of an example for each of the four institutional channels that is not given in the chapter.
6 Show the effects of emigration on employment, wages and social welfare if labor supply is not perfectly inelastic. How do the effects differ from the perfectly inelastic case shown in Figure 11.1?

Notes

1 India moved up to middle-income status in 2007, and China in 1999 (Sumner, 2010). For fiscal year 2015, the World Bank defines high-income countries as those with an average per capita income of $12,746 or higher and middle-income countries as those with per capita annual income between $1,045 and $12,745 (http://data.worldbank.org/about/country-and-lending-groups [4 August 2014]).

2 Researchers typically define low-skilled migrants as those with less than upper secondary school-ing (e.g., high school dropouts); medium-skilled migrants as those who have completed upper-secondary education (high school graduates); and high-skilled migrants as those who have completed post-secondary education and above.

3 The data are available at http://www.iab.de/en/daten/iab-brain-drain-data.aspx [20 September 2014].

4 Countries are categorized based on data from the World Economic Outlook Database (http://www.imf.org/external/pubs/ft/weo/2014/01/weodata/index.aspx) as of April 2014.

5 In addition, Clemens (2007) concludes that emigration may spur greater production of health care workers in Africa.

6 See Docquier and Rapoport (2012a) for a thorough review of the literature and discussion of these theories.

7 The World Bank measures remittances as the sum of workers' remittances, compensation of employees, and migrants' transfers (IMF, 2010a). Workers' remittances are current transfers by migrants who are considered residents in the destination country. Compensation of employees comprises wages, salaries and other benefits (in cash or in kind) earned by individuals in countries other than those in which they are residents for work performed for and paid for by residents of those countries. Employees include seasonal or other short-term workers (less than one year) and border workers who have centers of economic interest in their own countries (IMF, 2010b). Migrants' transfers are contra-entries to flows of goods and changes in financial items that arise from migration (change of residence for at least one year) of individuals from one country to another. The transfers to be recorded are thus equal to the net worth of the migrants (IMF, 2010a).

Internet resources

The Institute for Employment Research in Nuremberg, Germany, has created a dataset on immigration and emigration by education, available at http://www.iab.de/en/daten/iab-brain-drain-data.aspx.

The World Bank's resources on migration and remittances are available at www.worldbank.org/prospects/migrationandremittances.

Suggestions for further reading

Docquier, F. and Rapoport, H. (2012a) "Globalization, brain drain, and development." *Journal of Economic Literature* 50(3), pp. 681–730.

Gibson, J. and McKenzie, D. (2011) "Eight questions about brain drain." *Journal of Economic Perspectives* 25(3), pp. 107–128.

Yang, D. (2011) "Migrant remittances." *Journal of Economic Perspectives* 25(3), pp. 129–152.

References

Acosta, P. (2006) "Labor supply, school attendance, and remittances from international migration: The case of El Salvador." *World Bank Policy Research Working Paper* No. 3903. Washington, DC: World Bank.

Acosta, P.A., Fajnzylber, P.R. and Lopez, H. (2007) "The impact of remittances on poverty and human capital: Evidence from Latin American household surveys." *World Bank Policy Research Working Paper* No. 4247. Washington, DC: World Bank.

Acosta, P.A., Lartey, E.K. and Mandelman, F.S. (2009) "Remittances and the Dutch disease." *Journal of International Economics* 79(1), pp. 102–116.

Adams, R.H. and Page, J. (2005) "Do international migration and remittances reduce poverty in developing countries?" *World Development* 33(10), pp. 1645–1669.

Albrecht, D. and Ziderman, A. (1991) "Deferred cost recovery for higher education: Student loan programs in developing countries." *World Bank Discussion Paper* No. 137. Washington, DC: World Bank.

Amuedo-Dorantes, C. and Bansak, C. (2006) "Money transfers among banked and unbanked Mexican immigrants." *Southern Economic Journal* 73(2), pp. 374–401.

Aycinena, D., Martinez, C.A. and Yang, D. (2010) "The impact of remittance fees on remittance flows: Evidence from a field experiment among Salvadoran migrants." Mimeo, University of Michigan.

Bansak, C. and Chezum, B. (2009) "How do remittances affect human capital formation of school-age boys and girls?" *American Economic Review Papers & Proceedings* 99(2), pp. 145–148.

Batista, C., Lacuesta, A. and Vicente, P.C. (2012) "Testing the 'brain gain' hypothesis: Micro evidence from Cape Verde." *Journal of Development Economics* 97(1), pp. 32–45.

Beine, M., Docquier, F. and Rapoport, H. (2008) "Brain drain and human capital formation in developing countries: winners and losers." *Economic Journal* 118(4), pp. 631–652.

Beine, M., Docquier, F. and Schiff, M. (2013) "International migration, transfer of norms and home country fertility." *Canadian Journal of Economics* 46(4), pp. 1406–1430.

Bhagwati, J.N. and Hamada, K. (1974) "The brain drain, international integration of markets for professionals and unemployment: A theoretical analysis." *Journal of Development Economics* 1(1), pp. 19–42.

Bhargava, A. and Docquier, F. (2008) "HIV pandemic, medical brain drain, and economic development in sub-Saharan Africa." *World Bank Economic Review* 22(2), pp. 345–366.

Cervantes, M. and Guellec, D. (2002) "The brain drain: Old myths, new realities." *OECD Observer* No. 230. Paris: OECD.

Chami, R., Fullenkamp, C., Cosimano, T.F., Gapen, M.T., Montiel, P. and Barajas, A. (2008) "Macroeconomic consequences of remittances." *IMF Occasional Paper* No. 259. Washington, DC: International Monetary Fund.

Chand, S. and Clemens, M. (2008) "Skilled emigration and skill creation: A quasi-experiment." *Center for Global Development Working Paper* No. 152. Washington, DC: Center for Global Development.

Chauvet, L. and Mercier, M. (2014) "Do return migrants transfer political norms to their origin country? Evidence from Mali." *Journal of Comparative Economics* 42(3), pp. 630–651.

Clemens, M. (2007) "Do visas kill? Health effects of African health professional emigration." *Center for Global Development Working Paper* No. 114. Washington, DC: Center for Global Development.

Clemens, M. (2009) "Skill flow: A fundamental reconsideration of skilled-worker mobility and development." *Center for Global Development Working Paper* No. 180. Washington, DC: Center for Global Development.

Clemens, M.A. (2011) "Economics and emigration: Trillion-dollar bills on the sidewalk?" *Journal of Economic Perspectives* 25(3), pp. 83–106.

Collier, P. (2013) *Exodus: How Migration is Changing Our World.* Oxford: Oxford University Press.

Coronado, R. (2004). "Workers' remittances to Mexico." *Federal Reserve Bank of Dallas Business Frontier* 1.

Costaldo, A. and Reilly, B. (2007) "Do migrant remittances affect the consumption patterns of Albanian households?" *South-Eastern Europe Journal of Economics* 5(2), pp. 25–54.

Defoort, C. (2008) "Long-term trends in international migration: an analysis of the six main receiving countries." *Population* 63(2), pp. 285–317.

Docquier, F., Lohest, O. and Marfouk, A. (2007) "Brain drain in developing countries." *World Bank Economic Review* 21(2), pp. 193–218.

Docquier, F. and Rapoport, H. (2012a) "Globalization, brain drain, and development." *Journal of Economic Literature* 50(3), pp. 681–730.

Docquier, F. and Rapoport, H. (2012b) "Quantifying the impact of highly skilled emigration on developing countries." In: Boeri, T., Brücker, H., Docquier, F. and Rapoport, H. (eds.) *Brain Drain and Brain Gain: The Global Competition to Attract High-Skilled Migrants.* Oxford and New York: Oxford University Press, pp. 209–296.

Ferrant, G. and Tuccio, M. (2014) "South-South migration and gender discrimination in social institutions: A two-way relationship." Mimeo, University of Southampton.

Gibson, J. and McKenzie, D. (2011) "Eight questions about brain drain." *Journal of Economic Perspectives* 25(3), pp. 107–128.

Gibson, J. and McKenzie, D. (2012) "The economic consequences of 'brain drain' of the best and brightest: Microeconomic evidence from five countries." *Economic Journal* 122(560), pp. 339–375.

Gibson, J., McKenzie, D. and Rohorua, H. (2006) "How cost elastic are remittances? Evidence from Tongan migrants in New Zealand." *Pacific Economic Bulletin* 21(1), pp. 112–28.

International Labour Organization (2013). *Global Wage Report 2012/13: Wages and Equitable Growth.* Geneva: International Labour Organization.

International Monetary Fund (IMF) (2010a) *Balance of Payments Manual* 6th edn. Washington, DC: IMF.

International Monetary Fund (IMF) (2010b) Balance of Payments Statistics Database. Washington, DC: IMF. Available at: http://www2.imfstatistics.org/BOP/ [11 August 2014].

Kugler, M. and Rapoport, H. (2007) "International labor and capital flows: Complements or substitutes?" *Economics Letters* 94(2), pp. 155–162.

Li, X. and McHale, J. (2009) "Emigrants and institutions." Mimeo, World Bank.

Mbiti, I. and Weil, D.N. (2011) "Mobile banking: The impact of M-Pesa in Kenya." *National Bureau of Economic Research Working Paper* No. 17129. Cambridge, MA: National Bureau of Economic Research.

Mendola, M. (2008) "Migration and technological change in rural households: Complements or substitutes?" *Journal of Development Economics* 85(1), pp. 150–175.

Mercier, M. (2013) "The return of the prodigy son: Do return migrants make better leaders?" *IZA Discussion Paper* No. 7780. Bonn: Institute for the Study of Labor.

Mishra, P. (2007) "Emigration and wages in source countries: Evidence from Mexico." *Journal of Development Economics* 82(1), pp. 180–199.

Morawczynski, O. and Pickens, M. (2009) "Poor people using mobile financial services: Observations on customer usage and impact from M-PESA" CGAP Brief Online. Available at: https://www.cgap.org/sites/default/files/CGAP-Brief-Poor-People-Using-Mobile-Financial-Services-Observations-on-Customer-Usage-and-Impact-from-M-PESA-Aug-2009.pdf [14 September 2014].

Nenova, T., Niang, C. T. and Ahmad, A. (2009) *Bringing Finance to Pakistan's Poor: Access to Finance for Small Enterprises and the Underserved.* Washington, DC: World Bank.

OECD-UNDESA (2013) "World migration in figures." *OECD/United Nations Department of Economics and Social Affairs.* Available at: http://www.oecd.org/els/mig/World-Migration-in-Figures.pdf. [Retrieved November 14, 2014].

Opiniano, J. and Castro, T.A. (2006) "Promoting knowledge transfer activities through diaspora networks: A pilot study of the Philippines." In: Wescott, C. and Brinkerhoff, J. (eds.) *Converting Migration Drains into Gains Harnessing the Resources of Overseas Professionals.* Manila: Asian Development Bank, pp. 73–95.

Rauch, J. E. and Trindade, V. (2002) "Ethnic Chinese networks in international trade." *Review of Economics and Statistics* 84(1), pp. 116–130.

Saxenian, A. (1999) *Silicon Valley's New Immigrant Entrepreneurs.* San Francisco: Public Policy Institute of California.

Saxenian, A. (2002) *Local and Global Networks of Immigrant Professionals in Silicon Valley.* San Francisco: Public Policy Institute of California.

Shrestha, S.A. (2011) "Effect of educational returns abroad on domestic schooling: A British Gurkha army experiment." Mimeo, University of Michigan.

Spilimbergo, A. (2009) "Democracy and foreign education." *American Economic Review* 99(1), pp. 528–543.

Sumner, A. (2010) "Global poverty and the new bottom billion: What if three-quarters of the world's poor live in middle-income countries?" *Institute of Development Studies Working Paper* No. 349. Brighton, UK: Institute of Development Studies.

Woodruff, C. (2007) "Mexican microenterprise investment and employment: The role of remittances." *Integration and Trade* 11(27), pp. 185–209.

World Bank (2006) "Global economic prospects 2006: economic implications of remittances and migration." In: *Global Economic Prospects and the Developing Countries (GEP)*. Washington, DC: World Bank.

World Bank (2010) "An analysis of trends in the average total cost of migrant remittances." *Remittance Prices Worldwide* Issue 2.

Yang, D. (2011) "Migrant remittances." *Journal of Economic Perspectives* 25(3), pp. 129–152.

Part 5

Frontiers in Immigration Research

12   Frontiers in the Economics of Immigration

Much of the economics of immigration focuses on how immigration affects specific markets, such as the labor market, the housing market, markets for tradable and nontradable goods and the public sector via fiscal effects. But the economics of immigration is much broader than those topics. Immigration may affect the happiness and health of immigrants and natives. It may encourage or discourage natives from acquiring more education, and it may increase or decrease the fertility rate. Immigration-induced changes in education levels or fertility rates have long-term fiscal implications. Immigration may affect the crime rate or be connected to human trafficking operations and drug cartels. This chapter introduces all of these exciting areas of on-going research in the economics of immigration.

Happiness

Research on the relative well-being, or happiness, of individuals and societies is a booming area in economics. If someone were to ask you to rank your average level of happiness, what would you say? Your response probably depends on many factors, including your perception of your happiness relative to others around you, the extent to which you are an optimistic person, the current state of your health and other personal factors. Researchers ask questions like this in order to compare happiness levels between different types of people, across countries and over time.

Studies show that countries such as Colombia and Tanzania have citizens who report being relatively happy compared with their counterparts in rich, developed countries. Table 12.1 reports a standard measure of happiness using data from the World Values Survey between the years 1981 and 2004.[1] The World Values Survey asks the following question: "Taking all things together, would you say you are: 1) not at all happy, 2) not very happy, 3) quite happy, or 4) very happy." People in Colombia are the happiest of the countries surveyed. Some of the least happy countries during this period were Eastern European countries (Bulgaria and Romania) and former Soviet Union countries (Ukraine and Latvia).

Importantly, the richest countries are not necessarily the happiest countries. This contradiction—that increases in income are not necessarily associated with increases in happiness—is dubbed the Easterlin Paradox.[2] Within a country, people with higher incomes are more likely to report being happy. However, in international comparisons, happiness is not correlated with income after the point where basic needs are satisfied. For example, consider

Table 12.1 Ranking of countries by happiness, World Values Survey Sample

Country	Average happiness	Country	Average happiness
Colombia	3.65	Israel	3.02
Tanzania	3.50	Uganda	3.01
El Salvador	3.47	Uruguay	3.00
Venezuela	3.45	Brazil	2.99
Vietnam	3.41	Pakistan	2.98
Puerto Rico	3.40	Germany	2.98
Iceland	3.40	India	2.97
Ireland	3.37	East Germany	2.97
Netherlands	3.37	Algeria	2.96
Saudi Arabia	3.35	Bangladesh	2.96
Denmark	3.34	China	2.96
Northern Ireland	3.34	Bosnia & Herzegovina	2.95
Australia	3.34	Italy	2.94
Switzerland	3.32	Korea	2.94
Sweden	3.31	Peru	2.93
United States	3.31	Jordan	2.91
Singapore	3.30	Greece	2.91
Belgium	3.30	Portugal	2.91
Philippines	3.29	Azerbaijan	2.88
Luxembourg	3.28	Poland	2.86
Nigeria	3.28	Czech Republic	2.86
New Zealand	3.28	Croatia	2.85
United Kingdom	3.26	Hungary	2.82
Canada	3.26	Macedonia	2.81
Austria	3.23	Iran	2.81
Norway	3.22	Serbia	2.80
Taiwan	3.19	Slovenia	2.80
France	3.17	Georgia	2.72
Indonesia	3.15	Zimbabwe	2.67
Finland	3.13	Iraq	2.66
Malta	3.12	Slovakia	2.65
Mexico	3.12	Estonia	2.65
Turkey	3.12	Lithuania	2.63
South Africa	3.11	Armenia	2.55
Japan	3.10	Romania	2.52
Chile	3.09	Belarus	2.52
Egypt	3.06	Russia	2.49
Argentina	3.06	Latvia	2.46
Dominican Republic	3.05	Moldova	2.46
Kirghizstan	3.04	Bulgaria	2.45
Spain	3.04	Ukraine	2.44
Morocco	3.04	Albania	2.43

Source: Polgreen and Simpson (2011); average happiness reported on a 1–4 scale, with higher numbers indicating a higher average level of happiness.

the difference between El Salvador and the United States. El Salvador has a happiness index of 3.47 and had a per capita GDP of $3,790 in 2012. Compare this with the United States, a country with a happiness index of 3.31 and a per capita GDP of $51,749.[3] Given the stark differences in income, many Salvadorans should have an incentive to immigrate to the United States. However, if you consider their happiness level, people in El Salvador report being happier than people in the United States. Thus, differences in the relative level of happiness across countries may partially explain why we do not observe even more immigration to wealthy countries from poor countries.

There is some evidence that the relationship between happiness indicators and the flow of emigrants is non-linear. Linnea Polgreen and Nicole Simpson (2011) find a U-shaped relationship between the happiness of the source country and emigration rates: Unhappy countries have high emigration rates (many people leave unhappy countries) but beyond a certain level of happiness, emigration rates are higher as happiness increases (more people leave happier countries). Importantly, in obtaining this result, they control for income and income growth in order to isolate the relationship between happiness and migration.

There are other ways in which happiness is related to emigration. For example, emigrants may be a special group of people who are more optimistic about their lives and the potential that exists outside of their origin country. Imagine for a moment your own situation. What would it take for you to move to a foreign country with a different culture and language? In order for you to think that emigration is worthwhile, at least from an economic perspective, the gains from migration have to outweigh the costs. Those gains may seem bigger to an optimistic person than they would to a pessimistic person, causing the optimist to be more likely to emigrate. If optimism can be measured by happiness or well-being, then perhaps optimistic people in certain countries are self-selected to emigrate. If this is the case, the pool of emigrants will be relatively happy and optimistic compared with the pool of non-emigrants. Self-selection among emigrants may translate into economic effects on the destination country, such as more technological growth and innovation due to emigrants being more likely to own a business and have an entrepreneurial spirit (as discussed in Chapter 9).

Alternatively, perhaps emigrants are less happy in their home country. Emigrants may be "frustrated achievers," in which case their unhappiness drives emigration (Graham and Markowitz, 2011). Analysis of European data suggests this is the case: people dissatisfied with their lives have a greater intention to migrate both permanently and temporarily (Popova and Otrachshenko, 2011). Note here that the intent to migrate is different from actually migrating, but it captures individual traits that are related to migration behavior.

The migration process may change immigrants' happiness. Adjusting to a new society and culture can be difficult, and such challenges may make people less happy once they migrate. It is not clear whether migrating increases or decreases people's happiness, but research does indicate that immigrants' happiness depends on the degree of social integration in their new country, how they identify themselves and the reasons behind their migration (Amit, 2010). Many studies suggest that immigrants are less happy than natives in the destination (Bălţăescu, 2007; Safi, 2010; Bartram, 2011).

Economists have recently begun to study how immigration affects the happiness of the native population in the destination country. Immigrant flows to 26 European countries have a small but positive impact on the well-being of natives (Betz and Simpson, 2013). The most positive effects are from immigrant flows in the previous year, not from earlier flows. In Germany, immigration boosts natives' happiness, but the magnitude of the effect depends on immigrants' assimilation (Akay, Constant and Giulietti, 2014). The number of immigrants there who are not assimilated at all or who are fully assimilated has almost no effect on natives' well-being, while the number of immigrants who are somewhat, but not fully, assimilated has the most positive effect on natives' well-being. In both studies, recent immigrants have small positive effects on the happiness of natives.

Education

Immigration into a region can have a significant impact on the region's provision of public services, especially education. In most developed countries, education at the primary and secondary levels is mandatory and provided for free by the government. An influx of immigrants can therefore put considerable pressure on the education system. As discussed in Chapter 10, immigration can lead to fiscal costs via the education system and other publicly provided services. This section focuses on how immigration affects the educational attainment, or human capital investment, of natives.

There are two main channels through which immigration can affect natives' educational attainment, especially when focusing on primary and secondary schooling: school effects, and labor market effects. As Jennifer Hunt (2012) explains, the school effects channel is that enrollment of immigrant children puts pressure on schools in terms of class sizes, language services and resources per student. Funding may not keep pace with costs, resulting in crowd out of educational expenditures on natives. If educational expenditures on native-born students decrease, the quality of natives' education may fall.

Evidence on the school effects channel is mixed. A study of 19 countries over the period 2000 to 2009 finds a small but negative relationship between the share of immigrant pupils and the performance of 15-year-old natives in school, with the largest effects on female natives and those from a poor parental background (those with fewer books in the household than the national average) (Brunello and Rocco, 2013). A study of immigrants from the former Soviet Union who fled to Israel during the early 1990s finds that a higher concentration of immigrants in schools leads to higher drop-out rates and lower exam scores among Israeli natives (Gould, Lavy and Paserman, 2009). In New York City public schools, there is a negative relationship between natives' test scores and the immigrant share in their school for children in third through eighth grade, but there is a positive relationship between the two variables within a classroom (Schwartz and Stiefel, 2011). The scores that U.S. natives living in California and Texas get on the Scholastic Achievement Test (SAT) are not significantly related to the immigrant share of SAT-takers from their high school (Neymotin, 2009).

The other channel through which immigration may affect natives' educational attainment occurs through the labor market: If most immigrants are low-skilled, wages for low-skilled workers may decrease. The drop in low-skilled wages may encourage natives to invest in acquiring more education so that they do not directly compete with low-skilled immigrants in the labor market. Thus, immigration may lead to an increase in the educational attainment of natives. The converse may occur if immigrants are highly educated and high-skilled wages fall as a result of immigration.

Hunt (2012) finds that both channels are at work in the United States, but the net effects of immigration are positive. Her results suggest that a 1 percentage point increase in share of immigrants between the ages of 11 and 64 leads to a 0.3 percent increase in the fraction of natives who complete high school. The effect is largest among U.S.-born blacks. For U.S.-born Hispanics, educational attainment decreases as the number of immigrant children whose parents are less educated increases, but rises as the number of immigrant children with more-educated parents increases; the net effect is zero. Thus, the effect of immigration on the educational attainment of natives is positive overall, particularly for blacks.

Higher education

Immigration may also affect the ability of natives to enroll in and complete college. Similar to the case of primary and secondary education, foreign-born college students could crowd out natives from universities by increasing the price of education and thus the cost to natives. A demand and supply model of education shows the crowding-out effect. Students are the demanders of higher education, and universities are the suppliers of higher education, which is at least partially subsidized by governments. In many developed countries, such as Australia and those in Europe, higher education is almost completely subsidized by the government, making the government an important part of the market for higher education.

Figure 12.1 graphs the supply and demand for higher education. Notice that the supply of higher education is relatively inelastic, as economic research indicates is the case. John Bound and Sarah Turner (2007), for example, report that the supply elasticity of higher education is less than one in the United States. As immigration increases the demand for higher education, the price of higher education rises more than the quantity rises. Thus, by increasing the demand for higher education, foreign-born students put significant upward pressure on prices, crowding out some natives from attending college.

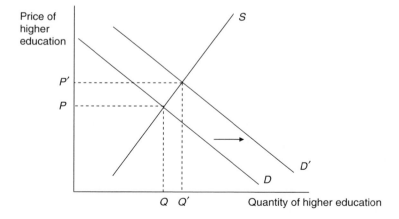

Figure 12.1 Effects of immigration on the market for higher education.

As immigration increases the number of students who want to enroll in college, the demand for higher education increases. The price of higher education increases to P′ and the quantity to Q′.

The effects of publicly provided primary and secondary schooling are somewhat different since the supply of public education is nearly perfectly elastic. In most developed countries, public schools are required to accommodate all students. In this case, an increase in the demand for schooling would have very little effect on the price of education but large effects on the quantity of students receiving education. In addition, the quality of education may adjust, as discussed earlier.

Economists Caroline Hoxby and George Borjas find evidence of crowding-out effects in higher education. Hoxby (1998) finds that foreign-born students crowd minority natives out of U.S. colleges and universities through two channels: by competing with high-need students for scarce resources, and by competing in affirmative action since institutions do not always differentiate between natives and non-natives when making decisions aimed at ensuring racial or ethnic diversity. Borjas (2007) studies the effect of foreign students on natives' enrollment in U.S. graduate programs and finds little evidence of crowding out for the typical native. However, there is an adverse effect on white American males.

Some policymakers question the merit of allowing, or at least subsidizing, foreign students' enrollment in higher education. Is it the role of the government to subsidize foreign-born students' education? As Borjas states, "If immigration policy is supposed to benefit the native population, it may be difficult to justify a subsidy system that limits educational opportunities for many native students unless the economic gains from foreign students are very large" (p. 148). In fact, large shares of foreign students who receive college or graduate degrees remain in the United States after graduation. These graduates often contribute to the advance of science and technology, which may create jobs for natives and boost economic growth, as discussed in Chapter 9. Once again, it is critical to analyze the costs (in this case, lower educational attainment among some natives) and the benefits (the gains to society from the skills acquired by immigrants).

On the other hand, low-skilled immigration could "crowd in" natives to higher education. Low-skilled immigration represents a decrease in the relative supply of high-skilled labor, thus increasing the relative wage of high-skilled labor. In this case, the marginal benefit of higher education, and thus natives' demand for college, would increase. Research on the United States indicates that this is the case: state-level increases in relatively low-skilled immigrant labor raise the proportion of natives going to college (Jackson, 2011).

Health

Immigration may affect health outcomes among both immigrants and natives. As Chapter 4 discussed, a number of studies document the healthy immigrant effect, or the fact that immigrants appear to have better health outcomes than natives in the destination or than non-migrants in the origin. This health advantage tends to narrow as immigrants' time in the destination country increases, as noted in Chapter 5.

Few studies have examined whether immigration affects natives' health. Immigration may affect natives' health through several channels. As with education, immigrants may crowd natives out of health care by increasing demand and raising the price of health care. Immigration also may reduce the quality of health care that natives receive if health care providers adjust services along a quality dimension instead of a price or quantity dimension.

Alternatively, immigration may increase the supply of health care if immigrants are disproportionately health care providers. This would reduce the price and increase the quantity of health care. In the United States, more than one-fourth of doctors and one-fifth of dentists and pharmacists are foreign born (Orrenius and Zavodny, 2010). More than one-fourth of doctors in England's National Health Service are foreign born as well.[4] These numbers exceed immigrants' population share in both countries.

Research suggests that immigration may affect natives' health through the labor market. As discussed in Chapter 7, immigrants may have a comparative advantage in manual labor jobs, while natives may have a comparative advantage in communication-intensive jobs. Low-skilled immigrants may replace low-skilled natives in physically demanding jobs that take a toll on workers' health. In Germany, immigration appears to lead to improvements in natives' health by improving their working conditions and reducing their workload (Giuntella and Mazzona, 2014).

Fertility

The size of a country's population depends on several factors, including fertility and mortality rates, average life expectancy and net migration flows. This section focuses on the various linkages between fertility and migration.

The total fertility rate represents the number of children the average woman is expected to have during her lifetime.[5] According to World Bank statistics from 2012, Japan and Italy have total fertility rates of 1.4, the lowest in the world.[6] In comparison, the United States and the United Kingdom have total fertility rates of 1.9. India has a relatively high total fertility rate of 2.5, while Uganda and Nigeria have total fertility rates of 6. Notably, as countries become richer, fertility rates fall. Figure 12.2 plots fertility rates in 2012 against GDP per capita. The negative relationship between GDP per capita and fertility is clear. Countries such as Niger, Mali and Chad have among the highest fertility rates and lowest per capita GDP, whereas rich countries such as Australia, Denmark and Norway have low fertility rates.

Differences in fertility rates across countries have important effects via immigration. Immigrants from countries with high fertility rates tend to have more children in the destination country than natives of that country (but due to selection or assimilation, such immigrants typically have lower fertility rates than women in their home country, as discussed in Chapter 5). Consider the case of the United States and Mexico. Immigrants from Mexico have more children than U.S. natives, a pattern that increases the overall fertility rate in the United States.

Low fertility rates and long life spans are problematic for rich countries with generous old-age pension systems. As populations in much of the developed world age, there are fewer young workers to support the older generation. Over time, as the size of the retired population grows, the tax system and the workforce cannot sustain government-funded retirement programs (Social Security, in the United States) at promised levels absent a major change. One controversial solution is to increase the size of the workforce through immigration.[7] Since immigrants tend to be working age, allowing more immigration increases the size of the workforce, which in turn increases tax revenues. In addition, since immigrants tend to have more children than natives, the size of the next generation increases.

Immigration is one of the reasons why the United States does not have the extremely low fertility rate experienced by most other developed countries; its large immigrant flows since

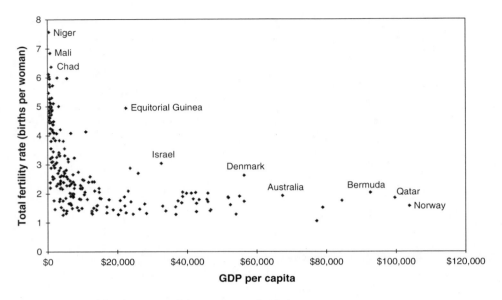

Figure 12.2 Total fertility rate and GDP per capital, 2012.

Source: World Development Indicators, http://data.worldbank.org/indicator/SP.DYN.TFRT.IN.

the 1970s have created a larger, younger workforce. Japan, in contrast, has a strict immigration policy that allows very few immigrants—immigrants are only 2 percent of the country's population. The low immigration rate, low fertility rate and high life expectancy there combine to mean that Japan's population is predicted to shrink by one-third over the next 50 years.[8] Japan is considering changing its immigration policy to combat its shrinking population.

There is another channel through which immigration may affect fertility. By increasing the supply of workers in a country, immigration may drive down wages. An inflow of low-skilled immigrant workers into household services, such as day care and housecleaning, will lower wages and reduce prices in that sector. Cheaper daycare and housecleaning make it easier for native-born women to work and could incentivize them to enter the labor force or work more hours. In addition, cheaper household services make it cheaper and easier to have children. By lowering the costs of having children, increased immigration could lead to higher fertility rates among natives, especially among high-skilled natives who can afford these services and have relatively high returns to working in the labor force. Research finds this is indeed the case. Delia Furtado and Heinrich Hock (2010) show that the increase in low-skilled immigration to the United States during 1980 to 2000 led to higher fertility and labor force participation rates among highly educated U.S.-born women.

Crime

Crime is an increasingly popular area of study for economists. Economists believe that the decision to commit a crime is not unlike many other economic decisions: When deciding whether to commit a crime, people compare the benefits with the costs. The benefits of committing the crime are the rewards the crime provides. For property crime, for example, the value of the property that is stolen is the monetary gain to the criminal. The expected costs of committing a crime include the probability of getting caught and the resulting penalties, which often involve fines, legal fees and time spent in jail. Importantly, the lack of legitimate work opportunities is often cited as the leading reason behind why people commit crimes.

As discussed throughout this book, immigrants may face different labor market opportunities than natives. These opportunities depend on immigrants' country of origin, their language proficiency, their skill set and their access to immigrant networks, among other factors. All of these factors may affect the extent to which immigrants are likely to commit crime. Specifically, if immigrants face lower odds of employment or lower wages than natives, the opportunity costs of committing a crime are lower for immigrants than for natives, and they therefore are more likely to commit a crime.

Looking across areas within a country, the immigration rate may be positively related to the crime rate because immigrants may live in areas that are more prone to crime. In many developed countries, immigrants tend to live in more urban areas than natives, and they tend to live in poorer areas as well since their incomes are lower. It is difficult to determine whether immigration leads to higher crime rates or immigrants are just more likely to live in areas with higher crime rates (and those areas would have higher crime rates even absent immigration). Researchers have attempted to disentangle these effects using statistical techniques, like instrumental variables or natural experiments.

A significant cost associated with committing crimes is the stigma that a criminal experiences. Arrests and legal proceedings are usually public matters, and social norms usually dictate that people believed to have committed a crime are viewed negatively. For immigrants who are less connected to the community and feel more like an outsider, the stigma of committing a crime could be lower, thereby reducing the costs of pursuing illegal activity. Alternatively, immigrants may be less knowledgeable about local laws and penalties associated with committing a crime. The lack of information may cause immigrants to underestimate the costs of committing a crime.

Immigrants may be less risk adverse, or more willing to pursue risky activities. A very risk-adverse person would be unlikely to migrate abroad, whereas people who can tolerate more risk (or even search out risky activities) are more likely to migrate. The same personality traits that motivate some people to migrate to a different country may lead them to pursue criminal activity. In addition, many migrants are young men, the demographic group most likely to be involved in crimes.

There are also several reasons why immigrants may be less likely to commit crimes than natives. Immigrants have often given up a lot to move, and they may be unwilling to participate in any behavior that puts them at risk of having to return home. In the United States, immigrants who are not naturalized U.S. citizens are deported if they are convicted of a felony. Felonies include murder, rape, drunk driving and aggravated assault.

Immigrants may be targeted by law enforcement more often than natives and hence be more likely to get caught. Knowing this, immigrants may be careful not to commit any type of crime, no matter how petty. In fact, it is plausible that immigrants overestimate the punishments for crime, which would reduce their propensity to commit crimes. For illegal immigrants, any type of suspicious activity may lead to being deported back to their home country. In the United States, law enforcement officials check legal immigration status when processing people into jail; illegal immigrants are eventually handed over to the Department of Homeland Security to be deported. Illegal immigrants therefore may have a higher cost of committing crimes than legal immigrants because if they get caught, the penalty is more severe. Indeed, a common joke in Los Angeles is that the only people who drive below the speed limit are illegal immigrants. However, illegal immigrants may also face worse labor market conditions and hence lower returns to working at legitimate jobs.

People in developed countries often believe that immigrants increase crime rates. Table 12.2 reports public attitudes on whether immigrants commit crime from a 2010 survey conducted by the German Marshall Fund. About one-fourth of Canadians either strongly or somewhat agree with the statement that legal immigrants increase crime, while more than one-half of Italians think so. About one-third of people surveyed in the United Kingdom and the United States think that legal immigrants increase crime. Negative attitudes towards immigrants and crime are even higher in regard to illegal immigrants. With the exception of Canada, more than one-half of respondents in every country surveyed think that illegal immigrants increase crime.

Although much of the public appears to believe that immigration increases crime, economic research has reached mixed conclusions. The relationship between immigration and crime rates depends on the specific flow of immigrants and the type of crime analyzed.

Research by Kristen Butcher and Anne Piehl suggests that immigrants are less likely to commit crimes than natives in the United States. Although larger cities have more crime (because they are more populated), immigration does not necessarily increase crime rates in the largest U.S. cities (Butcher and Piehl, 1998b). The incarceration rate among immigrants is about one-fifth the rate among U.S. natives (Butcher and Piehl, 2007). Recent immigrant cohorts appear to have lower propensities to engage in criminal activity, relative to U.S. natives of the same age, than earlier cohorts did (Butcher and Piehl, 1998a, 2007). This is despite the fact that recent immigrants face worse employment opportunities than earlier cohorts. Piehl and her co-authors also document many interesting patterns about crime and immigration in the U.S. during the early 1900s, as discussed in Box 12.1, "Immigration and crime in early twentieth-century America."

A study by Brian Bell, Francesco Fasani and Stephen Machin (2013) examines crime and two large immigrant flows to the United Kingdom. The first wave consisted of asylum seekers who entered the United Kingdom in the 1990s and 2000s from Afghanistan, Iraq, Somalia and the former Yugoslavia. The second wave consisted of workers from the "A-10" European Union accession countries. In 2004, the United Kingdom began allowing workers from Cyprus, the

Table 12.2 Public attitudes about immigrants and crime, 2010

	Legal immigrants increase crime	*Illegal immigrants increase crime*
Italy	56%	57%
Germany	46%	63%
Netherlands	45%	66%
France	40%	55%
United Kingdom	33%	63%
United States	32%	58%
Spain	29%	70%
Canada	25%	43%

Source: German Marshall Fund (2010).

Box 12.1 Immigration and crime in early twentieth-century America

At the turn of the twentieth century in the United States, immigrants represented 15 percent of the population. Most of the immigration was concentrated in cities in the northeast, with New York City and Boston the most common destinations. Given that crime rates are usually higher in cities with high population density and that immigrants at the time tended to be young, unskilled males, immigrants were often associated with criminal behavior more than natives, as characterized in popular movies such as *Gangs of New York*. Some countries, such as Italy and Ireland, were blamed for exporting their criminals to the United States.

Of course, collecting reliable data from over one hundred years ago can be tricky, but researchers have used advanced techniques to carefully check and analyze historical data. Research on the topic by Carolyn Moehling and Anne Piehl suggests that crime rates were not as high among immigrants as popularized in the media. It is true that the overall immigrant population was slightly more likely to commit crimes than U.S. natives. In fact, young immigrants in 1904 were more likely to commit serious offenses than natives of the same age (Moehling and Piehl, 2007). However, this gap is concentrated among just a few groups. For the majority of immigrants, crime rates were comparable to natives.

Italian immigrants in the United States were often characterized as the worst offenders. Moehling and Piehl (2007) find that Italian immigrants were more likely to commit major offenses but less likely to commit minor offenses than other immigrant groups. For example, Italians were more than twice as likely to commit major offenses as the Irish, and three times as likely as the Germans. Much, but not all, of these differences can be explained by the younger age distribution of Italian immigrants. But even after taking the age distribution into account, Italian immigrants appear to have been disproportionately involved in serious crimes. The relative economic opportunities that immigrant groups experienced also contributed to the differences in their crime rates.

Immigrants at the turn of the twentieth century were also likely to assimilate to natives' incarceration patterns. Moehling and Piehl (2014) find that second-generation immigrants in the 1900 to 1930 U.S. censuses had similar incarceration rates as natives. Adult new arrivals were less likely than natives to be incarcerated, but their incarceration rates rose with years of residence in the United States. In other words, immigrants appear to have negatively assimilated towards natives in terms of crime, as proxied by incarceration rates. The same appears to be true today (Butcher and Piehl, 1998a).

By 1930, immigrants were less likely to be incarcerated for more serious crimes than natives at every age and across state and federal detention facilities (Moehling and Piehl, 2007). Some of this was due to changes in immigration law in the 1920s that reduced the number of immigrants from southern Europe and changed their selectivity (as Chapter 13 discusses).

Czech Republic, Estonia, Hungary, Latvia, Lithuania, Malta, Poland, Slovakia and Slovenia to freely enter legally. These were two very different groups of immigrants. The asylum seekers had relatively poor labor market opportunities, with high unemployment rates and low labor force participation rates, while the accession immigrants had even better labor market opportunities than UK natives. The researchers find no evidence of an increase in violent crime due to either immigrant wave. However, the asylum immigrant inflow led to an increase in property crime: the study's estimates suggest that a 1 percentage point increase in asylum seekers as a share of the local population was associated with a 1.1 percent increase in property crime. The authors find that immigration from accession countries actually led to less property crime.

A study of the United States by Jörg Spenkuch (2013) finds little evidence that immigration leads to more violent crime but some evidence that it leads to more property crime. The estimates suggest that the average immigrant commits 2.5 times as many crimes as the average U.S. native. In addition, the study finds that Mexican immigration leads to large effects on property crime. It concludes that those with the worst labor market opportunities in the destination country are likely to cause non-violent crime to increase the most, which is consistent with the economic model of crime.

Evidence from the United States on criminal propensities among illegal immigrants relative to legal immigrants and natives is mixed. An analysis of the 1986 Immigration Reform and Control Act that legalized approximately 2.7 million illegal immigrants in the United States concludes that it led to a sizable reduction in overall crime rates (Baker, 2011). However, the rollout of the Secure Communities program in the 2000s—which has resulted in one-quarter of a million illegal immigrants being detained, many of them ultimately deported—did not lead to any discernible change in crime rates (Cox and Miles, 2014).

Finally, immigration may incite crime. Researchers who study overall crime rates need to keep in mind that natives commit crimes, too, and their propensity to do so may increase if immigration worsens natives' legitimate labor market opportunities. Further, natives may commit crimes against immigrants. Hate crimes are often targeted at immigrants. Alan Krueger and Jörn-Steffen Pischke (1997) study crimes against immigrants in eastern and western Germany in the early 1990s. Their results indicate that the incidence of crimes against foreigners was higher in eastern German states than western states, and differences in the unemployment rate did not play a role in explaining crime rates against immigrants. In fact, xenophobic crimes against foreigners are on the rise worldwide. There is rarely a day that goes by when details of yet another hate crime against foreigners are not in the world news.

Human trafficking

"Trafficking is often migration gone terribly wrong," says David Feingold (2005, p. 32). The U.S. Trafficking Victims Protection Act of 2000 defines severe forms of human trafficking as:

> sex trafficking in which a commercial act is induced by force, fraud or coercion, or in which the person induced to perform such an act has not attained 18 years of age; or the recruitment, harboring, transportation, provision, or obtaining of a person for labor or services, through the use of force, fraud or coercion for the purpose of subjection to involuntary servitude, peonage, debt bondage or slavery.[9]

Examples of victims of human trafficking include children involved in the sex trade, adults aged 18 or over who are coerced or deceived into commercial sex acts, and anyone forced into various forms of "labor or services," such as domestic workers not allowed to leave a home or agricultural workers forced to labor against their will. Human trafficking is considered a form of modern-day slavery in which perpetrators profit from controlling people against their will. According to the Polaris Project, human traffickers generate billions of dollars in profits every year by victimizing millions of people, documented and undocumented, around the world, including in the United States.[10,11]

Human trafficking often goes undetected. As an "underground" crime, it is difficult to spot victims of human trafficking. Modern-day slaves may be all around us, hidden in plain sight. Threatened by their oppressors, many victims refuse to come forth for fear of possible retaliation and deportation. Working and living conditions of victims often include being unable to come or go as they wish, receiving little or no pay, working excessively long shifts without breaks, being recruited falsely or misleadingly and incurring large amounts of debt.

Statistics regarding the estimated size of the human trafficking industry are quite staggering. There are believed to be between 12 and 27 million victims of human trafficking in the world (Loftus, 2011). There are believed to be between 10,000 and 100,000 victims in the United States each year.[12] Regarding the sex trafficking industry in particular, estimates suggest that profits exceeded $39 billion in 2010, with an annual average profit of over $29,000 per slave.[13]

The United Nations began to recognize human trafficking as an international problem in 1998 and drafted the *Protocol to Prevent, Suppress and Punish Trafficking in Persons, Especially Women and Children*, also known as the Palermo Protocol. In 2000, the United Nations approved the Palermo Protocol, which focused on preventing human trafficking, punishing traffickers and protecting victims. Soon after, the United States adopted the Trafficking Victims Protection Act, which likewise includes provisions aimed at prevention, prosecution and protection. The United States has a "U visa" that grants temporary legal status to up to 10,000 people a year who have been victims of crimes, including human trafficking. A number of other countries, including Canada, Mexico and the United Kingdom, have also adopted laws aimed at combating trafficking.

Economists analyze the market for human trafficking much like any other market. The supply of human traffickers typically consists of the victims themselves, and the demand is comprised of the customers of the service provided by the victims. Traffickers are often modeled as the intermediaries between supply and demand (Omar Mahmoud and Trebesch, 2010).

On the supply side of the market for human trafficking, economic conditions in the source country that push people to migrate make some of them vulnerable to being trafficked. In countries where GDP is lower, the outflow of trafficking victims is higher (Akee et al., 2010; Akee et al., 2011). In addition, there is evidence that high unemployment rates among young women are correlated with more human trafficking of women for sexual exploitation (Danailova-Trainor and Belser, 2006). On the demand side, source countries that are wealthy, are more open in terms of trade and have more prostitution are more likely to host human traffickers (Akee et al., 2010; Akee et al., 2011).

Not surprisingly, there is an important link between flows of migrants and human trafficking. For countries such as Belarus, Bulgaria, Moldova, Romania and the Ukraine, higher emigration rates translate into more human trafficking (Omar Mahmoud and Trebesch, 2010).

Large migrant flows foster a shadow economy of illegal services, such as false documents, smuggling across borders or help procuring work abroad. Human trafficking is a market with low entry costs: the risks of detection, prosecution or arrest are much lower for human trafficking than for other illicit activities that involve transporting items across borders, such as the drug and arms trades (Omar Mahmoud and Trebesch, 2010). (Box 12.2, "Drug-related violence and migration," discusses the link between illegal drugs and migration.)

Box 12.2 Drug-related violence and migration

Some forms of illegal activity, such as the drug trade, are frequently linked to migration. It is not uncommon for drugs to be carried across the border by people, whether it is through an airport, in a car, on a boat or on foot. In 2005, the Mexican government published and distributed widely a comic book aimed at people who might try to cross the Mexico–U.S. border illicitly. The comic book had many warnings, including one to not trust people asking migrants to drive a vehicle or carry a package because the packages often contain drugs.[1] (The related comics are shown below.) As crossing the border has become more dangerous and more expensive over time, Mexican drug cartels have become increasingly involved in smuggling people over the border.

A rise in drug-related violence in Mexico since the 2000s has pushed a number of Mexicans to migrate to the United States. Tens of thousands of people—many of them innocent bystanders—have been killed in drug-related violence in Mexico since 2007 (BBC, 2014). Others have fled for their lives. The characteristics of this outflow of Mexican migrants are quite different than past migrant outflows from Mexico. Many of the migrants who left because of drug-related violence are more educated and more likely to be business owners than previous migrants were, and they move their entire families to the United States, often legally under programs for investors or skilled workers. U.S. border cities like El Paso have experienced a surge of new businesses started by these migrants.

---

[1]"Desconfía de todo aquél que te ofrezca pasarte al 'otro lado' y te pida que conduzcas un vehículo o que lleves o cargues un paquete por él. Regularmente esos paquestes contienen drogas u otras sustancias prohibidas. Por esta razón, muchas personas han terminado en la cárcel." Guia del Migrante Mexicano. 2005.   Mexico Secretariade Relaciones Exteriores.   https://www.cfif.org/htdocs/legislative_issues/federal_issues/hot_issues_in_congress/immigration/mexican-booklet.pdfAQ.

Final thoughts on frontiers

The effects of immigration extend beyond traditional markets. Immigration affects the happiness of immigrants and natives. Immigration also affects educational systems, both at the primary and secondary level and at the college and university level. In particular, immigrants may crowd natives out of education in terms of price, quantity or—perhaps most significantly—quality. Immigrants often come from countries with higher fertility rates, which can raise fertility levels in the destination country and help to support public coffers. The presence of immigrants can change natives' fertility as well. Immigrants are often perceived to have negative effects on society, such as increasing crime rates. Research by economists reveals that this is not necessarily the case. Understanding research findings on these broader effects of immigration is important not only for students of the economics of immigration but also for policymakers. The next two chapters provide an overview of immigration policy in the United States and around the world, with a focus on economic implications.

Problems and discussion questions

1   Analyze Table 12.1. Choose a relatively happy country and a relatively sad country from the table. Do these happiness levels make sense to you? Why or why not? Why is measuring happiness difficult for economists? Then, using United Nations data, calculate the annual rate of change in the migrant stock from 1990 to 2013 (http://esa.un.org/unmigration/TIMSA2013/migrantstocks2013.htm). Does your happy country attract immigrants? Does your sad country repel immigrants? What other factors in each of these countries (besides happiness) are likely to affect immigrant stocks?

2   Are immigrants more or less happy than natives? In answering this question, be sure to consider the comparison group (natives back home or natives in the destination country).

3   What are the costs and benefits associated with providing public education to immigrants? Do they differ for different levels of education (primary versus secondary versus tertiary)?

4   Draw a supply and demand diagram for the market for public primary education. Show how an increase in immigration would affect the supply and demand of public primary education. Also, discuss the effects of immigration on the equilibrium price and quantity of public primary education.

5   Make a list of the various types of crimes that people commit. For each type of crime, decide whether criminal propensities are likely to be higher among immigrants or natives and discuss why. Make sure to think about the costs and benefits of each crime.

6   Discuss the various ways in which migration facilitates illegal activities across borders, such as human trafficking and the drug trade. Would migration affect the supply or the demand for human trafficking and drug smuggling?

Notes

1 The data represent averages of the happiness indicator for each country-year available and were calculated using weights provided by the survey. See Polgreen and Simpson (2011) for details.
2 The Easterlin paradox was first developed in early work by Richard Easterlin (1974). Simpson (2013) summarizes recent empirical findings.

3 GDP per capita as reported by the World Bank's World Development Indicators, http://data.worldbank.org/.

4 http://www.theguardian.com/society/2014/jan/26/nhs-foreign-nationals-immigration-health-service.

5 Specifically, the total fertility rate reported by the World Bank's World Development Indicators represents the number of children that would be born to a woman if she were to live to the end of her childbearing years and bear children in accordance with current age-specific fertility rates. The birth rate is the number of births per one thousand women of reproductive age in a given year.

6 World Bank, World Development Indicators, Fertility Rates, http://data.worldbank.org/indicator/SP.DYN.TFRT.IN.

7 Storesletten (2000) estimates that the United States could continue with its (then) current tax and spending policies if it received an additional 1.6 million high-skilled immigrants aged 40 to 45 annually.

8 http://www.economist.com/blogs/banyan/2014/03/japans-demography [31 May 2014].

9 www.state.gov/j/tip/laws/61124.htm [22 September 2014].

10 http://www.polarisproject.org.

11 Human smuggling is not interchangeable with human trafficking, although the two may overlap. Human smuggling is a transportation-based act, while human trafficking is exploitation-based. Human smuggling is the importation of people into a country while deliberately evading immigration laws. This includes bringing illegal aliens into a country as well as the unlawful transportation and harboring of aliens already in a country.

12 International Justice Mission, http://www.stand-for-freedom.com/.

13 The CNN Freedom Project: Ending Modern-Day Slavery, http://thecnnfreedomproject.blogs.cnn.com/.

Internet resources

CNN has a blog with facts about modern-day slavery at http://thecnnfreedomproject.blogs.cnn.com/.

Suggestions for further reading

Bell, B. (2014) "Crime and immigration: Do poor labor market opportunities lead to migrant crime?" *IZA World of Labor* 33. Available at: http://wol.iza.org/articles/crime-and-immigration [2 August 2014].

Hunt, J. (2012) "The impact of immigration on the educational attainment of natives." *National Bureau of Economic Research Working Paper* No. 18047. Cambridge, MA: National Bureau of Economic Research.

Simpson, N.B. (2013) "Happiness and migration." In: Constant, A.F. and Zimmermann, K.F. (eds.) *International Handbook on the Economics of Migration*. Cheltenham, UK: Edward Elgar, pp. 393–407.

References

Akay, A., Constant, A. and Giulietti, C. (2014) "The impact of immigration on the well-being of natives." *Journal of Economic Behavior and Organization* 103, pp. 72–92.

Akee, R.K.Q., Basu, A.K., Chau, N.H. and Khamis, M. (2010) "Ethnic fragmentation, conflict, displaced persons and human trafficking: An empirical analysis." *IZA Discussion Paper* No. 5412. Bonn: Institute for the Study of Labor.

Akee, R.K.Q., Bedi, A., Basu, A.K. and Chau, N.H. (2011) "Transnational trafficking, law enforcement and victim protection: A middleman trafficker's perspective." *IZA Discussion Paper* No. 5412. Bonn: Institute for the Study of Labor.

Amit, K. (2010) "Determinants of life satisfaction among immigrants from western countries and from the FSU in Israel." *Social Indicators Research* 96(3), pp. 515–534.

BBC News (2014) "Who is behind Mexico's drug-related violence?" 10 February. Available at: http://www.bbc.com/news/world-latin-america-10681249 [31 May 2014].

Baker, S.R. (2011) "Effects of the 1986 Immigration Reform and Control Act on crime." *Stanford Law and Economics Olin Working Paper* No. 412. Stanford, CA: Stanford University.

Bălțăescu, S. (2007) "Central and Eastern Europeans migrants' subjective quality of life: A comparative study." *Journal of Identity and Migration Studies* 1(2), pp. 67–81.

Bartram, D. (2011) "Economic migration and happiness: Comparing immigrants' and natives' happiness gains from income." *Social Indicators Research* 103(1), pp. 57–76.

Bell, B., Fasani, F. and Machin, S. (2013) "Crime and immigration: Evidence from large immigrant waves." *Review of Economics and Statistics* 95(4), pp. 1278–1290.

Betz, W. and Simpson, N. (2013) "The effects of international migration on the well-being of native populations in Europe." *IZA Journal of Migration* 2:12.

Borjas, G.J. (2007) "Do foreign students crowd out native students from graduate programs?" In: Stephan, P.E. and Ehrenberg, R.G. (eds.) *Science and the University*. Madison: University of Wisconsin Press, pp. 134–149.

Bound, J. and Turner, S. (2007) "Cohort crowding: How resources affect collegiate attainment." *Journal of Public Economics* 91(5-6), pp. 877–899.

Brunello, G. and Rocco, L. (2013) "The effect of immigration of the school performance of natives: Cross country evidence using PISA test scores." *Economics of Education Review* 32, pp. 234–246.

Butcher, K.F. and Piehl, A.M. (1998a) "Recent immigrants: Unexpected implications for crime and incarceration." *Industrial and Labor Relations Review* 51(4), pp. 654–679.

Butcher, K.F. and Piehl, A.M. (1998b) "Cross-city evidence on the relationship between immigration and crime." *Journal of Policy Analysis and Management* 17(3), pp. 457–493.

Butcher, K.F. and Piehl, A.M. (2007) "Why are immigrants' incarceration rates so low? Evidence on selective immigration, deterrence, and deportation." *National Bureau of Economic Research Working Paper* No. 13229. Cambridge, MA: National Bureau of Economic Research.

Cox, A. and Miles, T.J. (2014) "Immigration enforcement and crime control: A study of Secure Communities." *Journal of Law and Economics*, 57(4), pp. 937–973.

Danailova-Trainor, G. and Belser, P. (2006) "Globalization and the illicit market for human trafficking: an empirical analysis of supply and demand." *ILO Working Paper* No. 53. Geneva: International Labour Organization.

Easterlin, R. (1974) "Does economic growth improve the human lot? Some empirical evidence." In: David, P. and Reder, M. (eds.) *Nations and Households in Economic Growth: Essays in Honour of Moses Abramovitz*. New York and London: Academic Press, pp. 98–125.

Feingold, D.A. (2005) "Human trafficking." *Foreign Policy* 150, pp. 26–32.

Furtado, D. and Hock, H. (2010) "Low skilled immigration and work-fertility tradeoffs among high skilled US natives." *American Economic Review Papers & Proceedings* 100(2), pp. 224–228.

German Marshall Fund (2010) "Transatlantic trends 2010." Available at: http://trends.gmfus.org/archives/transatlantic-trends/transatlantic-trends-2010/ [22 July 2014].

Giuntella, O. and Mazzona, F. (2014) "Do immigrants bring good health?" *IZA Discussion Paper* No. 8073. Bonn: Institute for the Study of Labor.

Gould, E.D., Lavy, V. and Paserman, D. (2009) "Does immigration affect the long-term educational outcomes of natives? Quasi-experimental evidence." *Economic Journal* 119(540), pp. 1243–1269.

Graham, C. and Markowitz, J. (2011) "Aspirations and happiness of potential Latin American immigrants." *Journal of Social Research and Policy* 2(2), pp. 9–26.

Hoxby, C.M. (1998) "Do immigrants crowd disadvantaged American natives out of higher education?" In: Hamermesh, D.S. and Bean, F.D. (eds.) *Help or Hindrance? The Economic Implications of Immigration for African Americans.* New York: Russell Sage Foundation, pp. 282–321.

Hunt, J. (2012) "The impact of immigration on the educational attainment of natives." *National Bureau of Economic Research Working Paper* No. 18047. Cambridge, MA: National Bureau of Economic Research.

Jackson, O. (2011) "Does immigration crowd natives into or out of higher education?" Mimeo, Northeastern University.

Krueger, A.B. and Pischke, J.S. (1997) "A statistical analysis of crime against foreigners in unified Germany." *Journal of Human Resources* 32(1), pp. 182–209.

Loftus, B.S. (2011) "Coordinating U.S. law on immigration and human trafficking: Lifting the lamp to victims." *Columbia Human Rights Law Review* 43, pp. 143–214.

Moehling, C. and Piehl, A.M. (2007) "Immigration and crime in early 20th century America." *National Bureau of Economic Research Working Paper* No. 13576. Cambridge, MA: National Bureau of Economic Research.

Moehling, C. and Piehl, A.M. (2014) "Immigrant assimilation into U.S. prisons, 1900–1930." *Journal of Population Economics* 27(1), pp. 173–200.

Neymotin, F. (2009) "Immigration and its effect on the college-going outcomes of natives." *Economics of Education Review* 28, pp. 538–550.

Omar Mahmoud, T. and Trebesch, C. (2010) "The economics of human trafficking and labour migration: micro-evidence from Eastern Europe." *Journal of Comparative Economics* 38, pp. 173–188.

Orrenius, P.M. and Zavodny, M. (2010) "From brawn to brains: How immigration works for America." *Federal Reserve Bank of Dallas Annual Report.*

Polgreen, L. and Simpson, N. (2011) "Happiness and international migration." *Journal of Happiness Studies* 12(5), pp. 819–840.

Popova, O. and Otrachshenko, V. (2011) "Life (dis)satisfaction and decision to migrate: Evidence from Central and Eastern Europe." *Osteuropa-Institut Regensburg Working Paper* No. 306. Regensburg: Osteuropa-Institut.

Safi, M. (2010) "Immigrants' life satisfaction in Europe: Between assimilation and discrimination." *European Sociological Review* 26(2), pp. 159–171.

Schwartz, A.E. and Stiefel, L. (2011) "Immigrants and inequality in public schools." In: Murnane, R. and Duncan, G. (eds.) *Whither Opportunity.* Washington, DC: Brookings Institution, pp. 419–442.

Simpson, N.B. (2013) "Happiness and migration." In: Constant, A.F. and Zimmermann, K.F. (eds.) *International Handbook on the Economics of Migration.* Cheltenham, UK: Edward Elgar, pp. 393–407.

Spenkuch, J. (2013) "Understanding the impact of immigration on crime." *American Law and Economics Review* 16(1), pp. 177–219.

Storesletten, K. (2000) "Sustaining fiscal policy through immigration." *Journal of Political Economy* 108(2), pp. 300–323.

Part 6

Immigration Policy

13 U.S. Immigration Policy

The United States is the world's top destination for immigrants. The country is often called a "nation of immigrants" since almost all of its population either migrated there themselves or is descended from people who migrated there within the past four centuries. One of the country's best-known images is the Statue of Liberty, which stands near the entrance to New York City's harbor where millions of immigrants entered during the 1800s and early 1900s. The statue's pedestal is engraved with the poem "The New Colossus," by Emma Lazarus, which includes the lines

> "Keep ancient lands, your storied pomp!" cries she
> With silent lips. "Give me your tired, your poor,
> Your huddled masses yearning to breathe free,
> The wretched refuse of your teeming shore.
> Send these, the homeless, tempest-tost to me,
> I lift my lamp beside the golden door!"

How immigrants enter the United States and where they come from have changed substantially since the Statue of Liberty was dedicated in 1886. Most now enter through airports, not sea ports, although some walk or ride across the United States' border with Mexico or Canada. Until the middle of the twentieth century, most immigrants to the United States were from Europe. Most immigrants now come from Latin America and Asia. One aspect of immigration that has not changed since the time of Lazarus's poem is why people migrate to the United States: in search of a better life.

U.S. immigration policy has changed substantially over time. When the Statue of Liberty was dedicated, entry into the United States was virtually unrestricted, with the notable exception of immigrants from Asia. The main goal of immigration policy for the country's first 150 years was attracting people to help settle a vast country. The goals of U.S. immigration policy have changed since then. Immigration policy today aims to foster family reunification, encourage economic growth, advance international diplomacy, ensure a diverse group of immigrants and allow people to seek refuge, among other goals. Potential immigrants now face a complex set of rules and regulations. Many of these policies are controversial, and some of them lead to unintended consequences.

This chapter provides an overview of how many people migrate to the United States, where they are from and how they entered the United States. As a starting point, Figure 13.1 shows the size of the foreign-born population in the United States at the start of each decade from 1850 to 2010 (the bars, measured using the scale on the left vertical axis) and its share of the U.S. population, or the immigrant share (the line, measured using the scale on the right vertical axis). As the figure shows, both the size and share of the foreign-born population have changed considerably over time. This chapter explains the policies that contributed to these changes.

The discussion in this chapter focuses on immigration policy regarding three groups of immigrants that are part of the foreign-born population: legal permanent residents, temporary worker or student visa holders and unauthorized immigrants. Legal permanent residents are allowed to live in the United States indefinitely as long as they do not commit a major crime. They can work almost anywhere in the United States (some jobs are restricted to U.S. citizens). They are eligible to apply for U.S. citizenship after a few years. In recent years, permanent residents who are not naturalized U.S. citizens account for 25 to 30 percent of the foreign born living in the United States.

Temporary visa holders can live in the United States for a specified period of time and under certain conditions, such as working or attending school. Some temporary worker visas restrict holders to working in a specific job or for a specific employer. Temporary worker visa holders typically must leave the country if they lose their job, and student visa holders must leave fairly soon after finishing school or adjust to another type of visa. People living in the

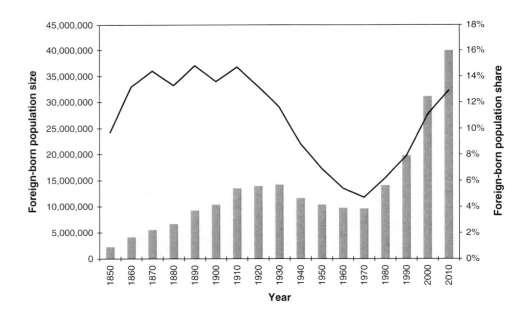

Figure 13.1 The foreign-born population in the United States, 1850–2010.

Source: U.S. Bureau of the Census (http://www.census.gov/population/www/documentation/twps0081/twps0081.html for 1850–2000; www.census.gov/prod/2012pubs/acs-19.pdf for 2000 [22 July 2014]).

United States with temporary visas, including temporary worker visas, account for a small share of the foreign born in the United States—about 5 percent in the early 2010s. Despite this small share, temporary visas are important because many permanent residents and eventual naturalized U.S. citizens first had a temporary visa. In addition, some sectors hire a relatively large share of their workers on temporary worker visas, and a growing share of U.S. college students are international students.

Unauthorized immigrants are foreigners who are not legally present in the United States. They either entered without a valid visa or violated the terms of their visa, such as not leaving when their visa expired. They are not allowed to work in the United States. Estimates suggest that unauthorized immigrants account for slightly over one-fourth of the foreign born living in the United States in the early 2010s.[1] All three of these groups of immigrants raise interesting issues, as this chapter discusses.

This chapter does not discuss immigration policy regarding several other groups, most notably naturalized U.S. citizens and temporary visitors. Chapter 5 discusses the economic issues regarding naturalization. U.S. policies regarding citizenship have changed little in recent decades. As of 2012, about 45 percent of the foreign born in the United States are naturalized citizens.[2] As discussed in Chapter 1, most researchers do not consider temporary visitors for business or pleasure to be immigrants—they do not live in the destination country. U.S. policies regarding visitors have changed over time, largely in response to national security considerations. Changes in these policies primarily affect tourism and related industries.

The evolution of U.S. immigration policy

The United States initially imposed few restrictions on immigration, and people entered the country in large numbers. As Figure 13.1 shows, the foreign-born population grew steadily from 1850 to 1910. This growth was largely due to massive waves of immigration, first from England, Ireland and Germany and then from southern and eastern Europe. Few immigrants came from the Western Hemisphere or Africa during this period. In 1882, Congress passed the Chinese Exclusion Act, the first in a series of federal policies that severely restricted immigration from Asia. (The U.S. Constitution gives the federal government the sole power to make U.S. immigration policy, and in 1891 the U.S. Congress officially gave the federal government—not state or local governments—the responsibility of enforcing immigration laws. Table 13.1 lists these and other milestones in U.S. immigration policy.[3])

The size of the foreign-born population in the United States changed little from 1910 to 1930. This was an abrupt departure from the steady growth in the number of immigrants that prevailed from 1850 to 1910. Immigration first largely ceased during World War I as a result of upheaval in Europe and the dangers of crossing the Atlantic Ocean during the war. It then remained low for several decades in large part due to policies put in place during the next decade.

During the 1920s the United States adopted a series of laws that restricted immigration from Europe. These laws put in place national origins quotas—limits on the number of immigrants admitted as permanent residents each year from each country—based on origin groups' shares of the U.S. population decades ago. The laws favored immigrants from northern and

Table 13.1 Milestones in U.S. immigration policy

1882	Chinese Exclusion Act
1891	Immigration Act
1921	Emergency Quota Act
1924	Johnson-Reed Immigration Act
1952	McCarran-Walter Immigration and Nationality Act
1965	Hart-Cellar Immigration and Nationality Act
1986	Immigration Reform and Control Act (IRCA)
1990	Immigration Act
1996	Illegal Immigration Reform and Immigrant Responsibility Act (IIRIRA) and Personal Responsibility and Work Opportunity Reconciliation Act (PRWORA)
2002	Enhanced Border Security and Visa Entry Reform Act
2005	Real ID Act
2007	Legal Arizona Workers Act (LAWA)
2012	Deferred Action for Childhood Arrivals (DACA)

western Europe at a time when most immigrants were trying to come from southern and eastern Europe. Specifically, the Emergency Quota Act of 1921 imposed annual quotas based on the national origins of the U.S. population in 1910. This law favored potential migrants from England, Ireland, Germany and other countries in northwestern Europe. In 1924, another quota law, the Johnson-Reed Act, was passed. This law based the quotas on the national origins of the U.S. population in 1890. The new quotas locked out most immigrants from southern and eastern Europe and virtually all immigrants from Asia. As a result of these laws, immigration began to decline dramatically. These restrictions led to the immigrant population size and the immigrant share falling between 1930 and 1970.

As World War II ended, pressure mounted on the United States to revise its immigration laws to accept more displaced persons from Europe. In 1952, the McCarran-Walter Act retained the national origins quota system but increased the number of permanent resident visas available. It added a preference system that classified applicants for permanent residence into three groups: immigrants with special skills and relatives of U.S. citizens, who were exempt from quotas; refugees; and other immigrants. The 1952 law ended the exclusion of Asian immigrants, although the national origins quotas that were still in place ensured that few Asians could become U.S. permanent residents.

Shifting from national origins to preference categories

An immigration policy based on national origins—in essence, on race and ethnicity—was viewed as inconsistent with the civil rights movement of the 1960s. Immigration policy at the time severely restricted the number of people from Asia and Africa who could receive permanent residence. In response to the civil rights movement, the United States adopted a new immigration policy in 1965 that opened the doors to immigrants from Asia, Africa and the rest of world. The new law, the Hart-Cellar Act, repealed the national origins quota system and replaced it with a preference category system that prioritized family ties. The system it created for granting permanent residence is essentially still in place today. The 1965 law placed annual caps on the total number of permanent resident visas granted and on the number of visas granted in various preference categories of family reunification immigrants, employment-based immigrants and refugees. The law also capped the number of visas granted to immigrants from each country. Immediate relatives (spouses, unmarried minor children and parents) of U.S. citizens were exempt from the preference category and country caps.

When the 1965 law was enacted, even its proponents considered it a fairly minor event. European immigrants were expected to continue to dominate a relatively small inflow of immigrants. But the law instead marked the beginning of a new era in U.S. immigration. The new policy led to sizable increases in the number of immigrants. As Figure 13.1 shows, the size of the foreign-born population and the foreign-born population share began increasing after 1970. Note, however, that even though the number of immigrants living in the United States is now at a record level, their share of the population is lower than it was during the late 1800s and early 1900s.

The 1965 law also led to an unexpected shift in where immigrants came from. Figure 13.2 shows the distribution of people who received legal permanent residence in the United States across five regions of origin by decade. During the early 1900s, the vast majority of new immigrants were from Europe—over 90 percent during the first decade of the twentieth century. The share from Europe began declining during the first half of the 1900s, and the share from Latin American and the Caribbean began rising. After the 1960s, the share of immigrants from Asia began rising substantially. The shares from Africa and Oceania (mainly

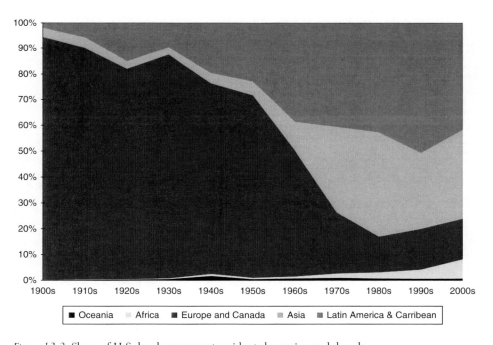

Figure 13.2 Share of U.S. legal permanent residents by region and decade.

Source: U.S. Department of Homeland Security (www.dhs.gov/sites/default/files/publications/immigration-statistics/yearbook/2012/LPR/table2.xls [22 July 2014]).

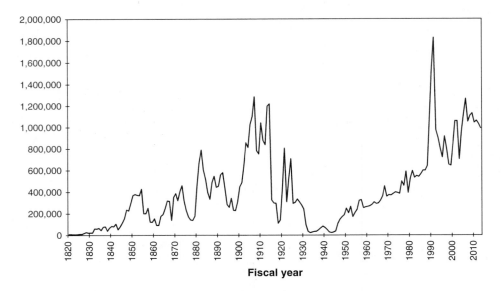

Figure 13.3 Number of persons granted legal permanent residence, 1820–2013.

Source: U.S. Department of Homeland Security (http://www.dhs.gov/yearbook-immigration-statistics-2013-lawful-permanent-residents [22 July 2014]).

Australia and New Zealand) are low, although the share from Africa has been increasing steadily since the 1960s.

Figure 13.3 shows the number of legal permanent resident visas ("green cards") granted per year for the period 1820 to 2013. The surge in immigration at the beginning of the twentieth century that led to the restrictions imposed in the 1920s is evident. Another surge occurred in the late 1980s and early 1990s because of a legalization program discussed in the next section. The 2007–2009 Great Recession appears to have led to a decline in the number of people receiving legal permanent residence, but it is too early to say for certain. (As discussed later, the Great Recession also appears to have led to a decline in unauthorized immigration.) In the 2000s, about one million green cards are awarded each year.

Addressing unauthorized immigration in the 1980s and 1990s

Until the 1980s, immigration policy focused primarily on permanent residents, not temporary migrants or unauthorized migrants. Neither group was large enough to merit much policy concern. One exception was a perceived need for temporary foreign workers during World War II. In 1942, the United States and Mexico created the *bracero* program, a temporary worker program that brought in about 200,000 Mexican workers a year until the program ended in 1964. The 1965 reforms initially exempted Mexico and other Western Hemisphere countries from the preference category and county caps and imposed only a total annual cap on permanent resident admissions from the region. Changes in the mid-1970s imposed the caps universally.

The preference category and country caps on permanent resident visas and the lack of a temporary foreign worker program meant not enough visas were available to accommodate the number of people who wanted to migrate from Mexico and the number of employers willing to hire them. As a result, unauthorized immigration from Mexico began to increase steadily, and the unauthorized population grew. After years of intense debate, the Immigration Reform and Control Act (IRCA) was passed in 1986.

IRCA attempted to address the contentious issue of unauthorized immigration with a three-pronged approach. First, it created two amnesty programs that ultimately legalized 2.7 million undocumented immigrants. Second, IRCA increased border enforcement levels and funding. Third, it required employers to ask new hires for documents that established their eligibility to work in the United States and imposed penalties on employers who know- ingly hired undocumented workers. (Prior to IRCA, hiring an unauthorized immigrant was legal under the so-called Texas Proviso.) It also created the H-2A program, which admits people to work in agriculture on a temporary basis.

IRCA quickly proved to be a failure at reducing illegal immigration. Employers and unau- thorized workers soon realized that IRCA's documentation requirements were easily circum- vented and that penalties were rarely imposed on employers. The unauthorized population resumed its upward trajectory. Apprehensions along the Mexico–U.S. border are a key indicator of the number of people trying to enter the United States illegally. As Figure 13.4 shows, apprehensions spiked in 1986 as migrants entered the United States in order to apply for amnesty. Apprehensions then fell for a few years as formerly undocumented migrants were able to cross the border legally. By the early 1990s, apprehensions had returned to their

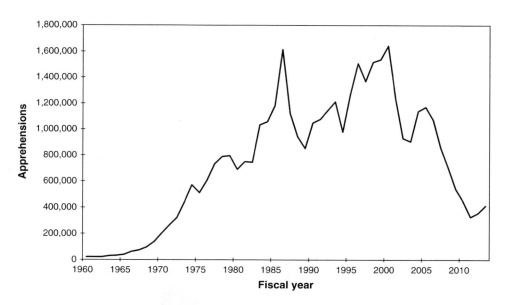

Figure 13.4 Apprehensions along the Mexico–U.S. border, 1960–2013.

Source: U.S. Department of Homeland Security (http://www.cbp.gov/xp/cgov/border_security/border_patrol/usbp_statistics/usbp_fy13_stats/ [12 September 2014]).

previous levels despite the fact that 2.7 million people had received legal status through IRCA. (The impact of the U.S. housing bust that began in 2006 and the Great Recession is evident in the figure as well. Illegal immigration fell as the number of jobs available in the United States declined.)

However, increased border enforcement did make it more difficult for migrants to cross the Mexico–U.S. border. Use of smugglers increased, and individuals began crossing (and dying) in more remote parts of the border. Unauthorized immigrants also began staying longer in the United States as it became more difficult to leave and then re-enter, and many were joined in the United States by their families. Given a ready source of relatively cheap unauthorized workers and few penalties for hiring them, agricultural employers made little use of the H-2A temporary worker program.

Unauthorized immigrants who were able to legalize their status under IRCA benefited in several ways. After they received legal permanent resident status, they were able to sponsor some of their relatives for permanent resident visas. They also became eligible to apply for naturalized U.S. citizenship after five years, after which they could more easily sponsor relatives to immigrate. As legal permanent residents (or eventually U.S. citizens), they became eligible for public assistance programs if they met the other program criteria. They also did better in the labor market. A number of studies that look at IRCA beneficiaries conclude that their wages increased by about 6 to 13 percent (Amuedo-Dorantes and Bansak, 2011; Amuedo-Dorantes, Bansak and Raphael, 2007; Kossoudji and Cobb-Clark, 2002; Rivera-Batiz, 1999). Much of the gains occurred because these immigrants were able to move into higher-paying jobs after gaining legal status. However, research by Cynthia Bansak and Steven Raphael (2001) shows that some Hispanic immigrants, both legal and illegal, faced increased discrimination in the labor market after IRCA went into effect.

Continued growth in the unauthorized population led to further measures aimed at reducing their numbers and fiscal impact. The federal government increased border enforcement significantly in the early 1990s, particularly at high-volume crossing points. In 1996, the Illegal Immigration Reform and Immigrant Responsibility Act (IIRIRA) further increased border enforcement levels and funding. IIRIRA also instituted three- and ten-year bans on re-entry for unauthorized immigrants. Before IIRIRA, some unauthorized immigrants living in the United States were able to adjust to legal permanent resident status, typically because a relative sponsored them. After IIRIRA, unauthorized immigrants were no longer able to adjust status. Instead, they were faced with a choice between remaining in the United States illegally or returning home and not being able to legally re-enter the United States for years. IIRIRA created Basic Pilot, an employment-eligibility verification system that was a precursor to E-Verify (which is discussed later).

The Personal Responsibility and Work Opportunity Reconciliation Act (PRWORA) of 1996—commonly referred to as "welfare reform"—made major changes to public assistance programs. PRWORA restricted the ability of legal immigrants who were not yet U.S. citizens to receive means-tested benefits. Unauthorized immigrants were already barred from virtually all public assistance programs, but PRWORA required verification of welfare recipients' legal status. As discussed in Chapter 10, some states responded to PRWORA by allowing immigrants to continue to receive welfare benefits, often at state expense, while others followed the new federal cutbacks.

Current immigration policy

Legal permanent resident visas

The 1965 immigration law created a preference category system for permanent residence that is still largely in place today. That law created annual (fiscal year) caps on the total number of permanent resident visas, on the number of visas issued under various preference categories and on the number of visas issued per country. The caps and preference categories were last changed by the Immigration Act of 1990. Table 13.2 lists the current preference categories and their caps. In addition, no more than 7 percent of family-sponsored and employment-based preference visas—or 25,620 annually—can go to immigrants from any one country.

As Table 13.2 indicates, there are four main categories for numerically limited family-sponsored immigrants. All of these categories require that potential immigrants have an eligible relative to sponsor them. The sponsoring relative must meet a minimum income requirement. Note that only certain types of relatives can immigrate—uncles, aunts and grandparents are

Table 13.2 Preference classes and annual caps for legal permanent resident status

Class	Annual cap	Average number, 2009–2013
Immediate relatives of U.S. citizens (spouses, unmarried minor children and parents)	None	476,673
Family-sponsored:		
Unmarried adult children of U.S. citizens and their minor children	23,400	24,656
Spouses, minor children and unmarried adult children of legal permanent residents	114,200	99,619
Married children of U.S. citizens and their spouses and minor children	23,400	25,899
Siblings of U.S. citizens and their spouses and minor children	65,000	64,565
Employment-based:		
Priority workers: persons with extraordinary ability, outstanding professors and researchers, and multinational managers or executives	40,040	37,105
Professionals holding advanced degrees and persons of exceptional ability	40,040	56,063
Skilled workers, professionals and unskilled (or "other") workers	40,040	40,047
Certain special immigrants (broadcasters, ministers and certain former U.S. government employees overseas)	9,940	8,588
Immigrant investors	9,940	4,936
Other:		
Diversity lottery	55,000	46,737

Source: U.S. Department of Homeland Security (http://www.dhs.gov/yearbook-immigration-statistics-2013-lawful-permanent-residents [22 July 2014]).

not eligible, nor are siblings or married adult children of permanent residents. The total number of family-sponsored permanent resident visas available is 226,000 per year.

There are five main categories for numerically limited employment-based immigrants. Most of these categories require that potential immigrants have a job offer from a U.S. employer. Only relatively skilled immigrants are eligible for most of the employment-based categories. Workers who do not have a college degree or work in a skilled occupation are typically only eligible for the third employment-based preference category, and the number of visas available for these unskilled (or "other") workers is capped at 10,000 per year.[4] The total number of employment-based permanent resident visas available is 140,000 per year. The spouse and minor unmarried children of a worker approved for an employment-based visa can receive a visa as well. These visas count toward the cap.

The diversity lottery category was created by the Immigration Act of 1990. The diversity lottery gives some potential immigrants who do not have a relative who can sponsor them or a qualifying job offer a way to receive permanent resident status. Applicants must have a high school diploma or equivalent and be from a country that sends relatively few immigrants to the United States (fewer than 50,000 during the previous five years). As discussed in Chapter 2, the diversity lottery is massively oversubscribed. About one-half of winners in recent years have been from Africa. The spouse and minor unmarried children of a diversity lottery winner can receive a visa as well.

There are a few additional categories not reported in Table 13.2, most notably refugees and asylees (successful asylum seekers). The number of refugees and asylees is not set by law. Since 1980, the president determines the maximum number of refugees the United States will accept each year. Refugees are eligible for legal permanent residence after living in the United States for one year. Courts evaluate asylum claims on an individual basis, and there currently is no cap on the number of asylees who can adjust to legal permanent resident status.

The caps presented in Table 13.2 are binding for some categories. All of the family-sponsored preference categories are currently oversubscribed—the number of applicants approved exceeds the number of visas available. A few employment-based categories are also oversubscribed, most notably the skilled workers, professionals and unskilled workers category. Approved applicants must wait for a visa to become available in the order in which their applications were approved, much like waiting in line at a store. Some approved applicants wait in their home country, and others wait in the United States while on a temporary visa. The wait can be as short as a few months or as long as a few decades, depending on the category and the country of origin. Immigrants from the four biggest immigrant-sending countries—China, India, Mexico and the Philippines—face longer waits because the country caps are binding for potential immigrants from those countries. Estimates suggest that more than three million approved applicants are waiting for a family-sponsored green card, and more than one million for an employment-based green card (Jasso et al., 2010). Box 13.1, "What's a green card worth?" sheds some light on why so many people want legal permanent resident status.

The last column of Table 13.2 shows the average actual number of permanent resident visas awarded by category during fiscal years 2009 to 2013. Some of the categories exceed their caps because of a complicated system of offsets—if one category is undersubscribed, those extra visas are awarded to another category specified by law. The most frequently used

Box 13.1 What's a green card worth?

Why do millions of people want legal permanent resident status? One important reason is the benefits it confers in the U.S. labor market. Many temporary worker visas impose restrictions that limit the visa holder to a specific occupation at a specific employer, while other visas make it hard to move to another employer if a better opportunity arises. Unauthorized immigrants may have difficulty finding an employer willing to hire them, and they may earn less than other workers when they are able to find a job. Legal permanent residents—"green-card holders"—are able to work in any job that does not require U.S. citizenship. As a result, they tend to earn more than temporary visa holders or unauthorized immigrants.

Economists have examined the value of a green card using several methods. A study that compares immigrants' earnings before and after they received their green card concludes that employment-based immigrants experienced an average annual wage gain of $11,860 (Mukhopadhyay and Oxborrow, 2012). Another study compares earnings among Mexican men married to a U.S. citizen—which automatically qualifies them for a green card—with earnings among Puerto Rican men married to a U.S. citizen; Puerto Ricans are U.S. citizens, so marrying a U.S. native does not change their immigration status (Chi and Drewianka, 2012). That study finds that being eligible for a green card boosts Mexican men's wages by 40 percent. The lifetime earnings gain is at least $100,000 in present discounted value. Research on Chinese immigrants who became eligible for green cards via the 1993 Chinese Student Protection Act concludes that eligible Chinese immigrants experienced sizable wage gains. Estimates range from 9 to 25 percent (Lan, 2013; Orrenius, Zavodny and Kerr, 2012). Research that looks at immigrants who were able to legalize their status through the 1986 IRCA or other legalization programs also finds evidence of substantial wage gains.

category is immediate relatives of U.S. citizens. The United States distributes about one million permanent resident visas in a typical year, and about 45 percent of them go to immediate relatives of U.S. citizens.

The preference categories and their caps are the subject of intense debate. People who want to be able to bring in more relatives argue that the family-based categories are too restrictive and the caps are too low. Employers and foreign workers argue the same for the employment-based categories. Some U.S. workers who believe that they compete with immigrant workers argue that the employment-based categories are too generous. Some people who are concerned that immigrants are a fiscal burden argue that the total number of visas awarded is too high, particularly for family-based immigrants or refugees who may not work. Others argue that the total number of visas awarded is too low.

The fact that immigrants who enter under different categories tend to have different characteristics fuels much of this debate, at least from an economic perspective. Permanent residents admitted via employment-based categories tend to have considerably more education than those admitted via other categories (Jasso et al., 2000). Diversity lottery immigrants tend to have more education than family-based immigrants, in part because lottery applicants must have at least completed high school. Not surprisingly, immigrants admitted via employment-based categories are more likely to work than immigrants admitted via other categories. Immigrants admitted via employment-based categories are also more likely than family-based immigrants to go to parts of the United States with better economic opportunities (Jaeger, 2008). The caps on various categories thus may affect the characteristics of permanent residents and, in turn, their labor market and fiscal impacts.

Temporary visas

A complicated system of temporary visas runs parallel to the complicated system of permanent resident visas explained above. Almost every foreigner who enters the United States for a stay of more than 90 days needs a visa, and people from most countries need a visa for shorter stays as well.[5] Types of temporary visas include visas for temporary foreign workers, student visas and visitor (tourist) visas. Again, researchers do not consider people with visitor visas to be immigrants because they do not live in the destination country (unless they overstay that visa, in which case they become unauthorized immigrants).

There is an alphabet soup of visas for temporary foreign workers. The H-1B visa allows foreigners to work in specialty occupations for up to three years. The H-2A visa allows foreigners from certain countries to work in seasonal agricultural jobs for up to ten months. The H-2B visa allows foreigners from certain countries to work in temporary or seasonal non-agricultural jobs for up to one year. The O visa allows people with extraordinary ability or achievement to work in the United States for up to three years. Artists, entertainers and athletes may enter the United States to perform or compete on a P visa. There are other types of temporary worker visas as well. Some temporary worker visa categories require that the U.S. Department of Labor certify that there are not enough qualified U.S. workers available and willing to perform the job that the temporary foreign worker will fill. Some of these visas have annual caps, and some of them do not allow a worker to switch to another employer without getting a new visa.

Debates about temporary worker visas center on concerns that immigrants, including those on temporary worker visas, adversely affect native-born workers. As discussed in Chapter 7, the basic economic model predicts that immigration will reduce natives' earnings and employment. Since temporary foreign workers are, by definition, in the United States to work, such concerns may be heightened for this group of immigrants. However, temporary foreign workers may not have an adverse impact if they complement native-born workers instead of substituting for them. For example, they may take jobs that few natives hold. Some temporary foreign worker programs include a "prevailing wage" requirement that requires employers to pay visa holders at least the average wage for the job they fill. Such requirements are an attempt to assuage concerns about adverse effects.

H-1B visas are perhaps the most controversial temporary worker visa. Most H-1B visas require that a worker have at least a bachelor's degree or work in an occupation that usually requires at least a bachelor's degree. The number of H-1B visas is currently capped at 65,000 a year.[6] In most years, the number of applications far outstrips the number of visas available. In 2012, more than 60 percent of H-1B visa holders were from India.[7] A similar share of H-1B visa holders worked in computer-related occupations, most of them as computer programmers. Their average annual compensation was $70,000. Research shows that H-1B visa holders tend to earn more than U.S.-born workers in similar occupations (Lofstrom and Hayes, 2011). Nonetheless, critics of the H-1B program charge that its existence has reduced the wages that computer programmers earn in the United States. Proponents of the program argue that it increases U.S. economic growth by increasing the number of workers in the information technology sector, a critical part of the U.S. economy, and by alleviating labor market shortages. A study shows that the H-1B program may even raise U.S. natives' earnings by increasing their productivity (Peri, Shih and Sparber, 2014). Box 13.2, "The effect of H-1B visa availability on students," discusses how the program may affect who attends college in the United States.

Most foreign students who study in the United States have a student visa called an F-1 visa. Student visa holders are not allowed to work off campus except in jobs related to their area of study, and they must receive approval from a designated official at their school before they can work off campus. After they graduate, foreign students are allowed to work for 12 months in a job related to their studies before they must transition to another visa; graduates in science, technology, engineering and math (STEM fields) can receive a 17-month extension.[8] Receiving a student visa was fairly straightforward until the 9/11 terrorist attacks. At least one of the hijackers had entered the United States on a student visa, and others had studied at U.S. flight schools despite not having student visas. After 9/11, scrutiny of student visa applications

---

Box 13.2 The effect of H-1B visa availability on students

Many H-1B visa holders graduated from college or university in the United States. After graduation, they adjusted from a student visa to an H-1B visa. While the number of student visas is unlimited, the number of H-1B visas is not. In 2004, the number of H-1B visas available per year fell from 195,000 to 65,000 visas. The cap of 65,000 has been binding every year since then. Foreigners may hope that studying in the United States is a pathway to working in the United States. But the H-1B visa cap may squash those hopes. If so, the cap may affect who chooses to study in the United States.

To examine this, Takao Kato and Chad Sparber (2013) look at the scores earned by foreign applicants on the SAT, a standardized test that many U.S. colleges and universities use for admissions decisions. They compare test scores among applicants from countries that are subject to the H-1B visa cap with test scores among applicants from countries that are not subject to the cap for various reasons (Australia, Canada, Chile, Mexico and Singapore). They look at average scores before and after the H-1B visa cap was lowered. They find that SAT scores fell among applicants from countries subject to the cap relative to applicants from countries not subject to the cap. The average math score fell by about 8.5 points, and the average verbal score fell by about 10 points. Their results suggest that some of the top foreign students were deterred from applying to U.S. colleges and universities by the greater difficulty they would face in getting an H-1B visa after graduation.

Box 13.3 How 9/11 affected immigrants in the United States

The United States enacted a number of changes after the terrorist attacks on September 11, 2001, that affected immigrants and immigrant inflows. The federal government extended immigration law enforcement powers to state and local police departments through programs called 287(g) and Secure Communities; created a special registration program for men from Muslim countries; and gave immigration authorities greater powers to detain non-citizens without judicial review, among other changes. The Enhanced Border Security and Visa Entry Reform Act of 2002 stepped up the use of biometric information, such as fingerprints, to better track who enters and exits the United States. It also increased funding for border security. Many states barred unauthorized immigrants from receiving driver's licenses and state identification cards, and the federal government adopted new standards for driver's licenses and identification cards via the Real ID Act of 2005.

Soon after 9/11, the federal government created a program that required many male non-U.S. citizens from 25 predominately Muslim countries living in the United States to register with the federal government. These men were required to report to immigration officials for questioning and to notify the government if they moved. More than 85,000 men participated in the program. Eleven of them were determined to have ties to terrorist organizations. The program was widely criticized as inconsistent with civil liberties. That program was scaled back in 2003 and ended in 2011.

Discrimination against immigrants, particularly those believed to be from the Middle East, increased after 9/11. Average earnings fell among first- and second-generation Arab and Muslim male immigrants in the United States (Kaushal, Kaestner and Reimers, 2007; Dávila and Mora, 2005). Increased stress and lower incomes appear to have had far-reaching consequences: poor birth outcomes increased among women with Arabic names after 9/11 (Lauderdale, 2006). The increased emphasis on having legal documents combined with greater discrimination against immigrants also led to worse labor market outcomes for unauthorized Hispanic immigrants. After 9/11, earnings and employment fell among Hispanic immigrants who were likely to be unauthorized (Orrenius and Zavodny, 2009).

increased considerably. Schools were eventually required to use a computer system called Student Exchange and Visitors Information System (SEVIS) to better track foreign students. Box 13.3, "How 9/11 affected immigrants in the United States," discusses other immigration-related changes in the wake of 9/11.

Unauthorized immigration and enforcement

Current U.S. immigration policy with regard to unauthorized immigration consists primarily of enforcement, both along the country's borders and in its interior. Border enforcement aims to prevent the entry of illegal immigrants. Border enforcement occurs at airports and seaports as well as the country's land borders with Canada and Mexico. It encompasses physical barriers, such as fences and walls; surveillance technology, such as motion detectors and drones; and personnel. People apprehended while trying to illicitly cross the border are usually returned or removed to their home country.

Interior enforcement includes enforcement at worksites, jails and prisons. Worksite enforcement includes raids on workplaces suspected of hiring unauthorized workers and audits of employers' records to ensure that employees are eligible to work in the United States. Jails and prisons check inmates' immigration status. In some areas, local law enforcement officials also check people's immigration status when making traffic stops or other interventions. People found to be in violation of immigration law are eventually transferred to Immigration and Customs Enforcement (ICE), an agency of the U.S. Department of Homeland Security, for removal from the country. During 2007 to 2012, more than 300,000 migrants were removed, or deported, from the United States each year.[9]

Policymakers balance a number of competing priorities when they determine enforcement levels. Increasing enforcement in order to reduce the number of unauthorized immigrants involves costs and benefits. These costs and benefits can be modeled using a basic marginal cost and marginal benefit framework, as shown in Figure 13.5. The horizontal axis can be thought of as having two dimensions, which go in opposite directions. The first dimension is enforcement, which increases from left to right. The second dimension is the number of unauthorized immigrants, which increases from right to left. The vertical axis is dollars, the units in which marginal costs and benefits are measured.

As enforcement increases, the number of unauthorized immigrants decreases. The marginal cost of enforcement increases as enforcement increases, while the marginal benefit of enforcement decreases as enforcement increases. Marginal cost increases as enforcement increases if each additional unit of enforcement costs more than the previous unit. For example, building

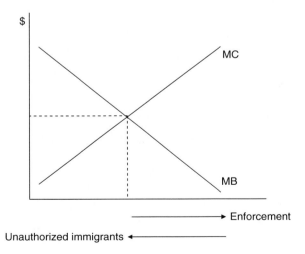

Figure 13.5 Marginal costs and marginal benefits of enforcement.

The horizontal axis has two dimensions: enforcement, which increases from left to right; and the number of unauthorized immigrants, which decreases as enforcement increases. The marginal cost of enforcement increases as the level of enforcement increases, while the marginal benefit of enforcement decreases as the level of enforcement increases.

a fence costs less than building a wall, which in turn costs less than using drones to patrol the border. Marginal benefit decreases as enforcement increases if there are diminishing marginal returns to enforcement. This means that each additional unit of enforcement is less effective at reducing unauthorized immigration than the previous unit. An important implication of Figure 13.5 is that it is unlikely that the optimal level of enforcement results in zero unauthorized immigrants. Reducing the number of unauthorized immigrants to zero would be extremely costly, and the marginal cost of doing so would almost certainly far exceed the marginal benefit.

State and local policies

The federal government has not passed any major laws regarding immigration policy since the mid-1990s. State and local governments, in contrast, adopted numerous policies regarding immigrants during the early 2000s. The continued increase in the number of immigrants combined with the increased geographic dispersion of immigrants across the United States led to a flurry of immigration-related activity at the state and local levels. Many of these new policies were aimed at unauthorized immigrants. Some were positive toward unauthorized immigrants, such as "sanctuary" policies under which municipal governments forbid their employees from asking people about their immigration status. Los Angeles, New York City and Washington, DC, are examples of cities with sanctuary policies.

Some states have adopted laws allowing unauthorized immigrant youths to pay in-state tuition at public colleges and universities. In 1996, IIRIRA made unauthorized immigrants ineligible for federally-funded financial aid. It also sought to make unauthorized immigrants ineligible to pay in-state tuition. (Students are typically eligible to pay in-state tuition at public colleges and universities in their state of residence. In-state tuition is often less than one-half the price of out-of-state tuition.) As of 2013, 18 states had laws or policies in place allowing unauthorized immigrants to pay in-state tuition.[10] In addition, three states offered financial aid to unauthorized immigrant students. Meanwhile, six states explicitly made unauthorized immigrants ineligible to pay in-state tuition. Several studies suggest that college attendance and completion among immigrants likely to be undocumented is higher in states that allow unauthorized immigrants to pay in-state tuition (Kaushal, 2008; Flores, 2010). Such policies do not appear to reduce financial aid, increase student debt or crowd out other groups of students from attending public colleges and universities (Amuedo-Dorantes and Sparber, 2014).

Many other policies that states and localities adopted were not positive toward unauthorized immigrants. In 2007, Arizona became the first state to require employers to verify that new hires are authorized to work in the United States. (Hiring an unauthorized worker is illegal everywhere in the United States, but IRCA only requires that workers present certain documents to their employers, not that employers verify those documents.) The Legal Arizona Workers Act (LAWA) requires that employers use a system called E-Verify. E-Verify compares an employee's name and Social Security number with federal records. The employer is notified whether the records match. LAWA requires employers to fire a worker whose records do not match if the worker cannot resolve the disparity. Arizona employers who do not comply with the law can lose their business license. As of 2013, 20 states had policies requiring some or all employers to use E-Verify.[11]

State laws that require employers to use E-Verify appear to have significant effects. Research shows that the number of Hispanics who are not U.S. citizens—many of whom are unauthorized immigrants—in Arizona fell dramatically after LAWA was passed in 2007 (Bohn, Lofstrom and Raphael, 2014). LAWA also appears to have pushed many unauthorized immigrants who stayed in the state out of the formal labor market into "black market" jobs or self employment (Bohn and Lofstrom, 2013). Employment and earnings among less-educated Hispanic immigrants have fallen in states that adopted E-Verify mandates (Amuedo-Dorantes and Bansak, 2012, 2013; Orrenius and Zavodny, 2014). Foreign investment has fallen in states that adopted E-Verify requirements (Amuedo-Dorantes, Bansak and Zebedee, 2014).

States and localities have adopted a number of other policies aimed at unauthorized immigrants. Such policies include requiring police and other government employees to ask about legal immigration status while conducting routine transactions (often called "show me your papers" policies); barring unauthorized immigrant children from public schools; and prohibiting landlords from renting to unauthorized immigrants, among others. Some of these policies have been upheld by courts, while others have been ruled unconstitutional.

Failed attempts at federal immigration policy reform

While states and localities have been busy adopting policies that affect immigrants, there has been a notable lack of action by the U.S. Congress since the mid-1990s. A tremendous variety of immigration-related legislation has been proposed in Congress, and some bills have passed either the House of Representatives or the Senate, but no major immigration-related legislation has passed both parts of Congress in years. Two attempts at immigration policy reform at the federal level are particularly noteworthy: the BSEOIMA Act, and the DREAM Act.

The BSEOIMA (Border Security, Economic Opportunity and Immigration Modernization) Act passed the Senate in 2013 but failed to pass the House of Representatives. The bill was what some policymakers call "comprehensive immigration reform" because it addressed multiple aspects of immigration policy. The bill proposed changes to the preference categories and caps for legal permanent residence visas; changes to several types of temporary worker visas; more funding for border enforcement; a requirement that all employers use E-Verify; and a legalization program for some unauthorized immigrants. Many opponents of BSEOIMA were concerned that the legalization program would encourage additional unauthorized immigration, but virtually every aspect of the bill had both supporters and opponents. Attempts at comprehensive immigration reform in 2006 and 2007 also failed to pass both parts of Congress.

The DREAM (Development, Relief and Education for Alien Minors) Act was first proposed in 2001. The DREAM Act would have created a legalization program for unauthorized immigrants who arrived in the United States as children. Most variants of the DREAM Act required beneficiaries to be enrolled in school, have graduated from high school or be serving in the U.S. military. Like many opponents of BSEOIMA, most opponents of the DREAM Act were concerned that it would have encouraged additional unauthorized immigration.

In response to Congress's failure to pass a DREAM Act, in 2012 President Barack Obama signed an executive order that contained several parts of the DREAM Act. The executive order created a program called Deferred Action for Childhood Arrivals (DACA). DACA allows some unauthorized immigrants to receive temporary legal status and a work permit.

To be eligible, immigrants must be under age 31, have arrived in the United States before age 16, have lived in the United States for five years, not have a criminal record and be currently attending school or be a high school graduate. Unlike the DREAM Act, DACA does not include legal permanent residency or allow beneficiaries to eventually apply for U.S. citizenship. DACA only confers temporary legal status for two years at a time. As of mid-2014, more than 550,000 DACA applications had been approved.

Final thoughts on U.S. immigration policy

As this chapter makes clear, U.S. immigration policy is a complex set of laws and policies at the federal, state and local levels. How U.S. immigration policy will evolve is uncertain. What economists do know is that policy matters. Immigration policy determines who is allowed to enter the country legally, and it influences who enters or stays in the country illegally. The next chapter explores the design of other countries' immigration policies, which tend to differ considerably from the United States.

Problems and discussion questions

1   Discuss the major shift in immigration policy in the United States in 1965. What were the long-run implications of the policy change?

2   How would a decrease in the marginal cost of enforcement, such as better and cheaper surveillance technology, affect the optimal level of enforcement and the number of unauthorized immigrants?

3   What would be the likely economic effects if the United States began requiring all employers to use the E-Verify system? Who would benefit, and who would lose? How might immigration patterns be affected?

4   Use data from the Department of Homeland Security's Yearbook of Immigration Statistics(http://www.dhs.gov/yearbook-immigration-statistics-2013-lawful-permanent-residents) to examine the ages and occupations of people obtaining permanent resident status in fiscal year 2013. How do the age and occupation distributions vary across broad classes of admission?

5   What are the likely effects of DACA on beneficiaries?

Notes

1 See http://www.pewresearch.org/2013/04/17/unauthorized-immigrants-how-pew-research-counts-them-and-what-we-know-about-them/ [12 September 2014].

2 See http://www.pewhispanic.org/files/2014/04/FINAL_Statistical-Portrait-of-the-Foreign-Born-2012.pdf [12 September 2014].

3 For the text of these and other immigration laws, see http://library.uwb.edu/guides/usimmigration/USimmigrationlegislation.html. For a good summary of current U.S. immigration policy, see http://www.immigrationpolicy.org/just-facts/how-united-states-immigration-system-works-fact-sheet [13 September 2014].

4 Since 1997, the number of "other" visas available has been capped at 5,000 until all immigrants who legalized status under a legalization program that year have been counted against the cap.

5 As of 2014, the United States had visa waiver agreements with 38 countries that allowed their citizens to enter the country without a visa for a short stay. See http://travel.state.gov/content/visas/english/visit/visa-waiver-program.html.

6 An additional 20,000 visas are available for masters or PhD recipients from U.S. universities. Non-profit research organizations are exempt from the cap.

7 See U.S. Department of Homeland Security (2013) *Characteristics of H-1B Specialty Occupation Workers.* http://www.uscis.gov/sites/default/files/USCIS/Resources/Reports%20and%20Studies/H-1B/h1b-fy-12-characteristics.pdf [22 July 2014].

8 This is called Optional Practical Training (OPT).

9 See Table 39 of http://www.dhs.gov/yearbook-immigration-statistics-2012-enforcement-actions. Removals do not count returns, or people apprehended crossing the border who are immediately returned to their home country.

10 See National Conference of State Legislatures, http://www.ncsl.org/research/immigration/in-state-tuition-and-unauthorized-immigrants.aspx [23 July 2014].

11 See National Conference of State Legislatures, http://www.ncsl.org/research/immigration/everify-faq.aspx#Table:States%20Requiring%20E%20Verify [23 July 2014]. Since 2009, the federal government has required some federal contractors to use E-Verify.

Internet resources

The U.S. Census Bureau publishes reports on the characteristics of immigrants in the United States at http://www.census.gov/topics/population/foreign-born.html.

The U.S. Department of State provides an explanation of permanent and temporary visas, including statistics, at http://travel.state.gov/content/visas/english.html.

There are a number of think tanks and other organizations that analyze U.S. immigration policy. Here are links to some of them:

American Enterprise Institute: www.aei.org

Brookings Institution: www.brookings.edu

Cato Institute: www.cato.org

Center for Immigration Studies: www.cis.org

Economic Policy Institute: www.epi.org

Manhattan Institute for Policy Research: www.manhattan-institute.org

Migration Policy Institute: www.migrationpolicy.org

Partnership for a New American Economy: renewoureconomy.org

Pew Research Hispanic Trends Project: www.pewhispanic.org

Urban Institute: www.urban.org

References

Amuedo-Dorantes, C. and Bansak, C. (2011) "The impact of amnesty on labor market outcomes: A panel study using the Legalized Population Survey." *Industrial Relations* 50(3), pp. 443–71.

Amuedo-Dorantes, C. and Bansak, C. (2012) "The labor market impact of mandated employment verification systems." *American Economic Review: Papers & Proceedings* 103(2), pp. 543–548.

Amuedo-Dorantes, C. and Bansak, C. (2013) "Employment verification mandates and the labor market outcomes of likely unauthorized and native workers." *IZA Discussion Paper* No. 7419. Bonn: Institute for the Study of Labor.

Amuedo-Dorantes, C., Bansak, C. and Raphael, S. (2007) "Gender differences in the labor market: Impact of IRCA's amnesty provisions." *American Economic Review Papers & Proceedings* 97(2), pp. 412–16.

Amuedo-Dorantes, C., Bansak, C. and Zebedee, A. (2014) "The impact of mandated employment verification systems on state-level employment by foreign affiliates." *Southern Economic Journal*, forthcoming.

Amuedo-Dorantes, C. and Sparber, C. (2014) "In-state tuition for undocumented immigrants and its impact on college enrollment, tuition costs, student financial aid, and indebtedness." *Regional Science and Urban Economics* 49(2), pp. 11–24.

Bansak, C. and Raphael, S. (2001) "Immigration reform and the earnings of Latino workers: Do employer sanctions cause discrimination?" *Industrial and Labor Relations Review* 54(2), pp. 275–295.

Bohn, S. and Lofstrom, M. (2013) "Employment effects of state legislation." In: Card, D. and Raphael, S. (eds.) *Immigration, Poverty, and Socioeconomic Inequality.* New York: Russell Sage Foundation, pp. 282–314.

Bohn, S., Lofstrom, M. and Raphael, S. (2014) "Did the 2007 Legal Arizona Workers Act reduce the state's unauthorized immigrant population?" *Review of Economics and Statistics* 96(2), pp. 258–269.

Chi, M. and Drewianka, S. (2012) "How much is a green card worth? Evidence from Mexican men who marry women born in the U.S." Mimeo, University of Wisconsin-Milwaukee Department of Economics.

Dávila, A. and Mora, M.T. (2005) "Changes in the earnings of Arab Men in the US between 2000 and 2002." *Journal of Population Economics* 18(4), pp. 587–601.

Flores, S.M. (2010) "State Dream Acts: The effect of in-state resident tuition policies and undocumented Latino students." *Review of Higher Education* 33(2), pp. 239–283.

Jaeger, D.A. (2008) "Green cards and the location choices of immigrants in the United States, 1971–2000." *Research in Labor Economics* 27, pp. 131–183.

Jasso, G., Massey, D.S., Rosenzweig, M.R. and Smith, J.P. (2000) "The New Immigrant Survey Pilot (NIS-P): Overview and new findings about U.S. legal immigrants at admission." *Demography* 37(1), pp. 127–138.

Jasso, G., Wadhwa, V., Gereffi, G., Rissing, B. and Freeman, R. (2010) "How many highly skilled foreign-born are waiting in line for U.S. legal permanent residence?" *International Migration Review* 44(2), pp. 477–498.

Kato, T. and Sparber, C. (2013) "Quotas and quality: The effect of H-1B visa restrictions on the pool of prospective students from abroad." *Review of Economics and Statistics* 95(1), pp. 109–126.

Kaushal, N. (2008) "In-state tuition for the undocumented: Education effects on Mexican young adults." *Journal of Policy Analysis and Management* 27(4), pp. 771–792.

Kaushal, N., Kaestner, R. and, Reimers, C. (2007) "Labor market effects of September 11th on Arab and Muslims residents of the United States." *Journal of Human Resources* 42(2), pp. 275–308.

Kossoudji, S.A. and Cobb-Clark, D.A. (2002) "Coming out of the shadows: Learning about legal status and wages from the Legalized Population." *Journal of Labor Economics* 20(3), pp. 598–628.

Lan, X. (2013) "The effects of green cards on the wages and innovations of new PhDs." *Journal of Policy Analysis and Management* 32(4), pp. 807–834.

Lauderdale, D.S. (2006) "Birth outcomes of Arabic-named women in California before and after September 11." *Demography* 43(1), pp. 185–201.

Lofstrom, M. and Hayes, J. (2011) "H-1Bs: How do they stack up to US born workers?" *IZA Discussion Paper* No. 6259. Bonn: Institute for the Study of Labor.

Mukhopadhyay, S. and Oxborrow, D. (2012) "The value of an employment-based green card." *Demography* 49(1), pp. 219–237.

Orrenius, P.M. and Zavodny, M. (2009) "The effects of tougher enforcement on the job prospects of recent Latin American immigrants." *Journal of Policy Analysis and Management* 28(2), pp. 239–257.

Orrenius, P.M. and Zavodny, M. (2014) "The impact of E-Verify mandates on labor market outcomes." *Southern Economic Journal*, forthcoming.

Orrenius, P., Zavodny, M. and Kerr, E. (2012) "Chinese immigrants in the U.S. labor market: Effects of post-Tiananmen immigration policy." *International Migration Review* 46(2), pp. 456–482.

Peri, G., Shih, K.Y. and Sparber, C. (2014) "Foreign STEM workers and native wages and employment in U.S. cities." *National Bureau of Economic Research Working Paper* No. 20093. Cambridge, MA: National Bureau of Economic Research.

Rivera-Batiz, F.L. (1999) "Undocumented workers in the labor market: An analysis of the earnings of legal and illegal Mexican immigrants in the United States." *Journal of Population Economics* 12(1), pp. 91–116.

14   Immigration Policy around the World

Setting immigration policy is extremely complicated, and countries all over the world regularly wrestle with determining the "right" immigration policy. Some countries have historical connections with another country that privileges immigrants from that country. Others have a general policy that applies to immigrants from all countries. Changing immigration policy is difficult for most countries, particularly those that are democracies. Although immigration policy is usually slow to change, public opinion about immigration can change quickly. Public opinion can become more negative when jobs are scarce during an economic downturn or when an event—such as a brutal crime committed by an immigrant—triggers a backlash against immigrants. Changes in the size or composition of immigrant flows may also ignite a national debate about immigration policy.

The world consists of a hodgepodge of immigration policies. In fact, there are so many immigration policies around the world that it is difficult even for people who study the topic to keep track of the variations! However, countries can be grouped into four general types of admission policies: policies that favor family ties and hence admit the majority of immigrants based on their relationship to people already in that country; point-based systems, which admit immigrants based on their characteristics, including age, education, experience and wealth; policies that give preference to immigrants from certain countries, regions or ethnic or cultural groups; and systems that largely limit immigration to workers on temporary visas. Most developed countries also have immigration policies regarding refugees, and some have programs aimed at helping immigrants integrate into their new country.

Brief recap of U.S. immigration policy

As discussed in the last chapter, immigration policy in the United States is complex. The U.S. immigration system gives preference to immigrants with family ties to U.S. citizens or permanent residents, although it does admit some immigrants based on their skills. Temporary worker visas are based on employer needs, whereas permanent visas are based primarily on family ties. Table 14.1 reports the number of legal permanent residents admitted to the United States in fiscal year 2013. About two-thirds of new legal permanent residents that year were admitted under family preferences. This compares with 16 percent admitted under employment-based preferences. Another 12 percent were refugees or asylees (successful asylum seekers), and the remaining 6 percent were diversity and other types of immigrants.

Table 14.1 Admission categories of U.S. permanent residents, 2013

Class of admission	Total	%
Immediate relatives of U.S. citizens	439,460	44.4%
Other family-sponsored preferences	210,303	21.1%
Employment-based preferences	161,110	16.3%
Refugees and asylees	119,630	12.1%
Diversity	45,618	4.6%
Other	13,876	1.4%
Total	990,553	

Source: U.S. Department of Homeland Security (2014) *Yearbook of Immigration Statistics: 2013* (http://www.dhs.gov/sites/default/files/publications/immigration-statistics/yearbook/2013/LPR/table6.xls [2 June 2014]).

The current U.S. system dates back to 1965, when the country changed from a system of national origin quotas to one that favors family ties. Although there have been some changes in immigration policy since then, U.S. immigration policy has remained steadfast in its emphasis on family ties. One result of this system is that the main source countries of immigrants change only slowly over time. An immigration policy based mainly on family ties heavily favors recent immigrants—they usually have close relatives abroad to sponsor to immigrate, whereas long-time U.S. citizens are unlikely to have close relatives abroad to sponsor. For the United States, the top five source countries of permanent residents in recent decades are, in descending order, Mexico, China, India, the Philippines and the Dominican Republic.[1] As discussed later in this chapter, a system of family-based preferences like the U.S. system differs significantly from policies that put more emphasis on employment or skill. Point-based systems are a case in point.

Point-based systems

Point-based systems are a form of skill-based preference systems. Although there are differences in the point-based systems used around the world, they are all similar in spirit. Countries allocate points for certain characteristics, and if a potential immigrant earns enough points, she receives—depending on the country—a permanent or temporary visa. A point system is essentially a scorecard, with points awarded based on age, language ability, education, occupation and so on. Exactly how points are allocated and what the passing threshold is differ across countries. Countries with a long history of point-based systems include Canada, Australia and New Zealand. This section describes their point-based systems and compares them with the U.S. system. A number of other countries, including the Czech Republic, Denmark, Hong Kong, Japan, Singapore, Sweden and the United Kingdom, have introduced a point system in recent years (Tani, 2014).

Canada

Canada has one of the most open immigration policies in the world, with about 21 percent of its population foreign born. In 1967, Canada became the first country to adopt a point-based system for awarding permanent residence to some groups of what it terms "economic class" immigrants. Table 14.2 reports the allocation of points in Canada, Australia and New Zealand in 2013. Canada's program favors immigrants with formal education and language proficiency. More than 50 percent of possible points are in those two categories. A maximum of 25 points out of 100 can be earned by a person who has a master's degree or a PhD and at least 17 years of full-time study. The lowest number of points available for education is five points for completion of high school. For language, a maximum of 28 points can be awarded to people who are highly proficient in both English and French. The number of points awarded depends on whether a person has basic, moderate or high proficiency. Written and oral tests are administered to gauge language ability in listening, speaking, reading and writing. Applicants must meet the minimum level in one of the two official languages in all four areas and can receive additional points for proficiency in the other official language.

Canada's system also awards points based on work experience, age (up to 45 years) and employer sponsorship. Importantly, individuals can make up points in one area by gaining points in another area. Notice that Canada does not assign points based on an immigrant's occupation. However, economic immigrants admitted under the point system must have work experience or a job offer in an eligible skilled occupation or have a PhD from a Canadian university, which effectively screens most applicants in that category on occupation.

Canada's immigration system favors highly educated workers. As reported in Table 14.3, about 57 percent of new legal permanent residents in 2013 were admitted as economic immigrants. About 31 percent were admitted under family preferences and 9 percent as refugees, neither of which are assessed under the point system. Comparing these figures with those for the United States (in Table 14.1), it is clear that the Canadian system emphasizes employment-based or economic immigration, while the U.S. favors family-based immigrants.

In 2012, the top three source countries for immigrants to Canada were China (32,990 immigrants), the Philippines (32,704 immigrants) and India (28,889 immigrants), according to Citizenship and Immigration Canada.[2] These three countries are known for sending educated immigrants to developed countries, including Canada and the United States.

Table 14.2 Allocation of points in Canada, Australia and New Zealand, 2013

	Canada	*Australia*	*New Zealand*
Language proficiency	28%	17%	Hurdle
Education	25%	17%	30%
Age	12%	25%	16%
Skilled occupation in host country	0%	Hurdle	32%
Work experience	15% (g)	17% (s)	16%
Sponsorship	10% (e)	8% (r)	0%
Other	10%	17%	6%
Pass mark	67%	50%	54%

Source: Tani (2014).

Notes: g = generic; s = specific; e = employer; r = state government. "Hurdle" means an applicant is automatically excluded if the standard is not met.

Table 14.3 Admission categories of Canadian permanent residents, 2013

Class of admission	Total	%
Economic class immigrants	148,037	57.2%
Family class immigrants	79,586	30.8%
Refugees	23,968	9.3%
Other	7,028	2.7%
Total	258,519	

Source: Citizenship and Immigration Canada, Preliminary tables – Permanent and temporary residents, 2013 (http://www.cic.gc.ca/english/resources/statistics/facts2013-preliminary/01.asp [27 August 2014]).

The Canadian experience has been that many point-based immigrants' skills do not transfer well from the destination country to the host country. Economic immigrants in Canada have tended to have worse labor market outcomes than expected given their skill levels. Abdurrahman Aydemir (2011) finds evidence that the Canadian point system is effective in attracting skilled immigrants, but this does not translate into higher labor force participation and employment rates, at least in the short run. Canada has taken several steps to combat this problem. In the 1990s, it created the Provincial Nominee Program, which allows provinces and territories to select immigrants. (In addition, the province of Quebec runs its own immigration system.) In 2008, it created the Canadian Experience Class, which grants permanent residence to skilled workers who have already lived in Canada on a student or temporary worker visa. Both of these new programs bypass the federal point system. In 2015, Canada is introducing an "expression of interest" system that will allow employers and the federal and provincial governments to view potential immigrants' qualifications. Canada will then invite selected candidates to apply for a visa.

Australia

Like Canada, Australia has a long history of immigration and a large foreign-born population share (28 percent in 2013). The permanent immigration program in Australia has two main components: the migration program, and the humanitarian program. The migration program consists of the skilled stream, the family stream and the special eligibility stream. For the skilled stream, Australia operates a hybrid selection system that includes both a point-based system and employer sponsorship. The goal is that immigrants are immediately employable. The system emphasizes specific skills that domestic employers want. Similar to the Canadian system, about two-thirds of immigrants are admitted based on employment-based preferences, and about one-third based on family preferences.[3] Australia is somewhat unique in that it adjusts its annual admissions cap on the number of permanent residents in response to changes in macroeconomic conditions.

As shown in Table 14.2, Australia allocates the most points on the basis of age (25 percent of total points) and then formal education, English proficiency and work experience (each 16.6 percent of total points). It requires at least vocational-level English and that applicants have an occupation on a list of skilled occupations. Potential applicants' post-secondary qualifications must be formally assessed before they can even submit an application for a point-tested skilled migration visa. Like Canada, Australia recently adopted an expression of interest model, called SkillSelect, which allows employers and the federal and state governments to view potential immigrants' qualifications. Selected candidates are then invited to apply for a visa.

A study by Deborah Cobb-Clark (2003) analyzes the effectiveness of Australia's point system in improving immigrants' labor market performance. In the late 1990s, Australia increased the emphasis on productivity-related skills in its immigrant selection process. Immigrants who arrived after the policy change had higher labor force participation rates and lower unemployment rates than immigrants who arrived before the change. Some of the improvement was due to other factors, including stronger labor market conditions in Australia and a change in public assistance policy to exclude most immigrants from social welfare programs during the first two years after they arrived in the country. Nonetheless, she concludes that the change in the point system played an important role in improving immigrant selectivity.

Barry Chiswick, Yew Liang Lee and Paul Miller (2008) compare the health status of immigrants who enter Australia under different visa categories. They find that immigrants who entered under employment-based preferences and those who enter under family reunification preferences have similar health. Refugees (those who enter under humanitarian preferences) have the worst health. Importantly, factors for which more points are awarded (more education, greater language proficiency, younger age, etc.) are associated with better health among immigrants. Countries with point systems that favor youth, high education and good language skills thus may not only have more-skilled immigrants who will earn higher incomes, but also relatively healthy immigrant populations.

Like a number of other countries, Australia allows wealthy immigrants to effectively buy their way into the country. Business innovators and investors who intend to invest or enter into business in Australia can receive a provisional visa and then a permanent resident visa; investors must invest at least AU $5 million in complying investments in Australia. The United States has a similar program for investors, the Immigrant Investor Program (also known as EB-5). The minimum investment is US $1 million, and the investment must create or preserve at least ten full-time jobs for qualifying U.S. workers within two years; there is a lower threshold if the investment is an economically distressed area. Canada ended its investor program in 2014.

In recent years, the Australian immigration system has been dubbed a two-step system because many of its immigrants enter on temporary visas and then adjust to permanent resident status after several years. The same is true of the United States—more than one-half of people receiving permanent residence there are adjusting status from a temporary visa. In Canada, about one-quarter of new permanents are transitioning from a temporary visa. In recent years, the number of temporary visas in Australia has outnumbered permanent settler visas by a ratio of three to one (Gregory, 2014). This has important implications for the Australian labor market. As Robert Gregory states:

> It is evident that a large pool of temporary immigrants, with work entitlements, has been created. This pool probably now accounts for three quarters of a million potential workers who, if all were employed, would be seven percent of Australian aggregate

employment. By way of contrast, annual permanent visa inflows, if all were employed, would account for just under two per cent of Australian employment.

(Gregory, 2014: 3)

Other point-based systems

The New Zealand point system, which began in 1991, favors skilled workers and work experience acquired locally through a temporary visa. New Zealand focuses on employability and demographic characteristics. As Table 14.2 indicates, formal qualifications also carry considerable weight, and immigrants must achieve a minimum score on a test of English proficiency.

In 2003, the United Kingdom created a point system with five different tiers. The system has become stricter over time, with increases in the qualifications required to receive a visa. Similar to the Australian and Canadian point systems, the UK system awards points based on age, work experience and qualifications. Unlike most other point systems, the UK system includes points based on previous earnings and awards points based on spousal characteristics. The five tiers are broadly defined as:

Tier 1: High-value migrants (entrepreneurs, exceptional talent, post-study employment and investors);
Tier 2: Skilled workers (skilled workers with a job offer in an area where there is a labor shortage, intracompany transfers);
Tier 3: Low-skilled workers (designed to fill temporary low-skilled labor shortages);
Tier 4: Students; and
Tier 5: Temporary workers

Most of the tiers require that the applicant have a job offer and be sponsored by an employer licensed by the UK Border Agency. Employer sponsorship means the employer is responsible for the foreign worker and must notify the UK Border Agency if the employee stops working. The United Kingdom has closed down or never opened a few of the tiers, and it has shifted much of its emphasis to having a job offer in an occupation determined to be experiencing a labor shortage. Typically, UK visas are temporary—they allow immigrants to work in the United Kingdom for a few years (usually three to five years, depending on the type of visa) but do not grant permanent resident status. Temporary residency may eventually lead to permanent residency. This is different from Australia, Canada and New Zealand, whose point systems all lead directly to permanent residency.

In 2011, Austria created a point system, dubbed the red-white-red card system, which has been lauded for successfully attracting high-skilled workers from non-EU countries. The red-white-red card point system is based on qualifications, work experience, language skills, age and studies completed in Austria. The visa is issued for 12 months, after which immigrants can apply for the "red-white-red card plus," which grants unlimited access to the Austrian labor market.

Even Japan, which has one of the strictest immigration policies in the world, adopted a point-based system in 2012 in response to its growing demographic problem (as discussed in Chapter 10). Figure 14.1 displays a recent flyer intended to promote Japan's new policy.

Figure 14.1 Leaflet for Japan's point system.

Source: Immigration Bureau of Japan, http://www.immi-moj.go.jp/newimmiact_3/en/pdf/leaflet_en.pdf [2 June 2014].

Drawbacks of a point system

A point system can be effective at targeting specific groups of high-skilled immigrants. This, in turn, can have positive effects on the labor market in the host country (as discussed in Chapter 7). It is also relatively transparent. Potential applicants can review the selection criteria and determine whether they can earn enough points to hit the threshold. However, a point system also has potential drawbacks, as discussed by Massimiliano Tani (2014). First, some categories may be somewhat subjective, such as assessments of language fluency. And, of course, which categories to include in the point system and how to award points are inherently subjective decisions. Policymakers may be able to justify the choices based on studies like those done by Cobb-Clark and Chiswick, Lee and Miller, but someone will almost certainly object to any conceivable allocation.

Another disadvantage is that a point system only selects immigrants based on observable factors, such as education, age, gender, experience and occupation. Applicants cannot be selected based on unobservable qualities, such as their work ethic and the quality and relevance of their skills. Such unobservable factors often play an important role in determining an immigrant's success in the host country. One way countries try to mitigate this disadvantage is by awarding points based on having a qualifying job offer. Employers may be able to screen potential immigrants based on factors that are hard to measure directly in a point system but that are apparent to employers. Another way to address this concern is to issue most permanent visas to people adjusting from temporary visas. Such migrants have presumably already demonstrated their ability to succeed in the host country.

A point system may not be flexible enough to deal with short-term labor shortages. If there is a shortage of workers with a particular skill set, the point system may not be flexible enough to meet that need, and alternative entry criteria may need to be developed. In particular, a point system that admits workers based on skill cannot be used to admit both high- and low-skilled workers—a country must choose a target group. A country that has chosen to target high-skilled immigrants may end up with a shortage of low-skilled workers, and vice versa. This may be true within skill levels as well. A country may target, say, doctors and end up with a shortage of engineers.

An advantage of a family-based admissions system is that family-based immigrants have an established network in the host country. Immigrants who are admitted based on skills may not have networks in the host country to help them find a job or housing. A lack of networks can lead to higher adjustment costs and worse economic performance in the short run.

Regular evaluation of the effectiveness of a point system—or any other immigrant admission system, for that matter—is important. However, collecting the data needed to measure immigrants' characteristics and their labor market outcomes in the host country over time is time consuming and expensive. Australia, Canada and New Zealand have longitudinal surveys that include thousands of immigrant respondents and contain hundreds of questions. Analysis of the data can inform the allocation of points in a country's point system. However, revisions to the point system may create uncertainty for employers and applicants alike. In addition, it is difficult for point systems that aim to respond to labor shortages to accurately predict and respond to future shortages. An immigration system that focuses on skills and employment must decide whether to emphasize short-run considerations, such as occupations experiencing a labor shortage, or long-run considerations, such as education levels and ability to integrate into the domestic labor market. Nonetheless, the list of countries with point systems has grown over time. This list includes several European countries that follow EU-wide immigration policy but also supplement the EU policy with their own policies.

European Union

Much like the United States, immigration forms a central component of European society. Of the 505 million nationals and legal foreign residents of the EU and Switzerland in 2013, some 52 million were born outside their European country of residence. In absolute terms, Germany has by far the largest immigrant population (9.8 million), followed by the UK (7.8 million), France (7.4 million), Spain (6.5 million), Italy (5.7 million), Switzerland (2.3 million) and the Netherlands (2.0 million), according to United Nations data.[4] As shown in Table 14.4, the proportion of foreign nationals and foreign-born persons within the

Table 14.4 Migrant stocks in the European Union, 2013

Country	Migrant stock	% of population
Germany	9,845,244	11.9
United Kingdom	7,824,131	12.4
France	7,439,086	11.6
Spain	6,466,605	13.8
Italy	5,721,457	9.4
Switzerland	2,335,059	28.9
Netherlands	1,964,922	11.7
Sweden	1,519,510	15.9
Austria	1,333,807	15.7
Belgium	1,159,801	10.4
Greece	988,245	8.9
Portugal	893,847	8.4
Ireland	735,535	15.9
Norway	694,508	13.8
Denmark	556,825	9.9
Hungary	472,798	4.7
Czech Republic	432,776	4.0
Finland	293,167	5.4
Latvia	282,887	13.8
Slovenia	233,293	11.3
Luxembourg	229,409	43.3
Estonia	209,984	16.3
Cyprus	207,313	18.2
Slovakia	149,635	2.7
Lithuania	147,781	4.9
Malta	34,455	8.0
Iceland	34,377	10.4
Monaco	24,299	64.2
Liechtenstein	12,208	33.1
Total	52,242,964	10.3

Source: United Nations, Department of Economic and Social Affairs, Population Division (2013) "Trends in International Migrant Stock: The 2013 Revision-Migrants by Age and Sex." (http://esa.un.org/unmigration/TIMSA2013/migrantstocks2013.htm?mtotals [2 June 2014]).

population of the 28 member states of the EU was about 10.3 percent in 2013, compared with 14.3 percent in the United States, according to United Nations data.

EU citizens are technically free to migrate across the member states of the European Union. The concept of free movement of persons came about with the signing of the Schengen Agreement in 1985 and the subsequent Schengen Convention in 1990, which initiated the abolition of border controls between participating countries. Cooperation has gradually been extended to include most EU member states as well as some non-EU countries. As they have abolished their internal borders, EU countries have tightened controls at their common external borders.

For visits of less than three months, all EU citizens have the right to enter another member state. For visits of more than three months, they must meet one of the following criteria: be engaged in economic activity (on an employed or self-employed basis); have sufficient resources and health insurance to ensure that they do not become a burden on the social services of the host country during their stay; be engaged in vocational training as a student and have sufficient resources and health insurance; or be a family member of an EU citizen who falls into one of the above categories.[5] EU citizens can gain permanent residency in another EU country after five years of uninterrupted legal residence in that country. This policy has not been without controversy, as exemplified by concern about Polish plumbers (see Box 14.1).

The European Union adopted EU-wide minimum standards regarding immigration by non-EU citizens (so-called third-country residents) as part of its Global Approach to Migration and Mobility (GAMM) in 2005. The initial focus of GAMM was the southern Mediterranean and sub-Saharan Africa. The focus has since expanded to cover countries in Latin America and the Caribbean as well as Central Asia and other parts of Asia. Growing discomfort with non-EU illegal (or "irregular") immigration has prompted discussions about the introduction of stringent selection policies for non-EU applicants based on each member state's domestic labor market needs.

In 2009, the EU created the "blue card" as a way of making the EU more attractive for high-skilled workers from non-member countries. The blue card (which was coined after the U.S. green card) offers a streamlined procedure for non-EU citizens to apply for a work permit. Work permits are valid for up to two years and can be renewed. Each country is allowed to set its own qualification criteria, but all countries must comply with the blue card's central principles. Three key conditions must be met in order to request an EU blue card visa: non-EU citizenship; completed higher education; and a work contract or a binding job offer. Workers who receive a blue card benefit from favorable family reunification rules and geographic mobility within the EU.

As of 2014, all EU member states except Denmark, Ireland and the United Kingdom participate in the EU blue card program. Those countries decided to opt out of the EU-wide system in favor of their own visa systems. Like the United Kingdom, Denmark has a point-based work visa program that aims to attract high-skilled workers, while Ireland grants work permits in skilled occupations experiencing labor shortages.

Outside of the blue card initiative, non-EU citizens face different entry criteria for each EU country. There are as many immigration policies in the EU as there are member states. The International Organization for Migration (2009) summarizes and compares EU countries' policies, which vary widely across countries and over time. However, the report notes that EU countries are making strides to better coordinate their policies. For example, an EU-wide directive is the creation of a single application procedure for third-country nationals to reside and work in member states. The EU has also mandated that countries issue a single permit for work and residence so that migrants are allowed to enter, re-enter and stay in the member country as well as pass through other EU countries. Furthermore, the EU has developed a common set of rights for third-country workers legally residing in member states so that migrants receive equal treatment across the EU.

Box 14.1 The Polish plumber

The free movement of workers across EU countries applied to the so-called A-10 countries that joined the EU in 2004. These countries were Cyprus, Czech Republic, Estonia, Hungary, Latvia, Lithuania, Malta, Poland, Slovakia and Slovenia. Workers in the accession countries were allowed to move freely to countries where wages were higher, such as France and the United Kingdom. The "Polish plumber" became a catchphrase in the run-up to the 2005 French referendum on the EU constitution.

The "Polish plumber" symbolizes fears of cheap East European labor threatening the jobs of West Europeans. Many Western Europeans feared that low-skilled workers from EU accession countries would replace native-born workers and drive down wages. But these concerns appear to be largely unfounded. A study by the European Commission (2008) concluded that the number of immigrants from Eastern Europe grew substantially after the EU enlargement in 2004, but wages did not fall and the immigrants made a "significant contribution to sustained economic growth." And they were not all unskilled workers. "The Poles aren't just picking apples or cleaning floors. There are many thousand in skilled jobs, and their departure could mean whole businesses packing up and following them," reported the BBC (2008).

However, when Bulgaria and Romania joined the EU in 2007, 15 of the 25 EU member states at the time (including the United Kingdom) kept their work permit systems that required most workers to be sponsored by an employer. This made it difficult for low-skilled Bulgarian and Romanian workers to gain entry.

Poland's response to the backlash was an ad featuring 21-year-old male model Piotr Adamski (see below). The ad beckoned French tourists to come to Poland.

Translation: *I am staying in Poland, do come over en masse.*

Guest worker programs

Many countries around the world have guest, or temporary, worker programs. Historically, industries experiencing labor market shortages have lobbied national governments to create temporary worker programs to help alleviate those shortages. Such programs are often limited to industries that experience seasonal fluctuations, such as agriculture, construction and tourism. More recently, guest workers have been used to satisfy demand in some countries for household services, such as cooking, cleaning and babysitting. An increasing number of guest workers worldwide are therefore women, whereas in the past they were predominantly men. Temporary worker programs require that workers return home after a specified amount of time. In most cases, guest workers have limited or no access to publicly funded social services, and they typically cannot bring their families with them.

Let's consider the economic theory behind the shortage of workers that motivates governments to create guest worker programs. If labor demand increases but labor supply remains the same, the equilibrium wage usually increases. A shortage of workers only occurs if for some reason the market wage does not increase in response to the increase in labor demand, as modeled in Figure 14.2. This might occur if binding contracts specify a wage, for example. After demand increases, quantity demanded exceeds quantity supplied if the wage does not rise.

One way to ease a labor shortage is to increase the supply of workers by admitting guest workers. When labor supply increases as guest workers enter, the supply curve shifts to the right. As Figure 14.3 shows, the equilibrium wage remains unchanged at $W*$ if the increase in labor supply—the number of guest workers—is big enough to fully satisfy the increase in labor

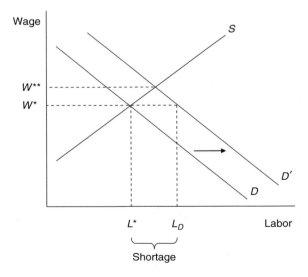

Figure 14.2 Model of a labor shortage.

Suppose labor demand increases and wages are fixed at $W*$ in the short run. The quantity of labor demanded (L_D) then exceeds the quantity supplied ($L*$), creating a shortage of workers ($L_D - L*$). In the long run, wages will adjust to $W**$.

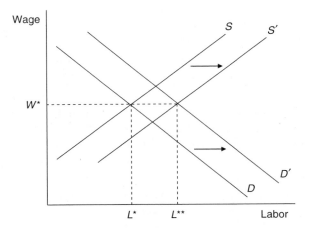

Figure 14.3 Model of labor supply increase in response to labor demand increase.

If the increase in labor demand is accompanied by an increase in guest workers, labor supply shifts to the right as well. The equilibrium wage remains *W**, and the quantity demanded equals the quantity supplied at *L***.

demand. In this scenario, the guest worker program fully accommodates employers' demand for additional workers. The wage therefore does not rise even though labor demand has increased. The number of native-born workers does not increase since the wage does not increase—all of the increase in labor demand is met by guest workers. The labor shortage disappears.

If instead labor supply does not increase enough to meet the increase in labor demand, wages rise. The increase in wages draws some native-born workers into the labor market, increasing the number of natives who are employed.

The design of guest worker programs varies significantly across countries. These programs are typically established to alleviate labor shortages. In some cases, however, guest worker programs are designed to minimize the flow of illegal immigrants between countries. Spain is an example of this, as discussed later in this chapter. In several countries, including Japan and the United Arab Emirates (along with other Gulf States), the majority of migrants enter through guest worker programs.

The United States has a long history of temporary worker programs. From the 1940s to the 1960s, the *bracero* program admitted Mexican workers on a seasonal basis to work in the agricultural sector. The program was created to ease labor shortages that arose during World War II and continued until concerns about abuses of workers gained prominence during the civil rights movement. As discussed in Chapter 13, the United States now has temporary worker programs for skilled workers, who work primarily in STEM (science, technology, engineering and mathematics) occupations, and for less-skilled workers in seasonal agricultural and non-agricultural jobs. Compared with the stock of more than 11 million unauthorized immigrants in the United States, the number of visas issued in U.S. temporary foreign worker programs, especially those for low-skilled workers, is minuscule.

Guest worker programs are small in most developed economies. Figure 14.4 plots the ratio of temporary workers to permanent immigrants for several OECD countries. The definition

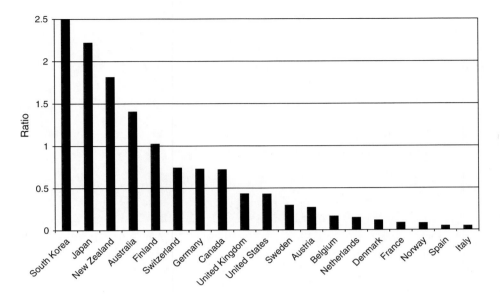

Figure 14.4 Ratio of temporary foreign workers to permanent immigrants, 2011.

Source: OECD (2013) *International Migration Outlook 2013*. Paris: OECD Publishing.

of temporary workers in the OECD dataset includes trainees, seasonal workers, intra-company transfers and other holders of temporary worker visas. The definition of permanent immigrants includes people granted a permanent resident visa, typically under employment-based, humanitarian or family preferences. As Figure 14.4 shows, a few industrialized countries admitted more temporary workers than permanent immigrants in 2011, including (in descending order) South Korea, Japan, New Zealand, Australia and Finland. Most European countries admitted relatively few temporary workers from outside the EU, including Italy, Spain, Norway and France. The United States admitted almost 460,000 temporary workers in 2011— the most of the OECD countries shown in the figure—but that number is well below the one million-plus people granted permanent residence there that year.

Germany

One of the earliest and best known guest worker programs was in Germany from the late 1950s until the early 1970s. Germany recruited and admitted large numbers of foreign workers, mostly from Turkey, in order to increase industrial production. The program was called *Gastarbeiter*, or guest worker. At the time, it was generally assumed that guest workers would eventually leave. Although the official guest worker program ended in 1973, many Turkish workers remained in Germany and brought their families. Today, immigrants represent approximately 12 percent of the German population, and Turks account for approximately one-quarter of all foreigners in Germany.[6] As Philip Martin and Michael Teitelbaum (2001) have quipped, there's nothing more permanent than a temporary foreign worker.

Since the end of the *Gastarbeiter*, German immigration policy limits immigration to skilled or highly skilled workers and admits low-skilled workers only for short periods. Until recently, the most popular temporary worker programs there admitted seasonal workers and workers used by foreign contractors. These programs brought short-term labor to Germany from Eastern Europe but became obsolete as more countries ascended into the EU.

Spain

Given the proximity of its southern border to Northern Africa and its colonial ties to Latin America, Spain has become a country of immigrants. Its migrant stock currently represents almost 14 percent of its population. This compares with a migrant stock representing about 2 percent of Spain's population in 1990. The switch from a country of emigrants to a country of immigrants has had profound social, economic, political, legal and cultural consequences. The majority of immigrants in Spain come from Africa, Latin America and Eastern Europe. Many of these migrants are low skilled and entered Spain on a temporary or seasonal work visa.

Spain is considered a test case for EU-wide guest worker programs. Spanish agreements with the governments of Senegal and Morocco allow workers to remain in Spain after their one-year visas expire, provided they are employed. The agreements

> put into practice many of the measures of circular migration that Brussels is promoting on a broader scale. Circular migration—allowing migrants to work temporarily in Europe—is meant to reduce illegal immigration and provide Europe with the farmhands and factory workers it needs, while avoiding integration costs
>
> (Gerson, 2007: 4)

Spain has also signed bilateral migration agreements with a number of other countries, including Bulgaria, Colombia, Dominican Republic, Ecuador, Mauritania, Morocco, Poland, Romania and Ukraine.[7]

Spain's guest worker program is complex. Workers and their sponsoring employers must satisfy a long list of eligibility conditions. For example, workers must be in good health and enrolled in the Spanish social security system. Employers must secure housing facilities for workers that are clean and in dignified condition. Employers must organize and pay for the trips to Spain and back to the country of origin.

The severe economic crisis that Spain has endured since the mid-2000s—deeper than in most European countries—has reduced the number of workers who want to come to Spain to work. With unemployment rates nearing 25 percent, few native- or foreign-born workers can find a job. Spaniards and recent immigrants are deserting the country in search of work. Some half a million people left Spain in 2012—60,000 of them Spanish nationals—and most of them to Latin America or elsewhere in Europe (Burgen, 2013).

Other countries

Low-skilled guest workers represent a large share of migrants in non-democratic developing countries, including the Gulf States, Hong Kong and Singapore. In Malaysia and Singapore, female guest workers employed as maids must take a pregnancy test every six months and are deported if they are pregnant. Most low-skilled workers in the Persian Gulf region are from poor countries in Asia and the Middle East, including Bangladesh, Egypt, India, Indonesia, Pakistan and Yemen. Box 14.2, "Migration and the United Arab Emirates," discusses guest workers in the one of the Gulf States.

Box 14.2 Migration and the United Arab Emirates

The United Arab Emirates (UAE) and its capital city of Abu Dhabi has become a popular destination for low- and high-skilled migrants. In 2013, a whopping 84 percent of the UAE population was foreign born, according to United Nations data. Most immigrants in the UAE originate from India, Bangladesh and Pakistan and are attracted by the UAE's high wages, relative political stability and modern infrastructure (Froilan, Malit and Youha, 2013).

In 1971, the UAE government introduced a temporary guest worker program called the Kafala Sponsorship System that allows citizens, companies and expatriates living there to hire migrant workers. The Kafala system has posed a number of challenges, many of which have attracted worldwide media attention. The challenges include ensuring economic opportunities for UAE citizens and addressing widespread concerns that migrants fall victim to labor and human rights abuses in the UAE.

The Migration Policy Institute, a think tank in Washington, DC, reports:

> Over the past several years, the UAE government has substantively reformed its laws to address the concerns of those who condemn the Kafala system for exposing migrant workers to abusive practices. Recent measures have ranged from outlawing employer confiscation of workers' passports to allowing workers to transfer employer sponsorship and introducing wage protection measures. Despite these efforts, human-rights and migrant organizations maintain that abusive labor practices have persisted at alarming rates, largely due to poor enforcement.
>
> (Froilan, Malit and Youha, 2013)

However, in May 2014, the *New York Times* reported abuse among migrant workers at the New York University (NYU) Abu Dhabi campus (Kaminer and O'Driscol, 2014). The *New York Times* reported evidence of "physical abuse, illegal recruitment fees, withheld passports, squalid living conditions and debilitating pay droughts, with minimal oversight from the university." Most of the men described having to work 11 or 12 hours a day, six or seven days a week, just to earn close to what they had originally been promised, despite a provision in the labor contract that overtime was voluntary.

One painter said he was promised a base pay of 1,500 dirham a month, or $408. After he arrived, he said, he found out it would be 700 dirham, about what other

Saadiyat Island construction workers have been reported to make. Overtime boosts that to 1,000 dirham, or $272. But food costs more than a third of that. Cellphones, the men's lifeline to the world they left behind, take another cut. And the annual raises they were promised have not materialized. Even working 11 hours a day, six days a week, they struggle to send home much more than $100 a month.

(Kaminer and O'Driscol, 2014)

Ironically, former U.S. President Bill Clinton was scheduled to give the commencement address to the first graduating class of NYU Abu Dhabi the week after the *New York Times* article was published. Despite pleas in the United States that he boycott the event in protest, Clinton delivered the address without any direct criticism of NYU or the UAE government (New York Times, 2014). However, Clinton did comment:

When this story came out, instead of going into an immediate denial, the university did something which reflects the values you have been taught here. The university, and the government, promised to look into the charges, to do it quickly, to do it honestly and, most importantly, among all the world's skeptics, to do it transparently and if the charges were well founded, to take appropriate, remedial action promptly.

(New York Times, 2014)

The media attention that surrounded the construction of the NYU campus shows how migrant workers can be at the center of worldwide labor abuse.

Refugee policies

Most migrants leave their home country voluntarily to seek a better life elsewhere. Refugees leave involuntarily—they flee because of the threat of persecution and cannot return safely to their homes. Immigration systems therefore often treat refugees differently than other migrants.

Early groups of refugees were often people fleeing religious persecution, such as the Puritans who left England and then the Netherlands, and the Huguenots who left France in the seventeenth century. These groups were dwarfed by the large-scale displacement of people in Europe during World War I and World War II. More than 2 million Armenians, Germans, Greeks and Poles were displaced across Europe during World War I. After World War II, there were more than 30 million refugees across Europe, and another 13 million ethnic Germans were expelled from eastern Europe and the Soviet Union (Hatton, 2013). Concern about these displaced persons led to the creation of the United Nations High Commissioner for Refugees (UNHCR) in 1949. Today, the UNHCR is the primary organization that protects and supports refugees at the request of a government or the United Nations and assists in their return or resettlement.

As Timothy Hatton (2013) discusses, the number of refugees swelled between the 1960s and the 1980s as a result of the Cold War, the Korean War and the Vietnam War. All three conflicts fueled refugee crises across the world. During the 1980s, conflicts in Afghanistan, Africa and Central and South America led to the displacement of yet more people. The collapse of the Soviet bloc starting in 1989 created a new pipeline of refugees in the 1990s. Today, conflicts in the Middle East and Africa are the primary source of refugee flows.

The United Nations defines refugees as people who are unable or unwilling to return to their home country because of a well-founded fear of persecution due to race, membership in a particular social group, political opinion, religion or national origin. War and ethnic, tribal or religious violence are leading causes of refugee crises. There were approximately 11 million refugees in 2013, according to the UNHCR (2014).

The source countries of refugees vary over time and change with the geographic location of conflicts, violence and wars. Table 14.5 reports the top 20 source countries for refugees in 2013, according to the UNHCR. Afghanistan is the top source of refugees, with more than 2.56 million refugees that year. Syria is the second largest source country, with 2.47 million refugees, followed by Somalia and Sudan. To give a sense of the volatility in these numbers, there were fewer than 20,000 refugees from Syria before the start of the Syrian conflict in early 2011. By 2012, the number of Syrian refugees had increased to 729,022, and then to almost 2.5 million by 2013! However, the long-lasting conflicts

Table 14.5 Top 20 source countries of refugees, 2013

Source country	Number of refugees
Afghanistan	2,556,556
Syria	2,468,369
Somalia	1,121,738
Sudan	649,331
Democratic Republic of the Congo	499,541
Myanmar	479,608
Iraq	401,417
Colombia	396,635
Vietnam	314,105
Eritrea	308,022
Central African Republic	252,865
China	195,137
Mali	152,864
Sri Lanka	123,088
Western Sahara	116,504
South Sudan	114,467
Palestinians	96,044
Côte d'Ivoire	85,729
Rwanda	83,937
Ethiopia	77,118

Source: UNHCR Statistical Online Population Database (www. unhcr.org/statistics/Ref_1960_2013.zip [24 August 2014]).

in Afghanistan have resulted in it being the leading source of refugees worldwide for three decades.

Where do refugees go? They tend to first go to countries that share a border with their home country. For example, about 95 percent of refugees from Afghanistan go to Pakistan and Iran. The Middle East and North Africa have approximately 2.63 million refugees. Asia hosts 3.5 million refugees, and Africa 2.9 million refugees (UNHCR, 2013). Table 14.6 reports the top 20 destination countries of refugees in 2013. Pakistan contains the most refugees, with 1.6 million, followed by Iran and Lebanon. Notice that the only high-income countries to make the list are, in descending order, the United States, France and Germany. Thus, the vast majority of refugees (nearly 90 percent in 2013) are hosted by low- and middle-income countries.

The preferred long-term solution to most refugee crises is voluntary repatriation, or that conditions improve enough that refugees choose to return home. However, some refugees cannot repatriate and remain in refugee camps indefinitely. Many refugees from Afghanistan, Burma, the Congo, Somalia and Sudan have been displaced for more than a generation. The average length of their stay in a camp was 17 years in 2003 (UNHCR, 2004). Worldwide, about 30 percent of refugees live in refugee camps (Hatton, 2013). Despite the best efforts of agencies like the UNHCR, conditions in most refugee camps are grim.

Table 14.6 Top 20 destination countries of refugees, 2013

Source country	Number of refugees
Pakistan	1,616,507
Iran	857,354
Lebanon	856,546
Jordan	641,915
Turkey	609,938
Kenya	534,938
Chad	434,479
Ethiopia	433,936
China	301,047
United States	263,662
Iraq	246,298
Yemen	241,288
France	232,487
Bangladesh	231,145
Egypt	230,086
South Sudan	229,587
Uganda	220,555
Venezuela	204,340
India	188,395
Germany	187,567

Source: UNHCR Statistical Online Population Database (www.unhcr.org/statistics/Ref_1960_2013.zip [24 August 2014]).

In some cases, third-country resettlement may be the best or only option. This resettlement is usually done by the UNHCR, often in partnership with local non-governmental organizations. However, international law does not require any country to accept refugees. Less than 1 percent of refugees are resettled each year.

Beginning in the 1980s and 1990s, when the number of refugees was increasing worldwide, many Western countries tightened their policies towards refugees and asylum seekers. (Asylum seekers are people who have arrived in another country seeking refugee status but whose claims have not yet been evaluated.) Countries such as Denmark, Germany and the United Kingdom passed legislation tightening asylum rules. In Europe, there was a "race to the bottom" of countries tightening their policies in order to discourage asylum seekers and deflect them to other countries (Hatton, 2013).

This policy tightening was effective in reducing countries' number of refugees and asylum seekers. Western countries that made it harder for potential asylum seekers to enter reduced their number of asylum applications by about 14 percent during 1997 to 2006 (Hatton, 2009). Meanwhile, Western countries that adopted tougher rules for processing asylum applications reduced their number of asylum applications by about 17 percent during that period. Macroeconomic conditions in potential destination countries can also affect the flow of asylum seekers. In Western countries, the number of asylum applications is negatively related to the country's unemployment rate, suggesting that many asylum seekers are economic migrants in disguise.

Most developed countries have an annual cap on the number of refugees they accept. Some countries have regional allocations that admit a certain number of refugees from specific regions or countries. In consultation with the U.S. Congress, the U.S. president annually sets the number of refugees to be accepted from five global regions and an unallocated reserve in case a country goes to war or more refugees need to be admitted regionally. In 2014, the total cap in the United States was 70,000. Actual refugee admittances there have varied between 60,000 and 80,000 in recent years. In addition, the United States has granted asylum to between 30,000 and 116,000 people per year in recent years. There is no cap on the number of people who can receive asylum each year in the United States.

In the United States, the Office of Refugee Resettlement works with local agencies to place refugees and provide them with services, including language instruction, job training, job placement services, housing and health care. Many refugees are intentionally placed outside of the main gateway cities in order to disperse them across the host country (such as in Utica, New York, as discussed in Box 14.3). One year after admission, a refugee in the United States may apply for permanent resident status. The most common origin countries of U.S. refugees in 2012 were Bhutan, Burma and Iraq, which together represented 71 percent of all refugee admissions (Martin and Yankay, 2013). Notice that none of these countries shows up on the list in Table 14.5—the United States is not currently admitting large numbers of refugees from the countries with the largest numbers of displaced persons.

The European Union has had a common system for asylum seekers, the Common European Asylum System (CEAS), since 1999.[8] The CEAS consists of three pillars: greater harmonization of standards of protection and asylum legislation; effective and well-supported practical

Box 14.3 Refugee resettlement in Utica, New York

In the United States, refugees are resettled across the country. Resettlement centers, which are funded by the U.S. government, help refugees adjust to their new life in the United States. Most refugees have already spent considerable time waiting in a refugee camp or a detention center for their entry visa to be approved.

Utica, New York, is a city of about 62,000 people located in upstate New York. Nearly 25 percent of its residents are refugees, giving it the fourth highest concentration of refugees in the United States (as a percent of the population). Utica was once a bustling industrial city with a population of over 100,000 people. However, as manufacturing plants moved south or overseas and an Air Force base closed, over 30,000 people left the city between 1960 and 2000. After four straight decades of dramatic population decline, Utica experienced its first population net increase between 2005 and 2010. Much of that increase was due to refugees.

The resettlement center in Utica is the Mohawk Valley Resource Center for Refugees (MVRCR). Since its inception in 1979, the center has assisted refugees from more than 30 countries, including Afghanistan, Bosnia, Burma, Cambodia, China, Czechoslovakia, Haiti, Hungary, Iran, Iraq, Laos, Poland, Romania, Somalia, the former Soviet Union, Sudan and Vietnam. About 15,000 refugees have come through the center in the past three decades, including 5,000 Bosnian refugees and their families who now call Utica home.

Like other resettlement centers across the United States, the MVRCR offers programs and services that teach refugees practical life skills which enhance their ability to integrate into the community; build individual and community capacity to integrate refugees into the Utica community; and foster an atmosphere of understanding and tolerance through the engagement of individual clients, the refugee/immigrant community and the local community.[1]

Refugees have had a significant economic impact on the city of Utica. Refugees have been a major factor in housing sales and the stabilization of housing values in the city. Refugee families have revitalized rundown neighborhoods and started small businesses downtown. There now is a vast offering of ethnic restaurants in Utica. Of course, there have been economic and cultural challenges as well, such as the cost of providing English-as-a-second-language classes. The Utica City School District—a district of fewer than 10,000 students—has students who speak 43 different languages. On balance, however, refugees have breathed new life into a struggling area.

---

[1] http://www.mvrcr.org/mission/

---

cooperation; and increased solidarity and sense of responsibility among EU states and between the EU and non-EU countries. Asylum flows are not constant, nor are they evenly distributed across the EU. They have varied between a peak of 425,000 applications for asylum in EU countries in 2001 and a low point of fewer than 200,000 in 2006. In 2012, there were 335,895 asylum applications in the EU.

Labor market outcomes of refugees

Given that refugees do not migrate for economic or work-related reasons and they are typically resettled somewhat arbitrarily within host countries, studying their success in the labor market in the host country is interesting. As Hatton (2013) states:

> [T]here are other reasons to think that the results for refugees might differ from those of other immigrants. The very fact that they come from different origins, under different circumstances, that they are admitted under different criteria and that they are sometimes subjected to a protracted processing period, suggest that their outcomes might differ.
>
> (pp. 464–465)

Refugees tend to have worse labor market outcomes than other types of migrants, especially in the short run. In Australia and Canada, for example, refugees have lower employment rates and higher unemployment rates than other types of migrants (Cobb-Clark, 2008; Aydemir, 2011). Research on refugees in Europe indicates that policies that place refugees in more remote locations with weak labor markets and poor job potential are one reason why refugees make relatively little labor market progress (Hatton, 2013). Refugees in Germany are less likely to work full time and have lower earnings than other immigrants, while refugees in Denmark earn less than other immigrants but have similar employment rates (Constant and Zimmermann, 2005a, 2005b).

Many refugees do not do well in the labor market because of their lack of education, skills and proficiency in the host country's language. Refugees from developing countries can experience severe culture shock if they are resettled in a developed country. In addition, refugees are often traumatized and have significant health issues arising from their experiences back home and in refugee camps. However, refugees have an incentive to thrive in their new country. The alternative of returning home is bleak: the situation in their home country is bad enough to motivate many of them to try to succeed in their new country.

Legalization policies

Some countries offer some form of legal status to unauthorized immigrants who have lived there for a considerable period. This is referred to as legalization or regularization (the latter term is commonly used in Europe). Some legalization programs are one-time events (or "one-offs"): They occur at a point in time in response to particular circumstances and often target certain types of immigrants. Other legalization programs are part of the immigration policy framework and are open ended. Chapter 13 discussed a large-scale, one-time legalization program in the United States, while this chapter focuses on legalization programs in Europe during the last few decades.

Between 1996 and 2010, approximately 5 million people were legalized (or regularized) in Europe. One-off legalization programs in Europe include five programs in Greece between 1998 and 2007 that legalized 650,000 immigrants; six programs in Italy between 1986 and 2006 that legalized 1.6 million immigrants; five programs in Portugal between 1992 and 2004 that legalized 300,000 immigrants; and six programs in Spain between 1985 and 2005 that legalized 1.1 million immigrants (Brick, 2011). Between 1997 and 2007, Greece, Italy and Spain accounted for almost 90 percent of all legalizations in the European Union. The majority of legalizations in Southern Europe were in response to the increased flow of workers from Eastern Europe and North Africa. These regularization programs typically allowed workers to receive a permit allowing them to live and work in that country for several years, not permanent residence or citizenship.

A number of European countries have legalized people who migrated there as asylum seekers, particularly people from the former Yugoslavia. For example, Austria, Belgium, France, Germany, the Netherlands, Sweden and the United Kingdom have legalized some failed asylum seekers—people who did not leave the country when their claims for refugee status were denied, or who never officially sought asylum—as part of their broad immigration policy (Brick, 2011). Other regularizations in Europe have focused on family reunification, such as France's 1998 Chevenement Laws that legalized 87,000 migrants.

The number and scope of legalization programs have slowed in Europe and around the world in recent years, mostly as a result of weak macroeconomic conditions. Legalization programs are more controversial in tough economic times, when immigrants are more likely to be viewed as a threat to the domestic workforce.

Policies regarding immigrants after arrival

Many developed countries have created programs to help immigrants integrate into the destination country in hopes of fostering economic success and cultural assimilation and reducing immigrants' reliance on public assistance over time. Ulf Rinne (2013) categorizes these programs into four broad groups: introduction programs, language training, active labor market programs and anti-discrimination policies.

Introduction programs

Introduction programs aim to ease the transition for new immigrants. These programs may encompass language courses, vocational training, job search assistance and even subsidized employment. They may also include courses about the history, norms, culture and traditions of the destination country. Introduction programs are common in Nordic countries. Humanitarian immigrants and tied movers (accompanying dependents of other immigrants) are expected or even required to participate in introduction programs in Sweden, for example. One reason why Nordic countries have extensive introduction programs is because many immigrants, especially humanitarian immigrants, have not succeeded in the labor market there in recent decades—immigrants' employment rates and earnings have been low and their reliance on public assistance programs high compared with other developed countries.

Language training

Language training may be part of an introduction program, but language training may also be provided as a separate program. Economists overwhelmingly view language skills as a critical determinant of immigrants' economic success in the destination country (Chiswick and Miller,

2014). Language skills are also critical to social integration. Most developed countries either require that immigrants have at least basic proficiency in the language spoken there or offer free or subsidized language training to immigrants. In Israel, for example, schools called *ulpan* are designed to teach adult immigrants basic Hebrew as well as providing cultural instruction.

Both introduction programs and language training specifically target immigrant populations. Active labor market programs and anti-discrimination policies, in contrast, typically encompass not only immigrants but the population as a whole.

Active labor market programs

Active labor market policies encompass a variety of programs that aim to increase employment and wages among disadvantaged groups in the labor market, such as the disabled, veterans or the unemployed. Immigrants are often overrepresented in these programs. Active labor market programs may include public employment services, training programs and subsidized employment.

Active labor market programs are quite popular in Europe and are often made available to immigrants. Studies of active labor market programs that involve intensified counseling, job search assistance, workplace introduction, subsidized employment and monitoring indicate that these types of programs increase employment rates and earnings among immigrants in Denmark, Finland and Sweden (Rinne, 2013). Studies of active labor market programs in Germany show that immigrants benefit more than natives from these programs, although there are differences by gender and ethnicity. In addition, German government subsidies that support start-ups and promote self-employment and entrepreneurial activity have significant positive effects among immigrants (and even larger effects among natives). Studies typically find that voluntary participation in these programs is vital—immigrants who are willing and active participants in these programs have the most success in finding and keeping jobs and improving their lifetime earnings.

Anti-discrimination policies

Immigrants may experience discrimination in the labor market, which may lead to lower employment and earnings. Policies such as anonymous job applications may help to minimize discrimination at the point of hiring. A Swedish study concludes that anonymous applications increase the likelihood that immigrants of non-Western origin get a job interview (Åslund and Skans, 2012).

Final thoughts

This chapter sheds light on the complexity of immigration policy worldwide. Countries take different approaches to selecting and admitting immigrants, dealing with unauthorized immigrants and helping immigrants integrate after they have arrived. Some countries admit the majority of their immigrants based on family preferences, while others use point systems to admit workers. Some focus on admitting permanent residents, while others admit most immigrants on a temporary basis. Some are more willing than others to welcome refugees and asylum seekers. After arrival, immigrants have different experiences in their host countries depending on the policies in place to help with integration and assimilation. Countries set different immigration policies to achieve different goals. The policies they set determine the size and composition of their immigrant inflows, which in turn determine the economic impact of immigration both at home and abroad. Those impacts, in turn, shape public opinion toward immigration, influence the number and characteristics of future immigrants and set the stage for future immigration policy.

Problems and discussion questions

1   Suppose after college graduation, you want to work in the EU. Using the blue card criteria at http://www.apply.eu/, what are the conditions for a work visa? Would you meet the conditions? If you do not meet the conditions for a blue card, what would you have to do to meet the conditions?

2   Discuss the costs and benefits if a country with a system based mainly on family preferences, like the United States, were to switch to a point system. Who would be the winners and losers?

3   Discuss immigration policy for the EU as a whole. Differentiate between policies for citizens of other EU countries and policies for citizens of non-EU countries. Then, choose one of the EU countries and, using the IOM report listed below or other resources, summarize its current immigration policy for non-EU citizens.

4   How are refugees different from other types of immigrants? Be sure to discuss differences in the reasons for migrating, the process of migrating and the effects on the host country.

5   Explain how integration policies are likely to affect immigrants and natives in the destination country. What are the justifications for these programs?

Notes

1   http://www.dhs.gov/sites/default/files/publications/immigration-statistics/yearbook/2013/LPR/table2.xls [30 August 2014].
2   http://www.cic.gc.ca/english/resources/statistics/facts2012/permanent/10.asp [30 August 2014].
3   http://www.immi.gov.au/media/fact-sheets/02key.htm [21 June 2014].
4   http://esa.un.org/unmigration/TIMSA2013/migrantstocks2013.htm?mtotals [2 June 2014].
5   http://europa.eu/legislation_summaries/justice_freedom_security/free_movement_of_persons_asylum_immigration/l33152_en.htm [1 June 2014].
6   https://www.destatis.de/EN/Methods/Census/2011Census.html [10 August 2014].
7   http://www.loc.gov/law/help/guestworker/spain.php [1 June 2014].
    http://ec.europa.eu/dgs/home-affairs/what-we-do/policies/asylum/index_en.htm [1 June 2014].
8   Ibid.

Suggestions for further reading

International Organization for Migration (IOM) (2009) "Laws for legal immigration in the 27 EU Member States." *International Migration Law* No. 16. Available at: http://publications.iom.int/bookstore/free/IML_16.pdf [15 July 2014].

Tani, M. (2014) "Using a point system for selecting immigrants." *IZA World of Labor* 24, pp. 1–10.

References

Aydemir, A. (2011) "Immigrant selection and short-term labor market outcomes by visa category." *Journal of Population Economics* 24(2), pp. 451–475.

Åslund, O. and Skans, O.N. (2012) "Do anonymous job application procedures level the playing field?" *Industrial and Labor Relations Review* 65(1), pp. 82–107.

BBC News (2008) "What if all the Poles went home?" *BBC News*, 27 November. http://news.bbc.co.uk/2/hi/uk_news/magazine/7316261.stm [1 June 2014].

Brick, K. (2011) *Regularizations in Europe: The contentious policy tool*. Washington, DC: Migration Policy Institute.

Burgen, S. (2013) "Spain youth unemployment reaches record 56.1%." *The Guardian*, 30 August. Available at: http://www.theguardian.com/business/2013/aug/30/spain-youth-unemployment-record-high [1 August 2014].

Chiswick, B.R., Lee, Y.L. and Miller, P.W. (2008) "Immigrant selection systems and immigrant health." *Contemporary Economic Policy* 26(4), pp. 555–578.

Chiswick, B.R. and Miller, P.W. (2014) "International migration and the economics of language." In: Chiswick, B.R. and Miller, P.W. (eds.) *Handbook of the Economics of International Migration*. Amsterdam: Elsevier.

Cobb-Clark, D.A. (2003) "Public policy and the labor market adjustment of new immigrants to Australia." *Journal of Population Economics* 16(4), pp. 655–681.

Cobb-Clark, D.A. (2008) "Leaving home: What economics has to say about the living arrangements of young Australians." *Australian Economic Review* 41(2), pp. 160–176.

Constant, A. and Zimmermann, K.F. (2005a) "Legal status at entry, economic performance, and self employment proclivity: A bi-national study of immigrants." *IZA Discussion Paper* No. 1910. Bonn: Institute for the Study of Labor.

Constant, A. and Zimmermann, K.F. (2005b). "Immigrant performance and selective immigration policy: A European perspective." *National Economic Review* 194(1), pp. 94–105.

European Commission (2008) "Free movement of workers is good for Europe's economy." IP/08/1729, 18/11/2008. Available at: http://europa.eu/rapid/press-release_IP-08-1729_en.htm [1 June 2014].

Froilan, T., Malit Jr., A. and Youha, A. (2013) "Labor migration in the United Arab Emirates: Challenges and responses." Washington, DC: Migration Policy Institute. Available at: http://www.migrationpolicy.org/article/labor-migration-united-arab-emirates-challenges-and-responses [15 June 2014].

Gerson, D. (2007) "Spain's guest-worker program provides test case for EU." *Christian Science Monitor*, 29 March. Available at: http://www.csmonitor.com/2007/0329/p04s01-woeu.html [31 August 2014].

Gregory, R. (2014) "The two-step Australian immigration policy and its impact on immigrant employment outcomes." *IZA Discussion Paper* No. 8061. Bonn: Institute for the Study of Labor.

Hatton, T. (2009) "The rise and fall of asylum: What happened and why?" *Economic Journal* 119, pp. F183–F213.

Hatton, T. (2013) "Refugee and asylum migration." In: Constant, A.F. and Zimmermann, K.F. (eds.) *International Handbook on the Economics of Migration*. Cheltenham, UK: Edward Elgar, pp. 453–469.

International Organization for Migration (IOM) (2009) "Laws for legal immigration in the 27 EU Member States." *International Migration Law* No. 16. Available at: http://publications.iom.int/bookstore/free/IML_16.pdf [15 July 2014].

Kaminer, A. and O'Driscol, S. (2014) "Workers at N.Y.U.'s Abu Dhabi site faced harsh conditions." *The New York Times*, 18 May. Available at: http://nyti.ms/1gXQSCd [18 May 2014].

Martin, D. and Yankay, J. (2013) "Refugees and asylees: 2012." U.S. Department of Homeland Security, Annual Flow Report, Office of Immigration Statistics. Available at: http://www.dhs.gov/sites/default/files/publications/ois_rfa_fr_2012.pdf [20 July 2014].

Martin, P.L. and Teitelbaum, M.S. (2001) "The mirage of Mexican guest workers." *Foreign Affairs* 80(6), pp. 117–131.

New York Times (2014) "Clinton lauds N.Y.U. graduates, and inquiry, in speech." *The New York Times*, 25 May. Available at: http://nyti.ms/1hoT1at [25 May 2014].

Rinne, U. (2013) "The evaluation of immigration policies." In: Constant, A.F. and Zimmermann, K.F. (eds.) *International Handbook on the Economics of Migration*. Cheltenham, UK: Edward Elgar, pp. 530–551.

Tani, M. (2014) "Using a point system for selecting immigrants." *IZA World of Labor* 24, pp. 1–10.

United Nations High Commissioner for Refugees (UNHCR) (2004). "Protracted refugee situations: The search for practical solutions." Geneva: UNHCR. Available at: http://www.unhcr.org/4444afcb0.pdf [21 September 2014].

United Nations High Commissioner for Refugees (UNHCR) (2013) *Global Trends 2013*. Available at: http://www.unhcr.org/5399a14f9.html [20 August 2014].

United Nations High Commissioner for Refugees (2014) UNHCR Statistical Online Population Database (www.unhcr.org/statistics/Ref_1960_2013.zip [24 August 2014]).

Index